LABOUR MARKETS IN ACTION

LABOUR MARKETS IN ACTION

Essays in Empirical Economics

Richard B. Freeman

Harvard University and National Bureau of Economic Research

HARVESTER WHEATSHEAF

New York   London   Toronto   Sydney   Tokyo

First published 1989 by
Harvester Wheatsheaf,
66 Wood Lane End, Hemel Hempstead,
Hertfordshire, HP2 4RG
A division of
Simon & Schuster International Group

Printed and bound in Great Britain by
BPCC Wheatons Ltd, Exeter

British Library Cataloguing in Publication Data

Freeman, Richard, *1945*–
    Labour markets in action:essays in empirical
    economics.
    1. Labour market. Econometric models
    I. Title
    331.12′0724

    ISBN 0-7450-0564-0

1 2 3 4 5   93 92 91 90 89

To Gary Becker, John T. Dunlop, Simon Kuznets,
H. Gregg Lewis and Martin Segal – mentors, critics, and catalysts.

CONTENTS

INTRODUCTION

Empirical economics? How do you learn anything? You can't do controlled experiments, so you can never be certain what you know. You can't test theory because the Invisible Hand, being invisible, can explain whatever you observe. And the way the economy changes, parameters are time-variant instead of constant. No one in his right mind can hope to find the truth in economics.

In graduate school I roomed with a physics student who viewed economics, and all social science for that matter, as something closer akin to tea-leaf reading than science. Unlike the great physicist Max Planck, who politely told John Maynard Keynes that he found economics too difficult to study, my friend minced no words about his suspicions of the field. No one could do science without experimental evidence. The high-powered theory and fancy econometrics that economists substitute for experiments were a joke. When I completed my PhD, he presented me with a laugh machine 'to be turned on whenever your nonexperimental data prove incomprehensible or recalcitrant'.

My friend – may his bubble chamber burst with new particles – was right about empirical economics. It is different than laboratory science. It is more difficult. Frustrating. Uncertain. Although economists do not like to admit it, we are closer to detectives than to physicists. We analyze how the world functions without experiments; assess hypotheses without decisive laboratory tests; reach conclusions from data generated for nonscientific purposes; and decide what caused what – 'whodunit' – in the economy from circumstantial evidence, often in the face of self-interested claims by actual participants. Reaching firm conclusions is not easy.

How do we learn anything? What do we do in lieu of turning on the laugh machine? The main purpose of this book is to set out the ways in which an empirical economist, specializing in what has become the quintessential inductive field in the profession, labor economics, deals with these problems of nonexperimental social science. My answer to what to do – the product of implicit responses to the nature of empirical economics rather than of any conscious model of how things should be done[1] – is embodied in the essays in this book and involves a five-fold approach:

First, to analyze markets when they experience sufficiently sharp exogeneous shocks as to create 'natural experiments'. I first became sensitive to the information content of natural experiments from the work of T. W. Schultz, who tested the claim that the marginal product of labor is zero in less-developed countries by examining output in Indian provinces that underwent typhus-induced declines in population.[2] Chapter 1's analysis of the market for physicists exploits the natural experiment that resulted from the 'sputnik'-induced increases in demand for scientific personnel and ensuing changes in government research and development (R&D) spending policies. Chapter 4's analysis of the age–earnings profile in the United States similarly exploits the natural experiment created by the birth-rate generated shifts in the supply of young workers while the Part II study of the changing economic status of black workers also makes extensive mileage out of shifts in demand that resulted from federal equal employment and affirmative action policies (Chapter 5).

Second, to focus on fundamental 'first-order economic principles and behavior, as opposed to the latest chalk twiggles from the theorists' blackboard. Given a choice between simple supply and demand analyses of phenomena and complicated stories about expectations formation, game-theoretic interactions, and the like, I invariably opt for the former. It is not just a question of Occam's razor. It is a recognition of the fact that without controlled experiments it is virtually impossible to pin down anything beyond first-order effects. Zvi Griliches once told me that this leads one toward factual reporting rather than deep analysis. Perhaps so. But Joe Friday always caught the villains on *Dragnet* by asking for the facts, ma'am, just the facts, and I prefer to start with facts than with speculations. To paraphrase Justice Holmes, in the current state of empirical economics it is better to determine the facts than to expatiate the obscure.

Third, to probe empirical findings with different data sets and alternative specifications. As all economics data have weaknesses – measurement error, unmeasured variables, sample survey quirks – and all model specifications are questionable, contaminated by data mining, any 'finding' ought to be replicated on several data sets and under alternative 'plausible' model specifications before one accepts it as valid. Replication with additional data and specifications contrasts sharply with the practice of econometricians who postulate a 'true' structural model, use maximum likelihood search procedures to extract its parameters from data, and stop, as if technical prowess rather than robustness of results was the key to credibility. In fact, as all practitioners know, any single piece of complex econometric analysis rarely convinces anyone, for the more sophisticated the econometrics, the greater the danger the results derive from the model than from the world. In economics, it is the cumulation of disparate lines of evidence, not the elegance of the statistical technology for a single estimator, that is compelling. In this book the studies of trade unionism in Part III best exemplify the procedure of confirming empirical claims by replication with different data sets.

Fourth, to gather new information through survey research when the available data sets do not adequately address the questions of interest. Many economists shy away from conducting their own surveys, but my experience is that the effort spent obtaining new direct information almost always pays off. In this volume I include three analyses based on original survey information: the determinants of the career decisions of college students (Chapter 3); the economic problems of inner city black youths (Chapter 6); and the permanence of homelessness among the very poor (Chapter 7). Though imperfect, each of the surveys generated interesting empirical results that one could not possibly derive from standard data sets and that contributed to the interpretation of the more econometric findings.

Fifth, to discuss issues and analyses with the participants in the markets under study. Since the Lester–Machlup debate of 1946[3] most economists have been leary of asking businessmen or workers about the factors that influence their behavior, fearing that people do not tell the truth or do not understand the economic forces that affect them. At Harvard John Dunlop taught the opposite: that one can obtain more valuable clues and hypotheses about the operation of markets through discussion with labor and management than from introspection or contemplating the blackboard. In a field lacking decisive tests of hypotheses, it is worth listening to what eyewitnesses and participants have to say. Given two equally plausible ways to interpret data, one which management and labor view as sensible and one which they view as crazy, my inclination is that the former is more likely to be right. Getting the opinions of the subjects of our research is also the only advantage we have over physicists. Quarks and gluons do not talk about what they do or why, not even to Richard Feynman.

Whether these approaches to the analysis of economic phenomenon – focusing on natural experiments; concentrating on first-order effects; probing results with numerous data sets and specifications; obtaining new survey information; discussing with labor and management – adequately address the criticisms of empirical economics raised by my physics friend, or whether I ought to have reached for the laugh machine more often, I hope the reader will judge.

The book, then, is organized into five areas which represent some of the major research topics on which I have worked: the market for highly educated workers; the economics of discrimination and poverty; the economics of trade unionism; comparative labor market institutions; and methodology of data analysis. Most of the essays are from technical economics journals, with a scattering from conference volumes and books. I introduce each section with a brief discussion of the substantive issues involved, the genesis of my interest, and the 'time variance' of the empirical findings. Full acknowledgments for each chapter are given in the Acknowledgements on page 343.

NOTES

1. For the most fruitful effort to lay out what is truly involved in economic data analysis, see Edward Leamer, *Specification Search* (New York: John Wiley, 1978).
2. Shultz's work is reported in T. W. Schultz, *Transforming Traditional Agriculture* (New Haven: Yale University Press, 1964).
3. The Lester–Machlup debate was carried on in the *American Economic Review:* see Richard Lester, 'Shortcomings of marginal analysis for wage/employment problems', *American Economic Review*, (March 1946), 36, pp. 63–82; and Fritz Machlup, 'Marginal analysis and empirical research', *American Economic Review*, (September, 1946), 36, pp. 519–54.

PART I

MARKETS FOR EDUCATED LABOR

In 1964 *Human Capital* was published (Becker, 1975), a book that offered a new vision of the role of economic rationality in the functioning of labor markets. In contrast to the industrial relations specialists who dominated the field through the mid-1960s (whose work I review in Chapter 16), Becker argued that labor supply decisions were not passive, irrational and sociological in nature but the result of rational optimizing investments in skills. He laid out a new research program for labor economics, which has transformed the field, as I have described elswhere (Freeman, 1986).

My first reaction to *Human Capital* was one of intellectual excitement. My second reaction was to ask the empiricists' question: how do I test to see if it is right? Did young persons make rational investments in human capital, as the theory postulated, or were their decisions based on the noneconomic factors stressed by the older generation?

The analyses of log earnings equations by Jacob Mincer (Mincer, 1974) and others that showed earnings rising with education and varying with age, while of fundamental importance in directing investigations of earnings in a fruitful direction, did not convince me that human capital was right: one does not need a theory of investment in human capital to expect education, age and work experience to affect earnings. My approach was to look, instead, for direct evidence of supply responsiveness to incentives among groups where such behavior seemed most likely to hold – among persons making the most significant investments in education, those choosing careers in highly specialized fields with long training programs, such as engineering, physics, doctorates in various fields. The results for engineering (Freeman, 1971; 1976) and physics (Chapter 1) provided great support for the notion of responsive labor supply investments in skill, and yielded evidence of a cobweb-type dynamics in which a strong job market attracts large numbers of students in a field, which in turn depresses the market. As part of my 'replication' strategy, I also examined similar models for other fields: accounting, business administration (MBAs of course respond to economic incentives), PhDs as a group, and later law, psychology, and biological sciences, with comparable results. When the economic rewards to college fell sharply in the United States in the early 1970s, I extended the analysis to college enrollments at the bachelor's level, and even risked using the model to forecast future returns to human capital and enrollments (Chapter 2). My other test was to survey students to see if they had information and subjective flexibility in career decision-making consistent with the econometric analysis and the human capital model. The results are summarized in Chapter 3.

The statistical and survey evidence did not, however, convince everyone knowledgeable of the scientific labor market that economics had a lot to say about the flow of young people into science. At the height of the employment crisis for physicists described in Chapter 1, the chairman of the physics department at Chicago asked me to present my analysis to his department, which I did. When I finished the presentation, the chairman shook his head, frowning deeply. Oh, Millie. Had I made some analytic blunder? A mistake in modeling? Where was my laugh machine when I really needed it? 'You've got us all wrong,' the chairman said gravely. 'You don't understand what motivates people to study physics. We study for love of knowledge, not for salaries and jobs.' 'But . . . ,' I was prepared to give the Chapter 3 arguments about market incentives operating on some people on the margin, when the students – facing the worst employment prospects for graduating physicists in decades – answered for me with a resounding chorus of boos and hisses. Case closed.

BIBLIOGRAPHY

Becker, G., *Human Capital* (second edition) (New York: National Bureau of Economic Research, 1975).
Freeman, R. B., *The Market for College-Trained Manpower* (Cambridge, MA: Harvard University Press, 1971).
Freeman, R. B., 'A cobweb model of the supply and starting salary of new engineers', *Industrial and Labor Relations Review* (January 1976), pp. 236–48.
Freeman, R. B., 'Demand for education' in O. Ashenfelter and R. Layard (eds), *Handbook of Labor Economics*, vol. 1 (Amsterdam: North-Holland, 1986).
Mincer, J., *Schooling, Experience, and Earnings* (New York: National Bureau of Economic Research, 1974).

1 · SUPPLY AND SALARY ADJUSTMENTS TO THE CHANGING MARKET FOR PHYSICISTS

Fluctuations in the market for scientists raise important questions about the way in which high-level labor markets adjust to sharp changes in economic conditions. What happens to salaries when demand for specialists declines greatly? How does the supply of new entrants respond to market ups and downs? What are the implications of the adjustment process for future manpower developments and current methods of manpower forecasting?

This chapter examines these questions with respect to physics, whose significant turnaround from relative shortage to surplus in the mid 1960s to early 1970s offers an especially fruitful case for study. It finds real salaries and the supply of new entrants to physics to be highly sensitive to market conditions. Economic responsiveness critically affects the likely future state of the field and should be taken into account in the standard forecast methodology. The first section outlines the principal post-World War II changes in the physics manpower market, the phenomenon under investigation. The second section analyzes the supply behavior of students and the determination of physics salaries in the framework of a recursive market model (Freeman, 1971). The estimated model is used to forecast the future state of physics manpower, yielding strikingly different results from those obtained by standard techniques. These differences highlight the sensitivity of the labor market as an allocative device and the critical role of supply and demand adjustments in manpower analyses. In the postscript I compare the actual market outcomes to the forecasts and find that the forecasts based on the supply responsiveness model were remarkably accurate while those based on mechanical extrapolations were orders of magnitudes off base.

THE PHYSICS JOB MARKET

The turnaround in the state of the physics labor market was marked by

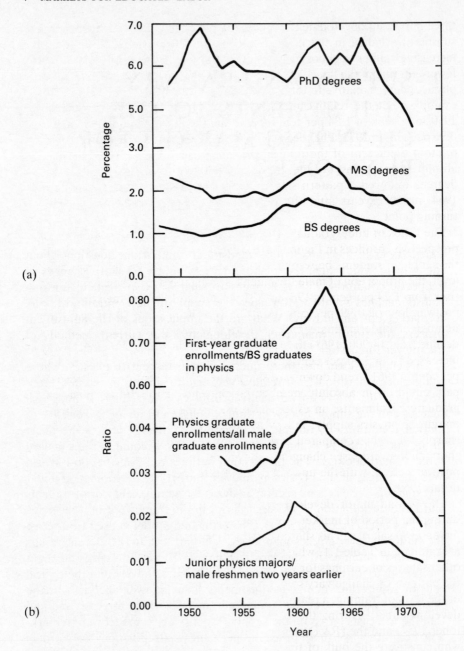

(a)

(b)

Figure 1.1 (a) Physics degrees relative to male degrees; (b) relative enrollments in physics.

Sources: Degrees, 1948–71, US Bureau of Census (1949–72); 1972 estimated using American Institute of Physics Pub. R-151.10 (1973). Enrollments, American Institute of Physics, Pub. R-151.10 (1973).

three important developments. First, as depicted in Figure 1.1, there was a substantial change in the flow of students into the field, with large and increasing numbers choosing physics in the late 1950s–early 1960s and fewer entering in the late 1960s. Figure 1.1(a) which records the number of physics degrees relative to total male degrees from 1948 to 1972, shows, for example, that the relative number of BS degrees in physics rose in the 1950s to a peak of 1.84 per cent in 1962 and then dropped nearly in half to 0.96 per cent in 1972. PhD degrees in the field plummetted downward from 6.7 to 4.6 per cent of the total in the late 1960s (1967–72) and declined absolutely at the onset of the 1970s (by 7 per cent from 1970 to 1972). MS degrees followed a pattern similar to that of BSs and PhDs, peaking in 1964, just two years after the BS peak and three years before the PhD turning point.

The ratios of undergraduate enrollments in physics to the population of prospective enrollees in Figure 1.1(b) reveal even more striking changes in the supply of students between the 1950s and 1960s. At the undergraduate level, the proportion of male freshmen selecting physics in their junior year rises from 1.24 per cent in 1953 to 2.31 per cent in 1960 and then drops to a postwar low of 0.99 per cent in 1972. Despite a near doubling in the number of undergraduate males, junior and senior year physics majors decline from 14,900 (1961) to 11,400 (1972). Graduate enrollments, having increased from 3.00 per cent of all male graduate students in 1955 to 4.14 per cent in 1961, trend downward sharply to 1.73 per cent in 1972 with a 24 per cent drop in absolute numbers at the end of the 1960s. First-year graduate enrollments, an especially sensitive measure of the adjustment margin of physics supply, fall by a third from 1961 to 1972 and decline sharply even when compared to the decreasing number of BS graduates. In short, there were large changes in the supply of students to physics in the postwar period, with the upward trend of the 1950s arrested and reversed in the 1960s.

The second major development was a significant fall in real salaries during the period of market downturn, after a decade or so of substantial increases in salaries. This sharp change in the economic status of physicists is examined in Table 1.1, which records percentage changes in physics and other salaries or earnings for various subperiods since World War II. While the patterns of change vary somewhat depending on the source of the data or the level of training, a reasonably clear picture emerges of physics salary developments.[1] During the 1954–62 period encompassing Sputnik (October 1957) and the (R&D) boom, the salaries of PhD and MS physicists, who constitute the bulk of the profession (80 per cent), and the starting salaries of BS physicists (but not the annual earnings reported by the National Science Foundation (NSF)) increased more rapidly than those of comparison groups. After 1962, by contrast, the rate of change of physics salaries fell increasingly behind that in male professional earnings, annual earnings of full-time employees, and average hourly earnings. Between

Table 1.1 Changes in physics salaries, 1948–73 (percentage change in current US dollar salaries)

	1951–4	1954–62	1962–8	1968–70	1970–2	1972–3
PhD						
Earnings	9.2	67.7	22.3	8.8	—	—
Starting salaries	—	54.4[a]	18.1	6.6	3.3	1.3
Starting salaries	—	—	—	12.0	−0.1	—
MS						
Earnings	21.4	55.4	26.0	11.9	—	—
Starting salaries	—	—	30.5	11.8	−0.3	2.8
Starting salaries	—	—	—	5.8	0.0	—
BS						
Earnings	28.6	37.2	25.0	15.9	—	—
Starting salaries	—	50.9[a]	30.6	10.1	−1.1	3.3
Starting salaries	—	—	—	10.0	−5.6	—
Comparison groups						
Male professionals	20.5	40.1	36.4	17.4	9.9[b]	—
Annual earnings	14.0	38.1	31.4	13.8	13.2[b]	—
Average hourly earnings	13.8	34.5	28.4	13.0	13.3	5.8[c]
CPI	3.4	12.6	15.0	11.6	11.9	—

Notes:
a Calculated from salaries of Massachusetts Institute of Technology graduates, with data obtained by the Placement Office at MIT. The PhD salaries from 1955 to 1961; BS salaries from 1955 to 1962.
b Extrapolation for 1971–2 at rate of increase of average hourly earnings.
c Estimated as change from April 1972 to April 1973.
Sources: Earnings from *NSF American Science Manpower*, various editions, except 1951, from US Federal Security Agency (1952). Starting salaries from *CPC*, 1960–73, except for 1954–62, as noted. Starting salaries from *AIP*, 1968–72a,b. Professional earnings, US Bureau of Census, 1948–72. Annual earnings, US Department of Commerce, 1966–72. Average hourly earnings and *CPI*, US Bureau of Census, 1948–73.

1962 and 1968, physics PhD earnings increased by 22 per cent, MS earnings by 26 per cent, and BS earnings by 25 per cent compared to a 36 per cent gain for male professionals. At the end of the 1960s and the onset of the 1970s, the income position of physicists declined more rapidly, with real as well as relative salaries falling. American Institute of Physics (AIP) surveys show, for example, no gain in starting PhD and MS salaries and a 5.8 per cent decline in BS salaries in the 1970–2 period when consumer prices advanced by 12 per cent; College Placement Council (CPC) data show rough stability in money salaries over the same period and into the 1973 recruitment season. The net effect of this decline is to reduce relative physics earnings to pre-Sputnik levels or lower: in 1954 the premium of PhD physics earnings over male professional earnings was 58 per cent; in 1962, 89 per cent; by 1970, it had fallen back to 57 per cent. From 1970 to 1972 the ratio of AIP starting rates to professional earnings records a further drop of 12 percentage points (1.25 to 1.13). It is apparent from these changes that relative salaries in physics have been highly sensitive to market conditions and roughly as responsive to market declines as to booms.

Third, there was a sizeable shift in federal expenditures on basic research and development, atomic energy, and graduate training which had an exceptional impact on physics and other scientific specialties. This shift appears to be the chief cause of the downturn in the science market of the early 1970s. Table 1.2 summarizes data pertaining to federal spending and activities that impinged on physics. Line 1 shows the postwar fluctuation of total R&D: the 1950s spurt in expenditures, the 1960s levelling of the rate of increase, and the 1968–72 decline in real and relative spending. A similar pattern is displayed in lines 2–5, which deal with activities more directly linked to physics: federally funded physics research (line 3), physical science basic research (line 4), percentage of physicists with federal support (line 5), and Atomic Energy Commission spending, which turns down in 1962 (line 2). Federal fellowship aid (lines 6–7) underwent a different path of increase and decrease, with the number of awards growing rapidly from 1962 to 1968 and declining thereafter. Because federal fellowships declined after the expenditure plateau, students supported in the 1960s graduated during the spending decline of the early 1970s, contributing to the manpower crisis of that time.

Table 1.2 Federal support of physics, 1951–72 (in constant 1957–9 millions of US dollars)

	1951	1954	1962	1968	1970	1972
Demand						
1 Federal *R&D* spending as percent	1,638	3,353	8,789	12,370	10,868	10,064
GNP	0.45	0.86	1.65	1.73	1.51	1.32
2 Atomic Energy Commission spending	547	1,110	2,558	2,069	1,851	1,702
as percent *GNP*	0.15	0.28	0.48	0.29	0.26	0.24
3 Federal physics research	—	137[a]	353	511	398	377
per physicist[c]	—	7	14	16	11	10
4 Federal basic physical science research	—	88[a]	573	876	781	809
per physicist[c]	—	7	23	27	22	22
5 Percent physicists with federal support	—	—	66	62	55	—
Supply						
6 Number of Physical Science Fellowships	—	406	1,684	5,960	4,459[b]	2,964[b]
as percent graduate enrollment	—	3	11	21	16	6
7 Average value of fellowship	—	1,688	3,767	3,856	3,420[b]	3,170[b]
as percent professional salaries	—	32	58	50	42	37

Notes:
a Used 1959, earliest year with data.
b Estimated from number or value of all federal fellowships, assuming constant ratio of physical sciences to total.
c In thousands.
Sources: (1) *NSF*, 1972b; (2) US Atomic Energy Commission, 1959–72; (3), (4) US Atomic Energy Commission, with number of physicists from *American Science Manpower*, various editions; (5) *American Science Manpower*, various editions; (6), (7) *Federal Interagency Committee on Education*, 1970, 1972.

The turnaround in the market for physicists and other scientific specialists described above and the impending 'demographic crunch' on higher education have spawned a crop of manpower requirements forecasts of the future (Cartter, 1971; Wolfe and Kidd, 1971) based on extrapolations of current and past developments. While useful in directing attention to possible supply/demand imbalances, the forecasts can be criticized for ignoring the effects of salaries and economic behavior on market developments,[2] possibly leading to erroneous or exaggerated statements of problems. The degree to which forecasts are potentially misleading 'depends, all else the same, on the way in which the science manpower market adjusts to changes in economic conditions. How responsive is the market mechanism? Are supply and demand adjustments to economic incentives first- or second-order effects in manpower forecasts?

MARKET ADJUSTMENTS AND FORECASTING IN A RECURSIVE MODEL

To answer these questions in the physics case, we analyze the observed pattern of change in enrollments, degrees, and salaries with a simple recursive model of the labor market and use the model to predict the number of PhDs in the field in the 1970–80 decade. Variants of the model, which exploit the time delay in the production of graduates due to lengthy training periods to identify supply and demand-adjustment processes, have been applied to other high-level occupations with some success (Freeman, 1971). In simplest form, focusing on starting graduates, the model contains a supply schedule linking the number of students entering a field to starting salaries and related incentives; a demand equation with the number demanded dependent on salaries and exogenous demand–shift variables;[3] and market clearing. Because of the lag in training specialists (upwards of 4–5 years for PhD physicists), the number of new entrants depends on past market conditions and is predetermined with respect to the demand and market clearing equations. This makes salaries rather than quantities the appropriate dependent variable in the demand equation and creates a recursive 'cobweb' structure that generates endogenous cyclical fluctuations. The recursive model differs greatly from the Arrow-Capron model of scientific markets wherein salaries, rather than supplies, react slowly to changes in the market. When, as seems reasonable, the disturbances in the supply and salary equations are independent, the equations are appropriately estimated by least squares.

Depending on data availability and the problems of concern, the model can be amplified to focus on the complexities of expectations formation (Nerlove, 1958; Muth, 1961), adjustments in salaries due to bargaining during recruitment, decisions to complete as well as initiate training, interactions between the salaries and demand for younger and older specialists, and so forth. The current chapter concentrates on the basic aspects of market adjustment: the responsiveness of students to market incentives, the factors determining starting salaries, and the 'cobweb supply relation' which links supply to past levels of supply and demand. The cobweb relation, obtained by substituting the salary equation into the basic supply equation[4] highlights the endogenous fluctuations that characterize the market.

Supply behavior

The decision to study physics is examined in Tables 1.3 and 1.4 which relate (in *log* form) enrollments and degrees to salaries and a measure of alternative opportunities (male professional earnings). The salary variables are dated at the June preceding the date of enrollments used in the enrollment regressions and at the June 3, 2, and 5 years earlier in the BS, MS, and PhD regressions, respectively. Enrollments and degrees provide alternative, related measures of the same underlying supply behavior, with the former reflecting the immediate, and the latter, the ultimate impact of market incentives on the number of new entrants. The dependent variable in Table 1.3 is the proportion of students in physics; the dependent variable in Table 1.4 is the absolute number of students, yielding somewhat different estimating equations.[5] The starting salary variables are viewed as proxies for anticipated lifetime incomes, appropriately discounted. Lagged dependent variables are used to estimate the time delay in supply responses in the framework of a simple lagged adjustment model. Because we lack a continuous series of salaries in physics over an extended time period, the calculations are based on a composite series obtained by linking overlapping NSF, CPC, and related data by least squares estimation.[6]

The computations of Table 1.3 reveal an extremely close relation between salary incentives and the number of physics students, suggesting that the ups-and-downs in supply shown in Figure 1.1 result from economically responsive behavior. Physics salaries obtain a sizeable positive coefficient in all of the regressions, and professional earnings a negative coefficient, often of similar magnitude. The salary variables account, by themselves, for three-fourths or more of the variation in the physics share of enrollments and degrees (odd-numbered regressions), with elasticities ranging from approximately unity (line 5) to over five (line 7). With the addition of the lagged endogenous variable, salary coefficients decline substantially (even-numbered regressions), indicative of different short- and long-run supply elasticities. Larger undergraduate than graduate elasticities presumably reflect the greater flexibility of persons not yet committed to science careers. The only divergent result in the table occurred in the PhD regressions where an initial calculation relating the physics share to salaries

Table 1.3 Regression estimates of the proportion of students in physics, 1954–72[a]

Dependent variable and period covered	Constant	Physics[b] salary	Professional earnings	Lagged proportion	R^2	SEE
1 Junior majors/male freshman lagged 2 years 1959–72	3.74	3.64 (0.70)	−3.50 (0.53)		0.76	0.12
2 Junior majors/male freshman lagged 2 years 1959–72	4.24	1.28 (0.56)	−1.54 (0.45)	0.69 (0.12)	0.93	0.06
3 Graduate enrollments 1954, 1957–72[c]	10.02	2.23 (0.37)	−3.24 (0.42)		0.86	0.10
4 Graduate enrollments 1954, 1957–72[c]	4.55	0.61 (0.36)	−1.04 (0.47)	0.87 (0.16)	0.97	0.05
5 First-year graduate enrollments/BS Physics graduates 1954, 1960–72[d]	5.66	1.05 (0.27)	−1.49 (0.31)		0.72	0.08
6 First-year graduate enrollments/BS Physics graduates 1954, 1960–72[d]	4.23	0.42 (0.37)	−0.82 (0.28)	0.73 (0.22)	0.90	0.05
7 BS degrees, 1957–72	8.06	5.53 (0.90)	−5.36 (0.73)		0.84	0.09
8 BS degrees, 1957–72	6.20	2.16 (0.61)	−2.41 (0.52)	0.68 (0.09)	0.97	0.04
9 MS degrees, 1956, 1959–72[e]	5.75	1.90 (0.41)	−2.49 (0.52)		0.70	0.09
10 MS degrees, 1956, 1959–72[e]	3.40	1.00 (0.44)	−1.31 (0.57)	0.59 (0.21)	0.84	0.07
11 PhD degrees, 1956, 1959–72[e]	3.93	1.22 (0.34)	−1.71 (0.39)		0.71	0.08
12 PhD degrees, 1956, 1959–72[e]	2.75	0.79 (0.35)	−1.03 (0.46)	0.68 (0.32)	0.81	0.06

a   The dependent variables are the logarithm of the proportion of students at the same level of training, unless otherwise specified. Independent variables are also in *logs*. Numbers in parentheses are standard errors of estimate.
b   BS salaries used in lines 1, 2, 7, 8; PhD salaries in lines 3–6, 11, 12; MS salaries in lines 9–10; all salaries deflated by *CPI*. Salaries lagged 3 years in lines 7–8, 2 years in lines 8–9, 5 years in lines 11–12.
c   Omitted 1958, 1959, 1961, and 1963 due to absence of physics salaries for the period of the supply decision.
d   Omitted 1961, 1963 due to absence of data.
e   Omitted 1960, 1961, 1963 due to absence of salary data for period of supply decision.
Source: See Tables 1.1, 1.2, and Figure 1.1, with salaries calculated by linking series as described in note 6.

Table 1.4 Regression estimates of physics enrollments and degrees, 1954–72[a]

Equation	Dependent variable	Constant	Physics salaries	Professional earnings	Lagged number	R^2	SEE
1	Junior majors 1957–72	3.46	1.15 (0.50)	−0.90 (0.28)	0.71 (0.11)	0.94	0.06
2	Graduate enrollments 1954, 1957–72[b]	0.70	1.02 (0.24)	−0.49 (0.23)	0.65 (0.16)	0.99	0.03
3	First-year graduate Students, 1954, 1960–72[b]	8.06	0.87 (0.60)	−1.04 (0.30)	0.42 (0.38)	0.81	0.06
4	BS degrees 1957–72	1.72	2.29 (0.88)	−1.26 (0.50)	0.40 (0.17)	0.96	0.04
5	MS degrees, 1956, 1959–72[c]	−1.10	0.93 (0.24)	−0.27 (0.36)	0.67 (0.10)	0.99	0.05
6	PhD degrees, 1956, 1959–72[c]	−0.68	0.82 (0.25)	−0.42 (0.38)	0.83 (0.11)	0.99	0.03

Notes:
a   Dependent variables are the number of students at the level specified. All variables are in *log* form. Numbers in parentheses are standard errors of estimate.
b   BS salaries in lines 1, 4; PhD salaries in lines 2, 3, 6; MS salaries in line 5; all salaries deflated by the consumer price index. Salaries lagged 3 years in line 4, 2 years in line 5; 5 years in line 6.
c   Omitted 1960, 1961, 1963, due to absence of salary data for period of supply decision.
Source: See Tables 1.1, 1.2, and Figure 1.1, with salaries calculated by linking series as described in note 6.

lagged five years (consistent with the other lag patterns) yielded weaker results than that given in the table with the two-year lag,[7] suggesting substantial economic responsiveness in the decision to complete the doctorate program. As the physics doctorate typically takes four or five years to complete, the effect of salaries on the initial enrollment decision and on eventual graduation is likely to involve complex lag structures, on which our limited number of observations provides little light.

Additional support for the economic interpretation of the changing supply of students to physics is given in Table 1.4, which focuses on the absolute rather than relative number in the field. Salaries are the key variables in these calculations, with the short-run elasticity of supply to physics salaries estimated at near unity for graduate students and over two for B.S. recipients. Interpreting the lagged dependent coefficients as adjustment parameters, the long-run elasticities of degrees to physics salaries range from 2.8 (MS) to 4.6 (PhD) and 4.8 (BS). The summary statistics, high R^2, small standard errors of estimate, show that the simple supply model does a surprisingly good job in tracking the market turnaround, which suggests its value in forecasting.

Provisos

Although the calculations in Table 1.3 and 1.4 support our analysis, they fall short of a 'complete' explanation of supply developments in several ways. First, fellowship availability was omitted from the calculations due to the absence of data, with a potential bias on the estimated salary coefficients. The direction of the bias, which depends on the correlation of fellowships with supply (presumed positive) and of fellowships with salaries is unclear,[8] for the latter would appear to have been positive in the 1950s and early 1960s but negative during the period of greatest increase in fellowship support (1962–8). Second, the quality of physics students and programs has also been ignored, again with unclear consequences. In this case, while the less-qualified are more likely to provide the adjustment margin in supply, high-quality institutions (heavily dependent on federal R&D programs) have reduced enrollment more than low-quality colleges and universities (see NSF, 1972a). Third, the simple lagged adjustment model is at best a crude first-order approximation to the underlying process of forming salary expectations and adjustment to new market conditions. Various alternative models allowing, say, for different lags with respect to physics salaries than to the broader professional earnings, have not been explored due to the lack of a complete salary series for the postwar period. Fourth, professional earnings have been used as a measure of the alternative opportunities facing students at various decision points, although in principle alternatives will vary by level of training.[9] These provisos notwithstanding, the evidence indicates significant student supply responsiveness to the changing science manpower market.

Cobweb supply patterns

An alternative perspective on supply behavior is given by the cobweb supply equation which links the career decision directly to the level of demand and predetermined numbers of graduates. The cobweb equation can be obtained, as noted earlier, by substituting the salary determination relation for salaries in the supply equation of the recursive model. It may also be obtained from a 'job opportunities' model of career decisions in which opportunities depend on the balance between levels of demand and persons seeking work. Information about opportunities as well as salaries is likely to be useful in evaluating the current state of the market and in forecasting future possibilities. Deletion of salaries from the supply equation permits estimation in the absence of 'good' salary data, which is especially fruitful in the case at hand.

Table 1.5 contains estimates of the cobweb supply relation in physics for the postwar period. In these computations, enrollments or degrees are regressed on the lagged dependent variable, professional earnings, R&D spending (indexing the level of demand), and degrees in the year of the supply decision. In the degree regressions, the explanatory variables are lagged three (BS, lines 1 and 2), four (MS, lines 3 and 4), and five (PhD, lines 5 and 6) years, with graduates sometimes lagged an additional year. Precise determination of the cobweb cycles caused by the negative impact

Table 1.5 Cobweb supply equation,[a] 1950–72

Equation	Dependent variable, time coverage and lag	Constant	Graduates[b] (0)	Graduates[b] (−1)	R&D	Professional earnings	Lagged number	R^2	SEE	Adjusted DW
1	BS degrees, 1950–72	7.20	−0.42 (0.05)		0.63 (0.11)	−0.87 (0.26)	0.76 (0.09)	0.989	0.043	1.77
2	BS degrees, 1950–72	8.24	−0.17 (0.14)	−0.24 (0.12)	0.78 (0.12)	−0.97 (0.25)	0.55 (0.13)	0.992	0.040	0.65
3	MS degrees, 1950–72	5.40	−0.13 (0.05)		0.64 (0.11)	−0.88 (0.33)	0.61 (0.08)	0.992	0.046	4.21
4[d]	MS degrees, 1951–72	8.15	−0.12 (0.03)		0.64 (0.06)	−0.81 (0.19)	0.60 (0.05)	0.999	0.035	—
5	PhD degrees, 1950–72	2.93	−0.14 (0.08)		0.45 (0.12)	−0.41 (0.55)	0.72 (0.08)	0.988	0.055	1.10
6[d]	PhD degrees, 1951–72	1.81	−0.15 (0.09)		0.40 (0.12)	−0.27 (0.59)	0.74 (0.06)	0.995	0.055	—
7	Junior majors, 1955–72	6.16	−0.37 (0.12)		0.44 (0.24)	−0.69 (0.42)	0.81 (0.16)	0.961	0.061	—
8[c]	Junior majors, 1956–72	7.53	−0.30 (0.12)		0.40 (0.21)	−0.63 (0.37)	0.83 (0.14)	0.965	0.064	—
9	First-year graduate students, 1954, 1959–72	7.08	−0.42 (0.12)		1.10 (0.11)	−0.76 (0.66)	—[e]	0.967	0.047	—[e]
10	Graduate students, 1955–72	0.94	−0.22[b] (0.12)		0.26 (0.19)	−0.08 (0.62)	0.87 (0.14)	0.990	0.044	2.38
11[d]	Graduate students, 1956–72	3.19	−0.18 (0.06)		0.27 (0.08)	−0.27 (0.30)	0.91 (0.06)	0.998	0.030	—

Notes:

a The dependent variable is the *log* of the number of degrees or enrollees, as specified. Independent variables are lagged by 3 years in lines 1 and 2; 4 years in lines 3 and 4; 5 years in lines 5 and 6; 1 year in lines 7–11. Numbers in parentheses are standard errors of estimate; all variables are in *log* form.

b BS graduates used in lines 1, 2, 7, 8; PhD graduates in lines 5, 6, 9–11; and MS graduates in lines 3–4. Graduates with zero (0) lag are lagged the same number of years as other variables; graduates with (−1) lag are lagged an additional year.

c Adjusted *DW* statistic calculated by Durbin procedure which takes account of lagged dependent variable. The statistic is distributed, asymptotically, as the standard normal.

d Non-linear least squares estimates, with autocorrelation coefficients of −0.66 (line 4); −0.41 (line 6), −0.24 (line 8), and −0.76 (line 11).

e Omitted as insignificant; standard *DW* statistic of 1.96 showed no serial correlation.

Source: See Tables 1.1, 1.2, and Figure 1.1, with salaries calculated by linking series as described in note 8.

of degrees on enrollments is not possible due to collinearity between degrees one year apart. In some regressions, the table shows 'best' results for graduates having the same lag as other variables (lines 3, 4, 10, 11); in other cases, an additional year lag does better (lines 5–9), while for BS degrees (lines 1 and 2), the cobweb effect is shared between the two. As evinced in lines 1 and 2, however, the estimated size of the effect is roughly the same regardless of the specific lag (adding the additional degree term in line 2 reduces the coefficient in line 1 from -0.42 to -0.17, increases its standard error, but gives the same total effect ($-0.41 = -0.17 -0.24$). Similar results are obtained for the other independent variables. Finally, the problem of negative serial correlation of residuals shown by the Durbin-Watson statistics adjusted to take account of the lagged dependent variable (see James Durbin) is treated in the non-linear least squares regressions of lines 4, 6, 8, and 11 where a one-period autocorrelation coefficient is estimated simultaneously with other coefficients, with little effect on the parameters of interest.

There are two important findings in Table 1.5. First, the key coefficient on graduates which must be negative by the model obtains the predicted sign in all regressions with especially large effects at the baccalaureate level (lines 1, 2, 7, 8) and for first-year graduate enrollments (line 9). The other explanatory variables are also accorded correctly signed and quantitatively plausible impacts on supply. Second, the regressions as a whole show that the cobweb relation provides about as good an explanation of degrees or enrollments as the supply regressions of Tables 1.3 and 1.4, with similar R^2 and standard errors of estimate.

Determination of physics starting salaries

The demand or salary side of the market is investigated in Table 1.6 which displays regressions of physics salaries on the level of demand measured by R&D and numbers of graduates lagged one and two years. These regressions lend support to the recursive model with R&D having a substantial positive effect, and degrees a substantial negative effect on all three salary variables. As shown, R&D is accorded a larger effect on PhD and MS than on BS salaries, presumably as a result of the greater concentration of R&D activity among higher degree recipients. The estimated coefficients have relatively small standard errors in regressions 1, 3, and 5 where only a single demand or supply variable is entered; addition of collinear variables in regressions 2, 4 and 6 reduces the coefficients and increases their standard errors, but (as in Table 1.5) preserves the sum. Hence the size but not the precise timing of the impact of R&D or degree on salaries is reasonably well determined: the elasticity of salaries to R&D ranges from 0.34(B.S.) to 0.54(M.S.) and the flexibility of salaries from minus 0.15 to 0.25.[10]

Table 1.6 Salary determination equations,[a] 1951–72

Equation	Dependent variable and time coverage	Constant	R&D (−1)	R&D (−2)	Degrees (−1)	Degrees (−2)	R^2	SEE
1	BS salaries, 1955–72	4.38	—	0.34 (0.05)	−0.16 (0.06)		0.95	0.047
2		4.15	0.22 (0.11)	0.14 (0.11)	−0.02 (0.08)	−0.13 (0.08)	0.96	0.021
3	MS salaries, 1951–72[b]	3.19		0.54 (0.03)		−0.26 (0.04)	0.98	0.030
4		2.97	0.20 (0.17)	0.36 (0.19)	−0.12 (0.10)	−0.13 (0.09)	0.98	0.029
5	PhD salaries, 1951–72[b]	3.57		0.44 (0.04)		−0.14 (0.04)	0.96	0.037
6		3.36	0.19 (0.26)	0.14 (0.24)	+0.05 (0.16)	−0.16 (0.12)	0.97	0.037

Notes:
a   The dependent variable is starting salary of the specified group; salaries and R&D are in 1957–59 constant dollars. Dependent variables are lagged 1 or 2 years as specified (−1), (−2). All variables are in *log* form. Numbers in parentheses are standard errors of estimate.
b   The years 1952, 1953, 1955, 1956, 1958, 1959, 1961, 1963 are omitted due to absence of salary data.
Source: See Tables 1.1, 1.2, and Figure 1.1, with salaries calculated by linking series as described in note 6.

The regressions also provide information enabling us to evaluate the relative importance of demand and supply forces in the changes in physics salaries shown in Table 1.1. As the variance of R&D and degrees about their means turns out to be nearly the same in the period covered, the larger R&D parameters in the regressions implies that changed demand, due primarily to changes in federal R&D spending, was the *chief source* of changes in physics salaries, though movements along the demand schedule due to supply developments are also significant.

Market adjustments and forecasting

To what extent do the preceding findings, which depict a highly responsive market adjustment process, lead to forecasts of future developments and problems that differ from those obtained by standard projection techniques? Table 1.7 contains predictions from the recursive model and other studies showing a marked divergence in forecasts, with strikingly fewer physics PhDs anticipated for the future in our model than in even the lowest standard projection. More precisely, the table uses two versions of the estimated model to generate forecasts. Variant A employs the supply of PhD degrees equation from Table 1.4 (line 6) and the PhD salary equation from Table 1.6 (line 5) to generate forecasts. Since the degrees lag salaries by four years, predicted salaries are not needed until the 1977

Table 1.7 Alternative forecasts of physics PhDs, 1970–80

Years	Office of education	Cartter	NAS–NRC	Model A	Model B
1969–70[a]	1500	1500	1500	1500	1500
1974–5	2153	1853	2153	1134	1189
1979–80	2492	2654	3350	731	786

Note:
a   The various projections use different base year numbers of PhDs due to differences in the source of data. National Academy of Science–National Research Council (*NAS–NRC*) data differ somewhat from those of the Office of Education. I have set the base year number as 1500 and made projections on the basis of implicit percentage increases in the actual forecasts. *Sources:* Office of Education, Cartter, *NAS–NRC* from Cartter; Models A and B, from the recursive model of Tables 1.4 and 1.5, as described in the text.

degree forecast. Variant B replaces the degree equation with an equation determining first year enrollments (Table 1.4, line 3), assuming a similar percentage increase in PhDs as in initial enrollments. In both models, R&D is assumed to increase at the postwar rate of growth of real GNP (3.7 per cent) so that the R&D to GNP ratio is fixed; professional earnings are postulated to increase at their postwar trend level of 2.8 per cent per year.

The important finding is that regardless of the precise equations used, our model predicts sizeable declines in physics doctorates while the other analysts foresee large increases. According to the recursive model, reductions in the supply of new entrants will ameliorate physics market problems; according to the standard calculations, increases in supply will exacerbate the potential imbalance of the 1980s due to the likely fall in demand for faculty. While different changes in exogeneous variables such as a sudden sharp increase in federal R&D spending on energy would significantly invalidate our forecasts, it is evident from Table 1.7 that economic responsiveness has a first-order effect on the market and should be taken into account in manpower analysis.

SUMMARY

The principal findings of this study can be summarized briefly as follows:

First, the number of physics students has varied greatly in the postwar period, declining in the recent collapse of the science market after a decade of rapid increase. These changes result from economic responses to salary or job opportunity incentives, with fairly large elasticities of supply for physics salaries ranging from about unity in the short run to 3 or 4 in the long run at the graduate level, and from 2 in the short run to 4 in the long run for BS recipients.

Second, salaries of physicists have fluctuated significantly relative to other wages and salaries, rising in the post-Sputnik boom period and falling rapidly in the late 1960s and early 1970s. The bulk of the change in salaries can be attributed to R&D expenditures and the R&D policies of the federal government, with changes in supply having a smaller, though significant, effect.

Third, developments in the physics market, as in several other high-level labor markets, appears to be well described by a simple recursive model which exploits the time delay in supply due to lengthy training programs. As a result of the recursive structure, large numbers of physics graduates create a market setting likely to reduce enrollments and future degrees in the field in accord with the cobweb scenario.

Fourth, in the absence of a sharp increase in demand in the near future, market adjustments, especially on the supply side, are likely to lead to far fewer PhDs in physics than indicated by standard forecasts. While the market still faces the major shock of a demographic-induced decline in demand for faculty in the 1980s, supply and salary adjustments will provide an important buffer to the decline.

POSTSCRIPT

The predictions in this article, shown in Table 1.7, turned out to be remarkably on target, confirming the value of the supply response analysis in understanding the market for physicists. In 1974–5 1,126 persons graduated with physics PhDs in the United States; in 1979–80 865 graduated with PhDs in the field, both in the range of the numbers predicted in the table, and out of the range of the forecasts that ignored responsive supply behavior. The greater number of physics PhDs in 1979–80 than predicted was due, moreover, not to any failure of the model to capture the supply behavior of American students, but to the increased number of physics PhDs granted to foreign students, whose decisions presumably depend on labor-market opportunities overseas. Remove those degrees from the total and the forecasts are within 5 per cent of the actual degrees granted in both 1974–5 and 1979–80. Economics does have something to contribute about the labor-market behavior, even of physicists.

NOTES

1. The major difference by level of training is the rapid increase of MS and BS salaries between 1951 and 1954 compared to the slow increase in PhD salaries. The major difference by source of data is between BS salaries reported by the National Register, which increases only moderately from 1951 to 1962, and those of starting physicists reported by placement offices, which increase rapidly in that period.

2. It should be stressed that the well-known Cartter forecast depends on a decline in the number of persons of college age in the 1980s, a relatively hard piece of evidence on which to base forecasts.

3. Selection of exogenous demand variables is difficult in analysis of factor demands. In the case of physics, federal R&D policies are taken as the major exogenous factor at work, making R&D expenditures exogenous.

4. Formally, with the simple model

$$S = aW(-1) \quad \text{(Supply equation)}$$

$$W = bS + cZ \quad \text{(Wage equation)}$$

where S = supply, W = wages, Z = level of demand. Substituting we obtain

$$S = abS(-1) + acZ(-1) \quad \text{(Cobweb equation)}$$

5. The equations differ because regressions with numbers as the dependent variables do not necessarily support the homogeneity postulate of the proportion regressions. Indeed, when the lagged number of physics students is entered in the regressions, the coefficient for all students becomes insignificant, and is dropped in the results shown in Table 1.4. As the homogeneity postulate remains *a priori* plausible, it was deemed fruitful to present the two sets of regressions.

6. Milton Friedman and Gregory Chow and An-loh Lin describe the optimal methods of extrapolation, interpolation, and linking series. In our case, the PhD and MS series are obtained by regressing CPC (1960–73) data on *NSF* data (1951, 1954, 1957, 1960, 1962, 1964, 1966, 1968, 1970) and using the predicted salaries for the pre-1960 years in which *NSF* figures exist. The BS salary series is obtained by regression of CPC figures on a series obtained from the MIT Placement Office for graduates of that school. All of the data are available on request.

7. The regression with the five-year lag yielded a coefficient for physics salaries of 0.73, with a standard error of 0.48 and one for professional salaries of −1.42, with a standard error of 0.63.

8. As Zvi Griliches shows, the omitted variable bias depends on the product of the least squares coefficients of the regression of the dependent variable on the excluded variable and of the regression of the included explanatory variable on the excluded variable.

9. In theory, the alternative income affecting decisions will change each year as cumulated human capital increases. One experiment designed to provide a better measure of alternatives (which is possible with available data) is to treat BS salaries rather than professional earnings as the relevant alternatives to graduate students. This is, however, by no means optimal since many undergraduate majors do not view BS physics work as the proper alternative. Calculations with BS salaries support the results in the text. The regression of first-year enrollments divided by BS graduates on PhD and BS salaries, for example, yields coefficients of 1.21 and −1.69, with standard errors of 0.93 and 1.23. The regression of the physics share of MS degrees on MS and BS salaries two years earlier yields 2.12 and −3.92 for the estimated coefficients, with standard errors of 1.04 and 1.32.

10. Note that the regression relates starting salaries to new entrants, not average salaries to total employment, and thus does not yield elasticities with respect to the stock of physicists. With ratios of graduates to employment of about 1 to 10, the flexibility coefficients for the entire stock would be ten times those in the text, which in turn implies that demand for all physicists is *inelastic*.

BIBLIOGRAPHY

American Institute of Physics (1968–72a), *AIP Graduate Student Surveys*, nos R-207.1–207.5 (New York: 1968–72).

American Institute of Physics (1968–72b), *Survey of Physics Bachelor's Degrees Recipients*, nos R211.1–211.4 (New York: 1968–72).

American Institute of Physics, *Physics and Astronomy Enrollments and Degrees in US*, no. R-151.10 (New York: March 1973).

Arrow, K., and Capron, W., 'Dynamic shortages and price rises: the engineer-scientist case', *Quarterly Journal of Economics* (May 1959), 73, pp. 292–308.

Cain, G., Freeman, R., and Hansen, L., *Labor Market Analysis of Engineers and Technical Workers* (Baltimore: 1973).

Cartter, A., 'Scientific manpower trends for 1970–1985', *Science* (April 1971), 172, pp. 132–40.

Chow, G., and Lin, A., 'Best linear unbiased interpolation, distribution, and extrapolation of time series by related series', *Review of Economics and Statistics* (November 1971), 53, pp. 372–5.

College Placement Council (*CPC*), 'Men's salary survey', (Bethlehem, Pa.: 1960–73).

Durbin, J., 'Testing for serial correlation in least-squares regression when some of the regressors are lagged dependent variables', *Econometrica* (May 1970), 38, pp. 410–21.

Federal Interagency Committee on Education, Student Support Group, *Report on Federal Predoctoral Student Support* (Washington: 1970, revised 1972).

Freeman, R., *Labor Market for College-Trained Manpower* (Cambridge, MA: Harvard University Press, 1971).

Freeman, R., 'Labor market adjustments in psychology', *American Psychologist* (May 1972), 27, pp. 384–93.

Freeman, R., 'Legal cobwebs: a recursive model of the market for lawyers', *Review of Economics and Statistics* (May 1975), pp. 171–9.

Freeman, R., and Breneman, D., 'Forecasting the PhD labor market: pitfalls for policy', National Board Graduate Education (Washington: 1974).

Friedman, M., 'The interpolation of time series by related series,' *Journal of American Statistical Associations* (December 1962), 57, pp. 729–57.

Griliches, Z., 'Specification bias in estimates of production functions', *Journal of Farm Economics* (February 1957), 36, pp. 8–20.

Muth, J., 'Rational expectations and the theory of price movements', *Econometrica* (July 1961), 29, pp. 315–35.

National Science Foundation, Reports of the National Register of Scientific and Technical Manpower, American Science Manpower (Washington: 1954–5, 1956–8, 1960, 1962, 1964, 1966, 1968, 1970).

National Science Foundation (1972a), 'First-year, full-time graduate science enrollment continues to decline' (Washington: 1972).

National Science Foundation (1972b), *National Pattern of R&D Reources, 1953–1972* (Washington: 1972).

Nerlove, M., 'Adaptive expectations and cobweb phenomena,' *Quarterly Journal of Economics* (May 1958), 72, pp. 227–40.

US Atomic Energy Commission, *Annual Financial Federal Funds for Research Development*, vol. 21, various editions (Washington: 1959–72).

US Bureau of the Census, *Current Population Reports*, Series P-60, various issues (Washington: 1948–72).

US Bureau of the Census, *Statistical Abstract of the United States*, various editions

(Washington: 1948–73).

US Department of Commerce, *The National Income and Product Accounts of the US, 1929–65*, (Washington: 1966).

US Department of Commerce, *Survey of Current Business*, July editions (Washington: 1966–72).

US Department of Labor, *Employment, Education, and Earnings of American Men of Science*, Bulletin 1027 (Washington: 1951).

US Federal Security Agency, *Manpower Resources in Physics 1951* (Washington: 1952).

Wolfe, D., and Kidd, C., 'The future market for PhDs', *Science* (August 1971), 173, pp. 784–93.

2 · FUNCTIONING OF THE COLLEGE GRADUATES' JOB MARKET

To understand the operation of a complex social system like the labor market for college graduates, in which numerous individuals and institutions interact to determine employment and wages, it is necessary to simplify reality and focus on the salient features of the system.

In the operation of the market for college graduates, there are, according to my analysis, five factors whose interplay determines the dynamic operation of the market over time.

RESPONSIVE SUPPLY BEHAVIOR ON THE PART OF YOUNG STUDENTS

The career and educational decisions of young persons and their families are critical in the operation of the market because these decisions ultimately determine the long-run supply of graduates to the economy. If the supply behavior of the young is highly sensitive to such economic incentives as salaries and job opportunities, the number of new graduates will be an important homeostatic device, helping equilibrate the job market. If, contrarily, the young are only slightly influenced by economic incentives, equilibration will be more difficult; the major brunt of adjustment will then fall, even in the long run, on salaries and on employers, possibly leading to extended disequilibria over long periods of time. How responsive are the young to labor-market incentives?

There is a substantial and growing body of evidence that, contrary to traditional views of student decision-making, young persons are highly sensitive in their educational and career decisions to the state of the labor market. For a wide variety of fields, ranging from law to physics to psychology to accounting, studies reveal a sizeable positive link between the number of students pursuing the area and salaries or related indicators of economic opportunities. In physics, for example, in the flourishing job market of the decade that followed Sputnik, enrollments at both the undergraduate and graduate level increased greatly; by contrast, in the deteriorating market of the late 1960s, despite a nearly twofold expansion in the size of the student body, junior- and senior-year majors declined from 14,900 (1961) to 11,400 (1971), while first-year graduate enrollments dropped by one-third. (See also Chapter 1.)[1]

More important in terms of the market depression of the 1970s, 'responsive supply behavior' appears to be the major cause of the dramatic fall in the fraction of young men choosing to attend college. Formal statistical analysis[2] indicates that over 95 per cent of the variation in the fraction of young men in college over the 1951–74 period can be attributed to two simple measures of the economic incentive to enroll: the income of graduates relative to other workers and relative employment opportunities. As Figure 2.1 shows, the pattern of change in enrollments 'predicted' by these variables does a good job of tracking the actual drop in the 1970s. Other factors that might be expected to influence enrollments – such as changes in the draft or the overall weakening of the economy in the mid-1970s–were important for only limited periods of time and appear to be dwarfed in importance by the continuous decline of the job market. The reduction in numbers called and eventual elimination of the draft, for example, may have played some part in the drop in enrollments from 1969 to 1970 but cannot be invoked as a cause of subsequent changes. Similarly, the rising unemployment and inflation that cut into real family income in the mid-1970s does not explain the fall in enrollments at the outset of the decade. Only the change in market opportunities covers the entire period.

Surveys designed to elicit the importance attached by students to economic factors in education and career decisions support the 'responsive supply' hypothesis. About two-thirds of male and one-half of female freshmen surveyed by the American Council of Education agreed, for example, that 'the chief benefit of college is that it increases earning power' (see Table 2.1). Seventy-seven per cent of men and 70 per cent of women were going to college, in large part, 'to get a better job' and 57 per cent of the men and 42 per cent of the women 'to make more money'–all of which suggests that when earning power declines, so too will enrollments. With respect to career choice, nearly one-half of the men and over one-third of the women regarded 'high anticipated earning' as very important in their decisions, while 42 per cent of the men and 52 per cent of the women also thought that 'job openings available' was very important. In addition, a relatively large percentage of students accorded considerable importance to the chance for steady progress and rapid advancement in their anticipated careers. These figures do not, however, mean that the labor market is the dominant factor in decisions, nor that it is critical to all persons. Because individuals have, as Adam Smith noted over 200 years ago, strong nonpecuniary preferences for specific kinds of work as well as having

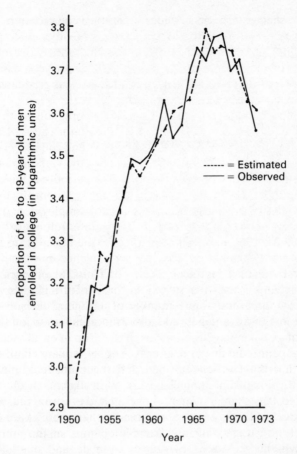

Figure 2.1 Proportion of 18- to 19-year-old men enrolled in college and proportion estimated from economic incentives, 1951–73.

Source: Based on regression estimates in R. Freeman, 'Overinvestment in college training?', *Journal of Human Resources* (Summer 1975), Table 5.

specialized abilities, the career decisions of many will not be affected by the market. Those with great love for certain jobs, for instance aspiring authors or priests, will choose that work at almost any 'living' wage. Others with special abilities – athletes, singers, chess champions, movie starlets– will select a career on the basis of their particular abilities. Even such sharp changes in the market as the downturn of the 1970s will have little impact on the behavior of these types of people. At the same time, however, many individuals whose abilities and preferences make several options feasible will alter their plans when relative wages change, moving–all else the same–from careers with contracting markets to those with expanding markets. The responsiveness of supply to economic incentives depends not

Table 2.1 Percentage of freshman students concerned with economic factors in educational and career decisions

	Male	Female
Agree that 'the chief benefit of college is that it increases earning power'	66	51
Factors reported as 'very important' in going to college:		
To get a better job	77	70
To make more money	57	42
Factors regarded as 'very important' in career choice:		
High anticipated earnings	48	35
Job openings available	42	52
Rapid advancement	40	30
Chance for steady progress	52	46

Sources: American Council of Education The American Freshman: National Norms for Fall 1971, *Ace Research Reports*, Vol. 6, No. 6, 1971, pp. 27–8, 35–6, and (with University of California, Los Angeles): *The American Freshman: National Norms for Fall 1974*, p. 20, 32.

on the existence of a mythical species of *Homo economicus*, who, like Scrooge McDuck, views life strictly in terms of the almighty dollar, but rather on the apparently large number of 'marginal decision-makers' for whom the other advantages and disadvantages of various occupations balance out.

The major consequence of responsive supply behavior on the part of the young is that the fraction enrolled and the number of new graduates become critical adjustment mechanisms. With a relatively elastic supply of students to colleges and universities overall and to various careers, changes in salaries and in employment opportunities, like those experienced in the early 1970s, are translated into sizeable changes in the number of new college graduates seeking work.

LONG WORKING LIFE

The mundane fact that people work for 40 or so years means that the vast majority of college graduates invested in their education and chose their specialties many years ago, making the total supply of graduates relatively inelastic even when the supply of the young is highly adaptive to new circumstances. When, as in the 1970s, there are many more young persons in the cohorts entering the labor market than there are graduates in the retiring age brackets, total supply will grow even if the fraction of the young enrolled in college falls. As a consequence, the movement toward a long-run balance of supply and demand for graduates in the entire population will necessarily be slow, permitting disequilibrium to persist for many years. In markets with long-lived factors of production, supply–demand disequilibria are likely to be long lived also.

Two factors ameliorate the problem of adjusting the total supply of graduates to changed market conditions. First is the fact that younger and older graduates often perform different work tasks, the former doing work directly related to their training, the latter more general managerial work. Because of different activities, graduates of different ages may be only moderately substitutable for one another, leading to more or less separate labor markets. As a result, the market for new graduates could improve rapidly as the supply of the young declines at the same time that the total college-trained population grows. The 'good news' is that the declining fraction of the young going to college may significantly alleviate the market for newly graduated workers in the next decade. The 'bad news' is that persons in the large graduating classes of the late 1960s and early 1970s may suffer from a relative excess of supply over their entire lives, creating a significant intergenerational equity problem.

The second factor easing the supply adjustment problem is the possibility of occupational mobility and other forms of adaptive responses to market incentives on the part of experienced workers. Although, because of their past commitments and training, the experienced react less to market ups and downs than do the young, they can still play a major role in the movement to equilibrium. Since there are many more experienced than new workers, even relatively small changes in the supply of the former can have a sizeable impact on the state of the market.[3] However, while the decisions of the experienced make the supply of college workers in different occupations more flexible, they have little impact on the total number of college workers in the entire economy, because decisions taken years ago to obtain education cannot be altered today.

Alleviating factors notwithstanding, the long working life of college manpower raises the possibility that, despite supply responses to the depressed market of the 1970s, a relative surplus of college workers in the population as a whole will persist for many years to come.

DEMAND AND EMPLOYER BEHAVIOR

The dynamic 'moving force' in the college job market is the demand for graduates, which is dependent on such basic economic forces as the structure of the economy, industrial activities and changes in technology, the possibility of substituting college graduates for other workers or for machines, and demographic changes. The structure of the economy is important because industries differ greatly in their relative employment of graduates, with, for example, 31 per cent of workers in finance in 1970 having college degrees compared to 6 per cent in the automobile industry. Whether industries that make intensive use of college manpower grow rapidly in the future, as they did in the 1960s when aerospace, the education sector and related industries enjoyed a boom, or slowly, as in the 1970s, will be a key determinant of market conditions. Industrial activities and technology are important because the relative employment of graduates within industries depends on what those industries do and how they do it. If resources are allocated to research and development or related activities that make extensive use of educated workers, demand for graduates will be high. Similarly, demand will also be high if, for whatever reason, new technologies are 'biased' (at given factor prices) in favor of relatively educated manpower. Empirically, there has been considerable variation in expenditures for R&D, causing sizeable shifts in the demand for college graduates, especially scientific and engineering personnel. On the other hand, there has been only modest change in the intraindustrial use of educated workers within periods of, say, a decade or so, and even over longer periods intraindustrial changes in the employment of graduates appear to be dwarfed by shifts in the composition of industries.[4] Demography is important because the age structure and rate of growth of the population are critical determinants of the size of the educational sector, which is the single largest industry employing graduates.

When, as in the 1970s, the relative wages of the college trained change, the possibilities of substituting better-educated for less-educated workers become critical in market adjustment. If substitutions are relatively easy to make, only modest declines in salaries will suffice to increase employment and equilibrate supply–demand imbalances. If substitutions are difficult, enormous changes in salaries may be required for a 'surplus' of graduates to find jobs.

Empirical evidence on substitutability is mixed. In the late 1960s, several scholars who compared incomes and employment across countries found surprisingly large 'elasticities of substitution', which suggests that only small declines in relative salaries are needed to increase greatly the employment of college workers. More recent work, including that of the Nobel Prize-winning Dutch economist Jan Tinbergen, indicates, however, that the possibilities of substitution are more limited and that significantly large changes in relative salaries are needed to have a major impact on employment. My work with time series finds sizeable but by no means enormous long-run elasticities of demand for all graduates, and smaller elasticities for such detailed specialists as engineers, R&D scientists, lawyers, physicists and biologists.[5] Perhaps the 1970s experience in the job market most decisively supports the moderate substitution hypothesis. It would be difficult to explain the sharp decline in the relative earnings of graduates by the economic forces of supply and demand if college-trained and other workers were such good substitutes that only minute adjustments in wages would be needed to equilibrate the surplus of new graduates that developed after 1969.

When employment of graduates in specific occupations is investigated, the possibility of increasing demand in response to lower salaries appears even more difficult. In 'good' college-level jobs, the percentage increase in employment caused by a percentage drop in salaries appears to be moderate, at best. Substitution possibilities are greatest in less desirable white-collar jobs, such as sales or clerical positions or lower-level management. The result is that, while lower earnings can resolve an unemployment problem, they do so by creating an underemployment problem that cannot be readily alleviated by cuts in salaries.

COBWEB DYNAMICS

Because four or more years are required to 'produce' a college graduate, the college market tends to follow the classic *cobweb feedback system* that has long been associated with the markets for corn or hogs. Like these agricultural products, the supply of graduates is determined by market conditions several periods earlier, due to the fixed time delay in educational production, and is thus a lagging function of the state of the market. Such a structure generates oscillatory ups and downs, with shortages changing into surpluses every four or five years. The reason for this pattern can be readily seen (Figure 2.2). If salaries and demand are strong in a specialty in, say, 1969, many students will be drawn into the field, becoming the new supply four or five years later. When they graduate in

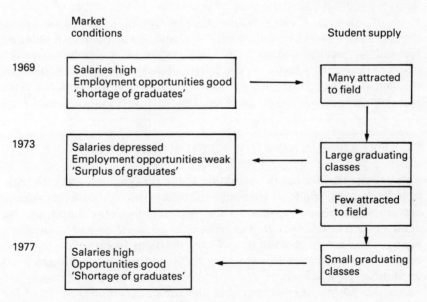

Figure 2.2 Cobweb dynamics in the college job market.

1973, unless demand has increased commensurately, they will 'oversupply' the market, depressing salaries and employment opportunities. With the decline in incentives in 1973, relatively fewer students will enroll in the field, causing a shortage in 1977, and so forth. Of course, other factors, notably shifts in demand, will also affect the market. What is important is that there is an underlying feedback structure tending to produce cyclical movements in the supply–demand balance. Econometric models based on the cobweb hypothesis have been quite effective in 'explaining' the labor-market experience of recipients of the Bachelor of Science (BS) in engineering, of graduates in accounting, and of Master of Business Administration (MBA) as well as law graduates, and those in other specialties in which there is a close one-to-one tie between education and occupation.[6] Cobweb dynamics help explain much of the recurrent shortages and surpluses of certain types of college-trained specialists in years past.

One other classic economic adjustment mechanism plays an important role in the market for graduates. This is the 'accelerator' adjustment process, which is traditionally viewed as governing capital goods production. In the case of the college trained, the fact that universities hire a relatively large number of graduates, particularly master's and doctoral degree recipients, means that demand depends in part on the number of students seeking academic careers. If many seek such careers, the demand for faculty and faculty salaries and employment opportunities will improve, leading to an increase in supply and further gains in demand. The situation tends toward instability, however, because once the number of students levels off, demand for new faculty will fall rapidly, causing a decline in the number of students considering academic careers, further reducing demand for faculty, and so forth. This feature of academia makes the market for university faculty and graduate studies exceptionally vulnerable to changes in the growth of enrollments. Academic stands on a revolving ball–you have to run to stay in place, and when you stop, you fall.[7]

GOVERNMENT AND EDUCATED MANPOWER

To complete the story of the operation of the college job market, the role of federal, state, and local governments must be brought into the picture. Governmental policies have a sizeable impact on both the supply and the demand sides of the market. The number of scholarships and fellowships, public subsidization and tuition policies, decisions to expand or contract educational systems, and moves to support students or provide grants to institutions have influenced and will continue to influence the supply of graduates–not only the quantity but also the composition in terms of the socioeconomic groups from which graduates are drawn and the specialties they choose. On the demand side, governments affect the market, directly as large employers of educated manpower and indirectly through their purchase of goods and services from the private sector. Some purchases, such as R&D, space programs, defense and health services, result in direct changes in demand. Other purchases have less immediate but still real impacts by the input–output linkages in the economy–the fact that industries purchase commodities from others, which employ graduates in turn, and so forth. Analysis of federal, state and local spending using the input–output table for the US economy created by a Nobel Prize winner, economist W. Leontief, shows that dollars of public expenditure, especially at the federal level, generate more demand for college-trained workers than do dollars of private spending.[8]

In years past, the dependence of the college market on governmental activities has had a significant destabilizing effect on the economic status of graduates, because federal, and to a lesser extent state and local, policies have changed greatly within short periods of time, causing sudden turnarounds in demand. Federal R&D spending, for example, shot up in the years surrounding Sputnik, giving a sharp spur to the demand for graduate scientists and engineers, then fell (in real dollars) equally sharply in the late 1960s and 1970s, contributing to the market turnaround. Private R&D spending, by contrast, rose modestly through most of the entire period. Similar pronounced changes in spending are found in the health sector, in defense, and in other programs. One possible reason for governmental overreaction to problems is the 'crisis mentality' of elected oficials whose time horizon, given the periodicity of elections, is short. Another is that fewer institutions are involved in the decision-making process than in private markets involving many firms. In any case, governmental activities have exacerbated rather than ameliorated problems in the college market and will undoubtedly continue to play a major role in future developments, for better or worse.

THE OVERALL MARKET SYSTEM

The preceding analysis paints a distinctive picture of the functioning of the college job market: a market in which young persons are exceptionally sensitive to economic opportunities; where the long working life of graduates makes overall supply adjustments sluggish; where demand changes substantially with changes in the structure of the economy, the demographic composition of the population, certain activities–like R&D–and governmental policies and expenditures; where employers substitute college graduates for less-educated workers in noncollege-level, white-collar jobs, in response to lower relative wages; where cobweb dynamics produce significant cyclical ups and downs; and where accelerator adjustments make one major employment area – the educational system – highly sensitive to changes in the rate of growth of enrollment. Given this model of the functioning of the college job market, what caused the depression of the 1970s? And what lies ahead?

WHY THE BOOMING SIXTIES BUST

The question of why the college manpower market deteriorated so suddenly at the outset of the 1970s can be turned around: why was the market so strong in preceding decades, despite the continuous growth of supply?

Two factors appear to answer both of these questions and explain the state of the market over the entire post-World War II period. On the demand side, the relative position of the highly educated was maintained in the 1950s and 1960s by large increases in demand due to changes in the industrial mix of jobs, the growth of R&D and the extraordinary expansion of the education sector. In the 1970s, all of these forces which had provided a significant upward push to the market, weakened or actually declined relative to the overall state of the economy.

The quantitative dimensions of the slackened demand are shown in Table 2.2 and Figure 2.3. Table 2.2 contrasts the growth of employment in industries that hire relatively large numbers of college graduates to the growth in those that employ relatively few. It covers both the booming sixties and the declining seventies. Among the industries with many graduates are the following: federal public administration, with one in six male graduates working for the national bureaucracy; professional services, ranging from law to welfare; finance, insurance, and realty; certain manufacturing industries, including ordnance, chemicals, petroleum, instruments, electronic computing, aircraft, electrical machinery; and, of course, education, which accounts for the employment of over one-half of female college graduates and one-tenth of male college graduates. Industries that hire very few college graduates include transportation, communication, agriculture, and the remaining areas of manufacturing.[9] The table reveals a marked slowdown in the rate of growth of college-manpower-intensive sectors relative to other sectors, between the 1960s and 1970s. During 1960–9 period, employment grew more than twice as rapidly in the college-intensive industries as in other industries – a differential rate of 2.4 per cent per annum. In the 1969–74 period, the sectoral growth rates converged, as employment in college-intensive industries slowed relative to the previous decade – resulting in a differential of just 0.8 per cent. The rate of change in employment in college-intensive manufacturing, in particular, which accounts for about one in nine male graduates, dropped from 3.6 per cent per annum in the first period to −1.2

Table 2.2 Compound annual percentage change in employment in college-manpower-intensive and other industries, 1960–9 and 1969–74

Industries	1960–9	1969–74
College-manpower-intensive	4.4	2.8
Noneducational:	3.8	2.3
Professional services[a]	5.4	5.9
Federal public administration, except postal service	2.0	0.0
Finance, insurance, and realty	3.7	3.2
College-intensive manufacturing[b]	3.6	−1.2
Education	6.2	3.9
All other[c]	2.0	2.0
National total	2.8	2.2

Notes:
a Excludes educational services: includes SIC codes 80, 81, 84, 86 and 89. Employment in 1969 in 84 and 86 is for March from Bulletin 1312–9, p. 685. Employment in 1960 is the mean for 1959 and 1961, also from p. 685. Employment in 1974 in 84 and 86 estimated by multiplying their share of total service employment in 1971 using data on p. 685 by actual employment in 1974.
b Ordnance, chemicals, petroleum, professional instruments, aircraft, electrical machinery, and electronic computing machinery, with 1960 electronic computing machinery estimated.
c Agriculture included, based on data for US Department of Commerce *Survey of Current Business* (July editions), with 1974 estimated.
Source: US Department of Labor, *Employment and Earnings 1909–1972*, Bulletin 1312–9, updated from *Employment and Earnings* (March 1975), Vol. 21, No. 9.

per cent in the second period, while that in federal public administration fell from 2 per cent to zero. This shows that the market decline cannot–as some have asserted–be traced solely to changes in the size of the education sector and to demographic shifts in the number of persons of school age. The rate of growth of demand for college workers in the 1970s decelerated relative to that for the less educated as a result of a more general shift in the industrial composition of employment–a shift involving slower growth in those sectors of the economy where relatively large numbers of graduates have traditionally been employed.

The changing pattern of demand is examined from a different perspective in Figure 2.3, which displays the proportion of GNP allocated to three college-manpower-intensive activities–R&D, defense and education. After increasing rapidly from the early 1950s through the Sputnik era, the proportion of GNP spent on R&D began to fall in the late 1960s. Actual R&D spending dropped significantly in deflated dollars in the early 1970s. Similarly, defense spending, which had fluctuated around 9–10 per cent in the 1950s and 1960s, fell to just 6 per cent of GNP in the 1970s. The proportion of GNP devoted to education also rose rapidly in the 1960s and then fell, from 8 per cent to 7.6 per cent, between 1971 and 1973, a drop of similar magnitude to the fall in the R&D share of GNP.

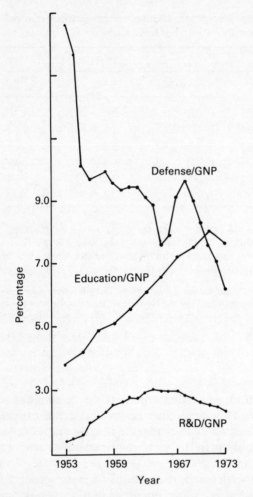

Figure 2.3 Share of GNP allocated to R&D, education and defense, 1953–73.

Sources: US Office of Education, *Digest of Educational Statistics 1974*, Table 172, p. 152; Ibid., Table 27, p. 26; Data for 1955 and 1960–73 from US Department of Commerce, *Statistical Abstract of the United States 1974*, Table 488, p. 306. Data for all other years calculated from *Statistical Abstract of the United States 1962*, Table 327, p. 248, and US Department of Labor, *Manpower Report of the President* (1974), Table G-3, p. 376.

On the supply side, there was surprisingly little net increase in the number of new college graduates seeking work during the period of rapid growth in demand. In the 1950s, the number of new college graduates fell somewhat, due to the diminished size of college-age cohorts – the result of falling birthrates some 20 years earlier. In the 1960s, when there were relatively many persons of college age, the enormous growth of graduate education delayed their entrance on the job market, so that the big increase in the supply of new college-trained workers did not occur until the end of the decade. Between 1958 and 1968, for example, despite a sizeable increase in the number of male bachelor's graduates, the 'net' number seeking work (defined as the number of graduates minus the number of first-year enrollees in graduate and professional schools), relative to the total male civilian workforce, *was halved*. The 1960s were a period of declining relative supply of new college workers, not–as is often thought – a period of increasing supply. In the late 1960s and early 1970s, by contrast, the number of new college graduates entering the job market increased greatly, as graduate education became less attractive. Between 1969 and 1972, the *net* number of new college graduates seeking work relative to the total male workforce increased threefold. Estimates by Allan Cartter of the ratio of students enrolling in professional and graduate schools for the first time (which differs from the number of first-year enrollees by excluding those who enrolled in previous years but had not completed their first year of study) to recent bachelor's graduates tells a similar though less drastic story. Cartter estimates that about 31 per cent of college graduates went directly to graduate and professional schools in the late 1950s, 41 per cent in the peak year of 1967 and 33 per cent in 1973. On the basis of these figures, which suggest larger increases in the supply of graduates entering the market in the 1960s than the 'net' estimates, the number of bachelor's degree recipients entering the job market per worker increased by 1.2 per cent per annum from 1959 to 1967, compared to 7.6 per cent per annum from 1967 to 1973.[10] However measured, it is apparent that the supply of new college graduates did not increase rapidly until the late 1960s and early 1970s, postponing the problem of adjusting to the large freshman classes of the 1960s.

The factors behind the increase in the number of young college graduates can be pursued further. As noted, demographic developments resulting from the post-World War II baby boom played a major role in increasing the number of college enrollments – and ultimately of degrees. Between 1950 and 1970, for example, the population aged 18 to 24 increased by over 9.5 million persons – in percentage terms, by a remarkable 65 per cent. All else the same, this change would have substantially raised the ratio of new graduates to total employment and created problems in the market for new entrants. Since the proportion of the young choosing college is highly variable, however, due to *responsive supply behavior*, demographic changes do not necessarily translate into comparable changes in college enrollments or degrees. During the 1950s, enrollment rose by 1.3 million, despite the constant college-age population, as a result of an increase in the fraction of the young choosing college. During the 1960s, both the college-age population and the

Table 2.3 Demographic and decision factors in the growth of college enrollments and the college workforce, men and women

	1950–60 (in thousands)	1960–70 (in thousands)
1. Actual change in enrollments	1,296	4,337
2. Change in enrollments predicted by growth of population of college age (assuming proportion enrolled fixed at initial year level)	2	1,884
3. Actual change in 25- to 29-year-old college graduates in the labor force	281	862
4. Change predicted by growth of population aged 25 to 29 (assuming proportion with degrees fixed at initial year level)	−39	309

Sources: US Office of Education, *Digest of Educational Statistics, 1972*, Table 86, p. 74. US Bureau of Census 1970 Census of Population, *Educational Attainment*, PC(2)-5B, Table 9, p. 74; 1960 Census of Population, *Educational Attainment*, PC(2)-5B, Table 4, p. 54, Table 5, p. 71; and 1950 Census of Population, *Education*, P-E No. 5B, Table 9, p. 74.

proportion of them choosing college grew, with a consequent doubling of enrollments and a gain of 4.3 million persons in college. The relative importance of these two factors in the 1950–70 growth in the number attending college and in the supply of graduates is examined in Table 2.3, where changes in enrollments predicted by demographic changes are compared to actual changes. Lines 1 and 3 of the table give the actual changes, lines 2 and 4 the changes predicted by the changing number of persons of the relevant age. The predicted values are obtained by multiplying the proportion in the age group enrolled or having a degree in 1950 (1960) by the change in population over the decade. Differences between these figures represent (a) the effect of supply behavior and (b) the interaction of changes in demography and the fraction choosing college. The data tell a clear story. In the 1950s, when the number of persons of college age was relatively steady (line 2) and the number of 25 to 29 year olds was declining (line 4), essentially none of the growth in enrollments or degrees can be explained by demographic forces. In the 1960s, despite the large increase in the number of the young, only 30 per cent to 40 per cent of the *change* is attributable to demography. Responsive supply behavior – decision factors – is more important than population factors in explaining the growing number of new college graduates on the market.

A SUPPLY–DEMAND ANALYSIS OF THE BUST

The preceding discussion suggests that the collapse of the college job market in the 1970s can be attributed to changes in the supply of and demand for graduates, with supply increasing rapidly and growth of demand leveling off at the turn of the decade. Figure 2.4 shows the way in which the timing of the shifts in demand and supply interacted to bring about the striking deterioration in conditions in the early 1970s. It graphs an index of the ratio of demand for college workers to the supply of new male bachelor's graduates. Demand is measured as a fixed-weight index of employment in industries, with the relative number of graduates used as a weight.[11] It captures the changes in demand that result from shifts in the industrial mix of jobs shown in Table 2.2. Supply is the estimated ratio of new bachelor's and higher-degree recipients seeking work to the male civilian labor force. Because of the distinctive features of supply and demand for female graduates, many of whom do not go on to seek employment, the figure deals solely with men. The year 1960 is taken as the base, with an index of demand to supply of 1. What stands out is the sharp deterioration in the demand – new entrants balance beginning in the late 1960s, after more than a decade of rough stability. Between 1968 and 1972, the ratio of demand to supply of new graduates fell by 46 per cent, due to the increase in supply and the slackened growth of demand. This change

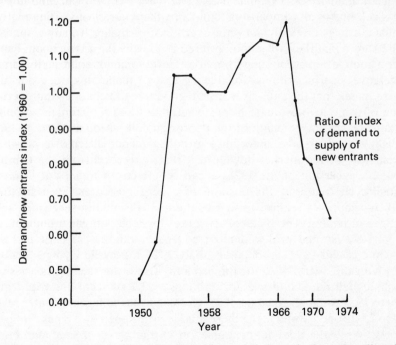

Figure 2.4 The deterioration of the demand–supply balance in the male college job market.

Source: Calculations in Freeman, 'Overinvestment in college training?', Table 6, Column 5, p. 306.

in the demand–supply balance in the college job market at the outset of the 1970s made the market ripe for a turnaround that would greatly depress salaries, job opportunities and employment, particularly of young graduates – as in fact occurred.

The supply–demand explanation of the market downturn can be examined more rigorously by comparing the actual post-World War II changes in the relative salaries of graduates to those predicted by a supply–demand model focused on the shifts outlined above. The results of such an empirical investigation are summarized in Figure 2.5, which reveals a close link between predicted and actual ratios of college starting salaries to the average annual earnings of full-time workers. While the ratio of college *starting* salaries to annual earnings of *all* workers is by no means the best relative income comparison to make (since it will be affected by changes in age composition of the workforce as well as in the position of graduates), the starting salary and annual earnings series are the only available data covering the entire postwar period. Surprising as it may seem, statistics on the starting pay of young high school graduates or of all high school and college graduates, which would provide better comparisons, have not been collected annually on a regular basis. The basic pattern of decline in the 1970s is found in all comparisons; however, the contrast of starting pay to, annual earnings probably does not overly distort reality. In any case, the figure shows that the explanation offered as to 'why the sixties boom bust' does a good job of accounting for market developments, tracking the drop in relative salaries with reasonable accuracy. While this does not, of course, mean that the analysis will yield good forecasts, it does suggest the value of using it to evaluate future possibilities and to estimate, at least tentatively, the likely length of the depressed college job market.

Finally, it is of some importance to note that one alternative possible explanation of the market downturn – that it resulted from the overall economic recession of the 1970s – can be effectively ruled out. Under normal cyclic patterns, the position of college graduates, even starting workers, improves relative to that of the less educated in recessions and declines in booms. The blue-collar worker loses his job when unemployment rises, not the professional or college graduate – at least in past economc declines. More detailed analysis of the cyclic changes shows that, with the overall state of the economy fixed, the starting salaries of graduates fell relative to average earnings by 3.5 per cent per year from 1970 to 1974, while the income of 25- to 34-year-old college graduates relative to 25- to 34-year-old high school graduates dropped by 3.6 per cent per year.[12] While this does not of course 'prove' that the depressed market of the 1970s represents a relatively long-term change in the market, it does support our overall interpretation of changes in terms of fundamental supply and demand shifts rather than normal cyclic or temporary peculiar circumstances.

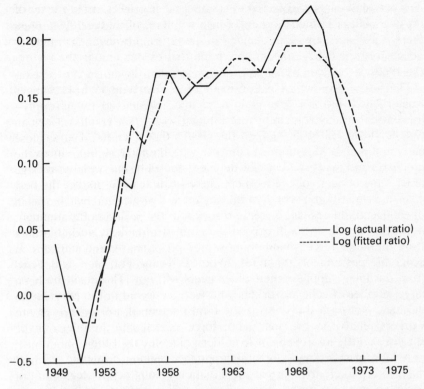

Figure 2.5 The ratio of college starting salaries to average annual earnings, actual and fitted, 1949–73, per full-time employee in industry.

Source: Based on computations in Freeman, 'Overinvestment in college training?'.

WHAT THE FUTURE MAY BRING

How long will the depression in the college job market last? Forecasts of the future economic situation of college graduates based on the model of the market given above suggest that, while the market is unlikely to return to the booming sixties, the relative economic status of graduates will level off in the near future and improve in the 1980s. On the basis of the type of analysis sketched out in this section, the economic standing of college graduates, barring unforeseen increases in demand, is expected to remain more or less at the depressed level of the mid-1970s until the end of the decade and then to improve moderately, at least for new bachelor's recipients, largely as a result of diminished growth in the number of graduates in response to the depressed market of the 1970s and to declines in the size of college-age cohorts. In the mid-1980s, the fall in the supply of new baccalaureates is expected to create a substantial boom in the market for new college-trained workers, which will level off in the 1990s. Unless there is a sharp increase in demand in the future, however, the boom will not restore the college income premium that existed among the young in the 1960s.

The future economic position of older graduates and of persons with master's and doctoral degrees in academic fields is less sanguine. First, it is unclear whether the improved job market for new graduates foreseen for the 1980s will 'spill over' to the classes that obtained degrees in the early and mid-1970s and must compete with the most recent 'vintages' of graduates in the 1980s. Lack of detailed studies of the substitutability of older and younger college workers makes it difficult to predict the result of such competition. Second, in the market as a whole, the relative number of college graduates will increase throughout the 1980s, as the number of new degree recipients will exceed the number of college workers retiring from the labor force, maintaining supply pressures for reductions in the economic position of graduates. Whereas young graduates will benefit from declining supplies, their older peers will not. There will be a very large number of college workers who were educated in the previous two decades. Not until the 1990s is the total number of college-trained male workers relative to the male labor force expected to grow less rapidly, suggesting little improvement for older graduates until then.

As for master's and doctoral graduates seeking academic jobs, the main forces likely to improve the situation among new baccalaureates – declining numbers enrolled in college – will operate to reduce demand for teachers. While reductions in the supply of new PhD and master's graduates should produce a more reasonable supply – demand balance than the catastrophe often given in forecasts that ignore individual responses to market reality, it is difficult to see how the relative economic position of these persons can fail to deteriorate through the rest of the 1970s and much of the 1980s. According to my analysis, the deterioration will come to an end in the late 1980s when college enrollments are likely to rise.

All of the forecasts are, moreover, best viewed as tentative and conditional estimates of likely future developments. They depend on various postulates about economic changes; they neglect many aspects of reality to focus on a few (important, in my analysis) behavioral and economic relations. At best they provide some notion of future possibilities and alert us to particular forces at work. *Caveat emptor.*

Forecasts for bachelor's graduates

Figure 2.6 sets out formal forecasts of the relative salaries of male bachelor's graduates, of enrollments in college, and of the college graduate share of the male workforce. The forecasts are obtained from the th equation recursive adjustment model described in detail in the Appenc ... In the forecasts it is assumed that future economic growth proceeds at post-World War II rates, so that the real earnings of fully employed, year-round workers grow significantly in the future but that the relative demand for new college graduates increases less rapidly than in the past – at the reduced rate of the 1970s, about 0.5 per cent per annum, compared to an overall post-war rate of 1 per cent per annum.[13] There are several reasons for favoring the slower demand rate: the education sector is, for demographic reasons, likely to decline in the 1980s; manufacturing industries that employ many graduates cannot be expected to grow at the rates of the 1950s and 1960s; there does not appear to be a major governmental defense or R&D initiative on the horizon. In addition, the larger relative supply of older male college graduates than in the past, including graduates of the 1970s unable to obtain college-level jobs, and likely increase in female graduates seeking work in traditionally male occupations will serve to depress the demand for new bachelor's men. If, in fact, demand for graduates increases more rapidly, however, the basic pattern of the forecasts remains much the same: more rapid increases in demand impart a moderate upward trend to the forecasts, yielding a greater improvement in the market than depicted in the figure but one which varies over time in the same manner. Conversely, if the relative demand for graduates is depressed further in the late 1970s and in the 1980s, the upswing is dampened and delayed. Still, as the number of new graduates drops in the 1980s, the market improves.

The timing of the onset of the upswing is only approximate. The forecasts abstract, as long-run projections often do, from business-cycle developments in the economy at large, so that the 1980s improvement could be displaced one or two years by the timing of recessions or booms. Continued weakness in the job market for non-college workers through the late 1970s due to weak recovery from the mid-1970s recession would, for example, improve the position of college graduates relative to other workers (who tend to be more affected by economy-wide ups and downs) and raise college enrollments through the end of the decade. When the overall rate of unemployment begins to fall, however, the relative position of the college-trained would decline, leading to reductions in the proportion enrolled, a decline in the number of new graduates four to five years later, and an ensuing upswing along the lines sketched out above.

Panel (a) of Figure 2.6 displays the forecast pattern of change in the ratio of the starting salaries of college men to average annual earnings. It shows a continued modest drop in the relative income of graduates until 1979–80, when the premium for new male baccalaureates begins a decadal increase, though one that does not restore the pre-1970s premium of over 20 per cent. The improvement in the market is especially large at the end of the

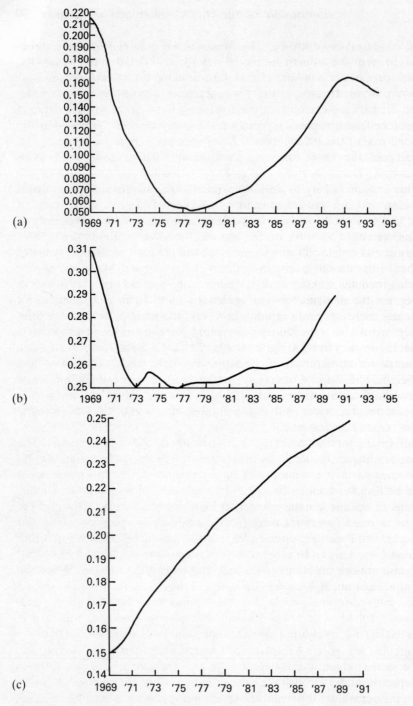

Figure 2.6 Forecasts of the state of the college job market, 1969–90: (a) log ratio of starting salary of male college graduates to earnings of full-time workers; (b) ratio of first-year male enrollments to number of 18- to 19-year olds; (c) college share of male labor force.

decade due to the sizeable fall in new bachelor's graduates in that period. Panel (b) gives the anticipated fraction of 18- to 19-year-old men enrolled as freshmen; because of the need to link initial enrollments to degrees, the numerator in Figure 2.6 is the number of first-year, degree-credit men, not – as in Figure 2.1 – the number of 18 to 19 year olds in college. According to forecasts, the propensity to enroll bottoms out in the late 1970s and then increases through the 1980s. Relatively many young persons in the demographically small cohorts of the 1980s are expected to go on to college, providing a buffer to the demographic swings. Panel (c) provides estimates of the impact of the changing number of new bachelor's degree recipients and the retirement of older graduates at age 65 on the college share of the total workforce. These estimates are obtained by assuming that all men aged 55 to 64 in 1974 will retire in the 1974–84 decade, while those aged 45 to 54 will retire in the succeeding decade, and that all young men will enter the labor force.[14] What is important here is that the college share of the male workforce continues to grow into the late 1980s, so that supply pressures for further deterioration in the economic position of graduates persist throughout the period. As a result, the economic position of older graduates, especially those who were in the large college cohorts of the 1970s, is unlikely to improve much in the next decade.

Alternative assumptions about the pattern of demand, retirement, cyclic conditions, and the like will yield – as noted earlier – somewhat different results, particularly with regard to the timing of changes. The general story, however, is clear: barring marked changes in the demand for graduates, overeducation in the job market will be a problem for the next decade or so, though the extent of the problem will vary over time and among graduates. The decline of 1969 to 1975 will slacken in the late 1970s; the market for new graduates will improve in the 1980s, especially in the latter half of the decade, though not by enough to restore the economic rewards of college training of the booming 1960s. The position of older graduates may, however, deteriorate even in the 1980s. All told, the United States is moving from a world in which higher education is a highly profitable endeavor offering great payoffs even with sizeable increases in the supply of graduates to one in which higher education is a more marginal investment for individuals and society.

POSTSCRIPT: WHAT THE FUTURE BROUGHT

The forecasts given in Figure 2.6 were published in 1976 on the basis of evidence through 1973, as indicated in the Appendix to this chapter. Social science forecasts of this type must, of course, be treated cautiously, for several reasons. First, even within the confines of the analytic framework employed, various simplifications have been assayed, in part to focus on what appear to be the critical forces at work and in part because of problems with data availability. Second, the track record of economists in forecasting even a few months into the future is notoriously poor, as the failure to predict the dimensions of the inflation and unemployment of the 1970s makes clear. With respect to college-trained workers, in 1949 Seymour Harris (then at Harvard) wrote a book predicting that the post-World War II period would be one of market glut. 'A large proportion of the potential college students within the next 20 years are doomed to disappointment after graduating as the number of correlated openings (in professional jobs) will be substantially less than the numbers seeking them.' Harris's expectations were falsified by the large increase in demand for graduates in the 1950s and 1960s, due, according to my analysis, to the shift in the composition of industrial employment, the spurt in R&D spending and demographic changes that led to the expansion of the education sector.[15] Similarly, prior to the market turnaround in the 1970s, human capital economists were concerned with reasons for the stability in the ratios of the incomes of educated to less-educated workers and sought relatively long-term or permanent rather than temporary reasons for the pattern. Third, because government programs, particularly R&D and defense, tend to employ relatively many college graduates, significant changes in governmental policies could substantially alter the demand for graduates and thus the forecast values even if the basic model is reasonably valid. A major increase in defense, R&D or related college-manpower-intensive activities would greatly reduce the problem of 'overeducation' in the job market and bring a much stronger upswing than I foresee in the 1980s.

Provisos and equivocations notwithstanding, the forecasts of the relative starting pay of college graduates and of the supply of students to American colleges turned again, like those for physicists, to be remarkably on target. The 1980s were characterized by a marked rise in the starting pay of college graduates relative to other workers and in the return to college-going in the United States (Murphy and Welch, 1988) which, if anything, exceeded the forecasts from the college labor-market model. Part of the rise can be attributed to the change in college-graduate supply on which Figure 2.6 focused (Katz and Revenga, 1989); part is due to a significant change in industry mix toward more college-intensive industries and to change in employment within high wage industries; and part is due to the declining wages of less educated workers as a result of the deunionization of the United States (discussed in Chapter 11) (Blackburn, Bloom and Freeman, 1989). In response to the rise in relative earnings, enrollments of young males rose substantially as a proportion of 18 to 19 year olds, as predicted in Figure 2.6(b), keeping total enrollments far above the levels predicted by analysts who neglected the supply responsiveness of young persons (Harrington and Sum, 1988). While the absence of laboratory conditions leaves open the possibility that the forecasts worked out for reasons other than those stressed in the analysis, the relative success makes one a bit more sanguine about the strength of empirical economics.

NOTES

1. Evidence on supply responsiveness is given in R. Freeman, *The Labor Market for College-Trained Manpower* (Cambridge, MA.: Harvard University Press, 1971); R. Freeman, 'Labor market adjustments in psychology', *American Psychologist* (May 1972), pp. 384–92; R. Freeman, 'Legal cobwebs: a recursive model of the market for new lawyers', *Review of Economics and Statistics* (May 1975), pp. 171–9; R. Freeman, 'A cobweb model of the supply and starting salary of new engineers', *Industrial Labor Relations Review* (January 1976).

2. The regression calculations are reported in R. Freeman, 'Overinvestment in college training?', *Journal of Human Resources* (Summer 1975), Table 5.

3. For example, if there are ten times as many experienced workers as new entrants, a 10 per cent drop in salaries that causes 1 per cent of the experienced workers to leave the occupation will alter the total number by the same amount, as will a 10 per cent drop in salary that causes a 10 per cent drop in the numbers of new entrants. Thus, even though new entrants evince ten times as great a responsiveness as the experienced, the salary change causes a similar reduction in supply.

4. Evidence that changes in distribution of workers are by industry, not in intraindustry coefficients, is given in R. Freeman, 'Manpower requirements and the skill composition of the US work force' (paper delivered at National Science Foundation Conference on Manpower Forecasting, Hot Springs, Virginia, April 1974); S. Dresch, 'Demography, technology, and higher education: toward a formal model of educational adaptation', *Journal of Political Economy* (March–April 1975), vol. 83 finds that only 30 per cent of the increased employment of college graduates from 1929 to 1969 was associated with increased employment of graduates within industries. While Dresch finds a greater role for intraindustry changes in the 1948–69 period, the 1948 figures are 'biased' by the World War II experience.

5. See S. Bowles, *Planning Educational Systems for Economic Growth* (Cambridge, MA: Harvard University Press, 1969), Chapter 3; G. Psacharapoulous and K. Hinchcliffe, 'Further evidence on the elasticity of substitution', *Journal of Political Economy* (July–August 1972), vol. 80, pp. 786–92; J. Tinbergen, 'Substitution of graduate by other labor', *Kyklos* (1974), vol. 27, no. 2, pp. 217–26; P. R. Fallon and R. Layard, 'Capital skill complementarity, income distribution and capital accounting', *Journal of Political Economy* (April 1975), vol. 83, no. 2; R. Freeman, 'Overinvestment in college training?', *Journal of Human Resources* (Summer 1975), pp. 287–310; R. Freeman, 'Demand for R&D scientists and engineers', in *Engineers and Scientists in the Industrial Economy*, unpublished report to National Science Foundation (1971), and studies by Freeman cited in Note 1.

6. The cobweb model of the job market is developed in R. Freeman, *The Labor Market for College-Trained Manpower* (Cambridge, MA: Harvard University Press, 1971). The studies by Freeman cited in Note 1 apply it to different professions.

7. More detailed analyses of the faculty are presented in A. Cartter, *PhD's and the Academic Labor Market* (New York: McGraw-Hill, 1976); R. Freeman, 'Demand for labor in a nonprofit market: university faculty', in *Labor in the Public and Nonprofit Sectors*, D. Hamermesh, ed. (Princeton, NJ: Princeton University Press, 1975), pp. 85–129.

8. Evidence on the impact of defense spending is given in R. Dempsey and D. Schmude, 'Occupational impact of defense expenditures', *Monthly Labor Review* (December 1971), pp. 12–15.

9. Data on the industrial employment of college graduates is presented in US Bureau of the Census' 1970 Census of Population, *Industrial Characteristics*, PC(2)-7B, Table 3; and 1960 Census of Population, *Industrial Characteristics*, PC(2)-7B, Table 21.

10. The 'net' data are from R. Freeman, 'Overinvestment in college education?', Table 6; and A. Cartter, *PhD's and the Academic Labor Market* (New York: McGraw-Hill, 1976). Cartter's figures are deflated by figures on the total labor force from the US Department of Labor, *Manpower Report of the President* (1975), p. 203.

11. More precisely, let α_j be the ratio of college to all workers in industry j in a given base year. Then the index is calculated as $\sum_j \alpha_j N_{jt}/\mathrm{I}$ where N_{jt} = employment in industry j in year t and I is the base year index. The indices are described more fully in R. Freeman, 'Overinvestment in college training?', *Journal of Human Resources* (Summer 1975); and R. Freeman, 'Manpower requirements and the skill composition of the US work force' (paper delivered at National Science Foundation Conference on Manpower Forecasting, Hot Springs, Virginia, April 1974).

12. See R. Freeman, 'The decline in the economic rewards to college education', *Review of Economics and Statistics* (February 1977), Table 5, pp. 18–29.

13. These figures are based on the fixed-weight index of demand described in Note 11 and in greater detail in the Appendix. Note that the index measures demand for all male college graduates and thus is likely to overstate the net demand for new bachelor's men when the supply of complementary graduates (women or recent baccalaureates lacking college-level jobs) is larger than in the past.

14. More precisely, I used data from US Bureau of the Census, 'Educational attainment', *Current Population Reports*, Series P-20, No. 272, Table 1, p. 15 to calculate the number of men 23 to 64 years old and proportion with four or more years of college in 1974. I subtracted the number of those 65 years old and over and added the number of those 22 to 24 years old to the reported numbers of those 25 years old and over. This yielded an estimate of 50,697,000 men 22 to 64 years old in 1974 and 9,251,000 college men. Comparable figures for earlier years were tabulated from relevant volumes of 'Educational attainment', To forecast future population, I subtracted away one-tenth the number of those 55 to 64 years old each year from 1975 to 1985 and one-tenth the number of those 45 to 64 years old from 1985 to 1990, on the assumption that an even proportion of these age groups retired each year; then I added the number of persons turning 22 years old, using data from Series P-20 No. 272 and from US Bureau of the Census' 1970 Census of Population, *United States Summary*, Table 50, p. 265. The former volume reports numbers in two-year groupings; they were divided in half to obtain the estimated number of those 22 years old; the latter contain figures by single year of age. The future number of college graduates was obtained by first

multiplying the number of those 22 years old in a year by the proportion expected to enroll four years earlier. Since the regression equation relates enrollment to persons 18 and 19 years of age, I multiplied the proportion by two, on the crude assumption that the two age groups have about the same distribution and enrollment probabilities. Finally, I multiplied the figure by 0.575, the proportion of men 25 years old and over with some college training in 1974 who actually graduated, according to Series P-20, No. 272, Table 1, p. 15.

15. Seymour Harris, *The Market for College Graduates* (Cambridge, MA: Harvard University Press, 1949). Harris also predicted that 'it may frequently not pay to be educated' (p. 17); that 'severe excesses of graduates would develop by 1968' (p. 19), and so forth. Clearly it is easy to be wrong in forecasting. On the other hand, however, Allan Cartter's 1964 analysis of the faculty job market has proved remarkably prescient. Not all economic forecasts look ridiculous ten or 20 years later.

BIBLIOGRAPHY

Blackburn, M., Bloom, D., and Freeman, R.B., 'Why has the economic position of less-skilled male workers deteriorated in the United States?', Brookings Institution Conference on Future Job Prospects (March 1989).

Harrington, P. E., and Sum, A.M., 'Whatever happened to the college enrollments crisis?', *The Journal Academe: Bulletin of the American Association of University Professors* (September–October 1988), pp. 17–22.

Katz, L.F., and Revenga, A.L., 'Changes in the structure of wages: the US vs Japan', National Bureau of Economic Research Mimeo (May 1989).

Murphy, K. M., and Welch, F., 'Wage differentials in the 1980s: the role of international trade', Mount Pelerin Society, unpublished (September 1988).

CHAPTER 2 APPENDIX
FORECAST MODEL

The forecasts used in this chapter are based on the following three-equation model of the job market for college graduates:

1. Supply of freshman males of college (1951–73):

$$FRSH = -2.02 + 0.88 \ POP + 1.31 \ [CSAL - ASAL] + 0.21 \ FRSH(-1)$$
$$\quad\quad\quad\quad (0.21) \quad\quad\quad (0.26) \quad\quad\quad\quad\quad\quad (0.16)$$
$$R^2 = 0.987 \quad\quad SEE = 0.049 \quad\quad dw = 1.79$$

2. Dependence of graduates on number of freshmen (1954–73):

$$BA = -0.63 + 0.71 \ FRSH[-4] + 0.29 \ FRSH[-5]$$
$$\quad\quad\quad\quad (0.2) \quad\quad\quad\quad\quad (0.2)$$
$$R^2 = 0.976 \quad\quad SEE = 0.061 \quad\quad dw = 0.55$$

3. Determination of college salaries (1951–73):

$$CSAL = -2.25 - 0.15 \ BA(-1) + 1.1 \ DEM + 0.31 \ ASAL + 0.45 \ CSAL(-1)$$
$$\quad\quad\quad\quad\quad (0.02) \quad\quad\quad\quad (0.51) \quad\quad (0.24) \quad\quad\quad\quad (0.11)$$
$$R^2 = 0.994 \quad\quad SEE = 0.018 \quad\quad dw = 1.51$$

where:

FRSH = number of first-degree, credit-enrolled males, as reported in US Office of Education, *Digest of Educational Statistics 1974*, Table 91, p. 77.

POP = number of 18- to 19-year-old men, as reported in US Bureau of the Census, 'School enrollment', *Current Population Reports*, Series P-20, various editions.

CSAL = a weighted average of college starting salaries taken from the annual survey of F. Endicott, 'Trends in employment of college and university graduates in business and industry', (Placement Center, Northwestern University). The weights are 0.05 for accounting, 0.35 for engineering, 0.20 for general business trainees and 0.40 for sales. They are designed to reflect the approximate distribution of college graduates in engineering and related sciences, accounting, bachelors of business administration and 'other fields', assuming that 'sales' jobs reflect nontechnical opportunities in other fields. Since the salaries move together, in general, alternative fixed-weight indices yield similar results.

CSAL is in 1967 dollars, deflated by the Consumer Price Index as given in US Department of Labor, *Handbook of Labor Statistics 1975*, Table 123, p. 314.

DEM = index of demand for college graduates, calculated by taking a fixed-weight index of employment in 46 industries. The weights are the proportion of men in each industry with college degrees in 1960, as given in US Bureau of the Census' 1960 Census of Population, *Industrial Characteristics*, PC(2)-7F, Table 21. The employment figures are from US Department of Commerce, *Survey of Current Business* (July edition).

BA = number of male bachelor's graduates, from US Office of Education, *Earned Degrees Conferred*, various editions, with 1972 from xeroxed sheets provided by the Office of Education. Where available, I used the figures that relate to bachelors only, not those that include first professionals. To estimate the number of baccalaureates' net of first professionals for the years preceding 1961, when the Office of Education first differentiated the figures, I subtracted the number of degrees in medicine and other health fields, theology, law, and architecture from the bachelors' and first-professional degree data to obtain a second series and spliced the two with 1961 as the overlap year. The major adjustment involves subtraction of medicine, law, and theology degrees from the bachelor series.

ASAL = average annual earnings of full-time workers in the United States, as reported in US Department of Commerce, *Survey of Current Business* (July edition). It is in constant 1967 dollars.

Numbers in parentheses after variables refer to the time lag for the variable, with (-4), for example, reflecting a four-year lag. Numbers in parentheses below variables are standard errors; dw = Durbin-Watson statistic; SEE = standard error of estimate; R^2 = percentage of variation explained by the equation. All variables are in logarithmic form. The years chosen for the regressions are dictated by data availability, with the immediate post-World War II period deleted from consideration due to the 'extraordinary' enrollments that resulted from the 'backlog' of demand from the war and the GI bill. The unavailability of degree figures for the years after 1972 dictated that the period end in 1973; estimated degrees were used for that year.

Equation 1 is the basic supply equation of the model, linking the number of men enrolling in the first year of college to the relevant population and to the differential between the income of starting male college workers and of all fully employed workers in the society, which is to be viewed as a rough index of the college income premium. The lagged number of freshmen is introduced to reflect lagged adjustments in the context of the usual partial adjustment model. The equation is a rough, first-order approximation to the underlying 'true' relation between economic incentives and enrollment in college. It ignores, largely because of the lack of adequate time-series data, tuition and fee charges. While this undoubtedly creates some problems, it is unlikely to bias seriously the results, because most of the costs of college occur in the form of foregone income, not tuition and fees.[1] The equation uses the ratio of college starting to average salaries as the measure of salary incentive rather than the more appropriate rate of return, whose calculation would require time-series figures on lifetime incomes that are not available on a year by year basis. The population data relate to 18 to 19 year olds, who constitute about 60 per cent of freshmen.[2] In a correctly specified model in which POP reflects the entire relevant group on 'potential' students, the coefficient on population should be unity; in the context of the lagged adjustment model, the coefficient divided by 1 minus the coefficient on the lagged term should be unity, as it is.[3] While Equation 1 is imperfect, it suffices to provide a rough 'test' of the hypothesized behavioral link between the job market and college enrollments and estimates of the relevant parameters.

Equation 2 simply relates the number of bachelor's graduates in a given year to the number of freshmen four and, because of delays, five years earlier.

Equation 3 makes the starting salaries of college graduates an inverse function of the number graduating and a direct function of the index of demand and of alternative salaries in the economy. The coefficient on BA measures the effect of a 1 per cent increase in the number of graduates on salaries. The $ASAL$ term is introduced to show the effect of economy-wide increases in wages on college salaries due to the shift in demand toward graduates when the wage of other workers rises. The lagged college salary variable, $CSAL(-1)$, measures the adjustment process in the market in the context of the usual partial adjustment model.[4] In this model, the short-term effect of independent variables on the dependent variable is given by the regression coefficients; the long-term effect is given by the coefficients divided by 1 minus the coefficient on the lagged dependent variable. The major weakness in this equation is the failure to treat the impact of the number of older college graduates and women on the starting salaries of men. In the absence of quantitative information about whether older and younger graduates are complements or substitutes and the extent to which women and men will compete in the same markets in the future, I eschewed analysis of these interrelations. While the good 'fit' of the equation indicates that concentrating on the relation between male BAs and starting salaries was not grievously wrong in the past, this problem with the structure of the equation may mar the forecasts and should, as stated in this chapter, be considered in evaluating them.

The three equations form a recursive system which is particularly amenable to forecasting.[5] The system is, to be sure, small, relying on very few variables and relations and thereby ignoring certain potentially important aspects of the world. While more complex and detailed models, along the lines of national econometric models or input–output models of the structure of the economy, would enhance our knowledge of the college market and illuminate the economics of the system, the present model suffices to indicate possible future developments.

The forecasts given in Figure 2.6 were calculated on a base of 1975. I calculated the change in college salaries for 1975 from the Endicott surveys for 1975 and 1974, using the predicted salaries.[6] The change in alternative salaries was estimated by the change in average hourly earnings from June 1974 to June 1975.[7] The change in first-year enrollments in 1974 was obtained from the Office of Education, while the change in 1975 was calculated by the model. Forecasts of changes in the population of 18 to 19 year olds were made from data on the age of men by single years, as given in the 1970 Census of Population.[8] I assumed that alternative salaries increase at its long-term trend rate of 2.4 per cent per annum in the future but that the growth of demand for college graduates increases at its 1970s' pace of 0.5 per cent per annum, as opposed to the pre-1970s' rate. As noted in this chapter, more 'optimistic' assumptions about the growth of demand for graduates yield forecasts that follow roughly the same time path as that in the figure but with a more pronounced upward trend in the 1980s. I experimented with other forms recursive three-equation models and obtained results also comparable to those in the figure: moderate decline in the job market for graduates through 1977–8, followed by a gradual upturn in the late 1970s and early 1980s and an ensuing boom in the late 1980s, followed finally by a leveling and modest decline in the early 1990s. Lest any of the forecasts be taken too seriously, I restate the warning that they provide only a rough notion of how certain factors are likely to affect the situation of graduates and can be readily invalidated by unforeseen shifts in demand due, say, to unpredictable structural changes in the economy, new technologies, government programs, wars or depressions. Experiments with related models at the MIT Center for Policy Alternatives have shown that failure to foresee sharp shifts in exogenous variables has led to sizeable divergencies between simulated and actual patterns, even though the basic model provides a good 'fix' on behavioral and market realities.

NOTES

1. G. Becker, *Human Capital* (New York: Columbia University Press, 1964), p. 75 estimated that forgone earnings made up 75 per cent of the full cost of college, a statistic that, has fallen, at most, moderately in recent years.
2. US Bureau of the Census, 'Social and economic characteristics of students', *Current Population Reports* (October 1973), Series P-20, no. 272, Table 15, p. 54.
3. In this model, a variable moves toward its equilibrium value by some proportion $(0 < \lambda < 1)$ of the difference between the equilibrium and past value. Formally, if X is the variable and $\bar{X}$ the equilibrium value we have

$$\Delta X = \lambda[\bar{X} - X(-1)]$$

or

$$X = \lambda\bar{X} + (1 - \lambda) X(-1)$$

where $X(-1)$ is the value in the previous period. For long-term equilibrium $X = \bar{X}$. The coefficient on factors that determine $\bar{X}$ are thus divided by 1 minus the coefficient on $X(-1)$ to obtain their long-term impacts.
4. See Note 3.
5. H. Wold, *Econometric Model-Building* (Amsterdam: North-Holland, 1967).
6. F. Endicott, *Trends in Employment of College and University Graduates in Business and Industry* (Northwestern University, 1975, p. 4 and 1974, p. 4).
7. US Department of Commerce, *Survey of Current Business* (August 1965), p. S-15.
8. US Bureau of the Census' 1970 Census of Population, *United States Summary* Section 1, Table 50, p. 265. I added the single years' figures to obtain 18 to 19 year olds comparable to the figures in the regressions.

3 · EXPECTATIONS AND MARGINAL DECISION-MAKING

The econometric evidence of responsive supply behavior given in the preceding chapters, and in studies of other fields, while valuable, do not pin down fully the micro-foundations of the economic theory of occupational choice and labor supply. They do not do this because they neglect an additional important source of information about behavior: direct survey data about the income expectations that are presumed to underly student decisions on fields of study and about the posited responses of the marginal decision-makers whose flexibility is needed to produce supply behavior consistent with the econometric estimates of supply elasticities.

This chapter presents survey evidence on these two points from a survey that I developed and analyzed in 1966–7. It compares student income expectations and perceptions of career characteristics to actual incomes and measures of the characteristics. Then it examines the career decisions of two groups of students whose behavior is especially relevant to the theory, those identified as marginal suppliers or as money-oriented.

EXPECTATIONS OF COLLEGE STUDENTS

Do students have reasonable income expectations? Do they consider forgone income in their educational plans? What weight do they *explicitly* place on monetary incentive?

Expectations of income opportunities

Survey evidence regarding the realism of student anticipations of future incomes, of the possibility of wealth, and of the variability of earnings are presented in Figure 3.1 and Table 3.1. The figure compares the average income that students expect for themselves in their chosen careers with income projections for three periods in the life cycle: at the start of

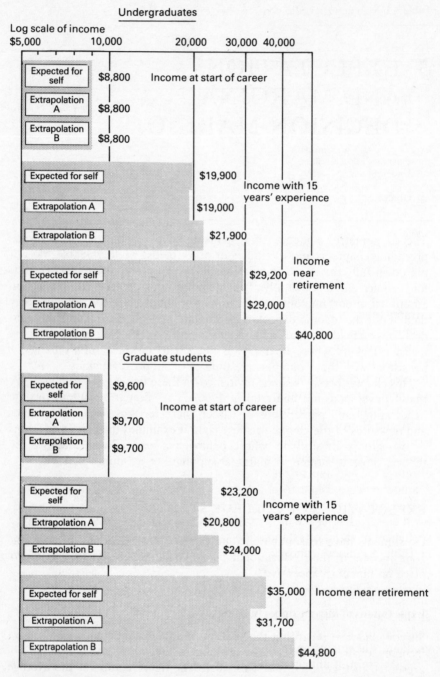

Figure 3.1 The incomes students expect in their career compared to extrapolations of 1966 incomes, by level of education and lifecycle status.

Table 3.1 Student expectations of income, 1967

	At start of career	Fifteen years later	Near retirement
Expected for average worker in career:			
1 Undergraduates	$8,350	$17,440	$23,700
	(0.376)[a]	(0.539)	(0.565)
2 Graduates	$9,030	$18,140	$25,000
	(0.288)	(0.523)	(1.826)
Expected for self, students with above-average expectations:			
3 Undergraduates	$9,100	$22,700	$35,400
	(0.419)	(0.718)	(0.886)
4 Graduates	$10,000	$27,800	$43,800
	(0.273)	(0.738)	(1.756)

Note:
a   Figures in parentheses are the coefficients of variation in expectations.

work, after 15 years' experience, and near retirement. The projections are extrapolations of the income of college graduates in 1966: extrapolation A assumes a 2 per cent increase in real income in the future, extrapolation B, a 3 per cent increase.

A close relation between expected and projected incomes is shown in the figure. For the beginning of their careers, the earnings that students expect for themselves are virtually identical to the extrapolated incomes. For periods further in the future, the personal income expectations lie between the A and B projections. Undergraduate expectations are especially close to the A projection, which assumed a 2 per cent rate of increase. Graduate students have more sanguine expectations. In both cases, the anticipations of future income appear reasonable.

Students were asked to estimate the income that the average college-trained worker in their field could expect as well as what they expected for themselves. The mean income foreseen for average workers and the coefficient of variation (standard deviation divided by the mean) are shown in Table 3.1, lines 1 and 2. These estimates diverge noticeably from the personal income expectations recorded in Figure 3.1. On the average, students expect other workers to earn less than they themselves. The differences range from a 5 per cent advantage foreseen by undergraduates at the start of work ($8,800 expected for one's self compared to $8,350 expected for average workers) to a 25 per cent advantage expected by graduate students when they approach retirement.

This pattern of anticipations is examined further in lines 3 and 4 of the table, which focus on students with above-average expectations. Approximately half of the respondents fit into this category. The greatest deviation in income expectations is for graduate students looking at the period near retirement. In this case optimistic students expect an 85 per cent personal premium.[1]

Two factors appear to underlie the higher personal income expectations of these students. First, many of those in the high-quality institutions covered in the sample probably possess the abilities, background, and knowledge needed for above-average income. The especially high incomes expected by optimistic graduate students, for example, are primarily due to several Harvard Business School students who plan to earn incomes associated with millionaire status. As very high earnings are not unheard of for graduates of the Harvard Business School, these intentions may reflect a realistic evaluation of market opportunities. A second reason for the anticipated personal premium may be what Adam Smith has termed 'the over-weaning conceit which the greater part of men have of their own abilities . . . (and) good fortune.'[2]

Relative income comparisons

As a second step in examining expectations, students were asked whether their careers offered higher earnings, greater variation in earnings, greater opportunity for wealth, and the prospect of greater increases in income than the *average college career*. Assuming that respondents are evenly distributed among fields, the distribution of careers must fall evenly about the median,[3] with the result that half view their careers as above average and half as below average.[4]

For the average level of earnings in a career, this pattern of evaluations prevailed: 52 per cent of students labeled as true the statement, 'Earnings in my career are higher than those in most college-level careers'; 48 per cent labeled it false. A similar distribution fits evaluations of the chance for great wealth. Approximately half of the respondents rated their careers as above average in the chance to earn great wealth while half did not. From these data it appears that students have reasonable perceptions of the relative income status of careers and of the relative opportunity to achieve wealth. For possible increases in income and the variation of income in careers, on the other hand, the survey responses suggest that students have a somewhat unrealistic perception of the market. Forty-six per cent anticipated more rapid increases of income in their intended careers than in other college level careers; 39 per cent anticipated the same rate of change; while just 15 per cent expected less rapid increases. Similarly, over two-thirds of the survey respondents regarded variation of earnings in their chosen careers as being above average – which, under the assumptions of the analysis, cannot occur in reality.[5] One possible explanation for students expecting greater earnings gains in their own career than in others is that this expectation, in fact, underlies their choice. Just as in the stock market where buyers expect prices to rise and sellers expect them to fall, in

Table 3.2 Variations in expected and actual income (coefficients of variation over the lifecycle)

Life cycle position	Expected income		Census income (1960)
	Undergraduate	Graduate	
Start of career	0.38	0.29	0.40
15 years' experience	0.54	0.52	0.85
Near retirement	0.57	0.74	0.90

the market for careers, students choose different fields in part because they expect their own to do better in the future.

Responses to other survey questions dealing directly or indirectly with increases in income and variation point to a realistic view of the market. With respect to changes, the expected increase implicit in anticipated levels of income conforms, according to Figure 3.1, to past rates of change. More significant, perhaps, despite the general tendency to overestimate relative changes, rankings of fields by expected and actual change are closely correlated (see p. 68). Similarly, the variation of expected incomes corresponds to the variation of actual incomes over the life cycle (see Table 3.2), and the ranking of fields by perceived and actual variation are in accord (see p. 64).

The picture of how students perceive changes in income and variation of income is thus mixed. They appear to exaggerate the position of their careers in relation to other college level careers but not the actual level of income or variation. It may be that the observed deviations from a symmetric distribution of responses simply reflect special concern about the potential variation of personal income in the risky future.

Forgone income

In addition to the income earned from work, the income lost by attending school should enter occupational and educational decisions. Accordingly, students were asked: 'What do you estimate your yearly (before-tax) earnings would presently be if you were not in school? Assume you were working today in a full-time permanent job.' Their responses are summarized in Table 3.3.

The student estimates compare favorably with the actual earnings of young workers. In 1966, 20-year-old high school graduates and college dropouts earned approximately $5,600–5,800 while college graduates aged 25 made about $7,800 per year.[6] Students thus appear to be well informed about the income opportunities lost through school attendance. Do they take account of these forgone earnings in career and educational decisions?

Table 3.3 Estimated forgone income, 1966–7 (frequency distribution in thousands of dollars)

Academic status	<$4	$4–5	$5–6	$6–7	$7–8	$8–9	$9–10	$10+	Average
Undergraduate	9.0	22.9	33.7	16.5	11.4	3.3	3.2	0.0	$5,700
Graduate	1.0	3.2	9.6	15.3	27.5	23.1	20.4	0.0	7,600

The survey question requesting students to list 'the cost or sacrifice' of school shows that many, though by no means all, are explicitly aware of forgone income. Roughly half of the graduate students and two-fifths of the undergraduates volunteered 'money,' 'time', or 'employment' as the cost of education. Each of these factors is an element in forgone income. An additional 40 per cent of the students listed 'living experience' as a cost. This is also related to forgone income. Finally, one-third mentioned tuition and one twentieth the postponement of marriage.[7]

Economic rationale of college

By comparing estimates of forgone income with expected future incomes it is possible to assess the economic rationale of attending college. If at reasonable rates of interest future earnings compensate for forgone income, the choice of college can be viewed as an economically rational decision; otherwise it is a decision to be explained by nonpecuniary factors.

At both undergraduate and graduate levels, student perceptions of the differential of future over forgone income are substantial and far in excess of the differentials required for an investment in education to payoff at 6 or 10 per cent. Undergraduates, for example, expect earnings after completing school to exceed current income forgone by 55 per cent; graduate students foresee a 26 per cent advantage to continued schooling. Assuming that undergraduates plan on four additional years of education and graduate students on two,[8] these figures can be compared with the 46 and 21 per cent required for education to pay off with a 10 per cent discount rate.[9] If students expect similar differentials for the entire working life, the implicit rate of return to education is 12–13 per cent in both cases. When the earnings of graduate students during school are added in, the return to graduate training rises to 16 per cent. These 'subjective' rates of return correspond to the actual rates. Thus the decision to attend college appears to be economically rational and based on a realistic view of the market.

Subjective importance of income

Table 3.4 presents some evidence on the subjective role of income and other characteristics in the choice of a career. The dominant factor in

Table 3.4 Perceived importance of job characteristics in choosing career

	Percentage of students who regard the characteristic as:			Percentage of students who perceive differences in the characteristic between chosen and alternative careers
	Very important	Somewhat important	Not important	
Characteristic		*Undergraduates*		
Earnings	16	49	35	84
Interest	82	12	6	83
Variety of places of employment	25	41	33	76
National need	14	39	47	75
Stability of earnings and employment	21	47	32	70
Years of education required	10	33	57	68
Sacrifice of entry	17	44	39	66
		Graduate students		
Earnings	13	46	41	84
Interest	84	10	5	87
Variety of places of employment	26	37	37	75
National need	13	48	49	67
Stability of earnings and employment	12	43	45	67
Years of education required	11	27	62	70
Sacrifice of entry	13	45	42	68

decisions is evidently *interest* in work. More than 80 per cent of the students rate interest as very important in career choice, compared to less than 25 per cent rating other characteristics as very important (column 1). Although interest in work dominates the career decision, income is still given a significant subjective role. First, to a sizable minority of students, income is a very important factor also. Second, income appears to have special significance in marginal comparisons. Column (4) of the table shows that income and interest are the principal factors that distinguish a chosen career from its closest alternative. At the same time, the majority of students report that when income differs between the chosen and alternative careers, it is *higher* in the former. While not conclusive, this suggests a marginal role for income in the career decision.

EXPECTATION OF INCOME BY SPECIALTY

To test the realism of income expectations and the reliability of labor-market information, this section turns to an examination of the interfield concordance of expected and actual income. The first step is to determine whether or not students with different majors or occupations have significantly different income expectations. Then the accuracy of expectations is tested by rank-correlating them with market salaries.

Levels of income

Tables 3.5 and 3.6 present the incomes expected by students according to their major field and intended occupation, respectively. The figures reveal significant differences in expectations for the start of work, after 15 years' experience and near retirement by area of specialization. Mathematics majors, for example, have much higher income expectations than language majors – $8,920 versus $7,180 at the start of their working life; $17,990 versus $14,580 after 15 years' experience; $24,480 versus $17,720 near retirement (Table 3.5, Panel A). Similarly, prospective doctors, businessmen, and lawyers generally expect higher earnings in their careers than do future teachers, social workers, and clergy (see Table 3.6). Statistically, the analyses of variance computations summarized in each table attribute a significant fraction of income variation to occupation or field of study, as the case may be. The array of mean expected incomes can thus be taken as a picture of how students perceive the structure of salaries.

Rank correlation comparisons of the expected incomes with incomes observed in the market point to a realistic formation of expectations and a well-informed body of decision makers. Despite difficulties in obtaining up-to-date measures of actual income for fields comparable to those in the survey,[10] all of the comparisons yield Spearman coefficients significant at 1 per cent or better.

First, the comparisons in Tables 3.7 and 3.8 show a very close correlation between the rank order of expected *starting salaries* and actual earnings of young graduates several years earlier. In Table 3.7 the expected salaries of students in 14 undergraduate majors is correlated with the actual salaries of graduates in these fields in 1960 at 0.67. In Table 3.8 the ranking of intended occupation by expected salary is correlated with the ranking of occupations by the 1960 earnings of young college graduates at 0.67.

Second, for the limited number of fields in which more recent data exist, both the level and rank order of expected salaries are closely aligned with actual earnings in the market. The correlation between student expectations and the 1967 rates given for nine sharply defined scientific–engineering fields by the College Placement Council is 0.85. With respect to levels of earnings, graduate students intending to work as engineers anticipate starting at $10,700, on the average, while surveys report that beginning MS engineers earned from $9,500 (Endicott placement data) to $10,000 (College Placement data) in industry in 1966–7. Since students are in contact with recruiters, with recent graduates, and through summer or part-time work, with prospective employers, accurate notions of the going rate for beginners is perhaps not surprising.

Further analysis of the connection between expected and actual salaries indicates that realistic expectations and accurate knowledge are not limited to starting rates. The incomes expected for 15 years' experience and near retirement are well correlated with the actual income of middle-aged and older workers. In particular, the rank order of salaries by intended occupation and by 1960 Census income in 18 comparable specialties produces the following Spearman coefficients:

Table 3.5 Incomes expected by students, according to field of study in 1967, and analysis of variance of expectations[a]

Panel A: Undergraduates

Major field	Income at start	Income after 15 years	Income upon retirement
All fields	8,350	17,440	23,690
Biology	9,510	20,940	26,850
Chemistry and geology	8,830	16,780	19,900
Engineering	8,840	16,840	23,900
Physics	9,520	17,760	23,360
Mathematics	8,920	17,990	24,880
Economics	8,270	18,130	25,320
Sociology	8,530	17,540	23,690
Psychology	7,710	16,330	20,590
Government	7,710	16,300	22,250
English	7,260	17,200	21,290
History	7,430	17,200	23,450
Languages	7,180	14,580	17,710
Arts and philosophy	6,920	14,780	21,610

Analysis of variance tables[b]

1 For starting salaries

Source of variance	Degrees of freedom	Sum of squares	Mean square
Major	12	793	66.08
Error	1,655	15,686	9.47
Total	1,667	16,479	

$$F = 6.97$$

2 For salaries after 15 years

Source of variance	Degrees of freedom	Sum of squares	Mean square
Major	12	6,213	517.75
Error	1,635	139,385	85.25
Total	1,647	145,598	

$$F = 6.07$$

3 For salaries near retirement

Source of variance	Degrees of freedom	Sum of squares	Mean square
Major	12	13,426	1,118.83
Error	1,581	271,971	172.024
Total	1,593	285,397	

$$F = 6.50$$

Table 3.5 (cont.)

Panel B: Graduate students

Major field	Income at start	Income after 15 years	Income upon retirement
All fields	9,020	18,140	24,980
Biology	8,932	17,020	21,460
Chemistry and geology	9,620	16,490	20,610
Engineering	10,710	18,370	23,490
Physics	10,400	16,660	20,240
Mathematics	9,000	16,260	21,110
Economics	8,910	16,460	22,880
Other social sciences	8,620	15,500	19,580
Government	7,720	14,670	19,910
Arts and philosophy	6,860	11,980	15,870
English–history Languages	7,950	13,780	17,600
Business	9,360	23,280	35,960
Education	7,410	13,360	16,640
Law	7,450	19,720	31,410
Medicine	9,600	26,500	34,290

Analysis of variance tables[b]

1 For starting salaries

Source of variance	Degrees of freedom	Sum of squares	Mean square
Major	14	1,519	108.50
Error	959	5,327	5.55
Total	973	6,846	

F = 19.38

2 For salaries after 15 years

Source of variance	Degrees of freedom	Sum of squares	Mean square
Major	14	12,693	906.64
Error	940	18,666	19.86
Total	954	31,359	

F = 45.65

3 For salaries near retirement

Source of variance	Degrees of freedom	Sum of squares	Mean square
Major	14	45,582	3,255.86
Error	914	272,389	298.02
Total	928	314,971	

F = 10.93

Notes:
a All income figures pertain to the average expected for the average worker in a career, not the income expected by the student for himself. Analysis of the personal expectations of students yields results similar to those in the table.
b The 1% levels of significance for the F-statistic are 2.20 (Panel A) and 2.09 (Panel B).

Table 3.6 Incomes expected by students, according to intended career in 1967, and analysis of variance of expectations[a]

Prospective career	Income at start	Income after 15 years	Income near retirement
All careers	8,690	17,800	24,350
Biology and agricultural science	8,440	15,600	20,270
Medical specialty	10,370	26,200	33,660
Chemistry	9,830	16,000	20,110
Government	7,610	17,590	24,260
Chemical engineering	9,000	15,910	22,520
Aeronautical engineering	9,500	16,000	22,000
Civil engineering	8,500	15,220	19,940
Electrical engineering	9,530	16,560	21,300
Metallurgical engineering	9,690	16,480	21,440
Mechanical engineering	9,630	17,390	25,290
Other engineering	9,520	17,630	29,540
Architecture	7,670	17,020	24,400
Physics	10,690	17,920	22,620
Mathematics and statistics	8,790	17,420	22,200
Social science	8,780	16,320	21,280
Social work	6,350	11,790	15,370
Geology and oceanography	8,320	13,130	15,180
Literary careers	7,130	17,320	24,440
Clergy	5,670	8,440	12,560
Business	8,810	20,520	31,550
Accounting	7,750	17,200	25,060
Law	7,760	19,530	28,700
Entertainment	7,040	20,380	24,810
Teaching	7,920	13,650	17,150
Scattered sciences	10,210	16,700	21,770

Analysis of variance tables[b]

1 For starting salaries

Source of variance	Degrees of freedom	Sum of squares	Mean square
Occupation	25	2,124	84.96
Error	2,574	18,859	7.33
Total	2,599	20,983	

F = 11.60

2 For salaries after 15 years

Source of variance	Degrees of freedom	Sum of squares	Mean square
Occupation	25	25,895	1,035.80
Error	2,537	202,773	79.93
Total	2,562	228,668	

F = 12.96

3 For salaries near retirement

Source of variance	Degrees of freedom	Sum of squares	Mean square
Major	25	42,436	1,697.44
Error	2,457	601,388	244.77
Total	2,482	643,824	

F = 6.93

Notes:
a   As in Table 3.3, all income figures pertain to the average income foreseen for the average worker in a career, not to personal income expectations.
b   The 1% level of significance for the F-statistic is 1.79.

Table 3.7 Rank order comparison of expected and actual starting salaries, by undergraduate major

Major	Rank of expected starting salary 1967[a]	Rank of actual salary of majors[a,b] 1960
Physics	1	2
Mathematics	2	6
Engineering	3	1
Chemistry and geology	4	5
Sociology	5	12
Economics	6	4
Business	7	3
Psychology	8	9
Government	9	7
History	10	11
English	11	13
Languages	12	14
Arts and philosophy	13	8
Education	14	10

Notes:
a   The rank correlation coefficient is 0.67. The 1% significance level is 0.64.
b   The 1960 salaries of the class of 1958 are likely to be good indicators of starting salaries.
Source: Actual salary figures from *Two Years After the College Degree*, National Science Foundation (Washington, DC).

At the start of career $r = 0.67$
With 15 years' experience $r = 0.60$
Near retirement $r = 0.86$

The 1 per cent significance level is 0.56.

From these correlations it appears that students have good information about earnings over the entire life cycle and realistic expectations about the distant future.

For a more refined test of student perceptions of earnings over the life cycle, the ratio of income expected near retirement to expected starting salaries was compared with the actual gradient of cross-sectional age–earnings curves. If students have correct knowledge of the life-cycle pattern of earnings in their chosen career, the ratios of expected incomes will mirror the actual ratios. The data in Table 3.9 indicate that this is the case. Students expect large gains in income over the life cycle (column 1) in occupations with steep age–earnings curves (column 2). The rank correlation coefficient is 0.84, significant at 1 per cent.

It can be concluded that students have the knowledge of life-cycle earnings posited in the human capital analysis of behavior.

Relative incomes

For a proper allocation of the workforce, individuals must correctly perceive income in alternative occupations as well as in their chosen

Table 3.8 Rank order comparison of expected and actual starting salaries, by intended occupation

Occupation	Rank of starting salaries expected by 1967 undergraduates[a]	Rank of 1960 earnings of young college graduates[a,b]
Physics	1	6
Medical specialty	2	1
Chemistry	3	12
Mechanical engineering	4	9
Electrical engineering	5	2
Other engineering	6	7
Aeronautical engineering	7	3
Business	8	4
Social science	9	11
Mathematics and statistics	10	8
Civil engineering	11	10
Biological and agricultural science	12	17
Teaching	13	16
Law	14	5
Accounting	15	14
Architecture	16	15
Government	17	13
Clergy	18	18

Notes:
a   The rank correlation coefficient is 0.67. The 1% level of significance is 0.56.
b   The earnings figures are for men aged 25–34 as reported in the US Census of Population.
Source: Actual salary figures are from US Census of Population (1960), *Occupation by Earnings and Education.*

specialty. At the least they should be aware of where their careers fit in the income array of high-level occupations. Table 3.10 summarizes the survey evidence regarding this assessment. Column 1 records the fraction of students who place their chosen occupations high in the income array; column 2 records actual 1960 incomes in those occupations. The rankings in columns 3 and 4 show a near perfect correlation between these measures of perceived and actual position. It appears that students are well aware of interfield differentials and have the facts needed for rational comparisons of alternatives.

PERCEPTIONS OF OTHER CHARACTERISTICS

Students have realistic perceptions of the economic characteristics of occupations other than income. The analysis described next shows that their evaluation of the variation in earnings, the chance for great wealth, likely increases in income, and opportunity for personal success correspond to the actual state of these characteristics as indicated in income distributions.

Table 3.9 Perceived and actual life-cycle earnings curves

Intended occupation	Ratio of salary expected near retirement to expected starting salary (1)	Ratio of the salary of specialists aged 55–64 to the salary of specialists aged 25–34[a] (2)	Rank of[b] (1)	Rank of[b] (2)
Law	4.21	3.07	1	1
Business	3.58	2.06	2	3
Medical specialty	3.25	2.42	3	2
Accounting	3.23	1.41	4	7
Government	3.19	1.51	5	4
Architecture	3.18	1.43	6	6
Mechanical engineering	2.63	1.30	7	11
Social science	2.43	1.50	8	5
Civil engineering	2.34	1.39	9	8
Aeronautical engineering	2.32	1.25	10	12
Electrical engineering	2.24	1.19	11	14
Clergy	2.24	1.23	12	13
Teaching	2.16	1.37	13	10
Chemistry	2.05	1.38	14	9

Notes:
a   The number of occupations for which comparisons of earnings by age, education, and occupation was limited to fourteen by the available census data.
b   The Spearman rank correlation coefficient is 0.84. The 1% level of significance is 0.65.
Source: Actual salaries: US Census of Population 1960, *Occupation by Earnings and Education.*

Variability of income and the chance for wealth

In Table 3.11 perceptions of income variability and the chance for great wealth in high-level occupations are compared with measures of these characteristics from the 1960 Census. Column 1 records the proportion of students rating a field high in variability; column 2, a measure of the variation among students in expected income; column 3, the interquartile deviation of incomes reported in the census. By inspection it is clear that these measures are in broad agreement about the extent of variability or risk in particular occupations. In each case, law and business are, for example, rated high in risk while scientific and academic specialties are viewed as safe, stable alternatives. Statistically, the rankings are significantly correlated at 1 per cent.

Columns 4, 5 and 6 of Table 3.11 show respectively the fraction of students rating a field high in opportunity for wealth, the proportion actually earning over $15,000 in the career in 1959, and the skew of the income distribution. Again, perceptions are in close accord with the observed phenomena. Nearly every student, for example, foresees a substantial opportunity for wealth in business and law, where earnings above $15,000 are frequent and where income is skewed to the right, while no one anticipates such opportunities in religious and social work. The

Table 3.10 Student perceptions of relative income position of intended occupations

Intended occupation	Percentage of students who view income as above the college average (1)	Income of men with five or more years of college, 1960 (2)	Rank of[a] (1)	(2)
Medical specialty	91	$19,794	1	1
Law	79	16,082	2	2
Electrical engineering	79	10,243	2	6
Aeronautical engineering	78	10,418	4	4
'Other' engineering	76	9,806	5	8
Mechanical engineering	75	9,844	6	7
Physics	72	10,409	7	5
Business	71	13,842	8	3
Chemical engineering	67	9,457	9	11
Mathematics & statistics	60	9,437	10	13
Accounting	56	9,669	11	9
Metal & mining engineering	50	8,968	12	14
Chemistry	47	8,931	13	15
Architecture	38	8,868	14	16
Social science	34	9,447	15	12
Entertainment	31	6,995	16	20
Literature	28	8,324	17	18
Government	27	9,661	18	10
Biology	25	7,387	19	19
Teaching	16	8,391	20	17
Clergy	6	4,611	21	21

Note:
a   The rank correlation coefficient is 0.88. The 1% level of significance is 0.52.
Source: Income figures, *US Census of Population, 1960.*

rank correlation of the percentage of students viewing a career as wealth-producing (column 4) with the percentage of specialists earning over $15,000 (column 5) or with the skewness of income (column 6) are significant at 1 per cent.

From the calculations it seems safe to conclude that students have a realistic view of the variation of income among careers and of the relative opportunities for earning large incomes.

Changes in income

Do students anticipate a continuance or a reversal of past changes in income? Is the extrapolation coefficient in an expectations equation positive or negative? This is an important question in assessing the validity of the cobweb model that guides Chapters 1 and 2. If students foresee a reversal of changes in income, presumably because they understand that careers in which incomes rise rapidly will face declines in relative incomes

Table 3.11 Measures of expected and actual variation in income and opportunities for wealth compared to variation and skew of income distributions, by occupation

Occupation	Perceived and actual variation of income			Perceived and actual chance for great wealth		
	Per cent of students who believe their career has greater than average variation in income (1)	Coefficient of variation of income expected by students after 15 years' experience (2)	Interquartile range of actual income divided by the median[a] (3)	Percentage of students who believe there is opportunity to become wealthy in their career (4)	Fraction of workers with incomes of $15,000 or more[a] (5)	Quartile measure of skew (minus sign means skewed left)[b] (6)
Biological and agricultural science	67	0.377	0.48	25	2	−0.03
Medical specialty	72	0.381	1.14	79	52	[c]
Chemistry	54	0.265	0.47	37	5	0.13
Geology	69	0.303	0.74	44	11	0.36
Chemical and petroleum engineering	47	0.220	0.44	32	9	0.00
Aeronautical engineering	59	0.248	0.46	38	8	0.06
Civil engineering	61	0.238	0.61	28	7	−0.02
Electrical engineering	58	0.271	0.43	35	7	−0.05

Metallurgical engineering	56	0.263	0.44	40	13	-0.10
Mechanical engineering	68	0.297	0.48	43	7	0.10
Other engineering	59	0.332	0.59	46	—	0.21
Architecture	86	0.355	0.73	67	19	0.29
Physics	55	0.267	0.51	20	11	0.08
Mathematics and statistics	76	0.348	0.74	26	6	-0.10
Social science	78	0.366	0.62	43	11	0.14
Social work	57	0.225	0.54	0	2	0.02
Government	66	0.266	0.58	20	6	0.12
Literary skills	85	0.422	0.78	58	12	0.11
Clergy	56	0.241	0.62	6	1	-0.14
Law	91	0.402	1.12	91	34	0.35
Business	89	0.608	0.86	87	41	0.27
Accounting	63	0.347	0.57	69	8	0.14
Entertainment	96	0.696	1.40	78	11	0.36
Teaching	55	0.372	0.45	14	7	-0.31

Notes:

a Actual income figures from *US Census of Population, 1960*.

b The quartile measure of skew is Bowley's statistic $(Q_3 - Q_2) - (Q_1 - Q_2)$ divided by Q_2 where Q_1 = first quartile income: Q_2 = median income and Q_3 = third quartile income.

c The large number of physicians and surgeons with incomes above $15,000 does not permit computation of the skew coefficient.

in the future as the supply of graduates expands, it would be better to model student income expectations with a more complex rational expectations analysis than with the adaptive expectations model used in those chapters and elsewhere.

Analysis of the number of students expecting average, above-average, and below-average gains of income points to a positive linkage between past changes and expected future changes in incomes. Students planning to work in occupations with substantial past increases – for example, mathematics – foresee sizeable increases. Those intending to enter occupations with moderate increases, on the other hand, expect small future gains. Overall, the rank correlation between past and expected changes in salary among fields is significant at 5 per cent, regardless of the precise sample or measures of income used.

Abilities and economic rent

An important characteristic of occupations is the opportunity afforded persons with special abilities to rise to the top. Table 3.12 presents the survey evidence regarding student perceptions of the opportunity for personal economic success and the potential return to special abilities in their chosen career. There is a wide variation in the perceived payoff to abilities among the occupations. The majority of students in the fields of law and business, for example, regard their careers as offering considerable opportunity for personal success or failure; approximately two-thirds expect to achieve above-average earnings, while less than two-fifths of the prospective doctors, teachers, and social workers (column 1) have such expectations.

There are also substantial occupational differentials in anticipated ability rents – the expected percentage differential between personal and average income in a career. In the fields of medicine and social work students who expect to do better than average foresee a maximum ability rent of 15–20 per cent (with 15 years' experience), while, on the other hand, persons entering entertainment occupations expect abilities to be very handsomely rewarded. In this case the percentage differentials between the income expected for the individual and that expected for the average worker in the field ('ability rents') are in the order of 300 to 500 per cent, which is probably a realistic evaluation of the return to talent in entertainment.

Overall, the perceptions of the potential payoff to ability shown in Table 3.12 correspond to the actual payoff indicated in the income distributions for the occupations. First the fields that rank highest in the fraction of students expecting above-average earnings or in 'anticipated ability rent' also rank highest in the dispersion, or skewness, of income. Rank correlations of the data in Table 3.12 with those in 3.11 yield Spearman coefficients significant at 1 per cent in all cases. Individuals thus expect

Table 3.12 Expectations of personal economic success

Intended occupation	Percentage of students expecting above-average earnings	Anticipated ability rents[a]		
		Start of career	With 15 years' experience	Near retirement
Biological and agricultural science	44	4	26	44
Medical specialty	37	1	17	20
Chemistry	44	8	26	26
Geology and oceanography	42	14	22	45
Chemical and petroleum engineering	73	12	22	22
Aeronautical engineering	57	18	25	32
Civil engineering	72	10	21	36
Electrical engineering	62	14	28	37
Metallurgical engineering	52	25	30	49
Mechanical engineering	46	17	35	35
Other engineering	53	11	24	33
Architecture	44	10	55	72
Physics	38	6	10	16
Mathematics and statistics	40	10	31	52
Social science	50	8	32	28
Social work	26	5	14	14
Government	49	13	33	60
Literary careers	46	8	29	45
Clergy	44	8	29	45
Law	60	20	76	118
Business	69	17	76	107
Accounting	50	9	9	28
Entertainment	33	12	306	531
Teaching	39	11	24	31
Scattered sciences	30	5	26	34

Note:
a   As defined in the text, ability rent refers to the percentage differential in the income a person expects for himself as opposed to the average worker in his career.

ability to be richly rewarded in fields with 'loose' income distributions. Second, in every field the percentage by which personal income expectation exceeds the average increases over the life cycle. This is in accord with the greater dispersion of income about its central tendency as a cohort ages.

MARGINAL DECISION-MAKING

The theory of labor supply is based on the response of persons initially indifferent among careers to economic stimuli. These marginal suppliers alter career plans when salaries change. Here we consider the survey responses of two groups of students with some of the characteristics of the marginal suppliers – those with very flexible career plans and those with special interest in income. Do these individuals respond to economic incentives in accordance with the economic theory of occupational choice?

Marginal suppliers and career plans

There are several (overlapping) groups of survey respondents whose career plans have the characteristics expected of marginal suppliers – students unsure of their career choice, those lacking strong interest in particular occupations, those dissatisfied with available information, those paying close attention to alternatives, and so on. From those categories I identify marginal suppliers as students expressing great likelihood of changing career plans upon receipt of new information. Students in this category appear willing to alter their plans when market conditions change. In addition, they exhibit other characteristics of marginality as well:

1. A tendency to give serious consideration to alternative careers while in college (82 per cent report such considerations, compared to 50 per cent of students unlikely to change careers with more information).
2. Great dissatisfaction with the adequacy of information.
3. A tendency to select a career at a relatively late date compared to other students. (Virtually all of the marginal persons make their career decisions during their college years and none in high school.)
4. A substantial likelihood of majoring in a field unrelated to their anticipated vocation (25 per cent do not expect to work in their major, compared to 10 per cent of other students).

There is thus a reasonable correspondence between these students and the marginal suppliers of economic theory.

The survey findings in Table 3.13 indicate that economic factors play an especially large role in the career decisions of students identified in this way. Many of these students weigh income heavily in their career decisions. Seventy per cent who are likely to change careers given new conditions view income as very or somewhat important compared to 56 per cent of those unlikely to respond to new information. Contrarily, interest in work is relatively less important to the marginal suppliers, with 74 per cent rating interest as very important compared to 90 per cent of their peers. For the population under study these differences are statistically significant.

The data in Table 3.14 provide further evidence on the role of income in the career choice of marginal suppliers. According to the table, these persons have relatively pessimistic income expectations, with lower anticipated incomes that other students for all periods of their working life. Not surprisingly, in view of this pattern, the marginal suppliers are also pessimistic about the possibility of receiving above-average incomes in their fields and of earning more than they could get in its closest alternative. Fifty-four per cent expect income below the college average com-

Table 3.13 Income in the career choice of marginal and other suppliers[a]

Student response to new career information	Importance of earnings in the career decision			Importance of interest in work in the career decision		
	Very	Somewhat	Not	Very	Somewhat	Not
Strong possibility of change in career plans	17	52	31	74	17	9
Career change possible but unlikely	16	50	34	84	11	5
Career change not very possible	15	41	44	89	7	4

Note:
a   Marginal suppliers are identified as those who report a strong possibility of changing career plans given new job information.

Table 3.14 Expected levels of income of marginal and other suppliers[a]

Student response to new career information	Expected income		
	At start	With 15 years' experience	Near retirement
Strong possibility of change	$8,060	16,530	22,630
Career change possible, but unlikely	$8,360	17,370	23,500
Career change not very possible	$8,840	19,320	26,240

Note:
a   For identification of marginal suppliers see Table 3.13, note a.

pared to 46 per cent of other students. Nearly a third believe that income is higher in the closest alternative to their present career choice. By contrast, just a quarter of students with a small likelihood of changing careers given new information foresee higher earnings in the alternative.

In short, it looks as though the marginal suppliers are dissatisfied with current income prospects and are searching for more lucrative careers. Income appears especially important in their career decisions, as predicted by the theory of choice.

Economic man

The one respondent in seven who rates income as very important in career decisions is akin to the proverbial 'economic man'. His decision should be particularly responsive to economic stimuli.

Comparisons of career decisions by the importance of income confirm this expectation. Money-oriented students choose occupations which offer especially high pay and in which income is expected to increase rapidly in the future. They are especially aware of the economic significance of education. Fewer than 10 per cent see no cost or sacrifice to college compared to 20 per cent of those uninterested in income. Moreover the economically oriented students report more flexible career plans than other students. Seventy-five per cent express a willingness to change careers upon the receipt of new information compared to 65 per cent of those with no interest in income. These differences suggest that the monetarily oriented are especially aware of and likely to respond to economic stimuli and thus provide part of the 'margin of adjustment' by which the market responds to changes in economic conditions.

Marginal incentive and career choice

The survey question asking students to compare incomes in their chosen career with the income in its closest alternative provides a final test of the marginal aspects of decision-making. All else being the same, careers in which many students expect incomes above those in alternatives are likely to be especially attractive and to recruit many new entrants, while the opposite should be true in fields where students expect incomes below those in close alternatives.

A comparison between changes in degrees in the period 1965–8 (or 1960–8) and the fraction of survey respondents viewing income as high relative to that in close alternatives confirms this implication of the marginal analysis. Taking fields with roughly comparable nonpecuniary advantages – the sciences and engineering, for example – increases in the number of degrees is positively rank-correlated with 'marginal income incentives,'[11] with a coefficient of 0.70, significant at 1 per cent. Thus the limited evidence available suggests that marginal income incentives influence plans in the expected way.

CONCLUSION

This chapter affirms the micro-foundations of the economic theory of occupational selection. As far as can be told from the survey responses, the theory rests on a firm foundation at the level of the individual decision-maker.

NOTES

1. These estimates are *not* based on the average income expected by students themselves relative to the average income expected for the career. Rather, for

each student expecting to do better, a ratio of ability rent was computed and the mean ratio calculated.

2. Adam Smith, *The Wealth of Nations* (Modern Library edition), p. 107.

3. The assumption that students are comparing their respective fields to the median may not be entirely valid, but is necessary for evaluating the reasonableness of responses. Obviously if 100 per cent of students thought their fields were above or below average, they would be unrealistic. Using the uniform distribution as a measuring rod is the best that can be done, given the wording of the questionnaire and available information.

4. Since the questions are worded as true–false, it is possible that uneven distributions of responses do not, in fact, reflect incorrect perceptions of the market. Some students may view their career as exactly average and thus be required to make a false comparison.

5. Exaggerated perceptions of characteristics are not infrequent in economic life. Professors, for example, have an exaggerated view of the quality of their departments. Cartter reports that they 'lean over backwards in rating their present university attachment . . . rating it on the average 17 per cent higher than outsiders did.' A. Cartter, 'Economics of the university', *American Economic Review* (May 1965), p. 487.

6. These estimates are backward extrapolations of the income of men with those levels of training in the age bracket 25–34. The basic data are from US Bureau of Census, *Current Population Reports*, ser. P-60, no. 56. 'Annual male income, lifetime income, and educational attainment of men in the US for selected years, 1956–1966' (Washington, DC: US Government Printing Office, 1968).

7. The percentages sum to more than 100 because students often listed more than one cost.

8. The average undergraduate in the sample was midway between his sophomore and junior years. Since most plan to enroll for graduate training, a reasonable estimate of the length of additional schooling is four years. The average graduate student in the sample was in his second year of study and would anticipate approximately two additional years of school.

9. The compensating differential was calculated by the formula $R = 100(1 + i)^t - 100$, where $t = $ the number of years of training and R is the compensating difference in income in percentage terms. See H. G. Lewis, *Unionism and Relative Wages in the United States* (Chicago, 1963), p. 122.

10. The principal noncomparability occurs between the final level of education foreseen by survey respondents and used in the income data. For example, our survey mixes MAT and EdD students in the graduate education category and compares their expectations with the income of PhD graduates. This probably explains the low rank of the field in expected income in the table.

11. The comparison described in the test can be improved in two ways. First, nonpecuniary income could be held fixed by focusing on the marginal incentive of students preparing the work in particular sectors of the economy – e.g. business or academic. Second, students could be surveyed in the future and their expression of marginal income incentive compared to that of the 1967 students. Presumably, changes in incentive will be correlated with a changed pattern of career choice.

4 · THE EFFECT OF DEMOGRAPHIC FACTORS ON AGE–EARNINGS PROFILES

The age distribution of the labor force varies greatly over time in response to long-term demographic changes. Historically, high birth rates produce a relatively large number of younger labor force participants and an age distribution skewed toward younger ages, while low birth rates have the opposite impact.[1] Because of the 'baby boom' that followed World War II and peaked in 1955–60 (US Bureau of the Census, 1977, p. 56), there was an especially significant change in the age structure of the US workforce in the late 1960s and early 1970s, when the number of young persons increased extremely rapidly. From 1966 to 1976, the number of labor force participants aged 20–24 grew from 9.7 million to 16.7 million, while the number aged 25–34 grew from 16.8 million to 23.0 million. The ratio of participants less than 35 years of age to participants 35 and over jumped from 0.46 to 0.67.[2]

What are the consequences for the wage structure of such sizeable changes in the age composition of the labor force? Does an increase in the relative number of young workers alter their wages relative to the wages of older workers? To what extent do cross-sectional age–earnings profiles respond to exogenous demographic shifts? What are the possible implications of the experience of the late 1960s and 1970s for the decade of the 1980s, when the number of young workers is expected to decline?

The answers to these questions depend on the degree of flexibility of relative wages by age or, in the context of standard labor demand analysis, on elasticities of complementarity which link changes in factor prices to changes in the supply of inputs. If the relevant elasticities are large, changes in the age composition of the labor force can substantially alter age–earnings profiles, whereas if elasticities are small, profiles will be relatively independent of the number of workers in different age groups.

This chapter studies the effect of changes in the age structure of the workforce on age–earnings profiles in the United States and provides estimates of the relevant elasticities of complementarity for young and older workers.

It focuses in particular on developments in the late 1960s and in the 1970s, when the relative number of young workers increased sufficiently rapidly as to provide a strong 'test' of the potential dependence of the profile on exogenous shifts in the age structure of the labor supply. The first section documents the magnitude of the change in the age structure of the work-force which constitutes the 'experimental' variation under study. The second section presents evidence from the Current Population Surveys of the US Bureau of the Census that the age–earnings profile of male workers changed in the period, with the ratio of the earnings of older men to the earnings of younger men rising sharply. The third section develops the re-levant labor demand and production function models needed to analyze the link between changes in the age structure of the workforce and changes in age–earnings profiles. The fourth estimates the extent to which shifts in age–earnings profiles can be attributed to demographically induced move-ments along labor demand schedules whose magnitude is reflected in the relevant elasticities of complementarity.

The principal finding is that the age–earnings profile of male workers, which has traditionally been viewed as a stable economic relation deter-mined by human capital investment decisions, appears to be significantly influenced by the age composition of the workforce. Apparently because younger and older male workers are imperfect substitutes in production, changes in the number of young male workers relative to older male work-ers substantially influence the ratio of the earnings of younger men to the earnings of older men. The effect of changes in the relative numbers of workers of different ages on age–earnings profiles is especially marked among college graduates. By contrast, the age–earnings profile of female workers, which tends to be quite flat, appears to be little influenced by the age composition of the female workforce, possibly because the intermittent work experience of women makes younger women and older women closer substitutes in production.

Whether the sizeable decline in the earnings of the large cohort of young workers entering the market in the 1970s relative to the earnings of older cohorts will persist, creating a lifetime 'size of cohort' earnings effect, or whether the new entrants of the 1970s will significantly catch up in earnings in future years remains to be seen.

The dependence of the age–earnings profile on demographically induced movements along a relative demand schedule suggests that standard human capital models of the profile, which posit that earnings rise with age or experience *solely* as a result of individual investment behavior, are incomplete. If, as found in this study, elasticities of substitution or com-plementarity among age groups are not infinite, human capital cannot be treated as a homogeneous input with a single rental price, whose 'units' of investment determine the age–earnings profiles. Differences in the activi-ties of younger and older workers and in the demand for those activities decisively influence the shape of the profile. To understand the relation between earnings and age, it is necessary to analyze the demand for workers by age and employer personnel policies as well as to analyze human capital investment decisions.

THE CHANGING AGE STRUCTURE OF THE WORKFORCE

The broad outlines of the remarkable change in the age structure of the workforce of the United States under investigation is examined in Table 4.1, which records the absolute number of workers aged 20–24 and 25–34 and the number aged 20–24 and 25–34 relative to the number of workers aged 35 and over for the period 1966 to 1976. The table treats male and female workers and college graduates and high school graduates separately. These patterns of change stand out in the table: a remarkable increase in the number of young workers in total, the result of the 'baby boom' that followed World War II; an even greater percentage increase in the number of young college graduate workers, the result of the unprecedented proportion of young persons choosing to enroll in college in the 1960s; and an especially marked increase in the number of young female workers, the result of a sizeable jump in the labor force participation rate of young women in the late 1960s and 1970s.

Among male workers, the numbers aged 20–24 and 25–34 increased by over one-third from 1966 to 1976, while the number of college graduates aged 20–24 and aged 25–34 more than doubled. As a result of these changes, the ratio of all male workers 20–34 to those 35 and over rose from 0.55 in 1966 to 0.78 in 1976, while the ratio of male college graduate workers 20–34 years of age to male college graduate workers 35 and over increased from 0.62 (1966) to 1.02 (1976). According to the figures in Panel B, the number of female workers aged 20–24 increased by 76 per cent, while the number aged 25–34 increased by 103 per cent. These gains outstripped the rate of increase of the older female workforce by sufficient magnitudes to raise the ratio of 20–24 to 35+-year-old female workers by 53 per cent and the ratio of 25–34 to 35+-year-old female workers by 76 per cent. Among college graduate workers, the number of young women aged 20–24 more than doubled, while the number aged 25–34 more than tripled. While less dramatic, the number of young female high school graduate workers also increased, particularly in the 25–34 bracket.

Data on the number of new high school and college graduates and on the number of new graduates entering the labor market tell a similar story about the influx of young persons into the workforce, though the timing of changes necessarily differs from that in Table 4.1. Between 1960 and 1970, the number of new high school graduates per thousand persons in the civilian labor force rose from 26.8 to 35.0.[3] From 1960 to 1972, the

Table 4.1 The changed structure of the workforce, by sex and education

	Workforce, by age				College graduate workforce, by age				High school graduate workforce, by age			
	Numbers (in 000s)		Relative to workers 35+		Numbers (in 000s)		Relative to college workers 35+		Numbers (in 000s)		Relative to 35+	
	20–24	25–34	20–24	25–34	20–24	25–34	20–24	25–34	20–24	25–34	20–24	25–34
A. Male workers												
1966	6,139	10,761	0.201	0.352	280	1,067	0.129	0.490	2,057	3,929	0.249	0.475
1968	6,788	11,376	0.221	0.371	290	1,137	0.131	0.514	2,066	4,220	0.232	0.473
1970	7,378	11,974	0.241	0.391	376	1,200	0.161	0.514	2,324	4,529	0.248	0.483
1972	7,795	12,806	0.257	0.423	567	1,393	0.232	0.569	2,772	4,792	0.288	0.497
1974	8,105	13,993	0.270	0.465	585	1,725	0.222	0.655	3,011	5,110	0.289	0.507
1976	8,421	14,990	0.282	0.502	686	2,203	0.242	0.779	3,334	6,309	0.330	0.525
% change 1966–76	37.2	39.3	40.2	42.6	145.0	106.5	84.7	59.0	62.1	60.5	42.2	11.0
B. Female workers												
1966	3,601	4,516	0.220	0.276	331	444	0.352	0.472	1,879	2,063	0.311	0.342
1968	4,251	5,104	0.251	0.301	436	526	0.397	0.479	2,104	2,358	0.317	0.356
1970	4,893	5,704	0.276	0.322	515	614	0.483	0.576	2,400	2,764	0.322	0.371
1972	5,337	6,525	0.298	0.365	620	801	0.540	0.698	2,593	3,068	0.331	0.392
1974	5,867	7,826	0.322	0.430	699	1,101	0.565	0.890	2,598	3,452	0.319	0.424
1976	6,339	9,183	0.336	0.487	757	1,388	0.565	1.04	2,935	3,958	0.346	0.466
% change 1966–76	76.0	103.3	52.7	76.4	128.8	121.6	60.5	120.3	56.2	91.9	11.3	36.3

Sources: Workforce data compiled from *Employment and Training Report of the President* (US Department of Labor, 1976) transmitted to Congress 1977, Table A-2, p. 137. Workers by education data compiled from 'Educational Attainment of Workers' (US Department of Labor, Bureau of Labor Statistics).

number of high school graduates and dropouts entering the job market grew from 13.2 per thousand members of the civilian labor force to 17.1 per thousand members of the civilian labor force.[4] For college graduates, the picture is more complex, as the tendency to enroll for graduate studies in the 1960s delayed the labor market entrance of the large classes of the 1960s until the following decade. From the late 1960s to the mid-1970s, however, the ratio of new bachelor's graduates on the market to the civilian labor force increased sharply.[5]

Because data on graduates refer to flows rather than stocks of persons in a wide age grouping, they reveal further the beginning of the decline in the number of young workers which marks the 1980s. From 1972 to 1977, the number of persons graduating from high school grew by a bare 4 per cent (US Bureau of the Census, 1977 p. 153). From 1974 to 1976, the number of persons graduating from college fell by 3.0 per cent (US Bureau of the Census, 1977, p. 153). The beginning of the demographic change from the large cohorts of young persons of the late 1960s and 1970s to the smaller cohorts of the 1980s can be seen in these figures.

While not a 'classical experiment' with all other factors held fixed, the sizeable increase in the number of young workers found in Table 4.1 and in the graduate data cited above and the concurrent change in the age composition of the workforce constitutes the type of exogenous shift in the age composition of the workforce that should provide a reasonably strong test of whether the age–earnings relation depends on factors beyond investments in training. Was the change in supply accompanied by changes in relative wages?

CHANGES IN THE RELATIVE EARNINGS OF YOUNG WORKERS

Evidence on earnings by age from the Current Population Survey of the Bureau of the Census provides an answer to this question. The CPS data show that for male workers, who traditionally have had steep cross-sectional age–earnings profiles, the demographic changes of the late 1960s and of the 1970s were accompanied by a substantial 'twist' in the age–earnings profile against the young. By contrast, among female workers, who have traditionally had flat age–earnings profiles, the demographic changes do not appear to have altered the relative wages of the young. While other factors may have also been at work, the concatenation of increases in relative numbers and decreases in relative wages in the period is highly suggestive of movement along a negatively sloped demand curve, with a moderate elasticity of substitution between workers of different ages.

Table 4.2 summarizes the CPS evidence on age–earnings profiles in terms of the ratio of the income or earnings of 45–54 or 45–49-year-old workers to the incomes or earnings of 20–24, 25–9, or 25–34-year-old workers, in toto and for high school graduates and college graduates taken separately. The figures in lines 1–8 are taken from the US Bureau of the Census's *Current Population Reports*, with the data for 1975 adjusted to take account of changes in the imputation procedure used by the Census. As discussed in *Current Population Reports*, Consumer Income Series P-60, No. 105, the Census made major changes in its method of computing incomes in 1975 when it introduced a new imputation procedure to estimate missing records. The new procedure tends to raise the average earnings of more educated and older workers relative to what would have resulted from the previous imputation procedure. For comparability over time, the 1975 data in the table are adjusted to a pre-1975 basis by multiplying the reported 1975 figures by the ratio of incomes in 1974 calculated from the old imputation procedure to incomes in 1974 calculated from the new procedure, using unpublished Census tabulations.[6]

Lines 1–4 treat the mean incomes of all workers who report greater than zero values for the year. These incomes are likely to be sensitive to cyclical changes in unemployment rates. Lines 5–8 are based on the incomes of year-round full-time workers, which should be less sensitive to the cycle and which should offer a better measure of rates of pay than the incomes of all workers. For women, the sizeable number of part-time workers and significant nonwage incomes makes interpretation of the incomes for all workers complex, suggesting that attention be focused on year-round full-time employees. The final lines of the table record ratios of usual weekly earnings. These figures have the advantage of referring to labor market earnings rather than total incomes and of covering narrower age groups. They suffer from lack of information on years of schooling.

The figures for male workers in the table show a substantial change in age–earnings profiles, with the income or earnings of older men rising sharply relative to the income or earnings of younger men. For all men, the data in lines 1 and 2 show an increase of 20 percentage points (9 per cent) in the ratio of the incomes of 45–54-year olds to the income of 20–24-year olds and an increase of 5 percentage points (4 per cent) in the ratio of the incomes of 45–54-year-olds relative to the incomes of 25–34-year olds. The comparable changes for year-round and full-time workers in lines 5 and 6 are 24 points (6 per cent) and 8 points (7 per cent). With the best measures of rates of pay, median usual weekly earnings, there is a rise in the ratio of the earnings of 45–49-year-olds to the earnings of 20–24-year olds not enrolled in school of 33 points (25 per cent) from 1967 to 1977 and a rise in the ratio of the earnings of 45–49-year olds to the earnings of 25–9-year olds of 15 points (14 per cent).

The figures for college and high school graduates show further that the 'twist' in male age–earnings profiles was most pronounced for college graduates. Between 1968 and 1975 the ratio of the incomes of 45–54-year-

Table 4.2 Ratios of the incomes or earnings of older to younger workers by sex and education, 1967–77

Income measure and group	Males			Females		
	1967–68[a]	1975[b]	1977	1967–68[a]	1975[b]	1977
Mean incomes of all workers						
1 Ratio of the income of persons aged 45–54 to the income of persons aged 20–24	2.30	2.50	—	1.38	1.48	—
2 Ratio of the income of persons aged 45–54 to the income of persons aged 25–34	1.18	1.23	—	1.16	1.05	—
3 Ratio of the income of persons aged 45–54 to the income of persons aged 25–34, high school graduates	1.21	1.30	—	1.24	1.13	—
4 Ratio of the income of persons aged 45–54 to the income of persons aged 25–34, college graduates	1.43	1.62	—	1.35	1.22	—
Mean incomes of year-round and full-time workers						
5 Ratio of the income of persons aged 45–54 to the income of persons aged 20–24	1.74	2.00	—	1.21	1.35	—

6	Ratio of the income of persons aged 45–54 to the income of persons aged 25–34	1.18	1.26	—	1.00	1.01
7	Ratio of the income of persons aged 45–54 to the income of persons aged 25–34, high school graduates	1.20	1.31	—	1.07	1.08
8	Ratio of the income of persons aged 45–54 to the income of persons aged 25–34, college graduates	1.38	1.63	—	1.05	1.14
	Mean usual weekly earnings, full-time white workers					
9	Ratio of the earnings of persons aged 45–49 to the earnings of persons 20–24 out of school workers	1.27	1.57	1.60	—	—
10	Ratio of the earnings of persons aged 45–49 to the earnings of persons 25–29	1.06	1.19	1.21	—	—

Notes:

a 1968 in lines 1–8; 1967 in lines 9–10.

b Figures for 1975 in lines 1–8 based on unpublished Census data which give incomes in 1974 and 1975 on a comparable basis. As discussed in Series P-60, No. 105, the Census used a different imputation procedure for estimating incomes in 1975. The new procedure tends to bias upward the earnings of more educated and older workers.

Sources: Current Population Reports, US Bureau of the Census, Consumer Income Series P-60, N. 66, Tables 39, 41; No. 101, Tables 53, 59; No. 105, Table 4. US Department of Labor, Bureau of Labor Statistics: unpublished tabulations from May 1967, 1975, and 1977 Current Population Surveys.

old year-round and full-time male college graduates to the incomes of
25–34-year-old year-round and full-time male college graduates rose by 25
percentage points (18 per cent), while the comparable ratio for male high
school graduates rose by 11 points (9 per cent). Similarly, for all male
college graduates, the ratio of the incomes of 45–54-year olds to the
incomes of 25–34-year olds rose by 19 percentage points (13 per cent),
while the ratio of the incomes of high school graduates 45–54 years old to
the incomes of high school graduates 25–34 years old rose by just 9
percentage points (7 per cent).

The data for women tell a different story. The mean incomes for all
workers show a rise in the income of women aged 45–54 relative to the
income of women aged 20–24, but do not show a rise in the income of
women aged 45–54 to the income of women aged 25–34 and depict a drop
in the income of older high school or college graduate women relative to
younger high school or college graduate women (lines 3 and 4). On the
other hand, the mean incomes for year-round and full-time workers show
an increase in the ratio of the incomes of 45–54-year olds compared to the
incomes of 25–34-year olds. The unclear pattern in the data may reflect the
general flatness of the age–earnings profile for women, particularly for
year-round and full-time workers. If the flat profiles result from high
substitutability between workers of different ages in production,[7] large
changes in the age structure of the population would have little or no
impact on the profiles.

Because age–earnings profiles differ markedly between men and women
and appear to have changed only for men in the period covered, the
remainder of this study will focus solely on male age–earnings relations.
The flat and apparently stable profiles among women suggest very different
economic processes at work, which merit separate detailed study beyond
the scope of the current inquiry.

Analysis of male earnings using CPS data tapes

More precise estimates of the extent of change in the age–earnings profiles
of males workers can be obtained by linear regression analysis of the effect
of age on earnings using the CPS data on individuals that underlie the
published aggregates. Regression analysis of the data for individuals has
several advantages over comparisons of published means: it permits investigation of labor market earnings (rather than of incomes, as given in
Current Population Reports Series P-60); it permits calculation of weekly
earnings (yearly earnings over weeks worked) as an indicator of rate of
pay; it allows for greater disaggregation of workers by age and education;
and it can be used more readily to make statistical tests of the significance
of observed changes.[8]

To estimate changes in age–earnings profiles among male workers in the period under study using CPS data on individuals, the following linear regression model was fit with the March 1969 and March 1978 tapes[9] (which give earnings for the preceding year):

$$\ln W_{ij} = a + \Sigma_{ij} b_{ij} E_i A_j + c R_{ij} + \mu_{ij} \tag{4.1}$$

where W_{ij} = weekly or annual earnings of workers in the ith education and jth age groups; E_i = dichotomous dummy variable that takes the value 1 for persons in the ith education group and the value 0 otherwise, with i covering seven education groups: 0–8 years of schooling, 9–11 years, 12 years, 13–15 years, 16 years, 17 years, and more than 17 years; A_j = dichotomous dummy variable that takes the value 1 for persons in the jth age group and 0 otherwise, with j covering six age groups: 18–24, 25–29, 30–34, 35–44, 45–54, and 55–64; R_{ij} = dummy variable which takes the value 1 for blacks; and μ_{ij} is assumed $N(0, \sigma^2)$. One interaction term is omitted to define the base group.

The results of the calculations are summarized in Table 4.3 in terms of *differences* between the coefficients on the log earnings of workers aged 45 to 54 and the coefficients on the log earnings of workers in younger age brackets for persons with 12 years of schooling (e.g., high school graduates) and for persons with 16 years of schooling (e.g., college graduates), taken separately. Comparable estimates for other education groups are also available, but for simplicity are not given in the table. In the left side of the table the dependent variable is the log of weekly earnings, the best measure of rates of pay on the March CPS files. The right-hand side of the table treats the log of annual earnings. The computations confirm the finding of a sizeable decline in the earnings of young workers relative to the earnings of older workers, particularly among the more educated. Among high school graduates, the log weekly earnings of 45–54-year olds is 0.18 log points higher relative to the log weekly earnings of 18–24-year olds in 1977 than in 1968; it is 0.17 points higher relative to the log earnings of 25–9-year-olds in 1977 than in 1968; is 0.09 points higher relative to the log earnings of 30–34-year-olds in 1977 than in 1968; and is 0.10 points higher relative to the log earnings of 35–44-year-olds in 1977 than in 1968. Among men with four years of college, the changes are greater, with increases of 0.30 log points in the difference between the log earnings of 45–54-year olds and the log earnings of 18–24, 25–29, and 30–34-year olds, respectively, from 1968 to 1977. In other education groups, the results are comparable. While not all of the changes in the difference in log earnings are significant at the 5 per cent level, those for the more educated group are highly significant.

The calculations using log annual earnings tell a similar story, with the earnings of the older workers rising relative to those of younger workers, especially among the college educated.

We conclude that there was, in fact, a substantial change in the

Table 4.3 Regression estimates and standard errors on the difference between the log of earnings of men aged 45–54 and of younger men, for college and high school graduates, 1968 and 1977

Education and age group	Coefficient and standard errors for earnings of 45–54 year olds relative to other group weekly earnings		Change in relative earnings	t-Test of change[a]	Coefficient and standard errors for earnings of 45–54 year olds relative to other group yearly earnings		Change in relative earnings	t-Test of change[a]
	1968	1977			1968	1977		
12 years of schooling								
18–24	0.60(0.03)	0.78(0.06)	0.18	2.57	0.95(0.03)	1.02(0.08)	0.17	1.89
25–29	0.13(0.03)	0.30(0.06)	0.17	2.43	0.17(0.03)	0.37(0.08)	0.20	2.22
30–34	0.02(0.03)	0.11(0.06)	0.09	1.29	0.02(0.03)	0.16(0.08)	0.14	1.56
35–44	−0.03(0.03)	0.07(0.06)	0.10	1.43	0.03(0.03)	0.08(0.08)	0.06	0.67
45–54	0.00	0.00	—	—	0.00	0.00	—	—
16 years of schooling								
18–24	0.83(0.05)	1.13(0.06)	0.30	3.75	1.18(0.06)	1.48(0.11)	0.30	2.31
25–29	0.28(0.05)	0.58(0.07)	0.30	3.33	0.37(0.05)	0.70(0.10)	0.33	3.00
30–34	0.10(0.05)	0.40(0.07)	0.30	3.33	0.10(0.05)	0.47(0.10)	0.37	3.36
35–44	0.01(0.04)	0.18(0.07)	0.17	2.14	0.02(0.05)	0.21(0.10)	0.19	1.73
45–54	0.00	0.00	—	—	0.00	0.00	—	—
Number of observations	30,231	29,842	—	—	30,231	29,842	—	—
R^2	0.248	0.272	—	—	0.297	0.284	—	—

Note:

a The significance for the t-tests are: 5 per cent level, 1.65; 1 per cent level, 2.33.

Source: Obtained by regression of the log of earnings on dummy variable for race and education by age, as described in the text. The regressions included age–education dummy variables for the following education groups: 0–8 years of education, 9–11 years of education, 13–15 years of education, 17 and 18+ years of education and for 55–64 year olds in addition to the groups in the table. The March 1969 and March 1978 Current Population Survey Tapes were used in the analysis.

age–earnings profiles for male workers during the period when the number of young workers increased relative to the number of older workers. Are these two changes causally linked? To what extent can the twist in the age–earnings profile against the young be attributed to the sharp increase in the relative number of young workers?

LABOR DEMAND AND AGE–EARNINGS PROFILES

In the framework of standard labor demand analysis, the impact of changes in the relative supply of workers by age depends on the substitutability of inputs. When labor of different ages is readily substitutable for other inputs, large changes in supply will cause only modest changes in wages by age. Conversely, when substitutability is limited, sizeable changes in age–earnings profiles are needed for demand to adjust to changes in the age composition of the workforce. Since the number of workers of different ages is taken as exogenously determined by demographic changes, the demand for labor schedule becomes a wage-determination schedule, linking factor prices to factor quantities. In such a model, Hicks's elasticity of complementarity, which relates factor prices to inputs (Hicks, 1970; Sato and Koizumi, 1973) is the appropriate elasticity concept, rather than the standard Allen elasticity of substitution. In this study I will concentrate on the inverse of the Hicks elasticity, defined as:

$$S_{ij} = (\dot{W}_i/\dot{L}_j)\, 1/\alpha_j \tag{4.2}$$

where W_i = wage of factor i; L_j = amount of factor j; α_j = share of factor j in cost; and where dots above variables represent log changes (i.e., $\dot{W}_i = d\ln W_i$) and where the elasticity S_{ij} is taken with other inputs held fixed but with output allowed to vary.[10] The 'own elasticity' of complementarity S_{ii} is implicitly defined as

$$\Sigma_j \alpha_j S_{ij} = 0 \text{ so that } S_{ii} = -\Sigma_{j \ne i}(a_j/a_i)S_{ij} \tag{4.3}$$

S_{ii} is negative for normal production functions.

When all inputs vary, the factor price determination equation of factor i can be written as:[11]

$$\dot{W}_i = \Sigma_{j \ne i}\alpha_j S_{ij}\dot{L}_j + \alpha_i S_{ii}\dot{L}_i = \Sigma_{j \ne i}a_i S_{ij}(\dot{L}_j - \dot{L}_i) \tag{4.4}$$

Equation 4.4 shows how changes in the quantities of all inputs or changes in the quantities of inputs relative to the input i alter the wage of input i. To see how changes in inputs alter relative wages, let i index one input (say, older workers) and k index another input (say, younger workers), then subtract the factor price equation based on equation 4.4 for input k from that for input i to obtain:

$$\dot{W}_i - \dot{W}_k = \Sigma_{j \neq i \neq k}[\alpha_j(S_{ij} - S_{kj})\dot{L}_j]$$
$$+ \alpha_i[S_{ii} - S_{ki}]\dot{L}_i - \alpha_k[S_{ik} - S_{kk}]\dot{L}_k \qquad (4.5)$$

When factors other than k and i do not affect the ratio of their marginal products, the elasticity of complementarity is equal to one divided by the standard Allen elasticity of substitution (Hicks, 1970; Sato and Koizumi, 1973), giving the following relative wage determination equation:

$$\dot{W}_i - \dot{W}_k = -(1/\sigma_{ik})(\dot{L}_i - \dot{L}_k) \qquad (4.6)$$

where σ_{ik} = elasticity of substitution between i and k, and $\sigma_{ik} > 0$.

Production functions and elasticities

The relevant elasticities of complementarity or substitution for workers in different age groups are estimated in this study assuming one of two functional forms for the production process: the constant elasticity of substitution (CES) form and the translogarithmic (TL) form.

The CES form has both desirable and undesirable features for empirical analysis of the effects of changes in the relative number of workers by age on age–earnings profiles. On the positive side, since the CES has only one elasticity of substitution, the appropriate relative wage equation is of the form of equation 4.6, which is reasonably simple to estimate and which provides direct information on the impact of relative quantities on relative earnings. The possibility that changes in relative wages, of the type observed in the 1970s, are due largely to cyclical rather than demographic changes can be readily examined with equation 4.6 by addition of variables measuring the business cycle. The major disadvantage of the CES is that it cannot be used to test the possibility that in a consistent production function framework changes in other factors, such as capital, may be influencing the relative demand for labor of different ages.

The translogarithmic (TL) production function provides an appropriate system for examining the effect of changes in the supply of several inputs on age–earnings profiles. The TL form yields a consistent system of demand equations with potentially different elasticities of complementarity (or substitution) between any pair of inputs. In the translog production system, the production function is:

$$\ln Y = A + \Sigma_i \alpha_i \ln L_i + 1/2 \Sigma_i \Sigma_j \gamma_{ij} \ln L_i \ln L_j \qquad (4.7)$$

The derived demand equations are:

$$\alpha_i = a_i + \Sigma_j \gamma_{ij} \ln L_j \qquad (4.8)$$

subject to cross-equation and within-equation restrictions on the parameters

$$\Sigma a_i = 1 \qquad (4.9)$$

$$\Sigma_j \gamma_{ij} = 0 = \Sigma_i \gamma_{ij} \qquad (4.10)$$

where α_i = share of input i in cost, and L_j = amount of input j. Equation 4.8 relates the share of each input in cost to the quantities of inputs; since quantities are given, the equations are in effect relative wage equations, dependent on how the wage components of cost change when quantities change. The Hicks elasticities of complementarity can be readily derived from the translog system by differentiation with respect to the relevant L_i. The resultant equations are:[12]

$$S_{ij} = (\gamma_{ij})/(\alpha_i \alpha_j) + 1 \qquad (4.11)$$

$$S_{ii} = (1/\alpha_i)^2 [\gamma_{ii} + \alpha_i^2 - \alpha_i] \qquad (4.12)$$

Equations 4.11 and 4.12 relate the elasticities of complementarity to the parameters of the equation and factor shares.

The TL system has one major advantage as a model of demand: it provides estimates of elasticities of complementarity for more than two inputs in a consistent production function framework. It has two disadvantages. First, specification or measurement error in the equation for a factor of only marginal concern, such as for capital in the case at hand, can greatly impact estimates of the demand equations for other factors. Second, the TL model is an equilibrium model that cannot be readily modified to allow for the effect of cyclical factors on relative demands.

Since neither the CES nor TL models of production or demand are without problems, the effect of the age composition on relatives wages by age will be estimated using both models. By using the two functional forms, each of which has weaknesses and strengths, I hope to obtain a better fix on the key demand relation under study than could otherwise be done.

DETERMINANTS OF CHANGE IN MALE AGE–EARNINGS PROFILES

Table 4.4 presents estimates of the impact of the ratio of the number of younger workers to the number of older workers, the state of the business cycle, and a general trend on the curvature of male age–earnings profiles. The dependent variables in the calculations are the log of the income of 45–54-year-old men relative to the income of the 25–34-year-old men (lines 1–5) and the log of the income of 45–54-year-old men relative to the income of 20–24-year-old men (lines 6–8). Lines 1–2 and 6–7 refer to the incomes of year-round full-time workers. As noted earlier, these incomes provide a better measure of wages than do the incomes of all workers; unfortunately they are not available until 1955. Lines 3 and 8 treat the ratio

Table 4.4 Demographic and trend determinants of the mean income of older to younger male workers, 1947–74

| Dependent variables (in ln units) | Constant | Coefficients and standard errors | | | R^2 | Durbin-Watson statistic |
		Cycle[a]	Relative number of workers by age	Time		
Income of 45–54-year olds relative to the income of 25–34-year olds						
1 Year-round and full-time workers, 1955–74	0.04	0.08 (0.26)	−0.27 (0.09)		0.34	0.33
2 Year-round and full-time workers, 1955–74	0.00	0.01 (0.11)	−0.14 (0.04)	0.005 (0.001)	0.89	1.79
3 All workers, 1947–74	0.09	−0.29 (0.14)	−0.20 (0.05)	0.003 (0.001)	0.54	1.70
4 Four-year college graduate workers, 1956–74[b]	0.09	−0.24 (0.64)	−0.51 (0.28)	0.006 (0.005)	0.33	b
5 High school graduate workers, 1956–74	0.15	−0.26 (0.12)	−0.07 (0.11)	0.003 (0.003)	0.48	b
Income of 45–54-year olds relative to income of 20–24-year olds						
6 Year-round and full-time workers, 1955–74	0.60	−0.72 (0.24)	−0.32 (0.04)		0.84	1.04

7 Year-round and full-time workers, 1955–74	0.69	−0.70 (0.25)	−0.41 (0.19)	−0.003 (0.006)	0.85	1.05
8 All workers, 1947–74	0.59	−0.71 (0.26)	−0.01 (0.05)	0.011 (0.001)	0.86	1.92

Notes:

a The measure of the cycle in lines 1–2 and 4–7 was obtained as the residual from the following regression of real GNP on time for the period 1955–74:

$$\log \text{GNP} = 8.32 + 0.039T \qquad R^2 = 0.983$$
$$(0.001)$$

The measure of the cycle in lines 3 and 8 was obtained as the residual from the following regression of real GNP on time for the period 1947–74:

$$\log \text{GNP} = 8.02 + 0.037T \qquad R^2 = 0.989$$
$$(0.001)$$

b The years 1957, 1959–61, and 1963 were omitted due to absence of data. Because of the omission, no Durbin–Watson statistic was calculated.

Sources: Income data and numbers from *Current Population Reports* US Bureau of the Census, Consumer Income Series P-60. The figures of mean incomes for the period 1947–60 are from US Bureau of the Census, *Trends in Income of Families and Persons in the United States: 1947–1960*, Technical Paper No. 7. Due to the absence of mean figures for the years 1961–4, mean incomes for those years were obtained by interpolation using least squares regression of the log of the mean incomes on the log of median incomes.

College incomes: *Current Population Reports* US Bureau of the Census, Consumer Income Series P-60, No. 92, Table A, p. 2, with 1965–7 ungrouped data spliced for consistency with 1967–72 grouped data using the 1967 overlap year. The missing year 1965 was obtained by applying percentage changes in median incomes from 1964 to 1965. 1973 and 1974 are taken from Series P-60, Nos. 97 and 101. Because the 1965 income figures were published only for men with 4+ years of college, I estimated the income of 4-year graduates in 1956 by regressing income for 4-year graduates on income for graduates with 4 or more years of college, using all the years after 1956, and extrapolating with the equation.

of the mean income of all men with nonzero incomes in the relevant age groups over the period 1947–74. These figures provide additional time–series variation in the data at the expense of potential confounding of changes in utilization of labor with changes in wages paid. Lines 4 and 5 consider the age–earnings profiles of college graduates and high school graduates separately for the limited number of years for which such figures are available.

There are three independent variables. The changing age structure of the workforce is measured by the log of the ratio of the number of male workers aged 45–54 to the number aged 25–34 (lines 1–5) or to the number aged 20–24 (lines 6–8). To test the possibility that changes in relative earnings by age are dominated by cyclical rather than demographic factors, the calculations also include a measure of the state of the business cycle, the deviation of the log of real gross national product (GNP) from its trend level: positive deviations reflect a strong economy, while negative deviations are indicative of recession conditions. This measure of the cycle is highly correlated with such alternative business-cycle indicators as the rate of unemployment or the difference between actual and potential gross national product (Freeman, 1973). Because of the operation of formal seniority systems and because older workers will have cumulated specific human capital while young workers will not, labor demand is likely to be more cyclical for young than for older workers, suggesting that the deviation of real GNP from trend will be negatively related to the ratio of income of older to younger workers. The third independent variable, a time trend, is introduced to control for any of a variety of factors (greater education of the young, gradual shifts in industrial structure) which might influence the demand for young as opposed to older male workers and thus the relevant income ratios.

The regression results suggest that, with trend and cyclical factors fixed, the relative number of older to younger workers has a significant impact on male age–earnings profiles. In the calculations focusing on the income of 45–54-year olds relative to 25–34-year olds, the measure of relative numbers by age obtains a significant negative coefficient, except among high school graduates (line 4). In line 1, which analyzes the incomes of year-round and full-time workers with the trend variable omitted, the log of the ratio of the number of 45–54-year olds to the number of 25–34-year old workers obtains a coefficient of −0.27, three times its standard error. Inclusion of the trend in line 2 reduces the coefficient on relative numbers substantively, but still leaves a significant relation between relative numbers by age and relative incomes by age. In line 3, which treats the income of all men over the period 1947–74, the coefficient on the relative number is a highly significant −0.20.

The regressions for the income of year-round full-time workers aged 45–54 relative to the income of year-round full-time workers aged 20–24 in lines 6 and 7 yield sizeable significant coefficients for the relative number of workers by age, though in these cases addition of the time trend raises rather than reduces the estimated coefficients. In line 8, by contrast, the ratio of the number of 45–54-year old workers to the number of 20–24-year-olds has no apparent impact on relative incomes. This is due largely to the trend term, which is highly collinear with the relative numbers variable over the period: with trend deleted, the coefficient on relative numbers in regressions explaining the ratio of the income of 45–54-year olds to the income of 20–24-year olds is -0.31 with a standard error of 0.09.

The business cycle indicator, the deviation of real GNP from its trend, has little impact on the income ratios of year-round and full-time male workers in lines 1 and 2, suggesting that the wages of 25–34-year-old men are no more sensitive to the cycle than are those of 45–54-year-old men. In the regression for all male workers in line 3, however, the cyclical variable is accorded a sizeable effect, which presumably reflects the greater cyclical sensitivity of the time worked of the younger men. Much stronger cyclical effects are obtained in the calculations for the income of 45–54-year-old men relative to the income of 20–24-year olds in lines 6–8, indicating that cyclical ups-and-downs have their greatest impact on the incomes of 20–24-year olds.

The regressions in lines 4 and 5, which focus on the age–earnings profiles of college graduates and high school graduates, respectively, suggest that the increased number of young male workers relative to the number of older male workers had an especially large impact on college graduates' profiles compared to only a modest impact on high school graduates' profiles. Similar results based on different models and data have also been obtained by other scholars. Using the Michigan Panel Survey on Income Dynamics, William Johnson found that the relative size of a cohort significantly reduced the impact of the earnings of college graduates but had little effect on the earnings of less educated workers (Johnson, 1978, p. 13). Using CPS Demographic files, Finis Welch (1979) found a significant effect of cohort size on earnings in all school groups, with, however, much larger elasticities for college graduates. All of these results suggest that younger and older workers are better substitutes in the lower schooling groups than in the college graduate group. This is consistent with an explanation of the 1970s fall in the rate of return to investment in college education in terms of the increased supply of young college workers.

The regression estimates in Table 4.4 can be used to gauge the impact of relative income of young workers by multiplying the coefficients on the explanatory variables by the observed changes in the variables.[13] For year-round and full-time workers whose incomes are closest to the wages of concern, such an analysis attributes most of the change to demographic factors (see Table 4.5).

According to these calculations, the regression model explains much of

Table 4.5 Predicted and actual changes in age–earnings profiles of male workers

	45–54-year olds/ 25–34-year olds	45–54-year olds/ 20–24-year olds
Actual change in log income ratios, year-round and full-time workers, 1968–74	0.06	0.18
Change predicted by regression model and actual change in independent variables	0.06	0.15
Due to change in relative number of workers by age	0.03	0.11
Due to cyclical change	0.00	0.06
Due to trend	0.03	−0.02

Source: Calculated from regressions 2 and 7 of Table 4.4 and actual changes in explanatory variables.

the 1968–74 increased curvature of cross-sectional age–earnings profiles in terms of the increased number of younger workers relative to the number of older workers. Half of the 0.06 increase in the log of the ratio of the income of 45–54-year-old to the income of 25–34-year-old workers is attributed to the increase in the number of 25–34-year-old workers relative to the number of 45–54-year-old workers, while 60 per cent (0.11/0.18) of the increase in the log of the income of 45–54-year olds relative to the income of 20–24-year olds is explained by the increased number of 20–24-year olds relative to the number of 45–54-year-old workers. The trend variable accounts for the remainder of the change in the income ratio of 45–54 and 25–34-year olds, while the cyclical variable explains most of the remaining change in the 45–54 to 20–24-year olds income ratio.

In sum, the estimated effects of demographic, cyclical, and trend factors using relative income equations based on CES-type functional forms suggest that the observed twist in the age–earnings profile against young men can be attributed in large part to the changed age structure of the workforce.[14]

Translog system estimates

The effect of changes in the ratio of the number of younger to the number of older male workers and of changes in the amount of other inputs on male age–earnings profiles can be analyzed with the translog system of derived demand equations (9)–(11). Such an analysis enables us to check on the robustness of the results of Table 4.4 under a different functional specification and to test two competing hypotheses about the causes of the observed twist in the male age–earnings profiles. First, that the twist results from increases in the amount of capital, which shifts demand for labor toward older as opposed to younger workers. Increases in capital would have such an effect on demand if, as seems reasonable, capital is relatively more complementary (less substitutable) with older than with younger workers. One reason for expecting relatively greater complementarity is that skilled labor has been found to be relatively more complementary with capital than unskilled labor (Griliches, 1969). Since older workers tend to be more skilled than younger workers, demand for the former could be expected to be relatively more complementary with capital. Another is that older workers presumably have also accumulated greater specific human capital, linked to physical capital. Second, that the twist in the male age–earnings profiles is due to the influx of female workers, who are better substitutes for young male workers than for older male workers. The reason for expecting greater substitutability between women and younger men than between women and older men is that women are more likely to be competing for entry-level or early career jobs than for more senior positions in firms. If women are better substitutes for the young, then increased numbers of women workers would raise the earnings of older men relative to younger men.

A translog derived demand system was estimated with the number of full-time-equivalent female workers aged 20–64, the quantity of capital, and number of full-time-equivalent male workers aged 20–35, and the number of full-time-equivalent male workers aged 35–64 as inputs. Workers below the age of 20 were eliminated due to serious problems in estimating their earnings. Male workers were divided into two groups because of the problems of estimating translog systems with more than four inputs using a limited number of observations. The younger of the two groups, 20–34-year olds, covers the 20–24 and 25–34-year olds treated in earlier tables.

The inclusion of women and capital in the analysis creates considerable data problems due to inadequate information on the amount and rewards of these inputs. The problem for women is that published CPS figures have historically reported incomes and the number of persons with income rather than labor market earnings and workers with earnings. Since many women have income but do not work in the labor market, it is imperative to adjust the data to take account of this difference. Comparison of the mean *earnings* of women to the mean income of women in recent years when both figures were published in the *Current Population Reports* shows small differences (less than 1 per cent in 1974, for example),[15] suggesting that the mean incomes provide reasonable estimates of mean earnings. Comparisons of the number of persons with income and with earnings, however, reveal a sizeable differential. In 1974, for example, 38 per cent more women were reported as having income than were reported as having earnings.[16] To take account of this problem and of the part-time work done by many women employees, the number of full-time-equivalent women working in the United States was estimated by adjusting data from the *Employment and Training Report of the President 1977* by estimates of weeks worked from the *Work Experience of the Population* reports of the BLS, as described in the table note. Comparable estimates of employment of men aged 20–34 and 35–64 were made from the same sources.

The problem with data on capital is that we lack good information on both the capital stock and user cost. An estimate of private capital was made from data on corporate and noncorporate investment in nonresidential business capital, provided by the US Department of Commerce (Musgrave, 1976) and unpublished data on government capital stock from the same source. The user cost of capital is based on methodology developed by Jorgenson and associates (Jorgenson, 1963). The particular measure used takes into account the differential tax treatment of equipment and structures and the presence of both equity and debt finance, and adjusts the cost of capital for depreciation and expected capital gains. It is based on a weighted average of the user cost of equipment and the user cost of structures, with weights taken as the share of each in total investment from the National Income and Product Accounts. The precise estimating procedure is described in detail in Clark and Freeman (1980).

The share of each of the inputs in cost was estimated by dividing the total factor payments to each by the sum of factor payments. In the sample the mean share of national income going to men aged 35–64 was 0.39; the share going to men aged 20–24 was 0.18; the share going to women aged 20–64 was 0.12; and the share going to capital was 0.31. Though the data leave much to be desired, they provide at least a crude means of examining in the context of the translog specification the effect of the increased supply of women and capital on the age–earnings profiles of men.

Estimates of the constrained translog system were made with an iterative version of Zellner's minimum distance estimator. Given the constraints, one of the factor share equations is redundant and can be dropped without affecting results: the capital share equation was deleted.

Table 4.5 records the estimated parameters of the system. Table 4.6 presents the elasticities of complementarity and of factor prices with respect to changes in quantities derived from the parameters at the *mean* value of the shares. In all cases the elasticities of input prices with respect to the quantity of the same input are negative, as required by the model. All of the labor inputs are complementary with capital (i.e., have positive elasticities of complementarity). As hypothesized, however, older men are relatively more complementary with capital and have a larger elasticity of factor price with respect to capital than do younger men (the relevant S_{ij}s are 1.76 for men aged 35–64 and 1.47 for men aged 20–34; the relevant factor price elasticities are 0.55 for men aged 35–64 and 0.46 for men aged 20–34). Contrary to expectation, the number of women is estimated to

Table 4.6 Estimates of derived demand equations of the translog production system, 1950–74[a]

	Share of inputs			
	Male workers	Male workers	Female workers	
	20–34	35+	20+	[Capital][b]
1 Constant	0.173(0.001)	0.404(0.003)	0.112(0.002)	0.301
2 In male workers 20–34	0.080(0.006)	−0.088(0.006)	−0.018(0.006)	0.026(0.009)
3 In male workers 35+	−0.088(0.006)	0.051(0.11)	−0.054(0.007)	0.092(0.011)
4 In female workers 20+	−0.018(0.006)	−0.054(0.007)	0.021(0.008)	0.052(0.012)
5 In capital	0.026(0.009)	0.092(0.11)	0.052(0.012)	−0.170(0.020)
6 R^2	0.767	0.674	0.861	—
7 SEE	0.0035	0.0110	0.0008	—
8 DW	1.52	0.49	0.69	—

Notes:
a   Numbers in parentheses are standard errors. Dependent variables are shares of inputs.
b   Capital equation omitted; estimated values obtained from constraints.
Sources: Income share calculated using incomes of workers from Current Population Survey, *Consumer Income Reports*, various editions, and number of workers employed from *Employment and Training Report of the President* (US Department of Health, Education and Welfare, 1977). Table A-14, p. 232. Because men and women workers are employed different numbers of hours over the year, the numbers used as explanatory variables were adjusted to reflect approximate hours worked. Data on weeks worked by part-time and full-time employees by sex and age were obtained from *Work Experience of the Population* (US Department of Labor, 1969), Table A-la, p. A-9: full-time-equivalents were calculated by estimating the mean weeks worked by full-time workers and part-time workers, with the former assumed to work 40 hours per week and the latter 20 hours per week. Estimates were made for a single year 1969 for men aged 20–34 and 25–34, men aged 35–64, and women aged 20–64. The mean weeks for the groups were: men 20–24, 35: men 25–34 and 35–64, 48; women 20–64, 37. Accordingly, the number of female employees was adjusted downward by 37/48 and the number of men 20–24 by 35/48. The figures were obtained from US Bureau of Labor Statistics, capital from Musgrave (1976) and unpublished US Department of Commerce data. The price of capital was obtained from Clark and Freeman (1979), as described in the text. Estimates were made by LSQ part of *Time Series Processor* program.

have a slight positive effect on the earnings of young men compared to a slight negative effect on the earnings of older men. The magnitudes of those elasticities of complementarity and of the elasticities of factor prices between the female workforce and the two age groups of men are, however, sufficiently slight as to suggest that male and female workers operate in essentially separate production processes. Given the problems noted above in estimating the input of female labor, however, little weight ought to be given to the link between the female workforce and demand for other factors.

The most important finding from the TL system regressions is that, consistent with our previous results, the earnings of men aged 20–34 depend critically on the number of young male workers. The elasticity

Table 4.7 Estimates of elasticities of complementarity and of the elasticity of factor prices to changes in the quantity of inputs, evaluated at the mean shares of factors in cost

	Change in the quantity of:			
	Men 20–34	Men 35–64	Women 20–64	Capital
The elasticity of complementarity S_{ij}, by group				
Men, aged 20–34	−0.209			
Men, aged 35–64	−0.25	−1.25		
Women, aged 20–64	0.17	0.15	−5.88	
Capital	1.47	1.76	2.40	−3.95
Elasticities of factor prices with respect to changes in quantities, by group				
Men, aged 20–24	−0.38	−0.10	0.02	0.46
Men, aged 35–64	−0.05	−0.49	−0.02	0.55
Women, aged 20–64	0.03	−0.06	−0.71	0.73
Capital	0.26	0.69	−0.29	−1.23

Source: Elasticity of complementarities calculated from the estimates of γ_{ij} and γ_{ii} in Table 4.7 using the formula

$$S_{ij} = (1/a_i a_j)\gamma_{ij} + 1$$
$$S_{ii} = 1/a_i^2(\gamma_{ii} + a_i^2 - a_i)$$

Elasticities of factor prices computed as $a_j S_{ij}$ and $a_i S_{ii}$.

of complementarity for the number of young men is sizeably negative and far in excess of the cross-elasticity between young and older men, implying that an increase in the number of young men would reduce their wage relative to the wage of older men. Most importantly, the estimated factor price elasticities indicate that changes in the numbers of male workers of different ages will substantively influence the earnings of younger and older men and thus are likely to alter male age–earnings profiles.

The quantitative contribution of changes in the various inputs on male age–earnings profiles in the period when the profiles changed sharply can be evaluated by substituting the estimated elasticities of factor prices with respect to quantities from Table 4.6 into the relative wage determination equation (4.5) and multiplying the resultant coefficients by the actual changes in the inputs. Let $\dot{L}_w$ = the log change in the input of female labor aged 20–64, and $\dot{K}$ = the log change in the capital input. Then plugging the factor price elasticities from the table into equation 4.5 yields:

$$\dot{W}_{35-64} - \dot{W}_{25-34} = 0.33\dot{L}_{25-34} - 0.39\dot{L}_{35-64}$$
$$- 0.04\dot{L}_w + 0.09\dot{K} \qquad (4.13)$$

as the appropriate equation determining the earnings of older men relative to younger men. From 1968 to 1974, the four inputs changed as follows:

Table 4.8 Decomposition of the change in relative incomes

Actual change ($\dot{W}_{35\text{-}64} - \dot{W}_{25\text{-}34}$), 1968–78	0.07
Change predicted by translog model and actual change in independent variables	0.09
Due to changed number of young men ($\dot{L}_{25\text{-}34}$)	0.08
Due to changed number of older men ($\dot{L}_{35\text{-}64}$)	0.01
Due to changed number of females ($\dot{L}_{w}$)	−0.01
Due to changed stock of capital ($\dot{K}$)	0.01

Source: Calculated using equation (4.13) and actual changes in explanatory variables.

$L_{25\text{-}34} = 0.24$; $\dot{L}_{35\text{-}64} = -0.02$; $\dot{L}_w = 0.17$; $\dot{K} = 0.11$; while $\dot{W}_{35\text{-}64} - \dot{W}_{25\text{-}34} = 0.07$. This yields the decomposition of the change in relative incomes shown in Table 4.8.

According to these calculations, the increased supply of young men was *the* principal factor depressing their earnings relative to the earnings of older men from the late 1960s to the mid-1970s.[17]

CONCLUSION

The analysis in this paper has shown that from the late 1960s through the mid-1970s when the number of young workers increased rapidly, the earnings of young male workers fell relative to the earnings of older male workers, altering male age—earnings profiles, particularly for college graduates. Demand for labor equations based on the constant elasticity of substitution production function and on the translogarithmic production function suggest that the increased number of young male workers was the major causal force underlying the increased earnings of older men relative to the earnings of younger men. Alternative factors that might explain the observed twist in male age—earnings profiles – the business cycle, general trends, the increased supply of women, and growth of capital – were found to have much smaller effects on age—earnings profiles.

The late 1960s to mid-1970s twist in male age—earnings profiles raises important questions about the effect of the size of a cohort on the earnings of the cohort and about the economic determinants of cross-sectional differences in earnings by age. Will the relatively low earnings of the large young cohorts of the 1970s be maintained in the future? Will age—earnings profiles change in favor of the prospective small youth cohorts of the 1980s? Do demographic swings produce significant intergenerational income inequality? How important are differences in the relative size of cohorts in determining the shape of cross-sectional age—earnings profiles?

Arguments can be advanced for and against the likely permanence of a 'cohort effect' on the earnings of the young (20–34-year old) male workers of the 1970s.

Three basic forces would appear to operate to create permanent cohort effects. First is the tendency of many firms to promote individuals by seniority along well-defined job ladders and to raise pay through 'standard' increases over starting rates. With this type of pay policy, a group that enters the market with low earnings compared to others will never catch up to the position it would have had had it entered with higher initial earnings. Second is the possibility that the large young worker cohort of the 1970s has been 'pushed' into jobs with flatter longitudinal age–earnings profiles than are normally chosen by young workers (as may have occurred among college graduates, some of whom have been unable to obtain 'college-type' jobs). While some of the young may be able to switch to jobs with steeper earnings trajectories in the future, the overall rate of increase in pay may still fall short of what would have occurred for a smaller cohort that obtained more desirable jobs at the outset. Third, to the extent that future promotions and raises will be depressed by competition from a large pool of persons in the same age groups, the large youth cohorts of the 1970s may actually lose ground in the job market relative to other cohorts in the future.

On the other side of the spectrum, if the low initial earnings of persons in the 1970s are given a strict investment interpretation, they suggest that young workers are making greater investments in on-the-job training than in the past, presumably through selection of 'learning jobs'. This will show up in especially steep longitudinal profiles for this cohort in the future and thus in significant catching up. Perhaps more realistically, the likelihood that substitution among workers of different ages increases with age suggests at least some diminution in the effect of cohort size over time (Welch, 1979).

Limited evidence on cohort earnings profiles in the past and on the jobs held by the new entrants of the 1970s suggests that some permanent effect of cohort size is likely. Ruggles and Ruggles's (1977) analyses of the social security (LEED) data file reveal a noticeable drop in the longitudinal profile for the cohort that entered the labor force in about 1930, apparently because 'the labor market conditions at the time of their entry had a significant depressing effect on their earnings relative to those who preceded them and were already established in the labor market,' whereas the earnings of the cohort born a decade later were 'high relative to the cohorts surrounding them and seem to have enjoyed this advantage continuously' (Ruggles and Ruggles, 1977, p. 124) Chamberlain's (1978) evidence on the return to schooling addresses directly the possibility that the relatively depressed position of young college graduates compared to high school graduates is a temporary phenomenon due to greater investments in on-the-job training. His estimates of the return to schooling at the 'overtaking point' (when earnings are no longer depressed by investments) suggest a drop from 12 per cent in 1969 to 7 per cent in 1973. Finally, the marked decrease in the proportion of new college graduates (Freeman, 1973, 1976) in professional and managerial jobs, where the profiles are traditionally the steepest, suggests that it will be difficult for young college workers to 'catch up' significantly in the future. Overall, while some catchup is likely, the large youth cohorts of the 1970s can be expected to continue to have lower earnings than the smaller cohorts that preceded them and the smaller cohorts that will enter the job market in the 1980s.

Developments in the 1980s should provide, at the least, an interesting test of alternative interpretations of the determinants of changes in male age–earnings profiles. If relative wages by age shift in favor of young workers when the number of young workers declines in the mid- to late-1980s, the importance of demographic factors as determinants of male age–earnings profiles will be given further support. If the large youth cohorts of the 1970s do not experience especially rapid longitudinal gains in earnings in the 1980s, the incompleteness of the standard interpretation of cross-section profiles in terms of investments in training will be further demonstrated. Opposite patterns will, of course, have contrary implications.

Finally, while the 1980s will provide further information concerning the importance of demographic and demand factors relative to investments in human capital as determinants of age–earnings profiles, the evidence presented in this study does suggest that greater consideration be given to demand for labor by age in analyzing male age–earnings profiles.

NOTES

1. For models of the link between birth rates and the age distribution of workers, see Keyfitz (1977).
2. All of the data in this paragraph are from US Department of Labor (1976), Table A-2, p. 137, and from US Department of Labor, various editions.
3. Figures on high school graduates are from US Bureau of the Census (1977), p. 153. Figures on the civilian labor force are from, US Department of Labor (1976), Table A-3, p. 139.
4. Figures on high school graduates and dropouts in the labor force are from US Department of Labor, 'Employment of June 1970 high school graduates', Special Labor Force Report no. 15, Table 2, and from *Handbook of Labor Statistics 1977*, Table 31, p. 77. Data on the civilian labor force are from US Department of Labor (1976), Table A-3.
5. See the estimates given in Freeman (1976), pp. 67–8.
6. Let W_{1974} = income of 1974 calculated by old imputation procedure, W_{1974} = income in 1974 calculated by new imputation procedure, and W_{1975} = income in 1975 calculated by new imputation procedure. Then the adjustment is $(W'_{1974}/W_{1974})(W_{1975})$.
7. This statement is simply a speculative hypotheses. Groups of workers could have similar earnings for any number of reasons unrelated to elasticities of

substitution. Moreover, a high elasticity of substitution need not produce similar wages for groups of workers.

8. The sampling errors reported in *Current Population Reports* (US Bureau of the Census) can be used to make statistical tests of changes in incomes, but are not well suited to test changes in ratios of incomes.

9. Unfortunately, there is no way to deal directly with the problem of changes in imputation procedures between the 1969 and 1978 CPS tapes. Prior to 1976 the public use tapes do not contain 'flags' for imputed earnings, making comparable regressions impossible. As the new imputation procedure appears to have greatly affected the earnings of workers by education but not by age, however, the results are unlikely to be seriously marred by this problem. Regressions with the March 1975 tape (which used the old imputation procedure) give, in any case, results much like those found with the March 1978 tape. For a detailed discussion of the imputation problems, see *Current Population Reports* (US Bureau of the Census), no. 105. That report shows that age comparisons are only modestly biased by the change in imputation procedure, but that education comparisons are seriously biased. There is a marked jump in the relative earnings of college graduates in the March 1976 tape due to the new imputation procedure.

10. Output must be allowed to vary in this experiment because the quantity of inputs is changing, which will change output.

11. To derive equation 4.4, rewrite equation 4.2 as $\dot{W}_i = a_j S_{ij} L_j$. This gives the change in W_i due to changes in L_j, all else the same. To get the change in W_i due to changes in all other factors, we sum $\dot{W}_i = a_j S_{ij} L_j$ across all j, which yields the expression (equation 4.4) in the text.

12. Since $a_j = L_j f_j/f$ (where f is the production function), we rewrite equation 4.8 as $f_j = f(a_i + \Sigma \gamma_{ij} \ln L_j)/L_i$. Then $f_{ij} = (f \gamma_{ij}/L_i L_j) + f_j (a_i + \Sigma \gamma_{ij} \ln L_j) L_i$. Since $f_i/f = (a_i + \Sigma \gamma_{ij} \ln L_j)/L_i$, the right-hand side of the expressions can be further simplified to $(f \gamma_{ij}/L_i L_j) + f_j f_i/f$. Multiplying both sides by $F/f_i f_j$ yields the expression in the text for S_{ij}. Serivation of S_{ij} is similar.

13. Let a_i be the estimated effect of variable S_i on relative earnings and let ΔX_i be the change in X_i in the period. Then the contribution of the change in X_i to the change in relative earnings is $\hat{a}_i \Delta X_i$.

14. While the regression calculations 'explain' the bulk of the variation in the income of older men relative to the income of younger men, it is important to recognize that some observations do not appear to fit the model. In particular, despite a relatively large number of younger workers in the late 1940s/early 1950s, the age–income profile was not as steeply sloped as the analysis would lead one to expect. This may be the result of the effect of the Great Depression and World War II on the employment experiences of workers or the result of the reduction in female participation at the end of the war. What is needed is a detailed study of the labor market for younger and older workers in that period to determine why relatively large numbers of young workers were 'absorbed' into the workforce with little reduction in the earnings of young workers relative to older workers.

15. In 1974 the mean income of all women was $4142. The mean earnings of women with no other income was $4101. See *Current Population Reports* (US Bureau of the Census) no. 101, Table 71, p. 145.

16. In 1974 there were 59.2 million women reporting income and 42.9 million reporting labor market earnings in the *Current Population Reports* (US Bureau of the Census) no. 101, Table 71, p. 145. These figures are similar to those in other years.

17.   Using a different data set, with different definitions of age groups and a different time period, Joseph Anderson (1978) also has found that a large fraction of the change in the relative wages of the young is due to their increased numbers. However, he also attributes a large portion of the change to geater complementarity between capital and middle-aged (25–54-year-old) workers than between capital and younger workers, those aged 14–24. While both Anderson's results and those in this study show a depressant effect of the increased relative number on the wages of workers, they differ in the estimated effect of capital, which may highlight the problems of measuring that variable. Differences in the age groups covered may also explain the moderately different results obtained between Anderson's data set and the one used here.

BIBLIOGRAPHY

Anderson, J., 'Substitution among age groups in the United States labor force', Williams College (December 1978).

Berndt, E., and Christensen, L., 'The translog function and the substitution of equipment, structures and labor in US manufacturing, 1929–1968', *Journal of Econometrics* (March 1973), 1, pp. 81–114.

Binswanger, H., 'A cost function approach to the measurement of elasticities of factor demand and elasticities of substitution', *American Journal of Agricultural Economics* (May 1974), 56, pp. 377–86.

Cartter, A., *PhD's and the Academic Labor Market* (New York: Carnegie Commission and McGraw-Hill, 1976).

Chamberlain, G., 'Omitted variable bias in panel data: estimating the returns to schooling', in *The Econometrics of Panel Data*, Colloque International du CNRS, Annales de *l'INSEE* (April, 1978), pp. 50–82.

Clark, K., and Freeman, R., 'How elastic is the demand for labor?', *Review of Economics and Statistics*, vol. LXII, no. 4 (November 1980), pp. 509–20.

Freeman, R., 'Changes in the labor market for black labor', *Brookings Papers on Economic Activity* (Summer 1973) (Washington DC: Brookings Institution).

Freeman, R., *The Overeducated American* (New York: Academic Press, 1976).

Griliches, Z., 'Capital-skill complementarity', *Review of Economics and Statistics* (November 1969), 51, pp. 465–8.

Hicks, J., 'Elasticity of substitution once again: substitutes and complements', *Oxford Economic Papers* (November 1970), 22, pp. 289–96.

Johnson, W. R., 'Vintage effects in the earnings of white American men' (University of Virginia: October 1978).

Jorgenson, D., 'Capital theory and investment behavior', *American Economic Review* (May 1963), 53, pp. 247–59.

Keyfitz, N., *Applied Mathematical Demography* (New York: John Wiley & Sons, 1977).

Musgrave, J., 'Fixed nonresidential business and residential capital in the United States, 1925–1975', *Survey of Current Business* (June 1976), 56.

Ruggles, N. D., and Ruggles, R., 'The anatomy of earnings behavior' in F. T. Juster (ed.), *The Distribution of Economic Well-Being* (New York: National Bureau of Economic Research, 1977).

Sato, R., and Koizumi, T., 'On the elasticities of substitution and complementarity', *Oxford Economic Papers* (March 1973), 25, pp. 44–56.

US Bureau of the Census, *Statistical Abstract of the United States 1977*, *Trends in Income of Families and Persons in the US 1947–1960* (Washington: US Government Printing Office, 1977).

US Bureau of the Census, *Current Population Reports*, Consumer Income Series P-60, various editions.

US Department of Health, Education, and Welfare, *The Condition of Education*, vol. 3, Pt. 1 (Washington: US Government Printing Office, 1977).

US Department of Labor, *Work Experience of the Population* (1969).

US Department of Labor, *Employment and Training Report of the President 1976*.

US Department of Labor, Bureau of Labor Statistics, 'Educational attainment of workers', Special Labor Force Reports, various editions.

US Department of Labor, 'Employment of high school graduates and dropouts', Special Labor Force Reports, various editions.

Welch, F., 'Effects of cohort size on earnings: the baby boom babies' financial bust', *Journal of Political Economy* (October 1979), vol. 87, 5, part 2.

PART II

DISCRIMINATION AND POVERTY

I don't give a damn what your numbers show. You are wrong, you leftwing, [rightwing] pointy-headed academic!

Several of the chapters in this section caused ruckuses. People feel deeply about discrimination, poverty, and the implications of economic analyses for policies to remedy these problems, and they react accordingly.

I discovered this when my first paper on the economics of discrimination (Freeman, 1973) was lambasted in the editorial pages of the *Washington Post* and attacked by some civil rights leaders. The paper made three claims: first, that the economic position of employed blacks, particularly the more skilled, had improved greatly following the Civil Rights Act of 1964; second, that black college students were moving into nontraditional careers in response to new opportunities, and third, that the equal employment and affirmative action efforts of the federal government was the most likely cause of the improvements. Why did the message that things were getting better arouse controversy? One reason, Paul Samuelson explained to me in a private letter, was that supporters of civil rights legislation feared that opponents would interpret the evidence as showing that government anti-bias programs, particularly affirmative action, were no longer needed, when in fact they were. A second possible reason was the implicit message in the paper, which I later made explicit, that elimination of discrimination might not, by itself, bring about racial income equality.

At the NBER conference at which I presented the technical version of Chapter 5 (Freeman, 1981) the attacks came from the opposite side, by persons who believed that government labor market interventions are generally not successful and attributed gains instead to 'supply side' changes in the quality of black workers due either to welfare programs removing the least able from the labor market or to improved schooling. These critics interpreted my evidence as indicating that government interventions, particularly affirmative action, were needed to maintain black economic progress, when in fact they were not.

Ensuing work has generally confirmed my commonsense reading of the evidence that government anti-bias programs did what they were supposed to do, improving the relative income position of black Americans (Leonard, 1984a, b), but has also made it clear that the employment prospect of one important group – young men from poor homes – has worsened rather than improved since 1964. Since existing data sets provided little information about these youths, I developed the National Bureau of Economic Research Inner City Youth Survey to illuminate their behavior and organized a research project around the survey. The essay on young blacks and jobs (Chapter 6) summarizes the results of that project (Freeman and Holzer, 1986).

The preprint to Chapter 7 – on homelessness – caused the biggest uproar of any research I have done. Advocates for the homeless had made unsubstantiated claims that 1 per cent of Americans were homeless; the Reagan administration estimated numbers a tenth as large, creating a rather nasty debate over numbers before the Congress and in the press. My analysis came down strongly on the side of the government. To the activists, this was like waving a red flag in front of a bull in Pamplona and they raced to Boston to denounce the research and researchers to the media: if the paper agreed with the Reagan administration on the numbers issue, the activists said, the authors must be evil heartless rightwingers, and the world had to be warned. In the ensuing hullaballoo the two key messages of the paper were lost: (1) that homelessness was increasing despite economic recovery and had become relatively permanent for many individuals; and (2) that increasing poverty and declining, low-rent housing stock caused most of the problem. There are times when one would prefer to deal with gluons and quarks.

BIBLIOGRAPHY

Freeman, R., 'Changes in the labor market for black Americans, 1948–72', *Brookings Papers on Economic Activity* (1973), 1, pp. 67–120.

Freeman, R., 'Black economic progress after 1964: who has gained and why?', in S. Rosen (ed.), *Studies in Labor Markets* (Chicago: University of Chicago Press, 1981).

Freeman, R., and Holzer, H. (eds), *The Black Youth Employment Crisis* (Chicago: University of Chicago Press, 1986).

Leonard, J., 'Employment and occupational advance under affirmative action', *Review of Economics and Statistics* (1984a), 66, no. 3, pp. 377–85.

Leonard, J., 'The impact of affirmative action on employment', *Journal of Labor Economics* (1984b), 2, no. 4, pp. 439–63.

5 · BLACK ECONOMIC PROGRESS SINCE 1964

It has become increasingly clear that black Americans have made substantial advances in the job market since 1964. Numerous recent studies, based on diverse data sets and analytic procedures, have reported sizeable declines in the differences between blacks and whites in earnings, education, and occupational position (see Bibliography, pp. 119–20). After decades of little or no improvement in the relative economic position of blacks, the advances of the 1960s and 1970s represent a major social achievement and suggest that national anti-discriminatory policies have successfully altered the job market for black workers. At the same time, however, economic parity between most groups of blacks and whites has not been achieved, nor has the high incidence of poverty, unemployment, and social ills in the black community been eliminated.

How sizeable has the decline in discrimination been since 1964? Which groups of black Americans have benefited most? Which continue to suffer serious socioeconomic ills? In what ways have blacks responded to the reduction in economic discrimination? To what extent have anti-discriminatory policies contributed to the changes? What are the lessons for policy? Because socioeconomic change is a complex phenomenon, these questions are not easy to answer. They have already generated considerable scholarly work and controversy, and will continue to do so in the future. Although the 'final returns' are not yet in, it is important to assess as best we can the economic developments that have in many ways changed the life of the nation.

MEASURING BLACK GAINS

The amount of black economic gains since 1964 depends, at least in part, on the statistical measures used to evaluate the relative position of blacks in the market.[1] Statistical measures of relative positions serve two separate, though related, purposes. The first is to estimate the extent of marketplace discrimination, defined as differences among similarly qualified workers in wages, employment, and occupational position that can be traced to the bias of employers, employees, unions, or consumers. The ideal experiment would be to change the race (or religion, sex, etc.) of an individual and then observe what happens to his economic position. A possible practical experiment would be to present employers with job applications from workers who differ solely in race, and find out who is hired and at what pay. In the absence of such experiments or more direct measures of productivity (e.g., a batting average in baseball), observed differences in economic position must be adjusted for differences in individual abilities or other characteristics (schooling, family background, training, etc.) that can be expected to influence earnings or productivity.

Measures of relative economic position are also used to evaluate the overall economic well-being of a group, particularly to determine whether it has a higher incidence of poverty than another group. Market discrimination and economic well-being, though related, are distinct phenomena requiring separate statistical measures. Labor-market discrimination in the United States, for example, has been most severe against highly qualified blacks, although the incidence of poverty is higher among less well educated and skilled blacks. On the other hand, a group might face discrimination but have high incomes (as do overseas Chinese in some Asian countries). For historical reasons, including past discrimination, a group can come to the job market seriously disadvantaged and thus be in a relatively poor position even in the absence of current discrimination. Changes in economic discrimination and economic well-being are likely to coincide, although they need not. For example, a decline in market discrimination, which raises the relative position of black workers, may have little or no effect on certain indicators of economic well-being, such as family income, which can change along with market opportunities, but also varies according to independent characteristics, such as the number of earners in a household.

Some of the confusion and controversy over the changing economic position of black Americans results from erroneously using family-income figures to measure market discrimination or, conversely, using the labor-market status of individuals to measure overall economic well-being. For example, little can be learned about the job market from comparing the income of middle-class black families, which often have two full-time workers, with that of white families, which do not, or from comparing the income of all black families, of which a large and growing number are female-headed, with that of predominately male-headed white families. On the other hand, comparing the economic status of individual black workers with that of otherwise comparable white workers reveals little about the relative economic position of black families. So it is necessary to make a sharp differentiation between the individual and the family, and between the measures appropriate to each.

A NEW JOB MARKET

Aggregate statistical measures of individual income or occupational position reveal sizeable gains for blacks relative to whites after 1964. Computerized cross-sectional and longitudinal data on thousands of individuals corroborate the aggregate picture. In contrast to earlier findings, evidence covering the late 1960s shows a marked convergence between the return on the educational investment of black males (especially the young) and that of white males. The impact of race on earnings fell sharply between the 1960 and 1970 Censuses. Detailed investigation of the National Longitudinal Survey shows that the occupational position of young black men entering the market after 1964 is essentially the same as that of young whites with similar backgrounds. The 1973 Occupational Change in a Generation (OCG) survey reveals marked advances in the relative position of blacks, particularly those aged 25 to 34, compared to the 1962 OCG survey. Several studies dealing with other labor-market problems have found that the traditional large negative impact of race on economic status is now much smaller than in the past.

Some of the statistical evidence that a 'new market' developed for black Americans is summarized in Table 5.1, which records the changes in several measures of the relative economic position of black (nonwhite) workers. Because of the likely impact of Title VII of the Civil Rights Act of 1964 and Executive Order 11246, and the intensification of anti-discriminatory activity in their wake (including court rulings, private actions, and those of the Equal Employment Opportunity Commission, state fair-employment-practices commissions, and the Office of Contract Compliance), the table differentiates between changes in relative position before 1964 and changes from 1964 to 1975. And since market discrimination reflects the demand for labor, which depends on relative productivity and wages rather than absolute differences, all of the measures are expressed as ratios of the position of blacks to that of whites.

Three related income measures are used in both sections (male and female) of the table: annual wage-and-salary earnings, which depend on both rates of pay and time worked, and reflect changes in unemployment over the business cycle, since most of the unemployed work some time during a year; the annual wage and salary earnings of 'year-round, full-time' workers, which is obtained by eliminating the unemployed and short-time workers over the year, yielding a better measure of wage rates; and 'usual weekly earnings' for all workers, including the unemployed – possibly the best available measure of rates of pay.

Table 5.1 Comparison of black and white economic positions and average annual changes in ratios

	Ratio of black (nonwhite) to white position		Annual change in ratio	
	1950	1975	1950–64	1964–75
Male				
Median wage and salary	0.50[b]	0.73	0.6[c]	1.2
Median wage and salary, year-round, full-time workers only	0.64[b]	0.77	0.1[d]	1.0
Median 'usual weekly earnings'	—	0.78	—	1.0[e]
Index of occupational position	0.76	0.88	0.3[c]	0.7
Relative penetration Professional, technical, and kindred	0.39	0.65	0.4[c]	1.8
Management	0.22	0.41	0.0	1.7
Crafts	0.41	0.71	1.2	1.2
Female				
Median wage and salary	0.40[a]	0.97	1.8[c]	3.5
Median wage and salary, year-round, full-time workers only	0.57[b]	0.99	1.3[d]	2.3
Median 'usual weekly earnings'	—	0.94	—	2.0[e]
Index of occupational position	0.49	0.87	1.4	1.6
Relative penetration Professional, technical, and kindred	0.47	0.83	0.9	2.1
Clerical	0.15	0.69	1.3	3.3

Notes:
a   Refers to the year 1949.
b   Refers to the year 1955.
c   Refers to the period 1949–64.
d   Refers to the period 1955–64.
e   Refers to the period 1967–75.
Sources: Calculated from Bureau of Census, *Current Population Survey*, and *Consumer Income Reports*, and from Department of Labor, *Handbook of Labor Statistics* and *Employment and Earnings*.

The fourth and fifth lines of both sections of the table turn from income to occupational statistics, which deserve particular attention since occupation is a relatively permanent phenomenon, involving long-term rather than transitory income. Unlike the income comparisons, which can be misleading if earners forgo their current income in order to invest in opportunities that have the potential for higher future earnings, the occupation figures can be expected to reflect enduring economic advances. In the fourth line of both sections of the table, I estimate the economic value of a given job, calculate the proportion of black and white workers in that occupation, and then divide the black by the white measure to obtain an index of relative standing. (The incomes of all male and female workers are used to measure the economic value of a given occupation for men and women respectively.) When the distribution of blacks, relative to that of whites, shifts toward higher-income jobs, the index will rise; it will fall when the black job structure deteriorates. The fifth line of both sections measures the 'relative penetration' of blacks into selected 'good jobs' – the professions, management, and crafts for men, and the professions, management, and clerical jobs for women – by comparing the fraction of all black workers in those categories to the fraction of all white workers. When the value is one, blacks and whites are proportionately represented in an occupation; when it is below one, blacks are less than proportionately represented; when it is above one, they are more than proportionately represented.

Since the data in the table relate to large groups of workers and are not 'corrected' for education, family background, region of employment, and the like, the comparisons are likely to overstate differences between blacks and whites that result from discrimination and to provide only rough measures of changes over time that result from changes in the job market. (More detailed analyses, based on multiple regressions, that tell much the same story as Table 5.1, are found in the various papers cited in the bibliographical note.)

There are three basic findings in Table 5.1. First and most important is the overall picture of relative black economic advance, especially after 1964. All of the indices show that black workers are markedly better off in 1975 than in the early postwar years. All but one of the measures (the relative penetration of black men into craft jobs) show much greater increases after 1964 than before, despite the smaller economic gap between blacks and whites before 1964 and the serious recession of the 1970s. Among men, there are at best modest increases in most of the measures before 1964, followed by sizeable changes thereafter. The income ratios rise by 0.6 and 0.1 points per annum after 1964 and by 1.3 and 0.8 points per annum thereafter. The overall index of occupational standing and the relative penetration of black males into professional, technical, and kindred jobs and managerial slots accelerated greatly after 1964. Among women, economic differences between blacks and whites declined rapidly before 1964 (in large part because of their movement out of household services into other jobs), but the table also shows a marked acceleration after 1964 in their relative median wage-and-salary income, which is roughly double the figure from the pre-1964 period, even with the rapid advances made earlier. The acceleration in the rate of relative black economic progress after 1964 is a necessary 'first fact' in determining the impact on the job market of the diverse anti-bias activities that intensified in the mid-1960s.

Second, the changes indicate that the gains made by blacks after 1964 (attributed by some to the economic boom of the late 1960s rather than to more fundamental shifts in market discrimination) did not erode in ensuing years. In fact, despite the largest labor-market downturn since the Depression, the relative income and occupational position of black workers continued to rise in the 1970s. In 1969, at the peak of the Vietnam war boom, the ratio of the median wage-and-salaries income of blacks to that of whites was 0.67 (for men), the ratio of year-round, full-time wages and salaries was 0.69, while the ratio of 'usual weekly earnings' was 0.71 – all figures much below those for 1975. The rate of advance by black males in the occupational structure also continued unabated in the recession, as did the income and occupational progress of black women. The fears that the changes first reported in my Brookings paper (Freeman, 1973) were purely cyclical has thus been completely disproven by later developments.

Finally, Table 5.1 reveals marked differences in the relative economic position of black men and women. Because of the more rapid gains achieved by black women in the postwar period, both before and after 1964, their income and occupational attainment are closer to those of white women than the economic position of black men is to that of white men. Within more narrowly defined groups of women, in fact, the statistics show that black women do almost as well as white women. For instance, among year-round, full-time workers, black women who are college graduates earned $10,104 in 1975, compared to $11,096 for their white counterparts; black females who are high-school graduates earned $7,230, compared to $7,400 for their white counterparts. In 1975, the principal obstacle facing black women in the job market was sex rather than race. Among men, by contrast, *overall* differences, though diminished from past levels, remain sizeable. Although the differences reflect too many factors to be attributed solely or even primarily to *current* market discrimination, the fact remains that overall economic parity between black and white men is far from established.

WINNERS AND LOSERS

Who gained from the improved labor market for blacks post 1964? Who remains seriously disadvantaged? Two groups of black men appear to have made the most substantial economic gains since 1964: the better educated and more skilled, especially the increasing number of highly qualified young black men who have entered colleges and universities; and those from more advantaged family backgrounds.

Consider first the economic position of black men with different levels of schooling. Prior to the late 1960s and early 1970s, the ratio of black income to white income *fell* as educational attainment rose. The rewards of going to college for black men were much below the rewards for otherwise comparable white men (perhaps accounting for some of the differences in enrollment rates). In the 1970s, the situation is quite different. At the top of the educational hierarchy, black PhDs appear to earn about as much as white PhDs ($21,200 versus $21,000 in 1973, according to National Science Foundation data). The median 'usual weekly earnings' of black men with five or more years of college averages 94 per cent of those of comparable white men; black graduates beginning in engineering and business fields earn about the national average; and incomes tabulated from the March 1975 *Current Population Survey* show black college men aged 25 to 29 earning 93 per cent as much as their white peers, compared to sizeable disadvantages for high-school or grade-school graduates. Estimates of the rate of return on investments in college education suggest higher returns for blacks than for whites (largely because of the poorer opportunities facing young black high-school graduates). Not surprisingly, although the proportion of 18- to 19-year-old white males going to college has dropped in the 1970s, the proportion of 18- to 19-year-old black males has risen. Overall, better-educated young black males fared better after 1964 than less-educated older black males.

Occupational figures provide further support for this generalization. The relative income of black male professionals and managers increased more rapidly than that of less skilled workers. The proportion of black college men obtaining managerial jobs – historically small, relative to whites – rose sharply: in 1964, a black graduate was 41 per cent as likely as a white to obtain a managerial job; by 1975, the likelihood had risen to 67 per cent. Indicative of the changing opportunities for highly qualified young black men is the marked shift in their career preferences and educational choices. In the early 1960s, black college men were over-represented in education. In the 1970s, they were over-represented as business and accounting majors with intentions to work in industry.

The economic advances of the period also apparently favored young blacks from better family backgrounds. Prior to the anti-discriminatory activity of the 1960s, sciological studies of the relation between background and economic position showed that parents played only a minor role in black economic achievement. Otis Dudley Duncan's analysis of the 1962 OCG survey showed that 'the Negro family [was] less able than the white to pass on to the next generation its socioeconomic status.' If you were black, it did not matter much what the socioeconomic status of your parents was; discrimination dominated your position in the labor market.

Studies of the period after 1964 show a very different pattern of 'status transmission.' A replication of Duncan's analysis by R. M. Hauser and

D. L. Featherman, using the 1973 OCG survey, reveals marked increases in the effect of background on achievement among blacks. In 1973, the impact of parental socioeconomic status on the education and labor-market standing of blacks was similar to that of whites. My analysis of older and younger men in the National Longitudinal Survey yields comparable results: Family background has only slight effects on the labor-market achievement of older black men but a sizeable impact on the position of young black men. A 10 per cent increase in the index of the occupational position of one's father in 1969 would have the effects on the hourly pay and occupational status of older and younger black and white men shown in Table 5.2.

The differential gains made by various groups of black workers can be attributed in part to the nature of the job market. Advances are concentrated among young workers because they constitute the effective 'margin of adjustment' in employment. The young are not significantly hampered in the job market by past discriminatory practices and human-capital-investment decisions, which 'lock' older workers into career paths and seniority ladders from which change is difficult. Improved opportunities for crafts apprenticeships or a college education will aid the 18- to 24-year-old black male but not the 45-year-old laborer. The sharp advances made recently by the highly educated and skilled also reflect the previous existence of discriminatory barriers that were most severe for the most highly qualified blacks, and the likelihood that they share the work attitudes of comparable whites. Blacks from more advantaged homes are also likely to have benefited more han poorer blacks from family investments in skills that make them more adept at responding to new opportunities. Black women have experienced a rapid improvement in economic position in large measure because experience, for whatever reason, has a lower impact on the earnings of women than men, so that improvements in starting jobs translate more rapidly into improvements in the relative incomes of women than of men.

Table 5.2 Estimated effect of a 10 per cent increase in the index of parental occupational position

	Hourly earnings	Occupational status
Older men (aged 48 to 62)		
Black	0.2%	0.3%
White	2.2	2.4
Younger men (aged 17 to 22)		
Black	1.7	2.0
White	1.6	2.3

Source: National Longitudinal Survey.

BACKGROUND DISADVANTAGES

The decline in market discrimination against young blacks and the increased role of family background in their achievement raises the possibility that differences between the backgrounds of blacks and whites – the lower income and education attainment of black parents, the greater incidence of fatherless homes among blacks, and the social ills associated with inner-city life – have become a much more important element in economic inequality than in the past. As long as background differences between blacks and whites have not diminished greatly, the drop in job-market discrimination implies that a larger proportion of economic differences between the two groups are attributable to the 'burden of background'. This is a major change in the nature of racial economic inequality, which suggests the need for different social policies to deal with it.

Estimates of the importance of family background for the educational and labor-market position of young blacks versus that of whites, based on data from the National Longitudinal Survey, are given in Table 5.3. In the calculations for education, background is measured by parental years of

Table 5.3 Estimated effect of background factors on the educational and economic attainment of young black men, 1969

	Years of schooling	Index of occupational attainment	Hourly earnings[a]	Yearly earnings[a]
Measure of difference between black and white attainment	1.6	0.20	0.33	0.44
Percentage contribution of background				
Parental occupation[b]	31%	25%	28%	7%
Parental education	25	—	—	—
Broken home	6	—	—	—
Home educational resources	44	—	—	—
Years of schooling		40	36	34
Region and place of residence	−6	15	24	11
Total contributions of factors	100%	80%	88%	72%
'Residual' differences	0.0	0.02	0.03	0.12

Notes:
a   Adjusted for years of work-experience lost because of the lower age of blacks in the survey and some patterns of intermittent work experience.
b   Because black workers have traditionally been paid less than whites in the same occupation, which is likely to affect the impact of the family on achievement, the occupational status of black parents is measured by nonwhite median incomes, while that of white parents is measured by total median incomes.
Source: Based on calculations from the National Longitudinal Survey.

education, median income in the occupation of the parent, presence of a male head of household, and three indicators of 'home educational resources' (presence in the home of magazines, of newspapers, and of a library card). In the calculations for labor-market position, background is measured by the median income in the occupation of the parent, since the other factors operate largely through education. By all of these measures, young blacks suffer a substantial disadvantage: The parents of the young black men in the sample average 7.9 years of schooling, versus 10.5 years for whites; 40 per cent of the blacks are from 'broken homes,' compared to 12 per cent of the whites; the index of parental occupational attainment reveals an 80 per cent black disadvantage; and 45 per cent of black homes have magazines, 69 per cent newspapers, and 47 per cent library cards, compared to 80 per cent, 92 per cent and 74 per cent of white homes, respectively.

The impact on the educational and labor-market attainment of young men in 1969 was calculated by multiplying each background difference by regression estimates of the effect of each factor. The first line of Table 5.3 gives a measure of the initial difference between young blacks and whites in 1969. The second line shows the percentage of the disadvantage attributable to specific background resources. The next-to-last line gives the total contribution of background factors, while the last line shows the 'residual' difference – usually termed discrimination.

While the table is too dependent on the specific models, measures of background, and samples used to present anything more than a rough estimate, it does tell a striking story. *All* of the differences in educational attainment appear to result from the poorer family background of blacks. Most, though not all, of the differences in occupational attainment, hourly earnings, and yearly earnings are atttributable to differences in parental background, years of schooling, and region and place of residence. The effects of 'residual differences' on occupational attainment and hourly earnings are relatively moderate, but high on yearly earnings. The markedly greater difference between blacks and whites in yearly compared to hourly earnings reflects the high incidence of unemployment among young blacks. For those with full-time jobs, 'residual discrimination' is modest, and could be readily attributed to any of several factors not examined in the analysis. So the big problem in the labor market is not wage or occupational discrimination within businesses but lack of employment altogether. For those 'in the system,' particularly those with more education and better backgrounds, the improvement in the job market after 1964 has greatly reduced economic differences between blacks and whites. For those who have not entered the mainstream of the labor market, for whatever reasons, sizeable problems remain.

As evident from Table 5.4, the decline in job-market discrimination after 1964 has erased only part of the enormous background disadvantage

Table 5.4 Differences between blacks and whites in family background

	1964	1969	1975
Ratio of black median family income to white			
All homes	0.54	0.61	0.62
Male-headed homes	0.57	0.71	0.75
Female-headed homes	—	0.61	0.64
Percentage of black families with female heads	23%	28%	36%

Source: Bureau of the Census, *Current Population Reports*, Consumer Income, Series P-60, and Special Studies, Series P-23.

of young blacks. While there has been improvement in the relative economic position of the black family, the change has been slower than for individual earners and has essentially ceased with the recession of the 1970s (see the first line of the table). In 1969, the ratio of black median family income to white stood at 0.61, 7 points higher than the pre-Civil-Rights-Act level of 0.54; between 1969 and 1975, the ratio remained roughly stable at 0.62. Why did family incomes rise differently than individual incomes? The major factor has been the increased proportion of black families headed by women. Between 1964 and 1969, the proportion of black homes with female heads rose from 25 per cent to 28 per cent; between 1969 and 1976, the proportion increased further to 36 per cent. Throughout the period of decline in job-market discrimination and improved income ratios, the 'deterioration' of the black family structure, which Daniel P. Moynihan first stressed in 1965, continued at a rapid pace, with an adverse impact on the rate of change of median family incomes. As the table shows, the ratio of black incomes to white among families with fixed demographic characteristics actually rose in the 1970s.

For the young person, what matters is the position of his family. With the problems of crime, quality of education, and life in the inner cities, the differences in family income and structure create a barrier to the socioeconomic progress of young blacks. Discrimination aside, disadvantages of these magnitudes can be expected to produce sizeable labor-market differences between blacks and whites, ranging from 10 per cent to 20 per cent, which by their nature cannot to eliminated by anti-bias policies in the labor market and which promise continued economic inequalities in the foreseeable future.

THE EMPLOYMENT PROBLEM

Lack of jobs for less qualified and disadvantaged black workers, including teen-agers, is a large problem that has been exacerbated by the recession of the 1970s. While there is some evidence that the recession has reduced black employment opportunities somewhat less than previous recessions, the fact is that blacks suffer excessively in economic declines, and the recession of the 1970s was particularly severe. Table 5.5 examines the employment problem in terms of the nonwhite share of various groups of men aged 16 and over and 25 to 34. While the nonwhite share of the population groups has risen, the nonwhite share of the labor force and of employed workers has remained roughly constant (or increased only slightly) from 1964 through 1976. As a consequence, the proportion of nonwhites employed has fallen relative to the proportion of whites employed. In 1964, 73 per cent of nonwhite men aged 16 and over were employed; in 1969, 73 per cent; and in 1976, 62 per cent. By contrast, the proportions of whites employed in those three years were 78 per cent, 78 per cent, and 73 per cent. As can be seen in the fourth and fifth lines, the drop in the total of employed workers has taken the form *not* of an increase in the black share of the unemployed (which has fallen in the recession) but of an increase in the black share of those out of the labor force entirely.

These facts highlight the sharp divergence between black Americans whose qualifications and background have won them a place in the economy since 1964 and those left out of the mainstream — such as black teenagers, whose lack of jobs is even more severe and exacerbated by the recession. In 1964, the unemployment rate for 18- to 19-year-old blacks was 23.1 per cent, compared to 13.4 per cent for 18- to 19-year-old whites. In 1969, the rates were 19.0 per cent (black) and 12.5 per cent (white); in 1976, 34.0 per cent (black) and 15.5 per cent (white). In the high-school graduating class of 1976, the unemployment rate for blacks was 46.2 per cent as of October 1976, but 15.1 per cent for their white classmates. Even if teenage unemployment has no long-term consequences for the career prospects of young persons, the immediate impact is still severe. If, as is more likely, those who have an adverse labor-market experience as teen-agers suffer for much of their working life, the problem is even more critical.

Finally, it is important to remember that large groups of experienced black workers, as well as less qualified young persons, have benefited only modestly from the decline in job-market discrimination. Because male occupations require considerable investment in skills and experience and often have lengthy, formal seniority systems, experienced black workers face the problem not simply of gaining equal opportunities today but of making up past deficiencies in education and work skills. The ratio of black income and occupational standing to white among older workers increased only moderately since 1964. With some exceptions, black men aged 35 or more continued to earn much less than their white counterparts.

More striking, the labor-force-participation rate of experienced black men has declined sharply. In 1948, 95.6 per cent of black men aged 45 to 54

Table 5.5 Nonwhite proportion of population and labor-force groups, 1964–76

| | Males aged 16 and above | | | Males aged 25–34 | | |
	1964	1969	1976	1964	1969	1976
Population	10.1%	10.4%	11.0%	11.1%	11.0%	11.5%
Labor force	10.0	10.0	10.0	10.9	10.7	10.9
Total employed	9.6	9.8	9.8	10.4	10.5	10.4
Total unemployed	19.3	18.9	18.1	24.0	19.1	19.3
Non-labor-force participants	10.7	11.9	14.8	17.0	18.7	22.9

Source: Department of Labor, *Employment and Training Report of the President, 1977.*

were in the labor force; in 1964, 91.6 per cent; in 1969, 89.5 per cent; and in 1976, 83.4 per cent. This decline may relect the impact of the growth in female-headed families among blacks, which could be expected to reduce the incentive for men to work, or it could result from the uneven impact on male and female earnings of the lessening of discrimination, with the increased ratio of female income to male weakening the family system. The decline may also reflect the response of older black men to the recession of the 1970s. For some blacks, it may also be the result of increased Social Security Disability Insurance funds for disabled workers (disproportionately black) who leave the workforce. In any case, the job-market position of many black men has been only modestly improved by reducing market discrimination. Even if economic parity were to be established among the young, differences among older workers guarantee persistent differences between black and white workers in the foreseeable future.

THE LESSONS FOR POLICY

The magnitude and incidence of black economic gains after 1964, which have persisted in the 1970s despite the recession, and the relative increase in the number of black workers have several implications for current and future national policy toward those suffering discrimination or disadvantages. The changed job market after 1964 and the changes in corporate personnel policy and recruitment practices suggest that the national anti-bias effort, which became intense in the mid-1960s, has significantly altered the economic opportunities for black workers. Although it is hard to determine which policy instruments account for the new situation – equal-employment-opportunity laws, affirmative action, court rulings, renewed activity by state fair-employment-practices commissions – it is difficult to know what alternative explanation would be plausible. A cyclical explanation is ruled out by the continued relative progress of blacks in the 1970s. An explanation based on changes in supply is ruled out by the relative *increase* in the number of black workers. And discussions with corporate decision-makers make it clear that the change in job opportunities would not have occurred in the absence of the national anti-bias effort. Of course, this is not to say that current levels of spending or activity are satisfactory or, in the long run, socially desirable. Problems of Federal reorganization, administrative change, 'reverse discrimination,' and the like make it clear that there is nothing 'optimal' about current policies. But past efforts appear to have been effective in producing change.

Moreover, simply ending job-market discrimination and guaranteeing equal employment opportunity will not achieve parity between blacks and whites in the foreseeable future. Anti-bias policies along the lines of the 1964 Civil Rights Act and the 1972 amendments cannot alter the family structure, compensate for low social origins, or remove the burden of past discrimination. The advances of the 1960s and 1970s still leave sizeable black/white economic differences among all men (but not women) and among families.

The greater gains of blacks from more advantaged homes and the heightened impact of family background on black achievement suggest that the 'burden of background' will remain a major deterrent to socioeconomic equality. What responsibility should the society take for helping blacks to overcome long-run disadvantages? To what extent should it also help whites with disadvantaged backgrounds? Since part of the background disadvantage of blacks results from past discrimination, should they merit special compensatory or redistributive programs? Or should all disadvantaged persons be aided in the same manner?

The related problems of family compensation and income differences raise more complex and controversial issues. Subsidies to female-headed homes (for instance, Aid to Families with Dependent Children) create an incentive for family disruption, which of course should be minimized. Other income guarantees to families also create incentive problems. Society need not be concerned with differences in family income resulting from differences in the number of adult earners, but it must consider the effects on the children of low-income families. Perhaps the most reasonable policy, one used in many countries, would be to provide child allowances to bring about some equalization among the young. It is difficult to see how other, less purely redistributive policies can alleviate the effect of family-income differences on the young.

As for unemployment, although it will decrease among blacks along with economic recovery, rates of black unemployment are unlikely to fall to acceptable levels. New methods of stabilizing employment in a recession may have to be found. New policies toward youth unemployment are needed to help disadvantaged inner-city blacks find meaningful first jobs and appropriate schooling and training.

Finally, the apparent reduction of job-market discrimination must not be taken to mean that the equal-employment effort should be weakened. If discrimination is a recurrent 'disease', continual inoculations and monitoring are needed. On the other hand, the fact that past efforts have been reasonably successful does not imply that future efforts should be intensified or indicate which aspects of present policy should be stressed in the future. More detailed evaluations of the effects of public expenditures are required to make such judgments. Continued success in reducing market discrimination along the lines described is, in any case, unlikely to eliminate economic differences between blacks and whites in the foreseeable future. For those who remain seriously disadvantaged, anti-bias activity is not enough.

NOTE

1.   In this paper I use the term 'black', in referring to data that relate to nonwhites, 90 per cent of whom are black, as well as to data that relate specifically to blacks. Similarly, in several instances I use the term 'white' to refer to the rest of the population, 90 per cent of whom are white, as well as to whites only.

BIBLIOGRAPHY

Farley, R., and Hermailin, A., 'The 1960s: a decade of progress for blacks?', *Demography* (1972), no. 3, pp. 353–70.

Freeman, R., 'The changing labor market for black Americans', *Brookings Papers on Economic Activity* (1973).

Freeman, R., 'Labor market discrimination: analysis, findings and problems', in Intriligator, M., and Kendrick, D. (eds), *Frontiers of Quantitative Economics* (Amsterdam: North-Holland Publishing Company, 1974).

Freeman, R., 'The changing labor market for minorities' in Gordon, M. (ed.), *Higher Education and the Labor Market* (New York: McGraw-Hill, 1974).

Freeman, R., 'A premium for black academicians?', *Industrial Labor Relations Review* (January, 1977).

Freeman R., *Black Elite: The New Market for Highly Qualified Black Americans* (New York, McGraw-Hill, 1977).

Glazer, N., *Affirmative Discrimination* (New York: Basic Books, 1977).

Hall, R., and Kasten, R., 'The relative occupational success of blacks and whites', *Brookings Paper on Economic Activity* (Washington DC: Brookings Institution, 1973), pp. 781–98.

Hauser, R. M., and Featherman, D. L., 'Equality of access to schooling: trends and prospects', Center for Demography and Ecology, Working Paper No. 75–17 (Madison, Wisconsin: University of Wisconsin, 1975).

Hauser, R. M., and Featherman, D. L., 'Racial inequalities and socioeconomic achievement in the US, 1962–73', Institute for Research on Poverty, Discussion Paper No. 275–75 (Madison, Wisconsin: University of Wisconsin, 1975).

Vroman, W., 'Changes in black workers' relative earnings: evidence for the 1960s', in Von Furstenberg, G. (ed.), *Patterns of Racial Discrimination*, vol. 11

(Lexington, Massachusetts: Heath-Lexington, 1974).

Weiss, L., and Williamson, J., 'Black education, earnings, and interregional migration: some new evidence', *American Economic Review* (June 1972), pp. 372–83.

Welch, F., 'Black-white returns to schooling', *American Economic Review* (March 1973), pp. 893–907.

Welch, F., and Smith, J., 'Black/white male earnings and employment: 1960–1970' (US Department of Labor, R-1666-DOL, June 1975).

6 · YOUNG BLACKS AND JOBS

Black youths have traditionally fared more poorly in the job market than have white youths. The nature of their problems, however, has changed over the past 20 years. In the early 1960s, for example, black youths earned considerably less than otherwise comparable white youths, and received a lower return on their investments in schooling. While differences between blacks and whites in skill, family background, and location in the country explained some of the black disadvantage in the job market, a large part of the problem was attributable to discrimination. The picture changed in the 1970s and 1980s. Blacks made advances in occupation and education, and with the onset of equal employment opportunity, affirmative action, and related government and private efforts to reduce market discrimination, the wages of black youths have risen relative to those of whites. Yet, the employment problem of young blacks has worsened, reaching levels that can be described as catastrophic. In 1983 only 45 per cent of black males aged 16 to 21 who were out of school were employed compared to 73 per cent of whites in the same category.

FROM A WAGE PROBLEM TO AN EMPLOYMENT PROBLEM

The well publicized youth unemployment problem, then, has taken the form not so much of joblessness among white youths as of high joblessness among black youths. The magnitude of this employment problem is shown in Table 6.1. The first three lines give the rate of unemployment from 1954 to 1983 for youths through the age group 20–24. The data show the high levels of unemployment among blacks at every age group, and the comparatively modest rates among whites. It also shows something that is too often forgotten: It is only over the past two decades that this large gap has developed. In 1954 the unemployment rate scarcely differed for black

Table 6.1 Employment and unemployment rates, 1954–83

	Black and other					White				
	1954	1964	1969	1977	1983	1954	1964	1969	1977	1983
Percentage of labor force unemployed										
Age: 16–17	13.4	25.9	24.7	38.7	47.3	14.0	16.1	12.5	17.6	22.6
18–19	14.7	23.1	19.0	36.1	43.8	13.0	13.4	7.9	13.0	18.7
20–24	16.9	12.6	8.4	21.7	27.2	9.8	7.4	4.6	9.3	13.8
Percentage of population employed										
Age: 16–17	40.4	27.6	28.4	18.9	13.7	40.6	36.5	42.7	44.3	36.2
18–19	66.5	51.8	51.1	36.9	31.3	61.3	57.7	61.8	65.2	58.0
20–24	75.9	78.1	77.3	61.2	57.2	77.9	79.3	78.8	80.5	74.2

Source: US Department of Labor, *Employment and Training Report of the President,* 1982 and *Employment and Earnings,* January 1984.

and white youths. The rates rose for blacks in the 1950s and early 1960s, in part because of the movement of blacks into urban centers. In 1950, for example, 36 per cent of blacks lived in rural areas, and nearly a third of employed black youths worked on farms. In 1970, 19 per cent of blacks lived in rural areas, and just 4 per cent of black youths worked as farmers or farm laborers. As measured unemployment is primarily an urban phenomenon, the urbanization of black America explains some of the increase in unemployment during this period. The sharp rise in unemployment rates in the 1970s and the early 1980s, on the other hand, has no such simple cause; for by 1969 the proportion of blacks in rural areas was relatively modest.

The proportion of the population that is employed, shown in the bottom three lines of the table, is in some respects a more direct and better measure of the 'employment' problem, because it reflects not only high unemployment but also the low labor force participation rate of black youths – i.e., the high number who report themselves no longer looking for work and are therefore not counted in official unemployment statistics. Many of these youths, particularly those out of school, report that they 'want a job now' even though they have given up looking. It is thus more proper to count them as potential workers. The employment rates in the table show even greater black-white disparity than the unemployment rates. Even these differences, however, understate the problem, considering the fact that a substantial number of employed black youths hold part-time jobs when they would like full-time work (22 per cent compared to 13 per cent of white youths in 1983).

For the youngest age groups, some of the decline in the employment rate reflects increased school-going among blacks, and the fact that fewer black students than white students are employed. But while joblessness among students who seek work is undesirable, it is the group that is neither in school nor employed which represents the most serious problem. Thirty-two per cent of 16 to 24 year-old blacks and minorities fall into the latter group, compared to 18 per cent for whites.

Defining the nature of this job crisis and determining the causes of declining black youth employment are difficult tasks at best. And unfortunately official government data on the labor force activities of youths are not suited to this purpose. The Current Population Survey (CPS), which is the monthly information source on households, basically asks if youths are working or are in school. It asks little beyond whether they are or are not seeking jobs, and how those not in school and not employed spend their time; it provides no information on alternatives to work that may be quite important to these youths, notably crime (broadly defined to include working in the 'underground economy'). Finally, there is a serious 'respondent problem' in the CPS: one member of the household answers for others, leading, it seems, to a significant bias in answers for youths, as mothers appear unaware of some of the work activity of youngsters.

TAKING THE INNER CITY PULSE

Data more helpful for understanding the black youth employment crisis are, however, available now from the National Bureau of Economic Research (NBER).[1] NBER developed a set of questions specifically designed for inner-city minority youths and in 1979–80 surveyed over 2,000 black males, aged 16 to 24, in poor, primarily black areas of Boston, Chicago, and Philadelphia. Comparing results from this study with figures for all youths shows the severity of the problems faced by inner-city youths from families in poverty.

As can be seen in Table 6.2 these youths are much more likely to be unemployed and less likely to be employed than white youth or all-black youth. They tend to earn slightly lower wages than other youths and they work fewer weeks. In addition, these youths have far worse family backgrounds than others. One-third of them live in public housing, and almost one-half of them have a family member on welfare. Only 28 per cent of them report an adult male in their households. With respect to 'socially deviant behavior' 16 per cent of the NBER survey group reported committing crimes; 26 per cent reported drug use beyond marijuana; 20 per cent reported alcohol use. In short, the more narrowly one focuses on inner-city youth in poverty neighborhoods, the worse the problem looks.

At this point, it should be noted that the joblessness of black youths has characteristics not readily apparent in aggregate statistics. Persons can suffer from joblessness, for example, either because they have trouble finding jobs or because they are laid off or discharged frequently. Most black youths suffer from a combination of the two: in general, they find

Table 6.2 Inner-city youth compared to other youths

	NBER	NLS	
	Inner-city	All black	All white
Out of school youth			
Percent in labor force	80	90	94
Percent unemployed	41	33	20
Percent employed	48	61	76
Average wages	$4.26	$4.29	$4.53
Average weeks worked in year	26	29	37
Family background			
Man in household	28%	51%	69%
Household member working/in school	41%	56%	71%
Family on welfare	45%	—	—
In public housing	32%	10%	1%

Sources: Tabulated from *NBER Survey of Inner-City Youth*, and *National Longitudinal Survey of Young Persons.*

jobs with great difficulty, and these are short-term jobs that are followed by long, extended spells of joblessness. Twenty per cent of the youths may hold *no* job in the course of a year.

Much of the black youth employment problem is associated with this slow transition from nonemployment to employment. Still, the loss of jobs through layoffs and discharges is significant. In a society where relatively few people are discharged from work, one-quarter of the youths in the NBER survey were fired, many because of absenteeism. Overall, this higher layoff rate cannot be attributed to differences in human capital or the characteristics of the place of work. Part of the differences can in fact be attributed to lower job tenure itself: Black youths who remain with an employer for an extended period enjoy the benefits of increased job security as do other youths; however, since fewer blacks than whites obtain permanent jobs, more blacks are subject to a vicious circle of joblessness.

It is of course sometimes argued that the joblessness problem among minority youth is a *youth* problem that will disappear with age. This would make it a temporary phenomena, which, though serious, will cure itself. While it is true that the employment of black youths rises with age, the increased employment that comes with age is unlikely to be large enough to remove the problem. Indeed, if the rate of increase in employment with age remains at the level of the 1970s, those blacks 16 to 19 years old in 1979 will not achieve an 80 per cent rate of employment for over a decade, and their unemployment rate is unlikely to fall to 10 per cent until they reach their mid-thirties.

What has caused the disastrous increase in black youth joblessness? Some claim that the problem is one of declining skills and the weakening of the work ethic; others that it is a case of discrimination pure and simple. Sluggish economic growth, the general rise in unemployment during the 1970s, the movement of jobs from cities, the growing number of women and immigrants (legal or illegal) entering the labor force: All of these have been suggested as causes of declining black youth employment. Indeed, one can ask to what extent black youth employment has been adversely affected by the increase in black youth wages due, in part, to equal employment opportunity, affirmative action, and minimum wage legislation. With all these factors at work, it is not surprising that serious research can point to no single cause of this problem, much less suggest a cure-all. What we can do is sort out the contributing factors and attempt to evaluate the relative importance of each.

A useful framework for analysis is to examine the potential causes of high or increasing joblessness in terms of (a) factors likely to affect joblessness by altering the supply of labor, and (b) those likely to affect joblessness by altering the demand for labor. It is important to recognize, however, that changes in employment depend on both sides of the job market: a decrease in demand reduces employment or wages in magnitudes that depend on the elasticity or responsiveness of supply; a change in supply similarly will or will not affect employment depending on the responsiveness of employers' wage-setting policies and the extent to which employment expands when wages are reduced relative to other prices. It is clear that any remedy of the situation will involve changing or reversing several of these factors; policies that address only one element of the problem will not be sufficient.

If there is a single unifying theme that runs through the various analyses it is that black youth are quite responsive to various economic incentives and to their social and family environment. The magnitude of the fall-off in employment thus reflects in large part the high responsiveness of young blacks to negative incentives and social-family developments in the 1970s. This suggests that if young blacks were offered different incentives, their employment situation could be significantly improved. Developing policies to change these incentives is therefore the major challenge in any effort to improve the employment rate of black youth.

HELP NOT WANTED: DEMAND PROBLEMS

Among the major demand-side factors which could, to some degree, contribute to high black youth joblessness are the sluggish overall performance of the economy; minimum wage laws and equal employment activities, which raise the wages of black youths; the increasing number of women and immigrants who have entered the job market; and residual employer discrimination.

It is widely recognized that economic growth has been relatively poor in the past decade or so, and that the overall unemployment rate has drifted up. Weak performance of the economy has contributed to the upward drift in black youth joblessness, but we find that it is not a dominant cause. In 1959 and in 1979 the rate of unemployment among white males was approximately the same (4.6 per cent and 4.5 per cent respectively). The employment rate for 20 to 24 year old black male youths stood at 75.9 in 1959, compared to 65.7 in 1979. There was nearly a ten point drop in the rate at the same cyclical level of unemployment for white men. Put more dramatically, in spite of relatively sluggish economic growth, the US economy from 1970 to 1983 found jobs for 22 million new workers, hardly any of whom were black youths (see Table 6.3). In 1970 1.2 per cent of employed workers were black male youths aged 16 to 24, and despite increases in their share of the population only 0.1 per cent of the jobs created in the period went to black youths.

This is not to say that the condition of the labor market does not affect black youth employment. Researchers find that the state of the local labor market is, in fact, a major determinant of youth joblessness. In the NBER survey, for example, inner-city black youths in Boston, a city with a relatively strong labor market, had an employment rate some ten points above comparable youth in Chicago or Philadelphia. And analysis relating black youth employment to the overall state of the labor market shows that a one percentage point decrease in unemployment raises black youth employment, over time, by about two and one-half percentage points. Economic expansion will thus raise black youth employment significantly but will not, by itself, restore 1950s employment rates.

It is often claimed that some government programs designed to aid the disadvantaged have unintended consequences for those very groups. The minimum wage, for example, by raising the pay of less-skilled workers (particularly youths), reduces their employability by making them more expensive to employers. There is no doubt that black youth wages have

Table 6.3 Growth of employment, 1970–83

	Number of new workers (in thousands) 1970–83	Share of employment 1970	Share of growth in employment 1970–83
All workers	22,156	100.0%	100.0%
Women	14,359	37.7%	64.8%
Youths 16–24	4,277	20.1%	19.3%
Black male youth, 16–24	165	1.2%	0.1%

Source: US Department of Labor, *Employment and Training Report of the President*, 1982 and *Employment and Earnings*, January 1984.

been significantly affected by the minimum wage. The
youths working in 1980 held jobs paying at or about that
lower minimum wage for youth would increase the numb
the economy, and the number of inner-city black youth
still cannot reasonably blame changes in the minimum wa,
black youth joblessness in the 1970s, the simple reason
minimum wage has *fallen* relative to average wages. In 197 , ...ᴄ minimum
wage was 50 per cent of average private sector wages; by 1983 it was only
42 per cent of average private sector wages. This decline in the relative
value of the minimum wage would have tended to *increase* employment of
youths over the decade.

Similar questions can be raised about equal employment opportunity
and affirmative action. By raising black youth wages, have they possibly
reduced employment? The evidence that exists does not support such a
conclusion. First, the thrust of the law is to raise demand, not simply
wages; an employer who pays 'equal wages' but discriminates against black
youths (or other protected groups) in hiring is liable to legal suit. Affirmative action programs take equal pay as given and seek to raise employment
of protected groups. The most reliable assessment of affirmative action
thus far (Leonard, 1984) finds that companies with affirmative action do
indeed increase employment of protected groups more than do other companies. Finally, in the late 1960s, when black youth wages rose substantially, there was *no* deterioration in employment (see Table 6.1).

There has long been considerable speculation about the potential effect
of the rapidly growing number of immigrants and women in the job market
on the employment prospects of young blacks. To what extent does the
influx of other workers into the labor market fill up entry-level jobs that
might otherwise have gone to young blacks?

Studies show that cities whose work force includes a high proportion of
women have had the worst labor markets for young blacks. It is difficult
not to interpret this as evidence that the rising rate of female participation
in the work force, particularly in the service sector, has hurt the job
opportunities for young blacks. By contrast, there is no evidence to support the view that the rise in the Hispanic population (among which immigrants are concentrated) has significantly worsened the job prospects of
black youth since black youth joblessness does not differ greatly between
cities with large or small Hispanic populations.

Although the increase in black youth joblessness is often attributed to
the movement of jobs from cities to suburbs, a careful assessment of the
relation between location and employment in Chicago does not find this to
be a major factor. The black youth employment problem there is one of
'race, not space.' There are basically two clusterings of blacks in the
Chicago area, on the west side and on the south side. There are many
factories and jobs on the west side; the south side is mostly residential. On

basis of proximity to work, one would think that those youths on the south side would have far less employment experience than those living close to jobs on the west side. But there turns out to be very difference between them. Moreover, if one looks only at the borderline between black and white areas of the west side, one finds that the white youths get the jobs. The problem facing these black youths, then, is not a lack of jobs in their area; even when the jobs are nearby, the white youths still get them. The likelihood for success of an enterprise zone scheme must be measured against this fact. For these findings seem to suggest that to raise black youth employment, what is needed is an improvement in the aggregate level of demand for labor in a city, not intra-city changes in the location of jobs.

One way of assessing employer discrimination is through auditor studies, which present employers with the job applications of otherwise comparable black and white workers and observe how the employers treat the applications. Auditor studies in the 1970s have found that employers treat applications of black jobseekers as favorably as those of white jobseekers, that blatant discrimination by employers has effectively been eliminated. It is more difficult to determine if there are subtler ways in which employers may (perhaps inadvertently) discourage or discriminate against black youth. A pilot 'audit' project was conducted in Newark, New Jersey in which youths graduating or about to graduate from high school – some white and some black – were sent out, having been told, 'Here's a list of jobs that we've identified; go and see what happens. We'll pay you to come back and report to us what happens when you apply for these jobs.'[2] The audit project found that the black auditors were treated less courteously, in some respects, than the white auditors. For example, people were less likely to call them 'sir.' In addition, the project found that white youths had much better links to the job market, and that both white and black youths were what is called 'reference poor.' They would fill out forms that asked, 'Who do you give as a reference for yourself?' and they would list their friends at school. They would not report teachers or previous employers; this was true for both black and white youths. For whites, most of whom have jobholders in their families and connections to employers, this lack of references is not as critical a problem in job finding as it is for blacks.

The perception among black youths that employers discriminate, and the quality of jobs these youths hold, also affect their work performance. For instance, youths who claimed that their employers discriminated were more likely to be absent from their jobs. Several other characteristics of these jobs also affect rates of absenteeism among black youth. High wages and high job status lower the frequency of absenteeism; chances of finding work elsewhere raise it.

One of the more surprising findings of the NBER study was the response to questions concerning the ease of finding jobs. A rather large proportion of youths who were not employed and not in school thought they could find a job relatively easily: for example, 46 per cent thought it would be 'very easy' or 'somewhat easy' to find a job working as a laborer. And 71 per cent considered finding a minimum wage job to be very or somewhat easy.

This hardly means that there is no shortage of jobs in the inner city. On the contrary, while it may be easy for a given individual to find a low paying job, only a small fraction look for and are willing to accept these jobs at any particular moment. If all of these youths sought such jobs simultaneously and were willing to hold them for longer periods, these jobs would not be as easy to find. In some sense, these jobs are 'shared' among youths: They work for a few months at a hamburger joint, then leave.

ATTITUDES, ASPIRATIONS AND SKILLS: SUPPLY PROBLEMS

The supply side factors affecting black youth employment might be summarized by the layman as the youths' attitudes and abilities, their willingness to work and the skills they can offer employers.

Among the more intriguing findings on the supply side was that church-going and 'right' attitudes or aspirations are important in enabling youths to take steps toward escaping inner-city poverty. In the NBER survey youths were asked whether they attended church and whether they were members of church groups. The idea was that the church, as a major social institution in the black community, would be doing things to help these youths advance in society. Church-going turned out to be a significant factor in reducing such socially deviant activities as crime and drug use, in increasing school-going, and in increasing employment. Put simply, the youths who went to church behaved differently from those who did not go to church.

But does one interpret these results as the role of the church as a social institution helping youth, or is it that 'good kids' go to church, get jobs, stay in school, don't commit crimes? This problem is treated differently by different researchers. While it is not possible to declare conclusively that church-going is what social scientists would call an exogenous variable or, on the contrary, that it is simply a 'good/bad kid indicator', the NBER research found that church-going and various family factors have *different* effects on aspects of youth behavior. This suggests some independent causal role for the church, or as the old-fashioned might put it, that church-going builds character.

Apart from church-going and family characteristics, responses to questions on attitudes toward work showed that black youths with strong long-term career desires manage to find work, whereas those without such desires do less well. This implies that efforts to promote positive attitudes toward work (ranging perhaps from role models to Operation Push-type activities) can help reduce the black youth joblessness problem.

While the quality of schooling in inner cities leaves much to be desired, it is still true that staying in school longer benefits youths. Those who stay in school longer have a lesser chance of committing crimes, a greater chance of being employed, and are more diligent employees than those who drop out of school. In addition, students with better school records (more As and Bs than Cs and Ds) also do better in the job market.

Finally, recent experiments suggest that a well-developed job program can be effective if linked to school. In the Youth Incentive Entitlement Pilot Project, offers of a guaranteed minimum-wage job during the school year and summer to youths who continue school have managed to provide inner-city youths (and others) with jobs, in addition to prolonging their schooling.

In the National Commission for Employment Policy's Fifth Annual Report to the President and Congress, the Commission noted that the understanding of youth unemployment has been hindered by a lack of study on the links between labor market problems and illegal activities. The NBER analysis of the relation between youths' perceptions of market opportunities and penalties for crimes helps fill this gap in the data on youth employment. In the NBER survey youth were asked to compare their potential for making money on a job and 'on the street.' Thirty-two per cent of those surveyed saw greater opportunities for earnings 'on the street,' and tended to commit (i.e., admitted committing) more crimes. Indeed, about one-fourth of all income of inner-city black youths is from crime. Perceptions of the risk of crime were found to be a major factor in whether youths chose a legitimate job or crime. The youths who felt that the chances to make money illegally were pretty good and who saw little chance of being penalized tended to commit crimes. More often than not, they tended not to be employed, not to be in school, not to spend their time productively, and to be involved with drugs or gangs. Furthermore, when they held jobs, those engaged in criminal activity tended to perform poorly on the job.

Viewed in terms of supply behavior the elasticities of trade-off between crime and employment implied by the NBER analysis are fairly significant. This result is striking, given the scholarly literature on crime. Previous studies of the trade-off between unemployment and crime done on aggregate data for crime rates and unemployment rates have found very modest linkages. In this case better data has yielded a conclusion more in line with what common sense suggests. Crime and employment are alternatives: poor employment opportunities (or attractive criminal opportunities) can lead to participation in crime, which further reduces success in the legal labor market.

In 1964 Daniel P. Moynihan directed attention to the instability of the black family as a potential cause of economic and social problems for black Americans. Analysis of family factors in the NBER survey shows that, while youths from female-headed households do not do particularly worse in employment than youths from other families, certain characteristics of families matter greatly.

One of the more depressing findings of the NBER project was that persons whose families are involved with major public programs for disadvantaged families do worse in the job market. Youths from welfare homes, with the same family income and other attributes as those from non-welfare homes, do far worse in the job market; youths living in public housing projects do less well than youths living in private housing. Since the 'loss' of welfare benefits is slight when youths work, the problems of youth in welfare households cannot be explained as simply a 'rational' response to economic incentives. Instead they are more likely related to other factors, such as information and 'connections' or attitudes and 'work ethic.'

It is also noteworthy that young blacks are more likely to hold jobs when other members of the family are employed. Whether this represents an improved ability to find jobs due to better information, 'connections', etc., or a greater work ethic learned from knowing jobholders, is unclear. In either case, 'family-centered' factors that raise job holding and family stability among black adults may offer an important 'indirect' approach for improving the job chances in youths.

An important issue in evaluating youth joblessness is the wage at which they would accept work. The NBER survey asked youths specifically about the pay at which they would take a job: 'well, really, how willing are you to take a job at different levels of pay?'; and 'would you take a full-time job right now, if it were as a laborer in a factory at $2.50 an hour?' If yes, the interviewer went on to the next question. If no, the interviewer raised the hypothetical wage to $3.50 an hour and then to $5.00 an hour.

The answers to these questions highlight two aspects of the problem. First, the reservation wages of black youths (the lowest wages they say they would work for) turn out to be comparable to those of similarly aged white youth. Since the two groups differ in their possibilities of getting jobs, and there are some differences in the wages at which they do get jobs, a portion of the longer period that blacks are out of employment can be explained by the fact that they maintain relatively high reservation wages. Black youth should not necessarily lower their expectations, nor should they necessarily settle for lower wages than white youths (assuming, of course, that they can even find an employer willing to discriminate by making such an offer). But the fact that they don't adjust their wage expectations contributes to joblessness. Second, the number of youths who expressed willingness to take jobs as pay increased modestly was substantial, implying a high degree of responsiveness to better economic opportunities. In addition, youths made a definite distinction between the wage at which they were willing to take different types of jobs, being willing to accept low-wage or low-skill jobs only temporarily.

CHANGING LABOR MARKET INCENTIVES

The overall picture of the black youth employment situation that emerges from this research effort is one in which black youth clearly want to work, but only at jobs and with wages that are comparable to those received by their white counterparts. Unfortunately, in a weakened economy, with increased job market competition from women and other groups, and an increasingly disadvantageous family background, the youths have had trouble obtaining such jobs. As a result, many have been led into altern- ative modes of obtaining money 'on the street' and to leisure activities that will not get them back on track. The growth of welfare households in which no adults work seems also to have exacerbated the problem, either because of its effect on contacts and information or its effect on attitudes and 'work ethic'.

The possibility of a solution to the black youth employment problem rests, in large measure, on the responsiveness of the youths to labor market incentives. Provided with choices other than the ones they currently face, black youths will respond positively. However, public or private policies to aid the youths cannot, in our view, be limited to a single policy. They should include not only government jobs programs for youth and aggres- sive anti-discrimination activity, but also the efforts of a broad range of public and private social institutions, ranging from the welfare system to employers to schools, to the criminal justice system, and to families.

In recent years, we have seen rather sizeable changes in social and economic behavior in response to changes in economic incentives. If the right incentives are given to black youths, we may see equally rapid change in their employment status.

NOTES

1. The research in this article is based in large part on the NBER investigation of the economic status of inner-city black youth. This four-year study made use of a special survey of these youths by Mathematica, Inc. The individual studies are given in R. Freeman and H. Holzer, *The Black Youth Employment Crisis*.
2. Interestingly, the researchers had great difficulty finding white youths to participate, apparently because they had good job prospects, while black youths were much more eager to go through this process, hoping to find work.

BIBLIOGRAPHY

Freeman, R., and Holzer, H. (eds), *The Black Youth Employment Crisis* (Chicago: University of Chicago Press, 1986).

Leonard, J., 'Employment and occupational advance under affirmative action', *Review of Economics and Statistics*, (1984) 66, no. 3, pp. 377–85.

Leonard, J., 'The impact of affirmative action on employment', *Journal of Labor Economics* (1984) 2, no. 4, pp. 439–63.

7 · PERMANENT HOMELESSNESS IN AMERICA?

Men and women sleeping on park benches, on heating vents, in privately run and public shelters. Large numbers of persons seemingly incapable of earning enough to pay for the very basics of shelter and food. Families filling welfare hotels that cost hundreds of dollars per week of public moneys. A temporary blemish on the American scene due to the severe 1982–3 recession? Or a permanent scar if social and economic developments do not change dramatically?

When the reports of homelessness first exploded in the media in the early 1980s, the problem seemed at most at be a temporary phenomenon, likely to diminish rapidly as the economy improved.[1] The idea that a sizeable, permanent homeless underclass was beginning to develop in the United States seemed hardly credible – a nightmare from the Great Depression; a propaganda debating point by Gorbachev at the Summit – not the reality of modern-day America. While no one denied the sudden burst in homelessness, which generated the first Congressional hearings on the subject since Depression days, even the most basic facts about the problem – the numbers of persons, lengths of time spent homeless, the characteristics of the homeless – were shrouded in controversy, often of a partisan nature.[2] In 1980, advocates for the homeless claimed that 'approximately 1 per cent of the population, or 2.2 million people, lacked shelter', a figure that was widely accepted in the media and is still often cited as approximately correct, although even larger figures are occasionally mentioned.[3] By contrast, the report of the US Department of Housing and Urban Affairs (HUD), released on April 23 1984, estimated numbers 10 to 15 per cent as large.[4]

What is the approximate size of the homeless population in the United States today? Did homelessness decrease with economic recovery, as expected, or is homelessness becoming an endemic part of the American scene? To answer some of these questions, we developed a set of questions specifically designed to illuminate the nature of homelessness in the United

States, and in the summer of 1985 one of us (Hall) interviewed 516 homeless persons in New York City: 210 shelter dwellers; 101 heads of homeless families in welfare hotels; and 205 people living in the street. When we began the survey, many persons close to the homelsss problem warned us that we would have little success in interviewing this hard-to-reach population. This did not turn out to be the case. Eighty-one per cent of the homeless persons who were approached agreed to give interviews: most were eager to tell about their lives; and while we do not have a random sample, we have one of the largest data sets that includes street as well as shelter residents. Our findings – together with those of numerous studies for various cities in the country – go a long way toward answering some of the key questions regarding the nature of homelessness in the United States today.

Put broadly, our research demonstrates that the perception of homelessness as a temporary blemish on the American scene is seriously in error. Despite the substantial recovery from the 1982–3 recession, the number of homeless persons appears to be increasing. For many homeless persons, spells of homelessness tend to be quite long, on the order of six to eight years for individuals. And, while social programs move homeless families into housing relatively quickly, patterns of change in incomes, family structure, land prices and housing costs will produce a continuous stream of newly homeless families large enough to keep welfare hotels and family shelters filled for the foreseeable future.

In the absence of major economic and social changes or a new housing policy for the extremely disadvantaged, the United States is thus likely to be plagued by a long-term problem of homelessness of a sizeable magnitude.

HOW MANY?

As noted, the issue of how many homeless persons there are in the United States has been at the center of bitter dispute for some time. At one extreme is the 2.2 million persons figure suggested by homeless activists; at the other extreme is the 250–350,000 person estimate by HUD in its 1984 report. When the Subcommittee on Housing and Community Development of the US House of Representatives held hearings on the HUD Report in May 1984, numerous witnesses, often involved in helping the homeless, castigated the study as seriously understating the problem. Many saw the report as an effort (conscious or unconscious) to reduce the magnitude of the problem by an administration considered unfriendly to the plight of the poor. Given the complexity of counting the number of homeless on the streets (as opposed to those in shelters) and the subjectivity of some estimating procedures (of the four methods used by

HUD, two involved obtaining 'expert' opinions or newspaper reports rather than 'hard counts'), it seemed as if one could not choose between the two widely disparate estimates, and some observers have simply decided that reality must lie somewhat in the middle of the range.

Our survey data provide new information that can be used to evaluate the conflicting claims about the size of the homeless population. In particular, we asked homeless persons the amount of time they spent in shelters and the amount of time they spent in the street since becoming homeless. Assuming that future behavior mirrors past behavior, the proportion of homeless time persons spent in shelters in the past can be used to estimate the probability they will be in a shelter in the future. Given separate estimates of time spent in shelters for persons who are currently in shelters and for persons who are currently in the street, we can, in turn, estimate the proportion of the entire homeless population in shelters.

Formally, let

$P(S_t)$ = proportion of homeless in shelters at time t;
$P[S_t/S_{t-1}]$ = conditional probability that a homeless person is in a shelter in t, given that they were in a shelter in $t - 1$;
$P[S_t/\overline{S}_{t-1}]$ = conditional probability that a homeless person is in a shelter in t, given that they were in the street in $t - 1$.

Then, by conditional probability:

$$P(S_t) = P(S_t/S_{t-1}) \, P(S_{t-1}) + P(S_t/\overline{S}_{t-1}) \, [1 - P(S_{t-1})] \tag{7.1}$$

where $P(\overline{S}_{t-1}) = 1 - P(S_{t-1})$.

In equilibrium, $P(S_t) = P(S_{t-1})$, yielding an equation for the proportion in shelters in t as a function of the relevant conditional probabilities:

$$P(S_t) = P(S_t/\overline{S}_{t-1})/[(1 - P(S_t/S_{t-1}) + P(S_t/\overline{S}_{t-1})] \tag{7.2}$$

In our survey, individuals in shelters spent 55 per cent of their homeless time in shelters whereas individuals in the street spent 20 per cent of their time in shelters, yielding an estimate of $P(S_t/S_{t-1})$ of 0.55 and an estimate of $P(S_t/\overline{S}_{t-1})$ of 0.20. This in turn yields an estimated ratio of persons in shelters to the total homeless population of about 0.31. That is, based on the time that homeless persons report they spend in shelters and in the street, there are 3.23 (= 1/0.31) homeless persons for every homeless person in a shelter, or put differently, 2.23 persons living in the streets for every person in a shelter.

Is our figure, based on the population of homeless people in New York in the summer of 1985, reasonably applicable to the overall country? We have performed two checks to see if it is. First, we compared it with street-to-population ratios from sources based on street counts: our figure was *higher* than most others, possibly because, as is widely recognized, even the best street count will miss some street dwellers.[5] If our estimate is 'too high' we will be overstating the total homeless population. Second, to see if there is a regional bias to our ratio (possibly because street dwellers are more common in the southern or western states for reasons of weather or because those regions have built fewer shelters than in the east), we have compared the regional distribution of federal surplus food under the Temporary Emergency Food Distribution Program to the regional distribution of homeless persons estimated by HUD. If we found proportionally more persons in the south and west obtaining food support than in shelters, we would be suspicious that our ratio understates the street-to-shelter homeless population in those areas of the country. In fact, we find no such regional disparity; the south does get a greater share of food moneys than would be expected from its share of homelessness, but the west has a lower share of food moneys, suggesting no overall regional problem with our data.[6]

Finally, to turn our estimate of the ratio of the number of homeless persons to the number in shelters into an estimate of the total homeless population (see Table 7.1), we need one other number – the number of persons sheltered. On the basis of HUD's 1983 survey of shelters, we estimate that there were about 76,500 homeless individuals in shelters in the United States in that year; multiplied by 3.23, this number yields an estimated total number of homeless persons of 246,500. In addition, HUD reported that about 14,500 members of families were sheltered in 1983. This number, however, appears to exclude most homeless families receiving vouchers to live in welfare hotels or motels rather than in shelters.[7] For New York, as many as 10,500 persons in homeless families lived in welfare hotels in 1983. In other cities, the exclusion seems to have a much smaller impact; on the basis of discussion with officials in various cities, we estimate that outside New York perhaps one-third of homeless families were in welfare hotels and therefore were unlikely to have been counted by HUD. Adjusting for the omission of 10,500 families in New York and of homeless families in hotels elsewhere, we increase HUD's number of homeless family members to 32,000. Assuming, as seems reasonable, that all members of families were either in shelters or welfare hotels, we came up with a final estimate for 1983 of about 279,000 homeless persons in the US. This, we note, falls at the lower end of the range suggested by HUD (250,000 to 350,000) in its controversial report. While our figures are to be viewed as rough orders of magnitude only, it is important to recognize that they are strongly inconsistent with the claim that 1 per cent of Americans are homeless. For the number of homeless to be on the order of 2.2 million persons, the street-to-shelter population ratio would have to exceed our estimate by about tenfold, which even given the crude nature of our procedures seems highly implausible. In short, we find that the much-maligned HUD study was roughly correct in its estimate of the number of homeless persons in 1983.

Table 7.1   Estimated number and growth of homelessness in the United States, 1983–5 (average night estimates)

	1983	1985
1 Number of homeless persons		
(a) in shelters	76,500	92,000– 98,000
(b) in street	170,500	205,000–219,000
2 Number of persons in homeless families	32,000	46,000
3 Total number of homeless		
Our estimate	279,000	343,000–363,000
HUD estimate	250,000–350,000	
Popular advocate claim	2,200,000	

Sources: Line 1: For 1983, our 76,500 consists of HUD's 54,500 (equal to 69,000 × 79% reported as individual homeless persons) plus others not included as homeless in HUD's study:
1. Those homeless in detoxification centers, approximately 7,000 nationwide. This number was arrived at by taking the total number of homeless in detoxification centers in New York and Boston and comparing it to the number of individuals in shelters. This rate (detoxification/total individual) is then applied to the 54,500 to yield the 7,000. For New York City, the total shelter population for individuals in 1983 was 6,346 homeless, 5,846 in city shelters (*source:* Human Resources Administration) and 500 in other private shelters (*source:* various phone calls with local churches and knowledgeable sources). For Boston, there were approximately 939 sheltered (*source:* Emergency Shelter Commission). The homeless detoxification population was 518 in Boston (same source) and about 400 in New York City (*source:* various phone calls with local sources and detoxification centers). This represents a detoxification/individual population of 918/7,285. Applying this rate to the HUD figure yields about 7,000 homeless in detoxification centers, nationwide.
2. Those homeless in runaway youth shelters and shelters for battered women; using HUD's homeless/bed rate of 77% (69,000/91,000), we estimate that roughly 9,000 homeless are in runaway youth shelters (HUD reports 12,000 beds) and 6,000 battered or abused women in shelters (8,000 beds) (*HUD Report*, p. 34). The total shelter population for individuals, therefore, is about 76,500.
Line 2: For 1983, our estimate of 32,000 represents the 14,500 reported by HUD (0.21 × 69,000) plus the 10,500 in New York City, very likely to have been omitted by HUD and a very rough estimate of 7,000 others likely missed by HUD because they were in long term facilities. See note 7 for a detailed account.
1985: Figures for individuals based on estimated 1983–5 growth rates, from New York and Boston shelters. For individuals, the growth rate in Boston was 20.2% between 1983–5. The number moved from 1,457 to 1,752 (*source:* Emergency Shelter Commission). In New York, the number grew from 6,740 to 8,642 (*source:* Human Resources Administration).
1985: Figures for families based on estimated 1983–5 growth rates obtained as weighted average from New York and Boston shelters. In New York City, it grew from 10,520 to 14,970 (*source:* Human Resources Administration, Crisis Intervention Center). In Boston, the number of individuals increased from 120 to 420 (*source:* Emergency Shelter Commission) or by 87% per annum. Here we took a weighted average to obtain a 44.6% growth between 1983 and 1985.

The pattern of response to the homeless problem – in which activists raise an alarm with high, undocumented claims about the numbers involved, to which the government responds with a commissioned report that seemingly diminishes the severity of the problem – appears to be an unfortunate part of American public debate. It has also occurred in the area of the number of illegal immigrants and the extent of hunger in the country, among other issues. In the case at hand, it has had the unfortunate effect of making what should be seen as shockingly large numbers – over a quarter of a million Americans homeless in 1983 – seem moderate by contrast.

What about changes in the homeless population over time? After all, 1983 was a peak post-World War II recession year. Since then, has the number of homeless persons declined with economic recovery?

Using estimates of the shelter populations from New York and Boston to gauge the rate of increase in shelter populations nationwide in our table, the answer is no. Between 1983 and 1985 the numbers of persons living in shelters in New York increased by 28 per cent, while in Boston the number increased by 20 per cent. While in the absence of a new HUD survey, these figures should be taken solely as 'orders of magnitude,' their direction is consistent with reports from other cities, as indicated by the January 1986 study by the Conference of Mayors which concluded that in 22 of 25 cities the homeless population had increased while only in three cities had it remained constant (Conference of Mayors: 15). Even more striking, the number of homeless families seems to have increased especially rapidly since 1983. In Boston, where some 120 homeless family members were reported in 1983, there were about 420 in 1985. Elsewhere in the state, family homelessness also grew sharply, so that a major theme of the 1985 Massachusetts *Report on Homelessness* was that 'family homelessness is on the increase' (page 19). In New York, the 10,500 persons reported in homeless families in 1983 grew by about 4,000 through 1985. Our discussion with shelter providers in other cities confirms this increase elsewhere.[8]

Finally, we have examined data on the number of households obtaining food from food shelters on the hypothesis that if homelessness is increasing, one would also expect that the number seeking food from pantries, kitchens, etc. would also be increasing. Indeed, that is precisely what the data show (Food Research and Action Center, 1985).

Given our estimate of the street-to-shelter ratio and the apparent 1983–5 growth in the number of individuals who were homeless and/or in shelters, we estimate that the homeless population was on the order of 343,000 to 363,000 by 1985, 23 per cent to 30 per cent larger than in 1983.

The weakest part of the estimated growth is the assumed constancy of the street-to-shelter population ratio. It is possible that, given increased shelter capacity, homeless people are spending more time in shelters, which would lead our figures to overstate the growth of the homeless population. On the other hand, however, our data show that the homeless tend to spend more time in the street as their spells of homelessness increase, suggesting that the ratio of street-to-shelter population could rise over time. To see whether these biases seriously mar our picture of increasing homelessness we have examined the number of persons in particular shelters in New York during 'peak' times. In New York City, the 'peak' number of individuals sheltered during the winter of 1985–6 was 47 per cent greater than the 'peak' number sheltered in the winter of 1983–4, whereas the 'average' number sheltered per night increased by just 28 per cent. This pattern is inconsistent with the notion that the street-to-shelter ratio declined on average, for, if the ratio declined, one would expect the increase at peak times to be smaller than at average times since there would be relatively fewer street people to swell the peak. In addition, several cities have reported turning people away from shelters, further indicating that the observed growth of the shelter population is not simply a result of a movement of a fixed homeless population into shelters.

WHO ARE THEY?

What kind of persons end up homeless in America? Does the population of homeless individuals consist largely of 'skid-row' types? The mentally ill? Or does the homeless population include a large number of persons who could reasonably be expected to function in the society?

By including street persons as well as shelter residents in our survey we are able to provide a more representative picture of the homeless than is afforded by standard government reports that are limited to persons in shelters.[9] Moreover, to determine the potential impact of a given characteristic on the chance of being homeless (as opposed to the prevalence of the characteristics among the homeless) we have made use of the following probability formula:

$$P(H/C) = P(C/H)P(H)/P(C) \tag{7.3}$$

where

$P(H/C)$ = probability of being homeless given the characteristic;
$P(C/H)$ = probability of having the characteristic given that one is homeless;
$P(H)$ = probability of homelessness; and
$P(C)$ = probability of having specified characteristic.

From our survey and those of others, we determine $P(C/H)$. While $P(C)$ is taken from various national data sources. We then calculate $P(H/C)P(H)$ which measures the extent to which a characteristic raises/ lowers the chances of being homeless. For example, we see from the third column in Table 7.2 that blacks are more likely to become homeless than the comparison group as they are overrepresented in the population by a factor of 1.96.

As can be seen in Table 7.2, our data and those of other studies give a markedly different picture of homeless individuals than the typical stereotype of a skid-row alcoholic. We find the following:

Table 7.2 Proportion of homeless individuals and relevant total population with specified characteristics

	Relevant comparison		
	Homeless (1)	Population (2)	Ratio (1/2)
Age			
20–29	0.22	0.26	0.85
30–59	0.68	0.51	1.33
60+	0.10	0.23	0.43
Ethnicity			
New York			
Black	0.48	0.25	1.92
Hispanic	0.16	0.20	0.8
Boston			
Black	0.32	0.22	1.45
Hispanic	0.05	0.06	0.83
Education			
% not graduated high school	0.53	0.27	1.9
Family background			
Without at least one parent	0.46	0.15	3.1
With neither real parent	0.15	0.03	5.0
Social pathology			
Percent that ever spent time in jail	0.39		
Percent mentally ill	0.33	<0.02	>15
Substance abuse			
Alcohol abuse	0.29	0.13	2.23
Hard drug abuse	0.14	<0.01	>14
Income			
Some current income (any source)	0.18	0.98	0.18
Receiving either public assistance or SSI or government transfer payments	0.12	0.22	0.55

Sources: The data in this table are ours with the following exceptions: the comparison age data are found in US Bureau of the Census (1986): 24. The ethnicity data for Boston were acquired from information given (by phone call) by the Emergency Shelter Commission in Boston. The education, family and ethnicity information for the comparison group are found in US Bureau of the Census (1969, 1985, 1986). The family background information for the comparison group are for 1968, since that is approximately when a 1986 homeless person would have been in his/her home. The alcohol and drug abuse data for the homeless are taken from *Homelessness in New York State* (1984). The comparison data for alcoholism is taken from US Bureau of the Census (1985), where 13% of the population is reported to consume at least 60 alcoholic drinks per month. The comparison data for income is men aged 25 to 64 and is taken from US Bureau of the Census (1983b). The homeless information for income comes from Goldstein (1984b).

1. The homeless consist largely of men over 30 and below 60 years of age, with an underrepresentation of both the very old and the very young. There are few homeless persons among the aged presumably because of high mortality rates for homeless persons. There are few young homeless persons because most young persons still live in their

parental home. The average age of the homeless is approximately 40.

2. With respect to ethnicity, blacks are overrepresented among the homeless, while Hispanics are underrepresented. As our data show lengths of spells of homelessness to be the same for blacks and whites, homelessness is proportionally greater among blacks than whites.

3. The homeless are far less educated than the population as a whole, with over half having failed to graduate from high school compared to a little over a quarter of the comparison group.

4. The homeless are more prone to substance abuse and mental illness than the population as a whole. A figure that emerges from a wide variety of studies (US Department of Housing and Urban Development, 1984; Chrystal, 1982) is that approximately one in three homeless persons suffers from mental illness. In terms of the comparison group a rough estimate is that less than 2 per cent of the US population is mentally ill, which implies that the mentally ill are about 15 times more likely to become homeless than someone else.

5. The homeless are much more likely to have been raised in a one-parent family than the population as a whole, and are especially likely to have been brought up with neither real parent.

6. The homeless individual is unlikely to receive much if any 'welfare' benefits such as disability insurance, unemployment insurance, etc.

One of the most striking characteristics of the homeless population, which has been neglected in much popular discussion, is the frequency of criminal activity. In our survey, 39 per cent admitted to having spent time in jail, with an average time in jail of two years. Other studies show somewhat larger percentages spending time in jail and report sizeable numbers (13 to 26 per cent) having committed felonies or major crimes (Chrystal, 1982).

The obvious question that arises from these figures is whether crime is not only a 'result' of homelessness, but is also a 'cause' of homelessness. To answer this we asked the homeless about the timing of their periods in jail. Sixty-one per cent of time spent in jail occurred prior to becoming homeless, suggesting that (unsuccessful) crime leads to homelessness. However, the reverse may also occur. Indicative of the presence of crime among the homeless, many of those we interviewed expressed concern that their meager goods might be stolen and that they might be mugged by other homeless persons. 'It's dangerous on the streets' was how one homeless woman expressed the situation.

Finally, an important issue on which our survey provides new insight is whether or not the homeless in the street differ markedly from the homeless in shelters. In terms of age and ethnicity, there are notable differences. Persons living in the street in our survey were nearly a decade older and were much more likely to be white than those living in shelters.

More importantly, we find that the street population tends to be generally 'worse off.' Homeless persons in the street are more prone to substance abuse, spend more time in jail, and appear to be less employable. Whereas 29 per cent of shelter residents in our survey reported themselves unable to work, 44 per cent of the street residents said they were unable to work. Consistent with this, spells of unemployment were longer for the street people.

It is not surprising to find street people to be functionally less competent than persons in shelters, as conditions on the streets are much worse than conditions in the shelters. The more rational homeless person will consequently choose a shelter. In terms of policy this implies that any social assistance program operating through shelters may miss the most vulnerable and helpless of the homeless.

THE HOMELESS FAMILY

According to the New York and Boston figures on which we base Table 7.1, homelessness has increased the most since the HUD report among families. Whereas in the 1984 report of HUD the problems of homeless families were given little separate attention, by 1986 the situation had changed to such an extent that the problems of the homeless family have come to the fore of much policy discussion.

Homeless families differ significantly from homeless individuals. They consist largely of female-headed families. They tend to be predominantly black, with the black overrepresentation among families far exceeding black overrepresentation among homeless individuals. Even in a city like Boston where the majority of homeless individuals are white, the majority of homeless families are black. Moreover, in contrast to homeless individuals who receive little social welfare benefits, the bulk of homeless families obtain regular AFDC payments and food stamps.

By age, the heads of homeless families tend to be young, with half less than 25 years old. They also tend to have less education than otherwise comparable persons and are more likely to have come from female-headed homes themselves. Finally, just as the deterioration of the two-parent family is a major cause of poverty and welfare recipiency, the breakup of the family seems to be a major contributor to family homelessness. Forty per cent of homeless families report that they lost their residence because of family conflict, often involving a situation in which they had doubled up with friends or relatives.

The characteristics that differentiate homeless persons and families from others could, we note, just as easily be a summary of characteristics differentiating those with any social problem from the average. While a certain proportion of the homeless have mental or other behavioral problems that distinguish them from the rest of the poor in America, it is important to recognize that homelessness is endemic among the same groups of people for whom urban poverty, unemployment, living-on-welfare, and crime is also endemic. In this sense homelessness is not a 'bizarre' problem to be studied by itself but rather is part-and-parcel of the overall social problem of low incomes, income inequality, and social pathology in the United States that has gained attention from activists and analysts of all political philosophies.

PERMANENT OR TRANSITORY?

A key issue in understanding homelessness, and developing policies to alleviate the problem, is whether it is a transitory or long-term phenomenon. If it is transitory, the homeless are likely to resume normal life in short order, making temporary shelters an appropriate social remedy for their problem. If, by contrast, it is largely a long-term problem for a sizeable number of persons, a very different set of policies will be needed to deal with the problem.

In its evaluation of lengths of homelessness, HUD concluded that 'for most people who become homeless, their condition is recent and likely to be temporary.'[10] Our analysis indicates that for individual homeless persons HUD's conclusion is, for reasons given below, incorrect. Far from being temporary, homelessness appears to be a long-term state for large numbers. Moreover, as with unemployment and welfare recipiency, if we calculate the proportion of homeless person-days contributed by the long-term homeless we find that the bulk of homeless time is contributed by persons who are homeless for long periods. While family homelessness is of much shorter duration, due in part to public policies to move families out of welfare hotels and shelters, even here lengths of spells are considerably longer than is recognized.

There are four reasons why homelessness is erroneously thought to be a short-run phenomenon. First, most shelters report the amount of time persons spend in that shelter rather than total time spent homeless, suggesting that periods of homelessness are short and episodic. Time spent in particular shelters or places may, in fact, be short, but much of the movement of the homeless is between the street, shelters, detoxication centers, hospitals, and jail rather than from homelessness to normal residences. Second, surveys that report durations of homelessness give the amount of time persons have been homeless up to the survey date, not the amount of time until they leave homelessness. Assuming, as statisticians often do, that one catches persons midway in their spell, one must double the reported times to estimate the likely completed duration of homelessness for those in any survey. Third, most information on the homeless comes from shelter residents, who by our analysis tend to be much better off and much less likely to be homeless over a long period than persons living in the streets. Finally, because the homeless population is a growing one, tabulations of durations at a point in time will give a misleading picture of lengths of spells by showing a disproportionately high number of short beginning spells.

On the other side of the coin, however, is the fact that any survey at a moment in time tends to overrepresent persons with long spells. This is because the likelihood of catching persons homeless differs by the lengths of time they are homeless. For instance, given one homeless person with a spell of one year and one homeless person with a spell of one day, a survey on a random day in the year will 'catch' the former but will miss the latter unless the day happens to be one during which the latter is homeless. While this is not a problem if one is interested in spells of homelessness weighted by their importance (i.e., by length), it does bias estimates of the distribution of *all* spells.

Our effort to deal with these problems takes two forms. First, in contrast to studies done by public welfare agencies, we asked the homeless people not how long they have been in their current state but, rather, 'how long ago was the first day that you ever were homeless?' We then asked them the proportion of time since that data spent on the street, in shelters, and in a normal residence. As 96 per cent of reported time since the first date was spent in the homeless state, we believe our figures give a more accurate picture of the length of homelessness. Second, we calculate a diverse set of statistics to reflect the differing concepts of spell lengths.

Table 7.3 presents the results of our analysis. Line 1 gives the average duration of incomplete spells for persons in our sample, with street persons weighted more heavily to reflect their greater number in the population. The 4.1 years reflects past reported homelessness from inception to date and is thus the 'hardest' number of those in the table.[11] Line 2 adjusts the distribution of incomplete spells to take account of the large number of new beginning spells due to recent growth of homelessness. It represents our estimate of what the duration of homelessness would be if the homeless population had been constant over the period and may thus be viewed as providing a more meaningful indicator of durations of homelessness for a given population. It is nearly 50 per cent larger than the estimated duration which does not take account of this problem. Doubling the figures in line 2 yields an estimate of the 'length-weighted' mean years of homelessness for our sample, that is, the 'average' years homeless weighted so that longer spells count more heavily than shorter spells; this is also the expected mean years of homelessness for the homeless persons in our sample, adjusted for the beginning spells. Finally, we adjusted our data on the distribution of the homeless population by length of time of homelessness to take account of the approximate growth rate of the population, estimating a 'steady-state' distribution and approximate 'escape' rates from homelessness to normal shelter dwellings. On the basis of these calculations, we

Table 7.3 Alternative measures of the year's homeless among individuals

	Years homeless
1 Incomplete duration for persons in our sample	4.1
2 Incomplete duration for persons, corrected for growth of homeless population	6.1
3 Estimated completed duration for persons in our sample (also, the average length of homelessness weighted by its contributions to total time of homelessness)	12.2
4 Estimated mean length of all spells of homelessness, including very short spells	3.5

Sources: Line 1: based on our survey, with an average incomplete duration for street people of 4.7 years and an average incomplete duration for sheltered people of 2.9 years.

Line 2: correction obtained by adjusting the frequency distribution in our survey to take account of growth from 1979 to 1985 when homelessness spurted and of average population growth for earlier period. For the 1979–85 rate of growth, we took a weighted average of the annual growth rates for New York and Boston, as reported in Table 7.1. Our specific adjustment was to multiply the frequency 1 to 2 years by 1.115, 2 to 3 years by $(1.115)^2$, etc. Starting at 7 to 8 years, we apply the average population growth rate of 1.014. Therefore, the 8-to-9 years percentage would be multiplied by $(1.115)^6 (1.014)^2$. The corrected frequency was multiplied by the midpoint of the duration (i.e. 0.5, 1.5, 2.5, etc.), the numbers summed, and divided by the sum of the percentages. The numbers were calculated separately for street and shelter populations with the results of 7.2 (street) and 3.7 (shelter), then averaged to yield the figure in the text.

Line 3: multiplied by 2 on the hypothesis that 'corrected' for growth we are catching people midway in their homelessness spell.

Line 4: estimated by calculating transition probabilities from the adjusted frequency distribution of spells and then simply taking the mean duration. The calculation was performed separately for persons in shelters and those on the street, and then weighted. We experimented with various ways of smoothing the frequency distributions to obtain transition probabilities and obtained figures like those in the table, so that the particular method, while crude, does not critically determine the results.

estimate that the 'typical' *spell* of homelessness (including spells of persons not in our survey because they are especially short) is 3.5 years. This number is far below other estimates, because our data suggest that there are many very short homeless spells: roughly one-third of individuals who enter homelessness appear to exit within half a year.

By contrast, for families, comparable calculations yield estimates of homelessness closer to the HUD description: incomplete spells of homelessness average about one year. The 'long-term' nature of the problem here is not one of relatively permanent homelessness of individuals, but rather of the continued influx of new families into the homeless state.

WHY HOMELESSNESS IN AMERICA TODAY?

What could possibly underlie the sudden growth of homelessness in America? The most commonly cited cause, deinstitutionalization of mental patients, cannot explain the 1980s growth of homelessness for the simple reason that deinstitutionalization occurred for the most part in the 1960s. Indeed, deinstitutionalization began in the late 1950s to early 1960s with the inception of tranquilizing drugs, and was given particular impetus by the Community Mental Health Center Act of 1963. From 1955 to 1982 the average number of persons in psychiatric hospitals on a given night fell from 558,922 to 125,200 (Alter, 1984: 25). While some persons are, of course, let out of mental hospitals today, they do not constitute a large proportion of the homeless population. A New York study found that just 7 per cent of the homeless came *directly* from mental hospitals (*Homelessness in New York State*, 1984). Our survey found just 1 per cent in that circumstance.

While deinstitutionalization cannot, therefore, be cited as a significant direct cause of homelessness, it did create a population of 'noninstitutionalized' persons whose psychological and economic position made them particularly prone to fall into homelessness, given adverse circumstances. To evaluate the contribution of noninstitutionalization to the current homeless problem, we have estimated the number of persons who might have been institutionalized in the 1980s had we institutionalized persons with mental problems at 1955 rates. Our estimate shows that about 657,000 fewer patients were institutionalized in 1982 than would have been at 1955 rates of institutionalization. Assuming that about one-third of the homeless are mentally ill, we find that roughly 14 per cent of those who would have been institutionalized have ended up homeless.[12] That failure to institutionalize has contributed to homelessness should not, however, be taken to imply that deinstitutionalization itself has failed. By our estimates, 86 per cent of persons who might have been institutionalized are not homeless and, at least by that minimal criterion, are successfully integrated into society. Perhaps if Community Health Centers had been developed in the numbers envisaged in the 1963 Act – 2,000 were planned, whereas there were only 717 built by 1980 – the negative effects of the movement on the problem of homelessness would have been largely avoided.

If noninstitutionalization is not the primary cause of the rise in homelessness in the United States, what is? Our analysis highlights two sets of factors: the growing incidence of social characteristics that may be causally related to homelessness, and changes in the housing market that make it increasingly difficult for the poor to rent space.

CHANGING SOCIAL CHARACTERISTICS

By comparing the frequency of personal and social characteristics between the homeless and comparison populations, as in Table 7.2, we can make inferences about the impact of these characteristics on the likelihood an individual will be homeless. Moreover, to the extent that a particular characteristic that raises the probability of homelessness has increased over time, we can infer that it has contributed to the rising problem.

The two main characteristics which, by this line of reasoning, have increased homelessness are the growing number of female-headed homes and increased substance abuse. Our calculations suggest that these factors have outweighed the main factor working in the opposite direction – rising education – so that on net the changing characteristics of the population have made the homeless problem worse.

Since social characteristics change gradually, however, it is clear that such changes could not by themselves have caused the sudden increase in homelessness in the 1980s. They are best thought of as creating a 'risk' population rather than increasing homelessness per se.

The one factor that did, of course, worsen in the early 1980s and undoubtedly did contribute significantly to the burst of homelessness is the recession-related increase in the number of persons with exceptionally low incomes. In 1979, 11.8 per cent of men 18 and over in the Current Population Survey had incomes below $3,000 or were without incomes. In 1983, 16.2 per cent had incomes that were below $4,000 (approximately $3,000 in 1979 prices, given inflation) or were without incomes (US Bureau of the Census, 1983b). As persons with low income are especially likely to end up homeless, this increase certainly contributed to the 1979–83 growth of homelessness. The recession cannot, however, be the prime factor at work, for if it were, homelessness would have fallen rather than risen from 1983 to 1985. It is, in our view, the concordance of increased poverty and income inequality with housing market developments deleterious to the poor that best explains why the at-risk population suffered homelessness in the period.

HOUSING MARKET DEVELOPMENTS

An obvious place to look for causes of homelessness is in the market for housing – in particular, at potential short-run or long-run imbalances between the availability of low-rent units and the income of those at the bottom of the income distribution. Did rents rise and the stock of low-rent housing decline relative to the number of persons and families in poverty in the early 1980s?

The available evidence suggests that it did. Consider first the pattern of rent increases during the 1979–83 period. According to the Federal Government's housing survey, median rents in the United States increased from $217 to $315 from 1979 to 1983 — a 45 per cent increase over four years, or 6 per cent with an adjustment for inflation (US Bureau of the Census, 1979, 1983a). By comparison, from 1970 to 1979 median rents did not increase at all in real terms. In part, higher median rents represent increased rents for units of a given quality; in part, they represent changes in the distribution of the stock of rental units toward higher-quality units. Both changes create great problems for the poor to obtain housing when the number of the poor increases, as it did in the 1979–83 period.

To get a better fix on the potential imbalance in the housing market between low-income persons and the supply of low-rent units, we compare in Table 7.4 the changing numbers of persons and families below the poverty line with the supply of rental units below $200 per month (in 1979 dollars). The figures show clearly that at the same time the number of persons and families below poverty increased, the number of low-rent housing units in central cities fell sharply, even though the number of low-rent units in the country as a whole held roughly stable. By contrast, in the previous decade, the number in poverty fell at about the same rate as did the number of low-rent units (defined in constant dollars). (See US Bureau of the Census, *Current Population Reports*, 'Consumer income,' Series P-60, for poverty figures and US Bureau of the Census, 'Annual housing survey', for number of low-rent units.)

Underlying the decline in low-rent units are several important social developments, mostly in central cities: the movement of higher-income and middle-class people back to some cities, i.e., 'gentrification' (which is important in Boston and some other booming northeastern cities); the growth of condominiums (encouraged by the mortgage interest deduction in the federal income tax code and, in several cities, by rent control); and increasing land prices, which make it less profitable to develop low-income housing. While one could imagine a housing market where developers would respond to these changes and to the increased number of poor persons by producing lower-quality low-rent units, building codes and

Table 7.4 Number of poor families and low-rent units in the housing market, 1979–83

	1979	1983	% Δ
Families (in millions)			
Families below poverty	5.3	7.7	45%
Persons in families below poverty	20.0	28.0	40%
Unattached adults below poverty	5.7	6.9	21%
Rental units (in millions)			
Number of rental units <$200 (constant US dollars)			
US total	10.7	10.7	0.1%
Central city	5.3	5.0	−5.4%
Single room rental units	0.98	0.97	−0.9%

Sources: Tabulated from US Bureau of the Census, *US Statistical Abstract*, 1986; *Annual Housing Survey*, Current Housing Reports, Part A, 1979, 1983.

other regulations put a minimum cost beneath construction of low-rent dwellings. In New York, the city offered a bonus of some $6,000 to landlords for renting to homeless families for two years but found that relatively few landlord took advantage of the bonus. One reason is that the cost of bringing apartments up to City building-code standards may exceed that amount. In 1986 the city raised the bonus to $9,700 to see if that would encourage landlords to accommodate the homeless. If it requires nearly $10,000 extra to make it worthwhile for landlords of existing buildings to house homeless families, it is no wonder that builders do not find it profitable to construct low-rent units in sufficient numbers to alleviate the imbalance.

The nature of the housing problem faced by currently homeless people does, of course, differ among different types of persons. For the most dysfunctional of the homeless, the problem is not so much one of housing cost as inability to earn even a modicum of pay. Aside from small sums obtained by panhandling, most homeless persons in the street have essentially no income; many have not worked for years and are, on the face of it, incapable of working without extended help; in addition, they claim few of the welfare benefits that might enable them to rent space in single room-only places, were such rooms available. Those who are mentally ill, chronic substance abusers, and generally in poor physical and mental health are in many cases functionally incapable of demanding and competing for housing in the free market.

For the bulk of the homeless, who have greater potential for finding housing themselves, and for homeless families that receive welfare payments, the declining availability of low-rent units and increases in rent relative to incomes appears to be a major cause of their problem. In Boston, where the housing market is particularly tight, the newspapers report the existence of shelter residents who are employed but cannot find or afford housing, at least in the short run.

While we are loath to generalize from a single area, the pattern of rapidly rising land values, rents, and housing market problems for the poor in Massachusetts raises the possibility that future economic progress, including full employment of the type enjoyed in Massachusetts, may exacerbate rather than alleviate the housing problems of the poor. One can easily devise a scenario in which economic growth raises demand for land, inducing landlords to develop higher-quality properties, pricing out of the market those whose incomes do not rise with the rate of growth.

In addition to the broad supply and demand patterns in the housing market, however, other factors are likely to make it difficult for the private market to resolve the homelessness problem. For one, once a person is homeless, landlords are likely to view him or her as a higher-risk tenant than other persons. The probability that someone who has been homeless will pay rent regularly may reasonably be viewed as lower than for others.

Moreover, while only a minority of the homeless may suffer from serious behavioral problems that may lead them to damage units or engage in behavior that would upset other tenants, the behavior of even a small number can raise the 'expected' costs of renting to any member of the group.

EFFORTS TO DEAL WITH HOMELESSNESS

Homelessness is an issue that arouses considerable public concern, with the result that a wide variety of programs – often of a rather innovative nature – have developed in both the public and private sectors to help the homeless.

The first and foremost need has been, of course, to develop shelters so that the homeless have an alternative to the street. The federal government's Emergency Food and Shelter Program (EFSP), initiated by Congress in 1983, disbursed 210 million dollars in three phases to deal with the problem. Part of the money went to the states and part was distributed through a national board made up largely of charitable organizations. Assessing the operation of the program, the Urban Institute concluded that 'the EFSP met a great need for emergency food and shelter services,' with the private charitable part disbursing funds to the needy more quickly than the states (Urban Institute, 1985). At the state and local level, many areas have developed extensive shelter systems where none had previously existed. In Massachusetts, for example, the number of publicly-funded shelters increased from two in 1982 to 29 in 1986. Private organizations have also made significant efforts to raise money to aid the homeless, ranging from local church and community efforts to the massive 'Hands Across America' fund-raising effort on 25 May 1986. Our observation is that the smaller privately-run shelters tend to be better accommodations for the homeless than the larger, impersonal publicly-run shelters.

While provision of beds for the homeless is a necessary step in dealing with the problem, it is not adequate. As our analysis indicates, the bulk of homelessness arises from a relatively long-term homeless population, which, by definition, is unlikely to return quickly to normal living conditions. Additional services are needed to help these people attain self-sufficiency, an attempt some shelters have begun to make. In addition, for the most dysfunctional and helpless of the homeless, who live in the streets, outreach programs are necessary.

Moreover, to the extent that the private housing market fails, for whatever reason, to provide additional low rent units in the future, arresting the growth of homelessness and reducing numbers will require either rent subsidies, additional public housing, or some other form of intervention in the housing market of a permanent rather than emergency form.

Even with effective programs, however, one should not expect a sudden, sharp decline in homelessness. While evidence that the number of homeless persons is smaller than the 1 per cent bandied in the press makes the problem seem more manageable, our finding that homelessness is a long-term state with causes going far beyond the economic recession suggests that a quick solution is unlikely in the near future. Indeed, if ongoing changes in the distribution of income, in various social problems and pathologies, and in the housing market continue into the future, the 'at-risk' population is likely to grow rather than to decline. And one unhappy lesson we have learned from past efforts to resolve social problems is that while problems can arise quickly, cures often take longer to find and implement.

NOTES

1. Media articles on the homeless increased at an extraordinary rate in the early 1980s. In 1980 there were 13 articles listed in the indexes of *The New York Times, Los Angeles Times*, and *Washington Post*; in 1985, there were 428 articles listed in the three indexes.
2. The 1984 Hearings on the Homeless and on the HUD Report on Homelessness show the extent of controversy over the issue (Subcommittee on Housing and Community Development, 1984; US Department of Housing and Urban Development, 1984).
3. The source of the 1 per cent or 2.2 million persons number is the Community for Creative Non Violence (Hombs and Snyder, 1982).
4. The HUD report, as it has come to be known, has been criticized widely by activists for the homeless since it was released in 1984.
5. The HUD figures show an average street-to-shelter ratio of 1.78:1 (p. 17 of their report). Because their ratio came from actual street counts, where 'counters' are bound to miss at least some street dwellers, one should expect the actual ratio to be slightly higher, as our 2.23 is. A more recent Nashville study found a street/shelter ratio of less than 1, also suggesting that our 2.23 is not missing a large number of those in the West who never use the shelters (Wiegand, 1985: 34–7). While it is possible that our survey also missed an especially hard-to-get population, which potentially spends even less time in shelters than the 'street' people we surveyed, our street-to-shelter ratio would not increase greatly unless these persons were exceptionally numerous and spent virtually no time in shelters, thereby greatly altering our estimate of $P(S_t/S_{t-1})$. For example, if persons missed in our street count were as numerous as those in our survey, and if they spent half as much time in shelters as those in the survey, $P(S_t/S_{t-1})$ would be 0.15 instead of 0.20. This would yield a homeless population to shelter population of 4.0 rather than 3.23, raising the estimated size of the population by 24 per cent.
6. The HUD distribution of homeless (US Department of Housing and Urban Development, 1984: 20) is: South, 24 per cent; North Central, 22 per cent; North East, 24 per cent; West, 31 per cent. The 1982–6 distribution of surplus foods under the Temporary Emergency Food Distribution Program is: South, 30 per cent; North Central, 22 per cent; North East, 24 per cent; West, 24 per

cent (US Department of Agriculture, 1986). While the distribution of surplus foods shows a higher proportion of federal dollars in the South than does the distribution of the homeless, it shows a compensatory lower proportion of federal food spending in the West.

7. HUD's description of families not included in their 1983 study is sufficiently vague that we contacted the survey organization, which reported that families in 'welfare hotels' may not have been included because these facilities are not regarded as part of the regular shelter system. It seems, however, that in most cities in the United States (except New York) very few families were in long-term facilities or hotels in 1983. The types of shelters for families also vary greatly from city to city. Some examples:

> *New York*: Opened its first homeless shelter in 1983. Therefore, at this time, virtually all families were in long-term facilities that very likely were not counted by HUD. Because of this seeming omission, we have added all 10,500 individuals in homeless families to HUD's figure.
> *Boston*: In 1983, virtually no homeless families stayed in homeless hotels as the law did not permit it. By 1986, 78 homeless families had been moved to ˌ long-term facilities or homeless motels.
> *Philadelphia*: The City Department of Human Resources reports that in 1983, all homeless families were in shelters; therefore, they were likely to have been included by HUD.
> *Houston*: Most families, according to the United Way, stayed in shelters or missions and were likely to have been counted by HUD.
> *Washington, DC*: The Department of Human Services claims that almost all of the homeless families in 1983 stayed in long-term facilities and were likely to have been missed by HUD. A small percentage in the private sector may have been counted.

Note that omission of persons in welfare hotels is not a problem in the more subjective 'extrapolation' methods used by HUD.

8. Other cities do not have exact figures for family growth; however, sources we contacted in Washington, DC, Chicago, Los Angeles and Houston agree that the number of homeless families has grown more rapidly than the number of homeless individuals.

9. The statistics for our survey are based on a weighted average for persons in shelters and in the street. We have weighted the figures in order to get a picture of the typical homeless individual. The weights (0.39, shelter: 0.61, street) were chosen on the basis of our estimate of the distribution of the population between the two places.

10. We note that the HUD figures on homelessness for New York show longer spells for New York and Boston than for other cities (US Department of Housing and Urban Development, 1984: 29). Our disagreement with HUD is based not on the spells reported for cities but on the conceptual grounds, namely, that incomplete spells in a growing population are not the proper measure of lengths of time spent homeless.

11. To check on the plausibility of our estimates we have compared the incomplete durations in our survey with those reported elsewhere and find no reason to believe ours are overstated. As durations reported elsewhere are limited to shelter populations, we limit comparisons to that subset of our sample. A calculated mean duration of sheltered residents in a recent Boston Survey show an incomplete spell of 2.1 years compared with 2.9 for the similar group in our survey. Our source for Boston comes from a study of 785

sheltered individuals (Emergency Shelter Commission, 1986: Table 1). In contrast, HUD's study reports shorter spells of homelessness for sheltered residents. We believe that two reasons account for this discrepancy. First, their study was conducted in 1983 – a time closer to the period usually considered to be the beginning of the rise of homelessness. In using durations shortly after the 'homeless increase', HUD is likely to catch a shorter-term homeless population. Second, we calculated duration beginning with the 'first time that a person was homeless'. For instance, if a person had been homeless for 5 years, then found a home for 2 months, and then became homeless for another 4 months, we did not count only the recent spell of homelessness of 4 months but rather the entire 5½ years. We believe that only counting the most recent spell seriously underestimates the duration of homelessness as people tend to bounce in and out of homelessness and, according to our survey, only spend 4 per cent of their total time since becoming homeless in a home of any sort.

12. The number of patients in institutions in 1955 was 558,922; with population growth of 40 per cent between 1955 and 1982, the number would have increased to 782,491 with no change in policies. However, only 125,200 patients were institutionalized in 1982, leaving a gap of 657,291 – our estimate of the additional persons who would have been institutionalized at 1955 rates.

Assuming that approximately one-third of the 279,000 (or 93,000) homeless are mentally ill (and would be in institutions), we find a failure rate of deinstitutionalization of 93,000/657,291 or 14 per cent. This number represents the number not institutionalized that ended up homeless.

BIBLIOGRAPHY

Alter, J., et al., 'Homeless in America', *Newsweek* (January 1984).

Burbridge, L. C., et al., 'An evaluation of the emergency food and shelter program: national, regional, and state level analysis', *The Urban Institute* (November 1984).

Burbridge, L. C., et al., 'Local boards and intermediaries', *The Urban Institute* (January 1985).

Burt, M. R., and Burbridge, L. C., 'Evaluation of the emergency food and shelter program', *The Urban Institute* (January 1985).

Citizen's Committee for Children of New York, '7000 homeless children: the crisis continues' (October 1984).

City of Boston Emergency Shelter Commission, 'Emergency Shelter Commission: "The October Project" seeing the obvious' (October 1983).

Committee on Government Operations, 'The federal response to the homeless crisis', Third Report (18 April 1985).

Conference of Mayors, *Report on the Homeless* (Washington DC: 1986).

Chrystal, S., 'Chronic and situational dependency: long-term residents in a shelter for men', *Human Resources Administration of the City of New York* (May 1982).

Chrystal, S., and Goldstein, M., 'Correlates of shelter utilization: one day study', *Human Resources Administration of the City of New York* (August 1984a).

Chrystal, S., and Goldstein, M., 'Homeless in New York City shelters', *Human Resources Administration of the City of New York* (May 1984b).

Dietz, S., Light, H., and Marker, D., *Survey of Shelters for the Homeless* (Washington, DC: US Department of Housing and Urban Development, Office of Policy Development and Research, April 1984).

Emergency Shelter Commission and United Community Planning Corporation, 'Boston's homeless: taking the next step' (April, 1986).

Executive Office of Human Services, *Massachusetts Report on Homelessness* (Boston: 1985), p. 19.

Federal Task Force on the Homeless, *Regional Meetings Briefing Book* (March 1985).

Food Research and Action Center, *Bitter Harvest II: A Status Report on the Need for Emergency Food Assistance in America* (December 1985).

Hombs, M. E., and Snyder, M., *Homelessness in America, A Forced March to Nowhere* (Community for Creative Non-Violence, 1982).

Homelessness in New York State, A Report to the Governor (Albany, NY: 1984).

Massachusetts Report on Homelessness (Boston: Executive Office of Human Services, 1985).

Planning Committee of the Emergency Shelter Commission, 'Housing the homeless: a report on Boston's homeless adults and families' (Boston: December 1985).

Reiners, E., 'Homelessness: the explosion of media coverage on the homeless' (May 1986).

Salant, S. W., 'Search theory and duration data: a theory of sorts', *Quarterly Journal of Economics* (February 1987), pp. 39–58.

Society for Promotion of Area Resource Centres, 'We, the invisible: a census of pavement dwellers' (1985).

Stone, L., et al., 'Heartbreak hotels', *The Village Voice* (1 April 1986).

Subcommittee on Housing and Community Development of the Committee on Banking, Finance and Urban Affairs, House of Representatives, 98th Congress, Second Session, *Homeless in America II* (Washington, DC: January 1984).

Sumariwalla, R. D., and Woodside, C., 'An internal assessment of impact of United Way's role and participation in the programs on the United Way System', *United Way Institute* (May 1985).

Surber, M., et al., 'An evaluation of the emergency food and shelter program: direct service providers' (Washington, DC: 1985).

Urban Institute, 'Evaluation of the emergency food and shelter program', Survey, Conclusions and Recommendations (Washington, DC: 1985).

US Bureau of the Census, *Statistical Abstract of the United States* (Washington, DC: 1969).

US Bureau of the Census, *Current Housing Reports: Annual Housing Survey*, Part A (Washington, DC: 1979).

US Bureau of the Census, *Current Housing Reports: Annual Housing Survey* (Washington, DC: 1983a).

US Bureau of the Census, *Current Population Reports*, Consumer Income Series P-60 (Washington, DC: 1983b).

US Bureau of the Census, *Statistical Abstract of the United States* (Washington, DC: 1985).

US Bureau of the Census, *Statistical Abstract of the United States* (Washington, DC: 1986).

US Department of Agriculture, *Food and Nutrition Survey, Title 2 Commodities* (Washington, DC: 1986).

US Department of Health and Human Services, *Helping the Homeless, A Resource Guide* (Washington, DC: Summer 1984).

US Department of Housing and Urban Development, *A Report for the Secretary on the Homeless and Emergency Shelters* (Washington, DC: Office of Policy

Development and Research 1984).

Wickendon, D., 'Abandoned Americans', *The New Republic* (18 March 1985).

Wiegand, R. B., 'Counting the homeless', *American Demographics* (December 1985), 7, pp. 34–7.

PART III

MARKETS UNDER TRADE UNIONISM

I wrote my dissertation with John Dunlop, the master of institutional knowledge and creator of union maximizing models, and later studied with Gregg Lewis, predominant analyst of union wage differentials. Despite, or perhaps because of, this, I eschewed studying unions for the longest time. The field was divided between institutional case studies in the style of Dunlop and econometric wage studies of the Lewis School, and I could see no way to cut through this division. Then I was asked to deliver a paper on the relevance of my then-Harvard colleague Albert Hirschman's *Exit, Voice, and Loyalty* theory to labor markets (Chapter 8). While Hirschman paid little attention to labor in the book, his exit-voice dichotomy suggested to me a different way of looking at unionism: as the institution of voice in the market; and a series of empirical investigations of the theory, starting with the exit-voice tradeoff on which the theory hinged. So off I went and looked. And found massive union effects on quit rates and job tenure that supported the fundamental ideas of the theory (Chapter 9); and additional effects on the fringe share of compensation and on the dispersion of earnings readily explicable or consistent with it (Chapter 10).

Some reacted to these papers with enthusiasm: of course, unions did more than alter wages; of course, they had numerous beneficial effects. Others were critical because the Hirschman theory diverged from straight neo-classical analysis, and they knew that anything that diverged had to be wrong. But what was it – sample selection? unmeasured labor quality? simultaneity? hidden variables? One seminar hotshot proposed that unionism was associated with lower quit rates not because of the exit-voice tradeoff, but because union workers had low alternative wages: they were so incompetent they could not get a decent job elsewhere (the invisible hand in the guise of the unmeasured variable, being invisible, can explain anything). When several months later the same critic told me that he knew the real reason for the finding that unionized workplaces were more productive than nonunionized workplaces: namely that union workers were innately more competent than nonunion workers – they had to be since they received higher wages – it became clear that what was needed was a book that put together all of the results on unionism from the 'Harvard school'. Critics can take potshots at a single article, but not at the collage of evidence that constitutes a book. Chapter 10 gives the clearest summary of the findings of *What Do Unions Do?* for what unions do to the US economy.

BIBLIOGRAPHY

Freeman, R., and Medoff, J., *What Do Unions Do?* (New York: Basic Books, 1984).
Hirschman, A., *Exit, Voice and Loyalty* (Cambridge, MA: Harvard University Press, 1970).

8 · INDIVIDUAL MOBILITY AND UNION VOICE IN THE LABOR MARKET

Standard economic analysis of the impact of trade unions on the labor market is straightforward: unions are monopolistic organizations that raise wages and create inefficiency in resource allocation. Industrial relations experts tell a more complex story, stressing the diverse effect of unions on work rules, managerial decision-making, and 'virtually every aspect' of the activity of enterprises. To what extent do the nonwage effects of collective bargaining make the monopoly model incomplete or misleading? Do unions perform economically significant functions beyond altering wage rates?

This chapter examines the nonwage effects of trade unions in the context of the 'exit–voice' model of the social system developed by Hirschman (1970). Unions are treated as the institution of collective voice in the job market; voluntary quits as the expression of exit. Comparisons are made between the free market quit and union voice mechanisms for transmitting worker desires for conditions of employment, compensation packages, and rules of the workplace to employers; some empirical implications of the analysis are drawn and preliminary empirical findings described.

EMPLOYMENT RELATIONS AND CONDITIONS OF WORK

What makes the exit-voice framework a potentially fruitful way of looking at trade unions are 'the peculiarities of the employment contract . . . which distinguish it from other kinds of contracts' (Simon, 1957, p. 183). In a world of uncertainty, imperfect information, and transactions costs, employment involves an authority relation in which workers sell 'labor power' to enterprises for extended periods of time. As Ronald Coase (1952) puts it, 'the contract is one whereby the factor (labor) for a certain remuneration . . . agrees to obey the directions of an entrepreneur *with certain limits*' (pp. 336–7). Because of on-the-job skills specific to enterprises (a learning curve phenomenon) and the cost of mobility and turnover, there are gains to be had from regular employment, a continuing relation between firms and much of their workforce, in which allocative and remunerative decisions are not directly determined by the price mechanism.[1] Because workers care about nonpecuniary conditions of employment and rules of the workplace, and because different conditions, rules, and methods of organization have different costs, the labor contract tends to be complex and multidimensional, involving numerous issues beyond wages, including the 'social relations of production' (Hicks, 1973, pp. 317–18). Because workers have some control over their own activities and can affect the productivity of others, particularly in 'team' settings where monitoring of individuals is expensive, their attitudes or morale are potentially important inputs into the production process.

The complex, multidimensional and continuing nature of the employment relation creates a substantial information problem in the job market (Williamson, Wachter and Harris, 1975). Within firms, prices convey only crude information about preferences and costs. In the external market, workers and employers must appraise diverse conditions, rules, and compensation packages across enterprises. Over time technological changes continually alter the structure of the workplace and jobs while changes in real income lead workers to demand new conditions of employment and methods of compensation. Firms or organizations have continual need for information from workers not only as Hirschman (1970) stresses because of decline or decay but because of changes in opportunities and efficient modes of behavior.

From the perspective of the exit-voice framework information about conditions and preferences can be provided by: free market 'exit', consisting of quits and related behavior and/or by 'voice' consisting of the collective bargaining system by which workers elect union leaders to represent them in bargaining. Each mechanism has certain strengths and weaknesses, which must enter any welfare economics calculation. Each is, from the perspective of positive economics, likely to produce different market outcomes in the various aspects of the labor contract.

QUITS AS AN INFORMATION SYSTEM

Worker control of their own effort in workplaces creates several forms of 'exit-behavior': quitting, rejecting a job offer; absenteeism, the partial withdrawal of labor time; reduction of work effort in the form of malingering and slack or in extreme cases 'quiet sabotage.' Strikes, which involve temporary collective exit, are best viewed as a tool of voice since they involve expression of demands by union or union-like group organizations.

Employers can learn about worker preferences and the causes of discontent from individual quits either inferentially by linking different levels of exit to different or changing characteristics of the employment relation in what amounts to hedonic price type calculations or through direct questioning, 'exit interviews', of those who quit or make related decisions.

The amount of information provided by either channel is, unfortunately, likely to be small relative to the costs of processing the data. Inferring reasons for discontent from 'abnormally' high quits requires specification of underlying multi-dimensional characteristics of workplaces; a reasonably large sample; and sufficient variation in conditions or in changes in conditions to permit the assignement of causality. Inferences about the preferences of workers who quit may, because of 'selectivity bias', yield incorrect information about average evaluations or the evaluations of future potential quitters. The wider the variation in tastes among workers due to differences in preferences and position in the workplace (especially seniority) and the greater the different modes of expressing exit (the young quit, while older employees choose less drastic actions), the more difficult will the inferential process be. If all persons had the same tastes, introspection by managers or foremen would yield answers at no cost.

Exit interviews run into a different dificulty – that of motivating the worker who leaves to detail workplace problems. There is no gain to quitters from providing management with desired information about dissatisfaction, and there are possible losses via bad references – retaliation for conveying bad news. As a result, the leading personnel management text reports that 'it is extremely difficult to get reliable information by means of exit interviews' (Meyers and Pigors, 1973, p. 222). The information content in other forms of exit behavior will be even smaller. A worker guilty of absenteeism for reasons of discontent with work relations will hide the reasons for fear of being fired, while malingering or quiet sabotage are by their nature covert activities.

Finally, whatever information the quit mechanism provides about current conditions of work, it provides much less about changes in conditions and, more importantly, about the trade-offs workers are willing to make in wages or other conditions for desired improvements; especially when the changes involve more than marginal adjustments in the workplace. Innovations in the labor contract can be appraised only by potentially costly trial and error experimentation: changing conditions or compensation and observing outcomes.

Despite the high noise to signal ratio in labor market quits, the mechanism has desirable properties. Quit behavior depends solely on individual free market 'marginal decisions' and does not require collective organizations like unions. Such behavior has well-known efficiency properties. Over time, some employers will extract the signal from the noise in quits or by trial and error find the 'optimal' labor contract and come to dominate production or be imitated by competitors.

Certain features of the quit mechanism suggest, however, that there may be some divergence from optimum for extended periods of time. Since workers who leave an enterprise do not benefit from the improvement in conditions that may result, the extent of quitting to convey information may be suboptimal. That is when quits are effective in altering work conditions, the irreversibility of the decision provides too little incentive for workers to leave. Even if the level of quitting were optimal, however, the possibility that quitters differ in their evaluation of conditions from other workers (notably older or specifically trained persons who are unlikely to quit and whose position in the firm gives them a different set of interests) makes reliance on quits potentially misleading. Other forms of exit behavior must also be evaluated. In recessions or declining markets, moreover, quits will be ineffective as a mode of workers expressing preferences and obtaining desired changes.

Hirschman's analysis suggests other malfunctioning. Consider the situation in which all employers offer the same work conditions and where workers quit particular enterprises in the hope of attaining better conditions but in fact cannot do so. Each firm has a constant pool of applicants for jobs and a constant quit rate; no information is conveyed about what to change and there are no advantages in profitability. More generally, the same result would occur if the firms had different but similarly undesirable work conditions. Workers disliking bad condition A in firm A would move to firm B where they would find bad condition B and so forth. In this musical chairs equilibrium, quits are ineffective and excessive, at least until 'random mutations' by enterprises produce a better wage-benefits-conditions package, so that quits differ substantially among employers. As a result there will be a long period of adjustment to equilibrium.

From the perspective of workers, the information flow is especially likely to be faulty with respect to aspects of jobs, ranging from treatment by supervisors and coworkers to actual (as opposed to nominal) work responsibilities to evaluations of hazard (Viscusi, 1979), which cannot be calculated without actually accepting employment. Under the quit system, each worker, would, say, learn about the bad qualities of a job only after a trial period of work and quit. If all workers knew about the job, no one would apply (without larger compensating differentials), but the information each gains is lost.

The question is not, however, whether individual mobility ultimately provides enough information to attain something akin to the optimal labor contract in the long run but rather how it does relative to the alternative institutional mechanism of voice, to whose operation I turn next.

COLLECTIVE VOICE BY TRADE UNIONISM

The institution of voice in the labor market is trade unionism and collective bargaining. There are several reasons why collective rather than individual activity is necessary for voice to be effective within firms. First, the authority relation makes it difficult for individuals to express discontent due to the danger of being fired – it is clearly easier to retaliate against a single worker than the entire workforce. Even with unionization, however, some protection of voice is needed, particularly for activists, as is recognized in the Wagner Act, which makes it an unfair labor practice to fire or otherwise discriminate against persons for trade union activity. Second, the communal nature of work conditions and rules which apply to all workers in the establishment creates a public goods problem of preference relation. Individuals cannot bargain over plant-wide conditions nor trade wages for fringes when there are sizeable set up costs. They will not have the incentive to reveal their preferences when the activity of others may produce the public goods at no cost to them. Elicitation of preferences and determination of acceptable bargaining packages are one of the major tasks of trade unions and critical components in the operation of successful collective bargaining systems. Third, because of the regularity of employment, there is a need to 'police' or monitor contracts and thus for a collective agency specializing in information about the contract and in representation of workers. The ubiquity of grievance systems (found in 96 per cent of contracts) or grievance and arbitration (93 per cent) reflects the importance of contract interpretation in the operation of collective voice (US Department of Labor, 1972).

The major advantages of unionization are that it provides: a direct channel of communication between workers and management; an alternative mode of expressing discontent than quitting, with consequent reductions in turnover costs and increases in specific training and work conditions; and social relations of production which can mitigate the problems associated with the authority relation in firms.

Union voice proffers very different information about workers' preferences than individual mobility – specific facts about areas of discontent and actual tradeoff possibilities (albeit masked by negotiating strategies). It creates an institutional mechanism for innovation in labor contracts and what may be termed a 'new market' for labor contracts.[2] It focuses managerial attention and effort on labor issues on a regular basis, alerting firms to problems fairly continually rather than by sudden sharp outbursts of discontent. In large enterprises, union voice provides central management with information about local conditions and operations that is likely to differ greatly from that obtained from the organizational hierarchy.

By providing a mode of expressing discontent beyond exiting, direct information about worker desires and certain preferred work conditions that cannot be readily offered by nonunion establishments, union voice can be expected to reduce quit rates, absenteeism and related exit behavior. In the exit-voice model, there is *ceteris paribus*, a reasonably well-defined and economically significant tradeoff between the two mechanisms. The reduction in quits will reduce labor turnover and training costs and increase firm-specific investments in human capital and possibly have efficiency gains.[3]

One desirable nonpecuniary condition of work, an industrial jurisprudence system with formal grievance, arbitration and related protection against managerial authority in establishments, may be 'produced' only by unionization or some related mechanism. The essence of industrial jurisprudence is the dilution of the power of the foremen and other supervisors, which would presumably be difficult to attain in nonunion establishments where management has the 'last word.' Desire for such rules and procedures implies that union voice enters as a direct argument in utility functions (suggesting that in the absence of monopoly wage gains, workers would take lower pay for collective bargaining) and by affecting morale and the social relations in the firm, possibly in the production function as well.

On the negative side, the major disadvantage of union voice is that, as the standard monopoly model stresses, it creates monopoly power in the job market and wages above and employment below competitive levels. There are other costs to unionization as well: government, management, and workers invest considerable resources in bargaining which might have been spent on direct production; the productivity of the workforce may be reduced by 'featherbedding' (one possible exercise of monopoly power which would not show up in wages *per se*). Some work rules, like closed shops, may be 'inequitable' to some workers; and more generally as a 'political organization' unions may not reflect the desires of all members in a reasonable or 'fair' manner.

Accepting the costs of collective bargaining, the normative question is whether these costs exceed the benefits due to reduction in exit behavior, improved flow of information, and provision of protection against managerial authority. There is, in our analysis, a tradeoff: by providing information and a mechanism for potentially complex bargaining among workers and between workers and management that is more efficient than quits, collective bargaining is likely to yield a better mix among wages, work conditions, rules of the workplace and a reduction in turnover costs and increased firm-specific human capital, at the expense of higher price of labor.

UNION VOICE AND MARKET OUTCOMES

The fact that unions are 'political' organizations whose activities depend on the preferences of workers as a group has important implications regarding the impact of collective bargaining.[4] Whereas quits reflect the desires of marginal workers, voice reflects the demands of some average of workers. If as a first approximation the median voter model is applied to union behavior, policy will be set by the median member (who is the marginal voter) with the consequence that greater weight will be placed on the preferences of relatively immobile workers (such as older workers and the specifically trained) than under the quit mechanism.[5] Trade unionism transforms the supply side of the job market by making median (or some other average) rather than marginal preferences the 'determinant' of the labor contract. In the job market, individuals for whom there is a great gap between (pecuniary and nonpecuniary) wages in an establishment and opportunity wages are especially likely to exercise voice when work conditions change in an undesirable way. This contrasts with Hirschman's product market case in which those with higher consumer surplus are most likely to exit when quality of goods deteriorate.

The switch from a marginal to median (or other average) supply calculus might be expected to create inefficiencies since optimality criteria invariably require marginal first-order conditions. Because of the union's role in facilitating information flows and coordinating worker preferences in bargaining, however, the situation is more complex. Bagaining among workers (which would not exist in the absence of unions) and potential worker demands for public or lumpy goods at the workplace *could* offset inefficiency losses. Consider, for example, a situation in which management can choose one of two modes of organizing work, which, exclusive of their impact on workers, have equal profitability. Method A greatly reduces the well-being of immobile senior workers, while method B has no effect on them but displeases the mobile young slightly. In a market where information is conveyed by quits, the behavior of the young would lead management to choose method A, despite the loss of consumer 'surplus' to older personnel. In a market with collective bargaining, the union might arbitrage the differences in preferences, so that the firm will pick B, with a negotiated redistribution giving the young some compensatory benefit and the old a less onerous loss than under A. This scenario can be expanded, to take account of different frequencies of quitting under A and B with similar results. The greater the difference between the losses under the two modes, the greater is the possibility that a superior bargain could be struck through the voice mechanism. I do not claim that the union will, in fact, arbitrage worker preferences correctly for the behavior of the union will depend on its internal organization, organizational goals, and political power of the various groups which are neglected here. The possibility is, however, there.

A second situation in which average preferences may yield better outcomes occurs when desirable work conditions or fringe benefits involve substantial fixed costs. Marginal evaluation could, as is well-known, lead enterprises to reject provision of employment conditions which would pass a benefit-cost test.

Advantages or disadvantages of union voice aside, by providing a distinct market mechanism for imparting information, aggregating preferences, altering authority relations, and changing marginal to average evaluations, collective bargaining will yield outcomes that differ from those in competitive markets. I conclude by sketching briefly some of the empirical implications of the model and the evidence regarding them.

As noted earlier, unionization is expected to reduce quits and raise investments in firm-specific training. Studies of interindustrial variation in quits have generally found a negative relation (Stoikov and Raimon, 1968; Burton and Parker, 1969; Pencavel, 1970), as does my analysis of the relation between unionization and quits using disaggregate data files, which provide a superior test, though the route of the linkage remains to be determined. At least one potential proxy for commitment to an enterprise, years of tenure with an employer, is also positively affected by unionization (see Chapter 9).

Reversing lines of causality, the exit–voice model suggests that when quitting is nonviable, workers may be more prone to unionization. This is roughly consistent with Alan Blinder's evidence that older workers and those with family responsibility are more likely to be union members; with US trade union history, in which unionism has grown rapidly following major recessions or depressions; and with union activities in coal, lumber, and similar locales from which exit is costly. Other factors are obviously also important, however.

Trade unionsim can be expected to increase the fringe benefits share of total compensation, both for information considerations (Lester, 1967, p. 494) and preference aggregation reasons. Analysis of data on the fringe share of compensation from individual establishments finds a significant positive union effect (Freeman, 1981).

As a relatively permanent market institution, preserving information about work conditions that might otherwise be lost through individual quits, trade unions can also be expected to increase differentials for bad working conditions relative to the competitive market outcome, a result supported by Viscusi's analysis of compensating differentials for dangerous work.

Through the various nonwage effects outlined here, unions might be expected to alter the overall production process and worker productivity. Medoff and Brown (1975) find, in fact, positive trade union productivity effects in cross-industry, cross-state regressions, holding capital-labor and worker quality fixed.

Finally the model suggests that by directing attention to workplace problems and encouraging expressions of discontent and by keeping dissatisfied workers from quitting, unions, may increase job dissatisfaction, other factors (wages, conditions) held fixed. Investigation of job satisfaction in large data tapes finds such a relation (Chapter 11; Borjas 1979).

If the unionization-satisfaction result stands up to more detailed analysis, it has significant implications for understanding the entire voice mechanism. It suggests that voice, of necessity, produces 'dissatisfaction' by making individuals especially sensitive to and willing to criticize conditions. To be effective, voice cannot be silent, even when it may produce 'the goods'.

NOTES

1. Because I focus on the situation with regular work relations, the analysis is not directly applicable to the case of craftsmen who change jobs regularly.
2. Recent theoretical work on the existence of contingent claims markets and constrained transactions is thus relevant, surprising as this may be to the theorists, to analysis of the trade union institution (Green and Sheshinski, 1975).
3. Of course the reduction in quits could be too great with bad consequences for overall labor mobility.
4. While recognizing the political and organizational nature of unions, in this essay I neglect the effect of these factors on behavior, treating unions solely as an institution that conveys the desires of members. This omission will be rectified in future work.
5. The median voter model is used as the simplest voting model. With many dimensions to contracts and groups within unions, it is obvious that a more complex game-theoretic model is needed to explain actual events.

BIBLIOGRAPHY

Blinder, A., 'Who joins unions', working paper no. 36 (Industrial Relations Section, Princeton University, February, 1972).

Borjas, G., 'Job satisfaction, wages and unions', *Journal of Human Resources*, (Winter 1979), vol. 14, no. 1, pp. 21–39.

Brown, C., and Medoff, J., 'Trade unions in the production process', *Journal of Political Economy* (June 1978), vol. 86, no. 3, pp. 355–78.

Burton, J., and Parker, J., 'Interindustry variations in voluntary labor mobility', *Industrial and Labor Relations Review* (January 1969), pp. 199–216.

Coase, R., 'The nature of the firm', ch. 16 in American Economic Association, *Readings in Price Theory*, vol. VI (Chicago: 1952), pp. 331–51.

Freeman, R., 'The effect of trade unionism on fringe benefits', *Industrial and Labor Relations Review* (July 1981), 34.

Green, J., and Sheshinski, E., 'Competitive inefficiencies in the presence of constrained transactions', *Journal of Economic Theory*, 10 (June 1975), pp., 343–57.

Hicks, J., *Theory of Wages* (New York: 1973).

Hirschman, A. O., *Exit, Voice and Loyalty* (Cambridge, MA.: Harvard University Press, 1970).

Lester, R., 'Benefits as a preferred form of compensation', *Southern Economic Journal*, 33, no. 4 (April 1967), pp. 488–95.

Lewis, H. G., 'Competitive and monopoly unionism', in P. Bradlee (ed.), *The Public Stake in Union Power* (Charlottesville: University of Virginia Press, 1959).

Meyers, C., and Pigors, P., *Personnel Administration* (New York: McGraw Hill, 1973).

Pencavel, J., *An Analysis of the Quit Rate in American Manufacturing Industry* (Princeton: Princeton University Press, Industrial Relations Section, 1970).

Simon, H., 'A formal theory of the employment relation', in *Models of Man* (New York: Wiley, 1957), pp. 183–95.

Stoikov, V., and Raimon, R. L., 'Determinants of differences in the quit rates among industries', *American Economic Review* (December 1968), pp. 1,283–98.

US Department of Labor, *Characteristics of Agreements Covering 20,000 Workers or More*, bulletin 17.29 (Washington DC: 1972).

Viscusi, W. K., *Employment Hazards: An Investigation of Marker Performance* (Cambridge, MA: Harvard University Press, 1979).

Vroom, V., and Deci, E., *Management and Motivation* (Harmondsworth: Penguin, 1974).

Williamson, O., Wachter, M., and Harris, S., 'Understanding the employment relation: analysis of idiosyncratic exchange', *Bell Journal* (Spring 1975).

9 · THE EXIT–VOICE TRADEOFF IN THE LABOR MARKET: UNIONISM, JOB TENURE, QUITS AND SEPARATIONS

In the exit–voice model of the social system (Hirschman, 1970, 1976) individuals react to discrepancies between desired and actual social phenomena in one of two ways: by the traditional free-market mechanism of 'exiting' from undesirable situations; or by directly expressing their discomfort to decision-makers through 'voice'. While little attention is paid to the labor market in Hirschman's book (1970), the exit–voice dichotomy provides a potentially fruitful framework for analyzing the major employee institution of capitalist economies – the trade union. From the perspective of the dichotomy, voice is embodied in unionism and the collective bargaining system by which workers elect union leaders to represent them in negotiations with management, while exit consists primarily of quits. A major feature of the model is a predicted tradeoff between the two adjustment mechanisms: when workers have a voice institution for expressing discontent, they should use the exit option less frequently and thus exhibit lower quit rates and longer spells of job tenure with firms.

Is unionism associated with lower quit rates and higher job tenure of workers, as predicted by the model? To what extent can any reduction in quits due to unionism be attributed to union 'voice' as opposed to other routes of union effects, notably wage gains?

Despite a sizeable literature on labor turnover and on the economic effects of unions, extant empirical evidence provides no clear answer to these questions. The turnover literature has focused on quit rates for aggregated manufacturing industries, which provides only weak evidence on the behavior of individuals; has not treated job tenure or permanent separations as dependent variables; and has only rarely sought to estimate the effect of unionism (see Parsons (1972) for a useful summary). As a result, the impact of unionism on turnover has been at best estimated imprecisely, differing with sample and control variables (Burton and Parker, 1969; Stoikov and Raimon, 1958; Pencavel, 1970; Parsons, 1977; Kahn, 1977). The union literature has dealt almost exclusively with union wage effects. Summarizing the state of knowledge in his textbook, Reynolds concluded that 'it is questionable whether collective bargaining has produced a major change in the pattern of labor turnover' (1974, p. 568).

To provide a better test of the relation between unionism and exit behavior, this study analyzes data on *individuals* from three surveys – the National Longitudinal Survey (NLS), the Michigan Panel Survey of Income Dynamics (PSID), and the Current Population Survey (CPS) – which contain detailed information on the personal attributes of workers and characteristics of jobs that is better suited for analysis of individual behavior than industry aggregates. Longitudinal data in the NLS and PSID and retrospective data on the CPS allow for the analysis of the effects of union status and other variables on *actual quits or separations over time*, while survey questions relating to job tenure provide information on past exit behavior. By examining several bodies of information, each of which has certain weaknesses and strengths, I hope to obtain a better fix on the hypothesized behavioral relation from that given in previous studies.

The principal finding of the chapter is that, *with wages and other measures of pecuniary rewards held fixed*, trade unionism is associated with significant, large reductions in exit behavior. Diverse calculations designed to adjust the union effect for potential omitted variable biases relating to union monopoly power or selectivity do not eliminate the union effect. While interpretation of the impact of unionism in terms of 'voice' is open to some question, the empirical analysis provides support for the hypothesis that trade unions alter workplace relations and worker behavior in ways *not* captured by standard monopoly wage models of the institution. Some evidence is presented that the observed reduction in exit is at least in part attributable to the operation of unions as a voice institution in the job market, though the fact that all collective bargaining involves voice in negotiations and in day-to-day work activities makes any definitive separation from the other components of unionism exceedingly difficult.

The chapter is divided into five sections. The first sets out the reasons for expecting unionism to reduce exit. The second develops the methodology for the empirical analysis. The third and fourth sections present the empirical results, with the former focusing on the effect of unionism on exit, and the latter probing the voice interpretation. The chapter concludes with a brief evaluation of the economic consequences of the union-induced increase in the attachment of workers to firms.

UNIONISM AND EXIT BEHAVIOR

Trade unionism can be expected to reduce exit behavior through 'monopoly routes' of impact and through 'voice routes' of impact.

In the context of the standard monopoly model of unions, exit is likely to be lowered by union-induced improvements in wages, fringes, and work conditions. Since the union wage effect is nonnegligible and high wages are likely to reduce quits significantly, the 'monopoly wage' route of impact may be quite potent, and must be controlled in empirical analyses seeking to isolate the voice channels of concern. The major empirical problem in this study is to hold fixed monopoly wage effects of unionism, some of which may be unobserved, so as not to produce biased estimates of the union voice–exit tradeoff.

There are several ways in which the operation of unions as an institution of worker 'voice' is likely to reduce exit behavior, producing the exit–voice tradeoff that is central to the model.[1]

First, unionism creates distinctive mechanisms for treating industrial relations problems that offer a substitute for classical exit behavior. Perhaps the most important such institution is the *grievance and arbitration system*, which offers dissatisfied workers who are considering quitting an alternative means of expressing discontent and possibly changing work conditions. Ninety-nine per cent of major US collective bargaining contracts provide for grievance procedures and 95 per cent for arbitration (US Department of Labor, 1977, p. 94), making grievance and arbitration virtually synonymous with trade unionism. By contrast, only 30 per cent of nonunion firms in the Bureau of National Affairs Personnel Policies Forum have formal grievance procedures, and only 11 per cent allow outside arbitration to settle grievances not resolvable at lower levels (Bureau of National Affairs, 1968, p. 2). The potential impact of a grievance system is clear: workers who feel themselves unfairly treated or who believe their supervisors erred in interpreting work rules will seek a solution through the grievance procedure before invoking the more drastic exit remedy. If the grievance is successful, the incentive to quit will be removed. Even if it is not and the aggrieved ultimately leaves, the overall rate of exit will be reduced as a result of the *delay* in the quit decision during the grievance procedure.[2]

The regular process of collective negotiation of labor contracts can also be expected to reduce exit behavior. Workers wanting new conditions who, in the absence of a bargaining alternative, might have quit will instead seek first to obtain the particular changes through bargaining. If some of the worker demands are met, quits are likely to be lower than would otherwise be the case. For work conditions and rules that are 'public' to the enterprise, where standard public goods arguments suggest that enterprises would have great difficulty in eliciting true worker preferences, considerable mobility might be needed in the absence of unionism for these conditions and rules to be provided. Unions might obtain and aggregate preferences in such a manner as to produce the desired arrangements more efficiently, and with lower mobility in the market.

Union 'voice' may also reduce exit by creating particular work rules and conditions of employment (which may or may not be costly to employers, once unionism is 'in place') that are desired by workers, particularly what industrial relations experts call the *industrial jurisprudence system*. Under this system managerial authority is diluted by requiring that many work place decisions be made on the basis of *negotiated* rules, for instance seniority, as opposed to supervisory judgment (or whim). By straightforward application of compensating differential arguments, if workers desire these conditions and if they are provided largely by unions, then with *pay and other pecuniary benefits held fixed*, separation rates should be lower for union workers.

Voice in the absence of unions

If 'voice' institutions such as grievance/arbitration and individual jurisprudence are desirable work conditions that reduce turnover, the question naturally arises as to why nonunion enterprises do not generally adopt them as part of a profit-maximizing strategy.

One reason for the general absence of voice or industrial jurisprudence practices in the nonunion sector is that the essence of voice is to reduce managerial power and create a dual authority channel within the firm. Such a change in power relations would be difficult to attain in the absence of a genuine independent union or union-like organization. During the 1920s many firms experimented with so-called 'employee representation' plans designed to provide a nonunion voice mechanism for workers (see National Industrial Conference Board, 1933). Many of these plans ended in failure, despite the best intentions, as workers are unwilling to express their desires for fear of retaliation by management and because of their own lack of power to affect decisions. Other plans led to the formation of company unions, which, in several industries, became the building blocks of independent unionism in the 1930s (Galenson, 1963). Under current law, of course, company unions are illegal. The dilemma is that if management gives up power, it creates seeds of genuine unions; if it does not, employee representation plans face severe difficulties. This is not to say that *no* nonunion firm will have a grievance/arbitration system, for some have such systems, in part to reduce worker desire for unions.[3] The point is that it is more difficult (costly) to institute an effective system in the absence of unions or union-type organizations.

A second more subtle reason for the concentration of voice institutions in the organized sector relates to the nature of price signals in unorganized and organized markets. In the unorganized market, the desire of workers for a given condition of work is conveyed by the marginal evaluation of the condition by the marginal worker, as reflected in the reduction in wage he would take to obtain the condition. In the union market, the desire for the condition is conveyed by some average of preferences of workers: in a median voter model. By the (marginal) desire of the median worker; in a 'consumer (worker) surplus'-maximizing model, by the average intensity of preferences for the condition. Assuming that 'inframarginal' workers have greater desire for voice and industrial jurisprudence or that such systems generate worker surplus or both, there will be a more intense demand for the condition under trade unionism. Given fixed costs to setting up voice institutions, the profit calculus might reject their development, while a benefit–cost calculation using the benefits to the median worker or taking account of consumer surplus would favor their development.[4]

EMPIRICAL ANALYSIS

Exit behavior is measured in this study by three variables: by job tenure, defined as the number of years a worker remains with a firm; by quits in a specified period; and by total separations in a period. Each of these variables has certain strengths and weaknesses for analysis of the exit–voice tradeoff. Tenure has the advantage of reflecting longer run and more permanent behavior than quits or separations because it relates to attachment between workers and firms over an extended period of time. The main disadvantage is the absence of data on characteristics of the job years earlier. Quits are useful because they measure worker behavior, which is at the core of the union voice model, but face the problem that the distinction between worker and employer-initiated changes is at least partially arbitrary (an employer may harass a worker to quit; a worker may quit because of potential plant closings or may perform poorly until fired). Separations do not have this problem but include such forms of mobility as those due to plant closings, which are not directly relevant to the model. By examining each measure, we are able to obtain a firmer set of conclusions than would otherwise be the case.

The decision to exit is analyzed in the framework of a probability model in which each person has a specific propensity to exit in a given year Q, dependent on a set of explanatory factors X_i, including unionism. Because exit is a dichotomous variable and probabilities are bounded by 0 and 1, the logistic provides an appropriate functional form for the relation:

$$Q = \left(\left[1 + \exp - \sum_i (B_i X_i) \right] \right)^{-1} \quad \text{with} \quad \frac{dQ}{dX_i} = B_i Q (1 - Q) \quad (9.1)$$

Tenure is treated as a backward waiting time variable dependent on Q. When Q is fixed, the probability that tenure in year n, T_n, is a specific value t can be written as

$$PR(T_n = t) = (1 - Q)^t Q \quad (9.2)$$

which is a geometric distribution. Since T_n reflects behavior over $t + 1$ periods of time, while changes in one time interval reflect behavior over only one period, T_n conveys greater information about exit propensities than dichotomous quit or separation measures.

The mean of the completed tenure (T) distribution has a well-known relation to Q, which can be fruitfully used in analysis:

$$E(T) = \frac{(1 - Q)}{Q} = \exp\left(\sum_i B_i X_i\right) \tag{9.3}$$

If Q depended on the X's as in equation (9.1) and was independent of past tenure, the appropriate function form for T would be the exponential, $T = \exp(\Sigma_i B_i X_i) + U_i$, where U_i is a random error. With a fixed Q, renewal theory guarantees that the mean of the distribution of incompleted tenure equals the mean of the distribution of completed tenure, justifying use of the completed spell functional form. When, as appears to be the case, Q is not constant but depends on the length of tenure (separations fall as tenure increases), the exponential is no longer appropriate. The functional form of the tenure equation will depend on the slope of the hazard function (the relation between cumulated tenure and the probability of separation) and can be quite complex. The most useful way of analyzing tenure in this case is to use the linear form, which can be viewed as a first-order Taylor series approximation to more complex functions:

$$T = \sum_i B_i X_i + U_i \tag{9.4}$$

Calculations show that the linear function is much superior statistically to the exponential, presumably because of the dependence of Q on tenure.

Controlling for monopoly compensation effects

To isolate the nonmonopoly wage impact of unionism on exit, it is necessary to control carefully for other determinants of exit (themselves correlated with unionism), such as pecuniary and nonpecuniary compensation at the current job and at alternative jobs and personal characteristics like age or sex, which affect the transactions cost of mobility.

There are three problems in controlling for compensation at the current job. First, the surveys of individuals to be analyzed lack adequate information on fringe benefits, which are increased by unionism (Freeman, 1981) and can be expected to reduce exit. This problem is dealt with by adjusting estimated coefficients on unionism for the omitted fringe variable using standard omitted variable bias formulae and outside information on the effect of unionism on fringes. Second, measures of nonpecuniary work conditions (above and beyond those represented by the voice or industrial jurisprudence conditions) are notoriously poor. Detailed industry and occupation dummies are used to narrow some of the possible range of variation among workers. In addition, measures that might be taken to reflect worker evaluation of nonpecuniary conditions, such as indicators of job satisfaction, are entered when available. Some effort is also made to control for omitted work conditions (and other factors) in the context of an unobservables model to be described shortly. Third, when tenure is the dependent variable in the analysis, there is a clear dual causal relation with tenure raising wages at the same time that high wages reduce Q and raise tenure. Because of the likely magnitude of the coefficient on tenure in the wage equation, simultaneity can be expected to bias upward the estimated coefficient of wages on tenure.[5] This in turn is likely to bias downward the estimated regression coefficient on unionism. As inclusion of wages in the tenure calculations tends to work *against* the exit–voice hypothesis, I shall operate as if the causality were unidirectional and ignore the simultaneous bias.

Since the set of options facing a worker cannot be measured directly but must be inferred from his or her general characteristics, it is more difficult to obtain adequate measures of alternative compensation. The major indicators of alternatives are education, which should (wages fixed) raise exit propensities due to the better opportunities of the more educated or, in the context of a model of specific human capital, as a result of the inverse link between general and specific human capital at any fixed wage level; years of work experience, which should raise outside earnings and thus exit; and the state of the local labor market. Occupation and industry dummy variables can also be interpreted as reflecting outside opportunities. Because standard earnings regressions that include such variables as education, experience, and occupation rarely explain more than one-third of the variance in log earnings, however, it is unlikely that these variables will adequately index alternative opportunities. If, as seems reasonable, the unobserved components of alternative opportunities are correlated with current wages, as both current and alternative possibilities depend on omitted human capital or personal characteristics, statistical analyses will understate the negative effect of current compensation on exit and bias the estimated coefficient on unionism even if the unobserved alternative opportunities are uncorrelated with unionism.

The effect of the omitted components of alternative compensation on the estimated impact of wages and unionism on exit can be analyzed with regression formulae that do or do not control for the omitted factor. Let W = compensation on the present job; W_A = compensation in other jobs; U = unionism; and Q = the propensity to exit. Then, using subscripts to specify partial regression coefficients with the first subscript reflecting the dependent variable, the second the independent variable, and additional subscripts reflecting controls, the least squares coefficient relating Q to W and with W_A omitted [b_{QWU}] and the coefficient relating Q to U with W_A omitted [b_{QUW}] are linked to the 'true' coefficients with W_A included (b_{QWUW_A} and b_{QUWW_A}) as follows:

$$b_{QWU} = b_{QWUW_A} + (b_{QW_AUW}) (b_{W_AUW}) \tag{9.5}$$

$$b_{QUW} = b_{QUWW_A} + (b_{QW_AUW}) (b_{W_AUW}) \tag{9.6}$$

where all of the coefficient are conditional on the other variables in the equation. The difference between the estimated and 'true' coefficients, $(b_{QWU} - b_{QWUW_A})$ and $(b_{QUW} - b_{QUWW_A})$, depends on the signs and size of b_{QW_AWU}, b_{W_AWU}, and b_{W_AUW}. Increases in W_A should increase exit, making b_{QW_AUW} positive. The term b_{W_AWU} is positive, by the assumption that the omitted factors are positively correlated with current pay. With $b_{QW_AUW} > 0$ and $b_{W_AWU} > 0$, there will be a downward bias in the estimated coefficient on wages. To obtain some notion of the magnitude of the bias, assume that W and W_A have similarly sized but oppositely signed effects on exit $(b_{QWUW_A} = -b_{QW_AUW})$. Then equation (9.5) can be rewritten to obtain the 'correct' coefficient:

$$b_{QWUW_A} = b_{QWU}/(1 - b_{W_AWU}) \tag{9.7}$$

If the coefficient from the regression of W_A on W, conditional on U and all other variables is sizeable, say 0.5 to 0.7, then the true coefficient will be significantly above the estimated coefficient, suggesting that the coefficient on wages be raised considerably to estimate better the true wage effect.

The bias in estimating the effect of unionism on exit in (9.6) depends on b_{W_AUW}, whose sign in unclear. If union workers are more able than others, in ways not captured by W, b_{W_AUW} will be positive, producing a downward bias in the absolute value of the estimated coefficient. Conversely, if union workers are, for whatever reason, less able than others, the absolute value of b_{QUW} will overstate b_{QUWW_A}. Assuming, as before, that $b_{QWUW_A} = -b_{QW_AUW}$, we obtain for the relation between the estimated and true coefficients on unionism

$$b_{QUWW_A} = b_{QUW} + (b_{W_AUW}) (b_{QWUW_A}) \tag{9.8}$$

If, other factors fixed, b_{W_AUW} is about equal to the union wage effect, say 0.10 to 0.20, the bias would be relatively modest, unless b_{QWUW_A} were extremely large.

STATISTICAL ESTIMATES OF THE TRADEOFF

This section presents estimates of the impact of unionism on tenure, quits, and total permanent separations[6] for four individual data sets:[7] the NLS older male sample; the Michigan PSID sample; the CPS sample; and the NLS younger male sample. Maximum likelihood calculations are used to estimate the determinants of quits and separations; nonlinear and linear least squares are used to estimate the determinants of tenure. The analysis finds a sizeable effect of unionism on all of the indicators of exit propensity, which is maintained after the various adjustments and corrections suggested in Section II.

Older male NLS results

The estimated effect of unionism and other important explanatory variables on exit behavior in the older male NLS sample is given in Table 9.1. The table records the mean and standard deviation of the measures of exit for union and nonunion workers[8] and the coefficients on unionism (measured by an 0–1 dummy variable for workers whose wages are set by collective bargaining), log earnings, dummy variables for presence of a retirement plan (=1 when a firm has a plan), an index of job dissatisfaction, and on lagged tenure, entered as an explanatory variable in some quit or separations equations. As specified in the notes to the table, the sample is limited to workers who remained in the labor force in the period and thus excludes persons who retired.

What stands out in the table are the differences in the exit propensities of union and of nonunion workers. The means and standard deviations show that union workers have considerably more tenure than nonunion workers (17.4 years versus 13.2 years) and have much lower quit rates (a minuscule 1.0 per cent compared to 7.2 per cent for nonunion workers) and lower separation rates (7.0 per cent for union workers versus 14.0 per cent for nonunion workers). Since the absolute difference in quit rates between union and nonunion workers (6.0) is almost equal to the absolute differences in the total separation rates, which also include employer-initiated changes, there are essentially no differences in other separations between union and nonunion workers.

In the multivariate statistical analysis, where a wide variety of other factors is held fixed, the different exit propensities of union and nonunion workers are evinced in the sizeable significant coefficients accorded unionism.

In the linear tenure calculations, unionism obtains a coefficient that ranges from 1.8 to 3.6 years, indicating that upward of half of the mean difference in years of tenure is, in fact, attributable to trade unionism, other factors held fixed. Introduction of the retirement variable in line 2 reduces the union coefficient in the linear form but still leaves a sizeable significant effect. By controlling for retirement plans, which are more prevalent among union workers, the analysis assumes that all of the effect of unions on pensions represents monopoly wage gains and that none represents the effective transmission of worker preferences via voice, possibly understating the voice component of the union impact. The job satisfaction index, also entered in line 2 as a crude indicator of unmeasured nonwage aspects of the workplace or of alternative opportunities (which, if especially good, should decrease satisfaction, all else the same), obtains an

Table 9.1 Estimates of the effect of trade unionism and other variables on exit behavior: older male NLS sample, 1969–71[a]

Dependent variable	Mean and standard deviation		Estimated coefficient and standard error								R^2 (−In likelihood)
	Union	Nonunion	Union[b]	Log earnings	Years of schooling	Age	Retirement plan (1 = yes)	Job dissatisfaction[c]	Tenure 1969	Other controls[d]	
1 Tenure, 1969 (linear)	17.4 (10.6)	13.2 (11.0)	3.64 (0.58)	3.49 (0.59)	0.11 (0.08)	0.41 (0.06)				1–7	0.20
2 Tenure, 1969 (linear)			2.96 (0.58)	2.41 (0.60)	0.07 (0.09)	0.47 (0.06)	4.65 (0.57)	0.02 (0.29)		1–7	0.23
3 Tenure, 1969 (exponential form)			0.56 (0.35)	1.59 (0.29)	−0.00 (0.05)	0.15 (0.04)				1–7	0.03
4 Quit, 1969–71	0.01 (0.09)	0.07 (0.26)	−2.17 (0.43)	−0.26 (0.24)	−0.03 (0.04)	−0.10 (0.03)				1–7	(267)
5 Quit, 1969–71			−2.07 (0.43)	−0.01 (0.27)	−0.02 (0.04)	−0.10 (0.03)	−0.85 (0.30)	0.36 (0.14)		1–7	(259)
6 Quit, 1969–71	−1.85	−0.85	(0.44)	0.19 (0.30)	−0.02 (0.05)	−0.08 (0.03)	−0.24 (0.31)	0.35 (0.15)	−0.16 (0.03)	1–7	(228)
7 Separations, 1969–71	0.07 (0.26)	0.14 (0.35)	−0.87 (0.21)	−0.09 (0.18)	−0.03 (0.03)	−0.07 (0.02)				1–7	(521)
8 Separations, 1969–71			−0.81 (0.21)	−0.08 (0.19)	−0.02 (0.03)	−0.06 (0.02)	−0.51 (0.20)	0.27 (0.10)		1–7	(514)
9 Separations, 1969–71			−0.63 (0.22)	0.16 (0.21)	−0.01 (0.03)	−0.05 (0.02)	−0.14 (0.20)	0.26 (0.10)	−11 (0.01)	1–7	(463)

a Number of observations = 1,735. Sample consists of private wage and salary workers who reported earnings and other variables in 1969 and who were employed in 1969 and 1971. Coefficients in lines 1–2 based on linear equation $T = \Sigma B_i X_i$. Coefficients in line 3 are based on exponential equation $T = \exp \Sigma B_i X_i$. Coefficients in lines 4–9 are based on logistic equation $Pr(Q) = 1/(1 + \exp -\Sigma B_i X_i)$.

b Unionism measured by 0–1 dummy variable for whether or not wages are set by collective bargaining. This variable is virtually identical with a union member variable.

c Job satisfaction measured as standard normal deviation, with positive values reflecting greater than average satisfaction and negative values the converse.

d Other controls are defined as 1 = 9 dummy variables for industry; 2 = 6 dummy variables for occupation; 3 = race; 4 = number of dependants; 5 = 3 dummy variables for region; 6 = size of local labor market; 7 = rate of unemployment in local market.

Source: Based on National Longitudinal Survey data tapes for men aged 45–59 in 1966, 1973 tape version.

insignificant effect. In both lines 1 and 2, the coefficient on log earnings is large, of a similar magnitude to that on unionism. The estimated exponential tenure equation (equation (9.5)) in line 3 yields a smaller coefficient on unionism than on earnings but fits the data so poorly as to be readily rejected in favor of the linear form.[9]

The estimated effect of unionism on the probability of quits or total separations in lines 4–8 tells a similar story. In line 4, unionism obtains a sizeable highly significant coefficient of −2.17, which implies that unionism causes a sizeable reduction in the probability of quitting. Addition of the index of job dissatisfaction, which significantly lowers quits, and of the retirement plan variable in line 5 reduces the coefficient on unionism modestly. Comparable results are obtained in the logistic separation equations in lines 7 and 8, where the estimated effect of unionism varies from −0.81 to −0.87 with a standard error of 0.21. Given the higher level of separations in the sample (a mean of 0.11), these parameters translate into differences in the probability of separation of about 0.08. In sharp contrast to the sizeable significant impact of unionism, both the quit and separation calculations accord a small insignificant effect to wages, which makes the union–exit tradeoff look quite powerful by comparison.

In lines 6 and 9, the log of tenure in 1969 has been added as an additional control in the quit and separation calculations. Inclusion of tenure can be interpreted in two possible ways. In the simplest interpretation, tenure is just another control variable, reflecting the dependence of exit propensities on cumulated tenure. Alternatively, however, tenure can be taken to represent unobserved factors that affect both future quits and separations and past employment stability. Formally, let T and Q depend on some omitted person or job-specific factor (F_i) as well as on unionism:

$$T = \alpha^T U N_i + F_i + \epsilon_{iT} \tag{9.9}$$

$$Q = 1/[1 + \exp(-\alpha U N_i - \lambda F_i + \epsilon_{iQ})] \tag{9.10}$$

where T superscripts are used to denote coefficients in the tenure equation. In equation (9.9) and (9.10) the residuals have two parts: F_i which reflects the omitted factor (given a unit coefficient in (9.9) and a scaling of λ in (9.10)) and equation-specific components ϵ_{iQ}, ϵ_{iT}, which are themselves uncorrelated and are uncorrelated with the independent variables. The econometric problem is that F_i is correlated with unionism (and possibly other explanatory variables also).

Solving equation (9.9) for F_i and substituting into equation (9.10) yields

$$Q_i = 1/(1 + \exp[-(\alpha - \alpha^T\lambda)UN_i - \lambda T + \epsilon_{iQ} + \epsilon_{iT}]) \tag{9.11}$$

which removes the correlation between UN_i and the residual but introduces a correlation between T and the residual since $E(T\epsilon_{iT}) > 0$. If an instrument for T could be found, such as an independent variable that does not enter Q, consistent estimates of the coefficient on tenure could be made. In the absence of instruments, λ will be underestimated in equation (9.11) and given a positive correlation between UN_i and T_i, the coefficient on unionism overstated. As can be seen in equation (9.11), however, the coefficient on unionism with the inclusion of tenure is $\alpha - \alpha^T \lambda$, rather than α itself. Given $\alpha^T > 0$, this implies an underestimate of the effect of unionism on quits. Inclusion of tenure in the regressions does not totally resolve econometric problems but does set up a difficult test of the union impact. From this perspective, the continued sizeable effect of unionism in lines 6 and 9, where tenure is entered as an explanatory factor, can be viewed as highly supportive of the postulated union–exit tradeoff. Unionized workers are much less likely to quit or separate from employers than nonunionized workers who have the same job tenure and thus having the same 'stability' history.

To analyze the magnitude of biases due to inadequate controls on alternative opportunities, it is necessary to obtain estimates of $b_{W_A WU}$ and $b_{W_A UW}$. With such estimates, equations (9.7) and (9.8) can be used to evaluate the effect of the omitted part of alternative opportunities. The link between alternative wages and current wages and between alternative wages and unionism can be estimated, albeit crudely,[10] by examining workers who changed employers from 1969 to 1971, with W_A measured by wages on the new 1971 job. Regressions of log wages in 1971 on log wages in 1969 and union status in 1969 and the other 1969 control variables for the 11 per cent of the older male NLS sample who changed employers yield the following coefficients (standard errors in parentheses):[11] $b_{W_A WU} = 0.32\ (0.09)$; $b_{W_A UW} = 0.12\ (0.11)$. Using equations (9.7) and (9.8), these values of $b_{W_A WU}$ and $b_{W_A UW}$ imply a sizeable increase in the estimated effect of wages on exit and a modest increase in the effect of unionism on exit. Adjusting the figures in line 2, where wages were accorded a sizeable effect on tenure, for example, yields $b_{QWUW_A} = 1.47\ (2.47) = 3.54$ and $b_{QUWW_A} = 2.96 + 3.54\ (0.12) = 3.38$. Even with the adjustment, the estimated impact of unionism on tenure is large relative to the estimated impact of wages on tenure. Adjusting the quit and separation equations has even less effect on the results.

In sum, the data on the effect of unionism on job tenure, quits, and separations in the older male NLS sample show union workers to be much more attached to their firms than comparable nonunion workers.

Michigan PSID data set

Table 9.2 presents estimates of the effect of unionism on tenure and quits using data from the Michigan PSID sample. This data set covers the entire population and thus gives a more inclusive picture of the trade union impact than that in the older male NLS sample. In the PSID, information

Table 9.2 Estimates of the effect of unionism on exit, Michigan Panel Survey of Income Dynamics, 1968–74[a]

Dependent variable and # of observations	Mean and standard deviations		Coefficients and standard errors						$(-\ln R^2$ likelihood$)$
	Nonunion	Union	Union	Log wage	Schooling	Age	Lagged tenure	Additional controls[b]	
Tenure, 1968. All family units. $n = 2{,}597$ (linear)	5.8 (7.4)	10.2 (8.6)	2.72 (0.27)	2.24 (0.20)	−0.13 (0.03)	0.18 (0.01)		1–9	0.243
Tenure, 1972. All family units. $n = 2{,}322$ (linear)	6.6 (8.0)	8.8 (8.2)	1.06 (0.27)	2.60 (0.19)	0.04 (0.04)	0.22 (0.01)		1–9	0.320
Tenure, 1972. All family units. $n = 1{,}175$ (exponential)[c]			0.77 (0.17)	0.76 (0.14)	−0.01 (0.02)	0.09 (0.01)		1–9	0.160
Annual quits, 1968–74 $n = 21{,}173$	0.090 (0.286)	0.058 (0.235)	−0.469 (0.070)	−0.238 (0.051)	0.001 (0.009)	−0.045 (0.002)		1–9	(5.603)
Annual quits, 1968–74 $n = 21{,}173$			−0.438 (0.070)	−0.197 (0.051)	0.002 (0.009)	−0.040 (0.002)	−0.038 (0.005)	1–9	(5.570)
Annual separations 1968–74 $n = 21{,}173$	0.130 (0.336)	0.092 (0.289)	−0.412 (0.058)	−0.253 (0.042)	−0.009 (0.008)	−0.044 (0.002)		1–9	(7.272)
Annual separations 1968–74 $n = 21{,}173$			−0.379 (0.058)	−0.205 (0.043)	−0.008 (0.007)	−0.038 (0.002)	−0.043 (0.004)	1–9	(7.212)

a Sample consists of private wage and salary workers who reported relevant variables in the given years. Coefficients in lines 1–2 are based on linear equation $T = \Sigma B_i X_i$. Coefficients in line 3 are based on exponential equation $T = \exp \Sigma B_i X_i$. Coefficients in lines 4–7 are based on logistic equation $PR(Q) = 1/Q + \exp - \Sigma B_i X_i)$.

b Additional controls are defined as 1 = 5 industry dummies; 2 = 8 occupation dummies; 3 = dummy for shortage of workers in local areas; 4 = unemployment in local areas; 5 = dummy for whether wages are high (= 1) or low; 6 = number of dependants; 7 = sex; 8 = race; 9 = dummy for whether person was in special low-income sample.

c Sample size reduced due to computational problems in maximum likelihood search procedure.

Source: Based on Michigan Panel Survey of Income Dynamics, 1974 tape version.

on unionism and mobility is available on an annual basis for the years 1968 to 1974, which provides data on exit in each of five separate years (1968–9, 1969–70, and so forth). To obtain a single large sample covering all of the years, individual year observations were pooled into one data set, with observations consisting of dichotomous exit variables from year t to $t + 1$ linked to the characteristics of the worker and job in year t. The pooled sample contains 21,173 observations, with certain individuals deleted in particular years due to changes in the survey sample. Since quits can be treated as independent from year to year while tenure cannot, tenure is examined in the initial year 1968 and in the intermediate year 1972.

The calculations in Table 9.2 confirm the basic finding of a significant union–exit relation. The mean values of tenure and quits for union workers and nonunion workers show substantially less exit among unionists, uncorrected for differences in other factors. Union members had 4.4 years more tenure in 1968 and 2.2 years more in 1972 (when the sample was somewhat smaller due to deletions). Over the period 1968–73 union workers had an average annual quit rate of 5.8 per cent compared with 9.0 per cent for other workers, a quantitatively large and statistically significant difference. The separation rates also differed noticeably, with a rate for union workers of 9.2 per cent compared with 13.0 per cent for nonunion workers. In the regressions, which include controls for wages, years of schooling, occupation, local labor market conditions, age, sex, race, and industry, as specified in the table, unionism is always accorded a significant impact. In the OLS tenure regressions, the union coefficient varies noticeably between 1968 and 1972, but is large absolutely and relative to its standard error in both cases. While the linear form fits better than the exponential, the fit of the exponential in line 3 (limited to a smaller sample due to computational problems) is much superior to that in Table 9.1 and yields a union coefficient somewhat larger at the mean value of variables (1.32) then from the better-fitting linear form (1.06). In the pooled quit equations in lines 4 and 5, which first exclude and then include tenure in the precedent period, the estimated impact of unionism on the probability of quitting ranges from 0.036 to 0.038 points at the mean level of quits. Comparable results are obtained in the pooled separation equations in lines 6 and 7, with the union coefficient estimated to lower separation at the mean level by 0.044 with tenure excluded from the equation and by 0.040 with tenure included as an explanatory variable.

The magnitudes of the union and wage coefficients in the quit and separation equations in Table 9.2 differ noticeably from those in Table 9.1. The impact of unionism is smaller in the Michigan PSID than in the NLS Older Male sample, possibly because of the inclusion of younger workers and women whose exit behavior is less likely to be affected by unionism than that of older men; the impact of wages on exit is significantly negative in lines 5–8 of Table 9.2, in contrast to its weak effect in the estimates of Table 9.1. With a smaller union and larger wage coefficient, the union–exit tradeoff becomes relatively more moderate compared with the wage–exit relation.

The wage and union coefficients in Table 9.2 can be 'corrected' for potential bias due to lack of adequate data on alternative opportunities in the same fashion as done previously. Regressing log wages of persons who changed jobs in the Michigan sample on their previous wage and union status and other aspects of the job for each year yielded the following estimates for 1969–70: $b_{W_A UW} = 0.13$ (0.05); and $b_{W_A WU} = 0.38$ (0.04) and comparable (somewhat lower) estimates for other years.[12] These figures suggest that in the tenure equation of line 2 the wage coefficient be raised to 4.19 and the union coefficient raised to 1.60, while in the quit and separation equations in lines 5 and 7 the wage coefficients be changed to -0.39 and -0.33 and the union coefficients be changed to -0.52 and -0.42, respectively. Even with these adjustments, the union impact is sizeable relative to the wage impact: an increase in wages of over 100 per cent is needed to reduce quits (separations) by as much as unionism, while an increase in wages of over one-third is needed to raise tenure by as much as unionism.

Because the PSID sample lacks any information on fringe benefits, it is also important to adjust the coefficients for the potential bias due to absence of fringe data. To obtain some notion of the magnitude of the bias, consider the least squares equation linking partial regression coefficients to the coefficients that are not partial for the omitted variable:

$$b_{QUF} = (b_{QU} - b_{QF}b_{FU})/(1 - r_{FU}^2) \tag{9.12}$$

where

b_{QUF} = the coefficient corrected for the omitted fringe variable
b_{QU} = estimated coefficient on exit
b_{FU} = the regression coefficient linking fringes to unions
b_{QF} = the regression linking exit to fringes
r_{FU} = the correlation of fringes and unionsim

and where all the coefficients are partial with respect to the other variables in the model.

Available information and the likely magnitudes of the coefficients in equation (9.12) suggest only a moderate upward bias in the estimated effect of unions, of at most 25 per cent. For b_{FU} and r_{FU}, estimates in Freeman (1981, Table 3) indicate that, conditional on straight-time pay, industry dummies, and other control variables, $r_{FU} = 0.30$ while $b_{FU} = 0.11$. An extremely high estimate of b_{QF} would be the coefficient obtained on log wages in the regressions: since fringes constitute no more than one-third of the wage bill, this implies that a dollar of fringes is three times as effective in reducing exit as a dollar of wages. With these estimates, the union coefficient in line 2 of Table 9.2 (where wages have their greatest impact relative to unionism) is reduced to 0.79, while there is virtually no impact on the coefficients in other lines. Unless the magnitudes of the estimated coefficients linking unionism to fringes and fringes to exit are markedly off, correction for the omission of fringes still leaves a sizeable union coefficient.

CPS data set

The largest data set with information on union status and quit behavior is the Current Population Surveys for the month of May, which contain information on persons who quit and the unemployed at the time of the survey, an extreme form of exit, since most quitters have a job in hand, and information on unionism on the past or current job. These surveys have the advantage of offering an especially large sample size, which permits many industry, occupation, and area control variables but the disadvantage of relating to a distinct and relatively small group of quitters. To obtain as large a sample of unemployed quitters as possible, I amalgamated the May 1973, 1974, and 1975 CPS surveys into a single sample with over 98,500 persons. With this size of sample and with numerous controls for occupation and detailed industry, maximum likelihood estimation of the logistic function became computationally infeasible. Instead, a linear probability model was fit. The linear coefficients can be transformed to obtain a first-order inverse Taylor series approximation of the logistic parameters by multiplication by n/SSR, where n = sample size, SSR = estimated sum of squared residuals (see Nerlove and Press (1973) for a discussion of this transformation).

Estimates of the effect of unionism, earnings, schooling, and age on quits in the CPS sample are given in Table 9.3. The linear regression coefficient on union status gives the, by now familiar, result of a negative significant coefficient that is of approximately the same magnitude as the coefficient on log wages. With diverse characteristics fixed, unionism is associated with a 0.26 per cent lower quit (into unemployment) rate, which is of similar magnitude to the effect of earnings in the sample. Transformed into logistic curve parameters, the coefficient on unionism is about 50 per cent larger than that obtained in the quit calculation of Table 9.2 while the coefficient on earnings is roughly twice as great. Still, it would take almost a 100 per cent increase in the log of average hourly earnings to reduce the probability of quitting by as much as the switch from nonunion to union status.

If the partial correlations between W, W_A, and UN from the Michigan sample are taken to apply to the CPS sample as well (since both samples cover the entire population) and the CPS estimates adjusted for omission of W_A, the wage and union coefficients are raised noticeably. In the logit

Table 9.3 Unionization and quits in the current population survey tapes, May 1973–5[a]

Dependent variable	Mean and standard deviation	Coefficient and standard error	Approximate logistic coefficient[b]
Quit and unemployed	0.004 (0.007)		
Coefficients and standard errors on explanatory variables			
Union	0.23 (0.42)	−0.0026 (0.0006)	−0.62
Log hourly earnings	1.24 (0.60)	−0.0024 (0.0005)	−0.57
Schooling	12.3 (3.0)	−0.00001 (0.0001)	0.00
Age	35.9 (14.4)	−0.0014 (0.0002)	0.33
Other controls	*Numbers of controls*		
Industry dummies	46		
State dummies	26		
Sex dummy	1		
Race dummy	1		
Occupation dummies	11		
Number of dependants	1		
Marital status dummies	3		
Year dummies	2		

Notes:
a   Number of observations = 98,593. Sample consists of private wage and salary workers reporting relevant variables.
b   Estimated by dividing linear coefficient by SSR/n, where SSR = sum of squared residuals, and n = number of observations. See Nerlove and Press [1973] for discussion of this approximation.
Source: US Bureau of the Census, Current Population Reports, May 1973, 1974, 1975 tapes.

form the coefficient on wages rises to −0.74, while the union coefficient rises to −0.71. If, in addition, the union (but not the wage) coefficient is reduced for the omission of fringe benefits using the same procedure and data as before, the union impact drops to −0.68.[13] Even with these adjustments, the finding of a steep union–exit tradeoff remains; the switch from nonunion to union status reduces quits by as much as 0.92 log wage increase.

Young male NLS sample

Estimates of the effect of unionism on exit behavior were also made with the young male NLS survey, which contains information on the union status and tenure of men aged 17–27 in 1969 and in 1971. Because of a lack of direct information on the causes of job changes between 1969 and 1971, the analysis is limited to tenure and to separations, defined as having a different job in 1971 than in 1969. The analysis eliminates students and focuses on regular workers.

The discussion of the difference between the supply price in union and in nonunion markets of the first section suggested that unionism represents older 'average' workers to a greater extent than younger mobile workers. This in turn suggests that the impact of unionism on exit would be weaker among younger, more mobile workers than among others, and might even possibly by positive rather than negative. The calculations summarized in Table 9.4 show the expected weaker effects. The differences in mean tenure and separation rates between young union and young nonunion workers are proportionately smaller than in the previous samples. The estimated effects of unionism in the linear tenure regressions in columns 1 and 2 and in the logistic separation calculations in columns 3 and 4 also yield relatively small and moderate union effects, both absolutely and relative to the estimated effects of wages. While the coefficient on unionism in the 1969 tenure regression is larger than the coefficient on wages, in all of the other calculations, the coefficient on wages is larger, which contrasts to the general pattern in previous analysis. Adjustments in the coefficients for the omission of major components of alternative compensation enhance this greater effect of wages than of unionism on the exit behavior of the young. In the young male NLS sample, regressions of the log of wages of persons who changed employers from 1969 to 1971 on unionism, log wages in 1969, and the control variables in Table 9.4 yield estimates of $b_{W_A WU}$ of 0.43 (0.04) and of $b_{W_A UW}$ of 0.005 (0.03), where numbers in parentheses are standard errors.[14] Using the formula in equations (9.7) and (9.8) to adjust the coefficients in the table raises the estimated effect of wages by 75 per cent but leaves the union coefficients essentially unchanged. Because deferred fringes are likely to be received too far in the future to affect the young, further adjuestments are not warranted. The principal conclusion to be drawn from Table 9.4 is that unionism has a smaller impact on the exit behavior of young workers than on the exit behavior of older workers.

Selectivity versus behavior

The analysis thus far has shown that with monopoly compensation gains fixed, unionism raises tenure and reduces quits. Is the estimated reduction in exit, with wages held fixed, due to unionization of relatively more stable persons, or is it due to actual changes in behavior caused by the specific work relations associated with the union institution?

The longitudinal data files provide a possible means of differentiating between these two effects and isolating the behavioral aspects of unionism of concern. With longitudinal data on the same person over time, that person's exit behavior when he or she is unionized and when he or she is not unionized can be compared, thereby eliminating the personal propensity to be a stable worker. The most direct way of controlling for individual effects is to add individual constants to the logistic probability

Table 9.4 Estimates of the effect of unionism on tenure and separations: younger male NLS sample, 1969–71[a]

Dependent variable	Tenure 1969	Tenure 1971	Separations[b], 1969–71	Separations[b], 1969–71
Mean and standard deviation				
Union	1.88 (1.85)	3.12 (2.57)	0.47 (0.50)	
Nonunion	1.66 (1.93)	2.74 (2.65)	0.58 (0.49)	
Coefficients and standard errors on				
Explanatory variables				
Unionism	0.28 (0.11)	0.36 (0.14)	−0.20 (0.13)	−0.20 (0.13)
ln wage	0.23 (0.14)	0.62 (0.16)	−0.73 (0.18)	−0.67 (0.17)
Years of schooling	−0.01 (0.02)	0.00 (0.02)	0.01 (0.03)	−0.00 (0.03)
Age	0.08 (0.02)	0.16 (0.02)	−0.13 (0.02)	−0.08 (0.03)
Years of work experience	0.16 (0.02)	0.13 (0.02)	−0.001 (0.002)	0.02 (0.02)
Tenure				−0.11 (0.03)
Other controls				
Industry dummies	9	9	9	9
Region dummies	3	3	3	3
Occupation dummies	6	6	6	6
Race dummy	1	1	1	1
SMSA dummy	1	1	1	1
Number of dependants	1	1	1	1
R^2 (−ln likelihood)	0.252	0.243	1,050	1,076

Notes:

a Number of observations = 1,742. Sample limited to private wage and salary workers out of school in 1969 and 1971 who report relevant variables. Coefficients in columns 1 and 2 based on linear tenure equation $T = \Sigma B_i X_i$. Coefficients in columns 3 and 4 based on logistic equation $Q = 1/(1 + \exp - \Sigma B_i X_i)$.

b Separations 1969–71 calculated from 1971 tenure, with separation = 1 if person had less than two years of tenure.

Source: Based on National Longitudinal Surveys data tapes for men aged 14–24 in 1966, 1973 tape version.

Table 9.5 Fixed effect logistic model estimates of effect of unionism on quits

Explanatory variable	Coefficient and standard error in fixed effect logistic model of quits	Numbers of variables
Unionism	−0.462 (0.151)	
Log wages	0.128 (0.104)	
Individual constants		1,232

Sources: Based on National Longitudinal Survey data tapes for men aged 45–59 in 1966, 1973 tape version. US Bureau of the Census, Current Population Reports, May 1973, 1974, 1975 tapes.

function and estimate a 'fixed-effect logit model' (see Chamberlain (1980) and Freeman (1978) for detailed discussions of this model). The fixed-effect procedure has the advantage over possible random-effect models of not requiring knowledge of a particular distribution for the individual propensities. The fixed-effect model yields consistent estimates regardless of the distribution of individual propensities, whereas random-effect models based on specific distributions yield inconsistent estimates when that distribution is incorrectly specified.

The Michigan PSID data set provides sufficient number of observations on individuals over time for the fixed effect logit to be estimated and has, accordingly, been used to test the selectivity interpretation of the union effect. Since, with individual constants in the equations, the behavior of persons who remain in their job over the whole period or who quit in each period is explained entirely by the constant, the sample drops from that used in Table 9.2 to 1,232 cases, consisting of 877 cases of a single quit, 276 cases of two quits, 67 cases of three quits, and 12 cases of four quits.[15]

The results of the calculations, given in Table 9.5, yield coefficients on unionism of similar magnitude to those obtained in Table 9.2 but show a marked change in the coefficient on log wages, which changes from significant negative to insignificant positive.[16] Since controlling for individual propensities to quit has essentially no effect on the coefficient on unionism, we conclude that the union impact appears to operate by changing the behavior of the same person rather than by unionization of innately more stable persons. In an organized workplace a given individual is less likely to quit than in a nonorganized work place, wages held fixed.

THE UNION VOICE INTERPRETATION

The analysis thus far has documented the existence of a significant inverse relation between trade unionism and various measures of exit behavior, which exists separate from the effect of unions on wages and the selectivity of innately more stable workers by unions. Because of the lack of a direct measure of 'voice' components of unionism, however, the voice interpretation of the relation rests on the inability of other factors to explain the union effect, rather than on positive support for the hypothesis. This section considers some direct evidence on the link between one of the major components of union voice, the grievance and arbitration system, and exit behavior, and finds some support for the hypothesis.

One direct test of the voice interpretation is to compare the effect of unionism on the exit behavior of workers more or less likely to use the grievance system. Persons with grievances should evince a sharper drop in the propensity to exit under unionism than persons relatively pleased with their job. Empirically, in terms of the information on the longitudinal files under study, workers who report themselves dissatisfied with their jobs are most likely to raise grievances and thus be affected by the grievance procedure. Does unionism reduce the rate of exit of dissatisfied workers more sharply than that of satisfied workers?

To answer this question, the quit rates of workers with varying expressed levels of job satisfaction were tabulated for union and nonunion workers separately from the Michigan and NLS older male surveys. In the 1972 Michigan survey, workers were asked, 'in general, would you say that your job is very enjoyable, mostly enjoyable, . . . not enjoyable at all?' with five possible answers. In the NLS a similar question was asked ('How do you feel about your job?') with four categories of responses. For ease of presentation and to obtain a reasonably sized sample of dissatisfied workers (few express extreme dissatisfaction), the categories have been grouped into three classes: highly satisfied workers, moderately satisfied workers, dissatisfied workers; with the result shown in Table 9.6.

Measured by *absolute* differences in quit rates, unionism clearly has a greater effect on dissatisfied than on other workers. In the PSID, quit rates are 4.8 points lower for 'highly satisfied' union workers than for highly satisfied nonunion workers and 6.2 points lower among the 'moderately satisfied,' and 8.1 points lower among the dissatisfied. In the NLS older male sample, the greater impact of trade unionism is even more marked, with a 4.7 point difference in quit rates among the satisfied rising to differences of 6.5 and 22.1 points with increased dissatisfaction. Measured as logits of the rates, the picture is less clear. The logit of the quit rate of union workers increases more slowly than the logit of the quit rate of nonunion workers as dissatisfaction increases from highly satisfied persons to dissatisfied persons and from highly satisfied persons to moderately satisfied persons. However, the logits increase more rapidly for union workers in comparisons of moderately satisfied and dissatisfied persons. Interpretation of the evidence depends on the metric and group used to evaluate the differences.

A second way of evaluating the effect of grievance and arbitration on

Table 9.6 Effect of unionism on quits of workers by level of satisfaction

State	Frequency of quits				Logit of quit rates			
	PSID		NLS older male		PSID		NLS older male	
	Union	Nonunion	Union	Nonunion	Union	Nonunion	Union	Nonunion
Highly satisfied	4.8%	9.1%	0.8%	5.5%	-2.79	-2.30	-2.82	-2.84
Moderately satisfied	6.1	12.3	0.9	7.4	-2.73	-1.96	-4.70	-2.53
Dissatisfied	10.4	18.5	2.2	24.3	-2.15	-1.48	-3.79	-1.14
Change from highly satisfied to dissatisfied	5.6	9.4	1.4	18.8	0.64	0.82	1.03	1.70

Source: Michigan Panel Survey of Income Dynamics.

Table 9.7 Effect of grievance clauses on tenure of union workers

Survey (sample size)	Regression ceofficient and standard error for effect of percentage of contracts with nonrestrictive grievance clauses on tenure of union workers[a]
NLS older male (n = 728)	8.4 (2.2)
PSID (n = 801)	2.2 (1.6)

Note:
a   In the NLS other variables included six occupation dummies, three region dummies, education, age, a retirement benefit dummy, and In wage, dummies for SMSA and race, number of dependants and the percentage of contracts with layoff and seniority clauses. The R^2 was 0.146. In the PSID controls were the same except that they include seven occupation dummies, and a sex dummy and excluded the retirements benefit variable. The R^2 was 0.400.

exit behavior is to compare the exit behavior of unionized workers in sectors of the economy having different types of grievance systems. The more inclusive or stronger the system, the greater should be the reduction in exit. While detailed knowledge of the operation of grievance machinery is needed for a definitive evaluation, readily available data on collective bargaining clauses from the Bureau of Labor Statistics can be used to obtain a rough measure of the scope of grievance systems. The BLS divides grievance clauses into those with 'unrestricted' coverage (43 per cent of the total), defined as expressing or implying 'that any dispute or complaint could be processed as a grievance' and those with 'restrictive' coverage (57 per cent) because 'they limit the grievance process to disputes arising under or relating to specific terms of the contract' [BLS Bulletin 1425-1, p. 6]. The percentage of workers covered by unrestricted clauses varies sufficiently across industries to provide some indication of industrial differences in the scope of grievance procedures. Accordingly, the percentage of contracts with nonrestrictive grievance clauses reported by the BLS [Bulletin 1425, Table 1, p. 2] for 31 separate industries was added to the NLS and PSID data tapes and the effect of the new variable on the tenure of union workers estimated by linear regression analysis To eliminate the possibility that 'favorable' results would result simply from the distinctive work arrangements in construction (low tenure, limited grievance system), construction workers were deleted from the sample. To reduce the danger that the effect of other union work conditions correlated with nonrestrictive grievance systems might underlie any statistical results, two other measures of contracts were also entered in the calculations: the percentage of contracts with explicit layoff provisions; and the percentage with seniority provisions.[17] All of the various control variables used earlier, except for industry dummies, were also entered into the equation. The resultant coefficients on the grievance clause variable are given in Table 9.7. While the crude measure of differences in grievance procedures makes the results no more than suggestive, the positive impact of the scope of the grievance system on tenure is consistent with the model.

More direct evidence on the impact of a grievance system on turnover is given, for a limited number of hospitals, in a study by Sargent and Clawson (1974). In their data set, hospitals with a written grievance procedure had a yearly separation rate of 0.50 while hospitals without a grievance system had a separation rate of 0.81; the simple correlation of separation rates with the presence of written grievance procedures is −0.72; the partial correlation between separation and grievance procedures is −0.74, conditional on bed size of hospital and distance from the center of the nearest city.[18] While absence of other control variables makes these relations suggestive rather than definitive, the significant relation between turnover and grievance procedure supports our interpretation of the evidence on the data tapes for individuals.

Finally, the voice interpretation of the apparently sizeable nonwage effect of unionism on exit, while novel in some respects, is consistent with the corpus of industrial relations analyses and findings. Industrial relations studies of unionism have traditionally stressed the importance of grievance, arbitration, and related factors in the impact of the institution (Slichter, Livernash, and Healey, 1975; Dunlop, 1970; and Kerr, 1978). Analyses of why workers join unions almost invariably find that worker grievances, usually with specific managerial policies rather than possible higher wages, motivate organization (Seidman, Landon, and Karsh, 1957). Companies that face organizing drives are usually advised by labor-management legal consultants to concentrate on personnel policy issues relating to what could easily be labeled voice issues. At the other end of the spectrum, AFL-CIO propaganda places great stress on the role of unions as the 'voice' of workers. These pieces of information suggest that the interpretation of the depressant effect of unionism on exit given in this study is broadly consistent with the industrial relations picture of the operation of trade unions in the United States.

CONSEQUENCES AND IMPLICATIONS

The evidence that trade unionism appears to reduce the exit propensity of workers, with at least some of the effect due to the operation of unions as an institution of collective voice, has implications for the functioning of the job market and for future research on trade unions. It suggests that unionism is a major force in the creation of a relatively permanent enterprise workforce and thus of the types of market arrangements and adjustments to which permanent attachment gives rise (see Feldstein (1976) and the literature cited therein). For example, with quits playing a lesser role in labor force adjustments in the union sector, one would expect organized firms to make greater use of layoffs and recalls, as appears to be the case (Medoff, 1979). At the same time, permanent attachment of workers can be expected to reduce wage adjustments over the business cycle and enhance employment fluctuations (Feldstein, 1976). The composition of the compensation package is also likely to be affected, with the greater likelihood of remaining with a firm raising the deferred compensation share of the wage bill (Freeman, 1981). Investments in firm-specific human capital may also be increased by union-induced reductions in exit. In terms of productivity, the increase in job tenure and reduction quits can be expected to raise the efficiency of organized establishments by lowering the costs of turnover in the form of hiring and training expenses. Brown and Medoff (1978) find that a sizeable proportion of the relation between unions and productivity among two-digit manufacturing industries across states is, indeed, due to the lower quit rates of unionized workers.

Finally, with respect to research, this study has taken only a first empirical step in analyzing the nonmonopoly wage effects of unionism. The model and findings suggest that greater attention be given to the economic effects of unionism beyond the monopoly wage gains that are at the center of most modern empirical work.

NOTES

1. For a detailed discussion of unions as a voice institution, see Freeman (Chapter 8) and Freeman and Medoff 1984).
2. There are two conditions for the delay effect to operate. First, there must be some nonzero probability of redressing the grievance, so that the worker is willing to try the option. Second, the length of employment must be finite, for otherwise delays will not affect the steady-state solution. If, on average, the length of employment were initially, say ten years, then a delay in quitting for, say one half year, would reduce the quit rate from 0.10 to about 0.095, a nonnegligible though by no means large, effect.
3. In discussion with ten large nonunion firms with grievance systems, all but one reported that the system was instituted in part to reduce worker desires for unionism (private interviews, 1978).
4. This argument can be put more formally. Let $L(W,C)$ be the supply curve facing the firm, where C = desired condition of work, and L_W, $L_C > 0$. Then the 'supply price' for the condition, defined as the wage that is needed to maintain a given workforce L at various levels of C can be written as $W(L,C)$, where $W_C < 0$. The marginal evaluation of the condition is $W_C(L,C)$; the median worker evaluation is $W_C(L_m,C)$, where L_m is the median. The average of worker marginal evaluations is $[\int_0^L W_C(X,C)dX/L]/L$. If, as assumed in the text, $W_{CL} < 0$, then $W_C(L_m,C) < W_C(L,C)$, and $[\int_0^L W_C(X,C)]/L < W_C(L,C)$ so that whether the union represents the median worker or the average desire of workers, it will place a greater weight on the condition than the competitive signal. See Viscusi (1978) for elaboration of models of this type.
5. More precisely, let W = wages, T = tenure, U_w = error in the wage

equation and U_t = error for tenure equation. Then, ignoring other factors for simplicity, we have the equation with wages as the dependent variable:

$$W = aT + U_w \tag{1}$$

or rewritten with T as the dependent variable,

$$T = (1/a)W - (1/a)U_w = a'W + V_t \tag{2}$$

We also have the equation with tenure as the dependent variable:

$$T = \beta W + U_t \tag{3}$$

Now the OLS estimate is

$$\hat{\beta} = \frac{\sum WT}{\sum W^2} = \beta + \frac{1/N\sum WU_t}{1/N\sum W^2} \tag{4}$$

where N = number of observations. So

$$\text{plim } \hat{\beta} = \beta + \frac{\text{plim } 1/N\sum WU_t}{\text{plim } 1/N\sum W^2} \tag{5}$$

But since $W = (U_t - V_t)/(a' - \beta)$,

$$\text{plim}(1/N)\ WU_t = \text{cov}(WU_t) = (1/(a' - \beta))\sigma_U^2 \tag{6}$$

when the covariance between V_t and U_t is 0. Moreover, in this the denominator of the right-hand expression in (5) becomes

$$\text{plim}(1/N)W^2 = \text{var}(W) = (1/(a' - \beta)^2)\ (\sigma_v^2 + \sigma_U^2). \tag{7}$$

But then

$$\text{plim } \hat{\beta} = \beta - (\beta - a')\ [\sigma_U^2/(\sigma_U^2 + \sigma_v^2)]. \tag{8}$$

We assume that $a \approx 0.02$ so that $a' \approx 50$ and that β is much smaller. Thus plim $\beta = \beta$ + positive term $> \beta$. The bias is upward.

6. These are to be distinguished from temporary separations due to temporary layoffs.
7. For discussions of these data sets see US Department of Labor Research Monographs 15 and 16; Institute for Social Research (University of Michigan) and US Bureau of the Census.
8. Note that we can compare the exponential and linear forms directly because they have the same dependent variable T. Thus, the R^2 is the correct measure of fit.
9. A potential problem with this procedure is that it ignores possible selectivity bias in the group that separate from their job.
10. This equation included the same controls as in Table 9.1. The R^2 was 0.462 and the SEE was 0.552. Tenure was included as an explanatory variable. There were 207 observations.
11. These are based on 525 separations from 1969 to 1970. Comparable estimates for other years give smaller coefficients on unionism and, except in one case, on ln wages as well:

	$b_{W_A UW}$	$b_{W_A WU}$
1970–1 ($n = 473$)	0.04 (0.06)	0.41 (0.04)
1971–2 ($n = 493$)	0.10 (0.06)	0.32 (0.04)
1972–3 ($n = 590$)	0.11 (0.06)	0.36 (0.04)

In each regression, all of the control variables listed in Table 9.2 were included in the calculations. Tenure was excluded.

12. Adjusting for W_A we have

$$b_{QWUW_A} = 1.61(-0.57) = -0.92$$

and

$$b_{QUWW_A} = 0.52 + 0.13(0.92) = -0.74$$

Adjusting for the effect of fringes on the union coefficient yields

$$b_{QUF} = [-0.74 - 0.13(0.92)]/0.91 = -0.68$$

13. The equation included the same controls as Table 9.4. Tenure was excluded as an explanatory variable.

14. When a person never quits, the best estimate of his individual propensity in the fixed logit is that he has a constant term that is $-\infty$. When a person quits always, the model fits best with an individual constant of ∞. Hence, these persons drop from the sample.

15. The differential effect of the individual constants on the union and wage coefficients may reflect the fact that wages are more person-related than unionism, which is much more of a social phenomenon.

16. The highly satisfied group in the PSID consist of persons who responded 'very or mostly enjoyable' ($n = 2,566$); the moderately satisfied group were those who responded 'somewhat enjoyable' ($n = 868$); the rest were labeled dissatisfied ($n = 293$). In the NLS older men, highly satisfied persons answered 'like it very much' ($n = 899$); moderately satisfied said 'like it fairly well' ($n = 734$); while the rest were dissatisfied ($n = 102$). Numbers in parentheses are the number of respondents in those categories.

17. The percentage with layoff clauses was obtained from US BLS Bulletin 1425–14, Table 1, p. 32. The percentage with seniority clauses was taken from US BLS Bulletin 1425–13, Table 8, p. 53.

18. The figures reported are based on simple correlation coefficients reported in the Sargent-Clawson (1974) article.

BIBLIOGRAPHY

Brown, C., and Medoff, J., 'Trade unions in the production process', *Journal of Political Economy* (1978), LXXXVI.

Bureau of National Affairs, *Personnel Policies for Unorganized Employees*, Survey No. 84 of Personnel Policies Forum (1968).

Burton, N., and Parker, I., 'Inter-industry variation in voluntary labor mobility', *Industrial Labor Relations Review* (January 1969) XXII, pp. 199–216.

Chamberlain, G., 'Analysis of covariance with qualitative data', *Review of Economic Studies* (1980), pp. 225–38.

Dunlop, J., *Industrial Relations Systems* (Carbondale and Edwardsville: Southern Illinois Press, reprint, 1970).

Feldstein, M., 'Temporary layoffs in the theory of unemployment', *Journal of Political Economy* (October 1976), LXXXIV, pp. 937–57.

Freeman R., 'Individual mobility and union voice in the labor market', *American Economic Review* (May 1976), LXVI, pp. 361–8 (this volume, Chapter 8).

Freeman, R., 'A fixed effect logit model of the impact of unionism on quits',

NBER Working Paper No. 280 (1978).

Freeman, R., 'The effect of trade unionism on fringe benefits', *Industrial and Labor Relations Review* (July 1981), vol. 34, no. 4.

Freeman, R., and Medoff, J., *What Do Unions Do?* (New York: Basic Books, 1984).

Galenson, W., *The AFL Response to the CIO Challenge* (Cambridge, MA: Harvard University Press, 1963).

Hirschman, A., *Exit, Voice, and Loyalty* (Cambridge, MA: Harvard University Press, 1970).

Hirschman, A., 'Some uses of the exit-voice approach–discussion', *American Economic Review* (May 1976), LXVI, pp. 386–9.

Institute for Social Research, *A Panel Study of Income Dynamics* (University of Michigan, 1968–73).

Kahn, L., 'Union impact: a reduced form approach', *Review of Economics and Statistics* (November, 1977), LIX, 503–7.

Kerr, C., *Labor Market and Wage Determination* (Berkeley: University of California Press, 1978).

Medoff, J., 'Layoffs and alternatives under trade unions in United States manufacturing', *American Economic Review* (1979), LXIX, pp. 380–95.

National Industrial Conference Board, *Collective Bargaining Through Employee Representation* (New York: National Industrial Conference Board, 1933).

Nerlove, M., and Press, S. J., 'Univariate and multivariate log-linear and logistic models' (Rand, December 1973).

Parsons, C., 'Models of labor market turnover: a theoretical and empirical survey', in R. Ehrenberg (ed.), *Research in Labor Economics*, vol. 1 (Greenwich, CT: JAI Press, 1977).

Pencavel, J., *An analysis of the Quit Rate in American Manufacturing Industry* (Princeton: Princeton University Press, 1970).

Reynolds, L., *Labor Economics and Labor Relations*, 6th edn (Englewood Cliffs, NJ: Prentice Hall, 1974).

Sargent, B., and Clawson, D., 'The effect of selected factors on hospital turnover rates', *Personnel Journal* (January 1974), LIII, pp. 30–4.

Seidman, J., Landon, J., and Karsh, B., 'Why workers join unions', *The Annals of the American Academy of Political and Social Science* (March 1957).

Slichter, S., *Union Policies and Industrial Management* (Washington: Brookings, 1941).

Slichter, S., Livernash, R. and Healey, J., *The Impact of Collective Bargaining on Management* (Washington: Brookings, 1975).

Stoikov, V., and Raimon, R., 'Determinants of the differences in quit rates among industries', *American Economic Review* (December 1958), XLVIII, pp. 1283–398.

US Department of Labor, Bureau of Labor Statistics, Major Collective Bargaining Agreements, *Grievance Procedures*, Bulletin 1425–1.

US Department of Labor, *Characteristics of Major Collective Bargaining Agreements, July 1, 1975*, Bulletin 1957 (1977).

US Department of Labor, Manpower Research Monograph, No. 15, *The Pre-Retirement Years*.

US Department of Labor, Manpower Research Monograph, No. 16, *Career Thresholds*.

Viscusi, W. K., 'Unions, labor market structure, and the welfare implications of the quality of work', *Journal of Labor Research* (Spring 1980), 1, pp. 175–92.

10 · EFFECTS OF UNIONS ON THE ECONOMY

The impact of trade unionism on the economy has long been an area of contention among economists. There are those – Alfred Marshall, Sumner Slichter, Lloyd Reynolds, John Dunlop – who come up with generally favorable assessments of unions. There are those – Milton Friedman, Henry Simons, Fritz Machlup, Gottfried Haberler – with generally negative assessments.[1]

To buttress their beliefs analysts can, and have, cited various instances in which unions have been a positive or negative factor in the economy. A reading of the case study literature, ranging from the immense Slichter, Livernash, and Healy volume to smaller studies of individual bargaining situations, suggests that everything anyone has said – good and bad – about unions is true. There are situations in which unions and the collective bargaining process raise wages, improve personnel practices, lower turnover, and induce management to improve productivity. There are also cases in which unions harm the operation of individual companies, reduce productivity, and have a generally deleterious effect on the economy. There are unions that are democratic social institutions and unions that are nondemocratic and corrupt.

To provide a realistic assessment of the economic effects of unionism it is necessary to go beyond the recitation of good and bad cases to a broad statistical analysis that permits one to reach generalizations about the institution as a whole and to specify the conditions under which the positive or negative effects of the institution are likely to dominate.

In recent years the availability of computerized data files that contain vast amounts of information on thousands of individuals, establishments, and companies has for the first time offered students of unionism the opportunity for such broad quantitative analyses. While an overall assessment of what unions do to the economy requires one to weigh positive and negative impacts on diverse outcomes – on which reasonable persons may differ – it is possible to determine the direction and magnitude of union effects on key economic variables.

In this chapter I present evidence indicating that in addition to well-advertised effects on wages, unions alter nearly every other measurable aspect of the operation of workplaces and enterprises, from turnover to productivity, wage inequality, profits, and fringe benefits. The evidence indicates that unions have 'two faces': a 'monopoly wage-setting' face, with generally harmful effects to the overall efficiency of the economy; and a 'collective voice/management response' (voice/response) face with generally positive effects on the operation of the economy (Table 10.1).

In the United States in recent years the empirical evidence suggests that the voice/response face of unions dominates the monopoly face, with unions in most settings associated with greater efficiency, lower earnings inequality, and generally more desirable workplaces. The widely stressed monopoly effects of unions on resource allocation and on such macro-

Table 10.1 The two faces of trade unionism

	Union effects on economic efficiency	Union effects on distribution of income
Monopoly face	Unions raise wages above competitive levels, leading to too little labor relative to capital in unionized firms.	Unions increase income inequality by raising the wages of highly skilled workers.
	Union work rules decrease productivity.	Unions create horizontal inequities by creating differentials among comparable workers.
Collective Voice/institutional response face	Unions have some positive effects on productivity – reducing quit rates, inducing management to alter methods of production and adopt more efficient policies, and improving morale and cooperation among workers.	Unions standard-rate policies reduce inequality among organized workers in a given company or a given industry.
	Unions collect information about the preferences of all workers, leading the firm to choose a better mix of employee compensation and a better set of personnel policies.	Union rules limit the scope for arbitrary actions in the promotion, layoff, and recall of individuals.
		Unionism fundamentally alters the distribution of power between marginal (generally junior) and more permanent (generally senior) employees, causing union firms to select different compensation packages and personnel practice from those of nonunion firms.

Source: Based on R. B. Freeman and J. L. Medoff, 'The two faces of unionism', *The Public Interest* (Fall 1979), 57, p. 75.

economic factors as wage inflation are found to be relatively modest in quantitative terms, and the voice/response effects of unions on turnover, wage inequality, provision of fringe benefits, and productivity are found to be somewhat larger.[2]

Evidence suggesting that, on net, unions are a positive economic force does not, of course, mean that unions are beneficial to individual companies. Indeed, the opposite appears to be the case on average. The gains of unionism accrue to their members. The costs show up in lower profitability for many organized companies. The paradox of American unionism is that it is at one and the same time a plus on the overall social balance sheet (in most though not all circumstances) and a minus on the corporate balance sheet (again, in most though not all circumstances).

THE UNION MONOPOLY PAY EFFECT

That unions raise the level of pay of their members is hardly news. Some early observers of unionism, indeed, expressed fears that the union monopoly wage effect constituted 'an attack on the competitive system' (Lindblom), 'the rock on which our present system is most likely to crack up' (Simons), or 'the most important domestic economic problems' (Haberler). Empirical estimates of union wage effects and historical experience (including the successful operation of highly unionized economies throughout the free world) show these fears to be groundless (Lindblom, 1949; Simons, 1944; Haberler, 1959).

They are not groundless because the union impact on wages is slight. A seemingly endless number of empirical studies of union wage effects, which compare the pay of union and nonunion workers (establishments) with similar economic attributes, or which compare pay of workers before and after they have been unionized, show that the union effect on wages is quite sizeable, 15 to 25 per cent on average in post-World War II years.

The effect is not, of course, uniform across workers or industries. In general, the union wage effect has been larger in historically regulated sectors (such as trucking and air transport) and in sectors in which unions organized larger portions of the workforce. It has been larger for workers who tend to be lower paid and less skilled than for those who tend to be higher paid (see Figure 10.1).

The effect is, moreover, not constant over time. In the 1970s, when the economy performed particularly poorly, the union wage premium rose, as unions maintained or increased the real (inflation-adjusted) pay of their members, while other workers suffered from increases below the rate of inflation. During this decade the union wage effect rose by as much as 9 to 10 percentage points (from about 15 to 25 per cent) putting significant profit pressure on organized companies. The concession bargaining of the 1980s represents a return to more traditional union wage premium.

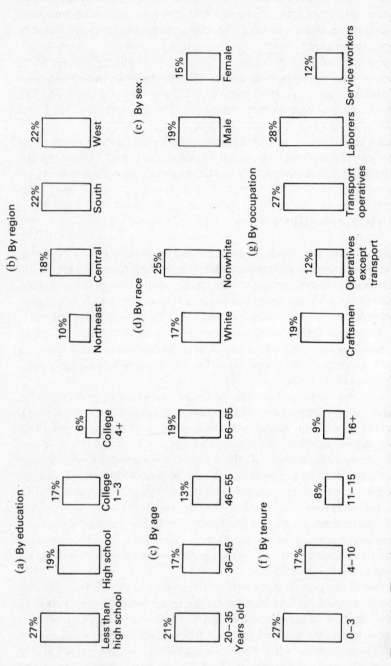

Figure 10.1 The union wage advantage by demographic group, for blue-collar workers, aged 20–65, 1979: (a) by education; (b) by region; (c) by age; (d) by race; (e) by sex; (f) by tenure; (g) by occupation.

Source: R. B. Freeman and J. L. Medoff, *What Do Unions Do?* (New York: Basic Books, 1984), p. 49.

While the union wage premium is sizeable, the adverse economic effects on resource allocation tend – virtually all analysts agree – to be slight. Indeed, empirical studies find only modest misallocative effects because the value of the output loss due to the monopoly increase in wages depends on the product of that increase and the number of workers whose employment is lost due to higher wages, which tends to be modest. Estimates based on the standard economic formula for evaluating the social loss due to monopolies suggest that union monopoly wage gains cost the economy 0.2 to 0.4 per cent of gross national product (GNP), which in 1980 amounted to about $5 to $10 billion dollars or $20 to $40 per person.[3]

Recent theoretical work on union contracts suggests that even this modest estimate may be too large. This work stresses the impact of union contracts on employment levels as well as wages and argues that an 'efficient contract' would redistribute company income from profits to workers without causing any social misallocative loss. A smart union leader and company bargainer could rewrite an existing contract to eliminate the social loss and raise either pay or profits or both. Consistent with this argument are studies which find union employment effects, (as opposed to wage effects) difficult to estimate in data.[4] As analysis of the 'efficient contracts' view of unionism has just begun, the safe conclusion is simply that traditional estimates of union misallocative effects which are modest probably overstate the true effects somewhat.

UNION WAGE GAINS AND INFLATION

It was once widely believed that union wage increases were a primary cause of cost-push inflation. Until the 'stagflation' of the late 1970s and early 1980s, the facts contradicted this belief. Far from outpacing other wages or salaries, union wages increased more slowly in inflationary periods, so that the union wage premium tended to fall. The usual explanation was that by negotiating contracts that set wages over extended periods, typically three years, union wage gains caused periods of inflation to last longer than they would have otherwise, but one could not reasonably blame unions for initiating cost-push inflation.[5]

The increase in the union wage premium in the highly inflationary late 1970s and early 1980s lent new life to the argument that unions cause inflation. In this period, union cost-of-living adjustment clauses may have created a new situation in which union wage policies tended to augment rather than to reduce inflationary wage pressures.

Just how important might the union wage gains have been to the inflation of the past decade? If union wage increases have no effect on the wages of other workers, it is relatively easy to demonstrate that unions can be blamed for only a minuscule share of inflation. To see this, note that:

Contribution of union
wage increases to
percentage change in = $\frac{\text{Union labor's}}{\text{share of costs}}$ × $\begin{array}{l}\text{Percentage change}\\\text{in union wage}\\\text{premium}\end{array}$
unit costs, and thus in
prices

Unionized labor accounts for about 25 per cent of total cost of national output, and the union wage premium rose over the entire 1975–81 period by a total of about 9 percentage points. The result was to add 2.3 percentage points of inflation to the observed 68 point increase in the GNP deflator. While it is still possible that union wage increases adversely affected inflation through 'spillovers' on other workers, no serious student of inflation believes this to be a major cause of the stagflation of the period. There simply is no evidence for such an assertion (Flanagan, 1976, 1984; Johnson, 1977; Mitchell, 1980).

STRUCTURE OF PAY: DISPERSION AND COMPOSITION

The impact of unions on pay goes far beyond altering the level of pay in organized jurisdiction. Anyone who compares union and nonunion firms is almost immediately struck by two marked differences in the structure of pay: the unionized sector evinces greater equality (less dispersion) of wages for comparable workers and it pays a larger proportion of compensation in the form of fringe benefits.

The effect of unions on equality of pay has long been at the heart of economists' evaluations of the institution. In *Capitalism and Freedom* Milton Friedman laid out the case that, for all the talk of worker solidarity, unions increase inequality:

> If unions raise wage rates in a particular occupation or industry, they necessarily make the amount of employment available in the occupation or industry less than it otherwise would be – just as any higher price cuts down the amount purchased. The effect is an increased number of persons seeking other jobs, which forces down wages in other occupations. Since unions have generally been strongest among groups that would have been high-paid anyway, their effect has been to make high-paid workers higher paid at the expense of lower-paid workers. Unions have therefore not only harmed the public at large and workers as a whole by distorting the use of labor; they have also made the incomes of the working class more unequal by reducing the opportunities available to the most disadvantaged workers (Friedman, 1962).

By contrast, industrial relations experts, beginning with the Webbs, have stressed union standard rate policies favoring 'equal pay for equal work,' within and across establishments, as a likely force reducing inequality of wages (Reynolds and Taff, 1956).

The issue is an important one. Many people champion unions in the belief that they are an egalitarian force, and if in fact unions increase inequality, the case for a positive role of unions in the economy would be greatly weakened.

The modern empirical analyses of union effects on inequality, summarized in Table 10.2, show the claim that unionism increases inequality to be wrong; on the contrary, unionism tends to be a powerful force for equalization of earnings in the economy. The earnings inequality claim is wrong not because the effect to which it directs attention – raising wages of some workers at the expense of other workers – does not occur. It does. The claim is wrong because the increase in inequality induced by monopoly wage effects is dwarfed by three other union effects on wages that reduce inequality; union wage policies favoring lower inequality of wages within establishments; union wage policies for equal pay for equal work across establishments; and union wage gains for blue-collar labor which reduce inequality between white-collar and blue-collar workers.

The effect of unions on inequality of wages within establishments results in large part from policies designed to force employers to pay workers on the basis of specified job rates, in which all workers classified in a given category are paid the same wage, as opposed to paying personal rates that depend on the supervisor's perception of workers. Unions favor job rates for three reasons. First, as a political organization whose policies reflect the preference of average workers, unions can be expected to adopt wage policies benefiting the majority of the workforce. In most situations the majority of workers have earnings below the mean level, suggesting that the majority will favor pay policies that accord greater gains to the lower paid. Second, unions are likely to favor single-rate policies because they replace managerial discretion and power at the workplace with more objective decision rules. Because the value of a worker's contribution to a firm is extremely difficult to measure and different supervisors may read the same facts in different ways, the union will seek to protect the membership from the uncertainty of arbitrary supervisory decisions by pressing for a one-rate-per-job pay policy. Third, unions are likely to seek equalized wages among workers doing similar tasks for reasons of worker solidarity and organizational unity. As the mid-1980s debates over two-tier wage systems indicate, unions are fearful that policies other than equalization will erode their organizational strength, dividing the higher paid from the lower paid.

Comparisons of wage policies and inequality of wages within establishments show that unionism has a significant impact toward equalization of pay. One study of thousands of plants has found that 68 per cent of union workers are paid by a single rate or automatic progression in pay compared to 35 per cent of nonunion workers, with a resultant lower inequality of wages in the union plants (Freeman, 1982).

Unions try to standardize wages in an industry or local product market

Table 10.2 Studies of the impact of unionism on wage inequality

Study	Nature of data	Finding
1 Freeman (1980)	Current Population Survey data on individuals and expenditures for employee compensation data for firms.	Unionized workers have 15 per cent lower standard deviation of log earnings than otherwise comparable nonunion workers; unionism reduces white-collar/blue-collar differential by 10 per cent. These effects produce a 2–3 per cent reduction in inequality among comparable workers.
2 Freeman (1982)	BLS *Industry Wage Survey* data on individuals working in nine industries.	Standard deviation of log (wages) in union sector is on average 22 per cent lower than in nonunion sector.
3 Hirsch (1982)	Cross-sectional analysis of 1970 census of population data on 3-digit industries.	Each percentage point of unionization lowered the variance of log earnings by 0.015 points.
4 Hyclak (1977)	Cross-sectional analysis of 1970 census data on earnings in SMSAs.	Each percentage point of unionization lowered the Gini coefficient 0.021 points.
5 Hyclak (1979)	Cross-sectional analysis of 1970 census data on male earnings in SMSAs.	Each percentage point of unionization lowered Gini coefficient for men by 0.038 points.
6 Hyclak (1980)	Cross-sectional analysis of 1950, 1960, and 1970 census data on family income in the 48 contiguous states.	Each 1 per cent increase in the mean for unionization lowered the mean of the percentage of families earning under $3,000 in 1970 by 3 per cent. Similar findings for 1950 and 1960.
7 Plotnick (1982)	Time series analysis of current population survey data for men.	Each 1 percentage point of unionization lowered variance of log (earnings) by 0.065 points.
8 Freeman (1984)	Analysis of inequality of workers before and after unionization in four data sets	Workers who join unions have declines in standard deviation of earnings of 0.03 to 0.09 points compared to workers who leave unions.
9 Freeman and Medoff (1984)	Analysis of total impact of unions on earnings inequality using various data sets	Unionism reduces standard deviation of log of earnings by 3 per cent.

Note: Some of these studies used the variance of log earnings; others used the Gini coefficient, a related measure of inequality; still others used the standard deviation of earnings. The different inequality measures should yield different reductions in inequality, as they do.

Sources:
1. R. B. Freeman, 'Unionism and the dispersion of wages,' *Industrial and Labor Relations Review* (October 1980), 34, pp. 3–23.
2. R. B. Freeman, 'Union wage practices and wage dispersion within establishments', *Industrial and Labor Relations Review* (October 1982), 36.
3. Barry Hirsch, 'The Interindustry Structure of unionism, earnings and earnings dispersion', *Industrial Labor Review* (October 1982), 36.
4. Thomas Hyclak, 'Unionization and urban differentials in income inequality', *The Journal of Economics* (1977), 3, pp. 205–7.
5. Thomas Hyclak, 'The effect of unions on earnings inequality in local labor markets', *Industrial and Labor Relations Review* (October 1979), 33, pp. 77–84.
6. Thomas Hyclack, 'Unions and income inequality: some cross-state evidence', *Industrial Relations* (Spring 1980), 19, pp. 212–15.
7. Robert D. Plotnick, 'Trends in male earnings inequality', *Southern Economic Journal* (January 1982), 48, pp. 724–32.
8. R. B. Freeman, 'Longitudinal analysis of the effects of trade unions', *Journal of Labor Economics* (1984), 2, pp. 1–26.
9. R. B. Freeman and James L. Medoff, *What Do Unions Do?* (New York: Basic Books, 1984), p. 91.

in order to 'take wages out of competition.' While there are notable exceptions in the form of concessions given to companies in trouble, multi-employer bargaining (which in 1980 was the practice in agreements covering 43 per cent of the major contract workforce) or multi-plant bargaining (the practice relevant to an additional 40 per cent) tend to produce uniform or near-uniform rates across establishments. The result is a distribution of pay among plants in a given sector that paradoxically seems to more closely mirror the competitive ideal of a single rate in the market than does the distribution of pay in the nonunion sector.

Finally, because unions tend to organize more blue-collar than white-collar workers and have a larger wage impact on blue-collar workers, they reduce white-collar/blue-collar pay differentials by approximately the same amount as they raise blue-collar wages. In the average nonunion establishment, the white-collar worker earns about one and a half times as much as the blue-collar worker. In the comparable union establishment, the white-collar worker earns about one-third more than the blue-collar worker, a considerably smaller premium (Freeman and Medoff, 1984). The union monopoly wage effect that is usually cited as a contributor to blue-collar inequality is at the same time a contributor to equality between blue-collar and white-collar labor.

Adding up the three inequality-reducing effects on wages among blue-collar workers indicates that on net unions reduce inequality. The effect depends, of course, on the size of wage effects, exceptions given to standard-rate policies, and the size of the union sector. With the rise of two-tier contracts, concession bargaining, and declining union density, the inequality-reducing effect of unions is likely to become less important.

FRINGE BENEFITS

Consider two workplaces where employers are equally skilled, one union, one nonunion. Which workplace is likely to have a pension plan, better health care plans, more fringe benefits by virtually every type?

The answer from modern empirical work is unequivocal. Unionism increases fringe benefits at workplaces. It increases fringes in part because it increase wages (which can be viewed as part of its monopoly wage impact). Also, however, it raises the fringe share of the pay of workers with the same total compensation, particularly toward pensions; life, accident, and health insurance; vacation and holiday pay see Figure 10.2. In 1979, 76 per cent of unionized private sector workers had pension plans compared to 35 per cent of nonunion workers.

In addition to increasing the number of fringes available to workers, unions affect the nature of those plans. Consider first the difference between union and nonunion pension plans: union pension plans tend to be defined-benefit plans, which promise workers definite amounts of retirement pay, rather than defined-contribution plans, which invest moneys and pay workers the return on the investment. Defined-benefit plans are generally favored by senior workers who enjoy the rewards of increased defined benefits without incurring the full costs. In the 1970s all but 10 per cent of union private pension plans were of the defined-benefit type, compared with a bare third of nonunion private pension plans. The union preference for defined-benefit plans also reflects the desire of unions and workers to avoid the risk of allowing retirement pay to depend on fluctuations in capital markets. In the life, accident, and health areas, union plants are more likely to include dental and eyeglass benefits, as well as to increase medical and life insurance expenditures.

The union effect on fringes is greater in smaller firms than in larger firms and is especially significant in industries where workers are more attached to occupations than to employers (construction, for example), or where firms are relatively small (such as trucking). This is primarily because fringe programs with sizeable set-up costs and deferred compensation require a large and permanent market institution to administer and maintain them, and in the above situations unions are the sole such institutions. Multi-employer programs, of the type initiated by unions, make benefits portable across employers and provide the size to reduce average set-up costs. The vast majority of multi-employer pension plans are union-run (68 per cent in the pension plan file of the Office of Pension and Welfare Benefit Programs, Department of Labor), and while a few have attracted attention for illicit practices (the Teamsters Central States Pension Fund being the most infamous case), most such plans provide workers with benefits otherwise unavailable in their sector.

Is the impact of unions in raising fringe benefits a plus or a minus to

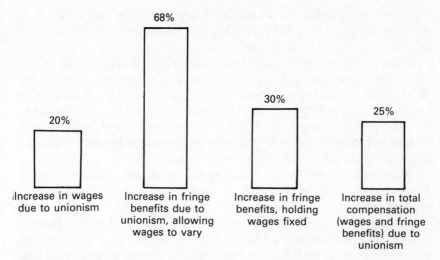

Figure 10.2 Estimates of percentage impact of unionism on wage, fringe benefits and total compensation.

Source: R. B. Freeman and J. L. Medoff, *What Do Unions Do?* (New York: Basic Books, 1984), p. 64.

the economy? In terms of the conventional 'monopoly wage' criticism of unionism, the part of the union effect on fringes that raises labor costs is an additional social cost of union monopoly power. In terms of the representation or voice role of unions, the increased share of fringes in compensation is likely to be an economic plus as it reflects the ability of unions to provide management with better information about worker preferences (through bargaining) and likely cost savings due to group purchase. Whether the positive or negative effects on the overall economy are more important is unclear. What is clear is that unionism has greatly altered the ways in which workers are paid.

EXIT-VOICE: TURNOVER

The effect of unions on labor turnover and creating relatively permanent committed workforces is central to understanding what unions do to the economy. In theory, unionism can positively influence the functioning of individual enterprise and the overall economy by providing workers with a 'voice' alternative to quitting when they are discontented with work conditions. In a non-union setting the unhappy worker 'votes with his feet' by quitting his job. In a union setting, he or she can negotiate changes in terms of work through collective bargaining and can obtain redress to individual grievances through the grievance-arbitration system. In addition, by serving as a mechanism for enforcing labor contracts, unions are likely to create greater opportunities for deferred compensation as part of labor contracts.

Because relatively permanent employees behave differently than short-term employees, the potential reduction in exit due to unionism has far-reaching implications for the operation of firms. How sizeable is the union-caused reduction in exit and increase in permanency of workforces? To what extent are the effects of unions on turnover due to the potentially socially deleterious monopoly wage effects and to what extent are they due to the potentially beneficial 'voice' effects?

Considerable research has been devoted to examining the relation between unionism and exit behavior. Some studies have compared the quit rates of workers with similar personal characteristics (age, sex, race, education), with similar wages, and in the same occupation and industry in the presence of unionism and in the absence of unionism. Other analyses compare the quit rates at establishments in industries that are heavily unionized with those in industries that are lightly unionized. Still others compare the number of years union and nonunion workers remain with the same firm. The most recent studies use work history files that follow people for as long as a decade to contrast the exit behavior of the same worker when he or she works union to what he or she works nonunion.

Regardless of their form the studies seek to control for the union wage effect by comparing workers paid the same wages. This is critical because union-induced monopoly wage increases which reduce quitting may be more harmful than beneficial to the economy, whereas reductions in quits due to better work conditions, grievance procedures, and the like are likely to be beneficial.

The evidence that unionism reduces quit behavior and creates a more permanent workforce is compelling.[6] Every study finds that, independent of raising wages, unionism substantially reduces quits and increases the years a worker stays with his firm. Virtually every study finds, moreover, that the effects of unions on quits is far in excess of the impact of the union monopoly wage increase on quits. On average unionism reduces the probability that a worker quits by from 31 to 65 per cent and correspondingly increases the number of years a worker stays with an employer from 23 to 32 per cent (Freeman and Medoff, 1984). Unionism is an important force in reducing turnover and creating permanent employment of the type that some believe contributes to the Japanese economic success.

Is the reduction in exit worth a lot to firms? To workers? How does the potential gain in social product from lower turnover compare with the monopoly cost of unionism?

For firms, a reasonable estimate is that the lower turnover due to unionism is equivalent to a 1 to 2 per cent reduction in cost, or equivalently, to a 1 to 2 per cent increase in productivity. While not negligible, these savings are dwarfed by the union wage effect, guaranteeing that firms will not invite organization to enjoy the benefits of lower turnover.

For workers, by contrast, the potential welfare gain from union work conditions is sizeable. Our best estimate is that unionism is equivalent to a 40 per cent wage increase: that is, one would have to pay nonunion workers 40 per cent higher wages to reduce their quit rate to the union level. Translating this into an economists' 'consumer surplus' yields a conservative estimate of the welfare gain of 0.2 to 0.3 per cent of GNP, which is of comparable magnitude to the social cost of unionism estimated earlier. There is, however, one difference between these social losses and gains: the benefit of voice accrues to organized workers only, whereas the costs come out of everyone's pocket. Even so, it is striking that the voice benefits, traditionally ignored in quantitative evaluations of unionism, are as large as the monopoly costs.

LAYOFFS AND CONCESSIONS

A firm faces a decline in demand for its product and must decide how to adjust its employment, wages, and hours. Should it lay off workers? Should it lower wages? Reduce work hours?

Trade unions are concentrated in highly cyclical parts of the economy – manufacturing and construction – so that union policies can greatly affect how the economy responds to the business cycle. In the United States, unions have generally opted for an adjustment pattern based largely on temporary layoffs rather than wage or hour reductions. Temporary layoffs typically last less than a month and generally end with the recall of the laid-off workers. Because workers are generally recalled or rehired, temporary layoffs are not as serious as permanent layoffs, which occur as a result of such permanent economic changes as the shutting down of an entire plant.

The difference between union and nonunion policies regarding temporary layoffs are substantial: layoff rates are two to four times higher in the union than in the nonunion sector, and union workers are 50 to 60 per cent more likely to be on temporary-layoff unemployment as a result (Freeman and Medoff, 1984).

Why do unionized workers and firms choose temporary layoffs rather than reductions in wages or hours? The most important reason is that temporary layoffs usually mean laying off junior workers, not the senior employees who have a greater influence on union policies than they would have on the policies of a nonunion firm. Faced with the choice of reduced earnings through fewer hours or lower wages or the unemployment of a junior worker, the senior worker will select the policy that is personally most beneficial. Except in cases where mass layoffs are threatened, this will lead him or her to prefer layoffs to the other forms of adjustment.

It is one thing to be laid off temporarily, knowing you will be recalled to your job in a few weeks. It is another matter entirely to face the danger of extended joblessness because of an event such as a plant closing or bankruptcy. In a temporary layoff, the senior worker is protected by inverse seniority layoff rules; when a shut-down threatens, all workers' jobs are seriously endangered. As a result, union policies with respect to shutdowns on prolonged economic distresses differ from their policies with respect to temporary layoffs.

Faced with the threat of shutdowns or related long-term company problems, unions in the 1980s have proven to be much more flexible in their wage-setting policies than most observers would have expected on the basis of earlier experiences. Unions in industries undergoing serious long-term economic problems have negotiated wage concessions. In some sectors they have agreed to two-tier systems of pay, which reduce the pay for new workers while maintaining the pay of incumbents. Profit-sharing schemes, once considered anathema among unionists, have been negotiated in several cases. The lesson is that when jobs of senior union workers are threatened unions are highly flexible and willing to adjust in order to save those jobs. The stereotype of the union as an inflexible institution on the wage side has been proven false by these developments.

PRODUCTIVITY

Few issues regarding the economic effects of unions have generated more controversy than what unions do to productivity. As Bok and Dunlop wrote in 1970:

> For more than a century and a half, economists have debated the effects of 'combinations of workmen,' or collective bargaining, on the efficiency of business enterprises. The literature is replete with conflicting appraisals of the impact of work stoppages, work rules, regulation of machinery, apprenticeship, and training on employee efficiency and managerial decisions (Bok and Dunlop, 1970).

Modern quantitative analysis of productivity in organized and unorganized industries and plants suggest that, on average, unionism is associated with higher productivity, by perhaps 6 to 10 per cent on average with however wide variation across sectors, plants, and time periods.

From one perspective the productivity findings are to be expected, at least in sectors where unionized firms compete with nonunion firms. Given that unionized firms pay higher wages, one should expect management to undertake activities that raise productivity; if they cannot do so, the firms will eventually be driven out of business. The surprise is that productivity seems to be higher in unionized settings not only because of traditional economic responses to higher wages, such as increased use of capital and less employment (which are socially undesirable) but also because of the reduction in quits and changes in labor practices which unions bring to workplaces (and which are generally socially desirable).

It should be stressed, however, that of all the findings of the modern empirical research the positive union effect on productivity (above and beyond monopoly-wage induced increases in capital per worker) is by far the most controversial. It is controversial in part because of the difficulty of comparing productivity across plants that often produce somewhat different outputs with somewhat different machines. It is also controversial because the routes by which unionized management and labor manage to raise productivity are difficult to specify. There is a modest gain from lower turnover already noted and a tendency for plants to bring in new management and supervisors and alter methods of management after unionization, but the quantitative impact of 'productivity targeting', 'more professional management', and so on have not been adequately measured.

Finally, the results are controversial because of evidence that the union effect on productivity is quite volatile, highly dependent on the nature of labor–management relations.

The changing pattern of productivity in bituminous coal provides a striking example of the volatile nature of the union productivity effect. During the period in which the United Mine Workers strongly pressed the John L. Lewis policies of mechanization, technological change, and rising wages, productivity in union mines was on the order of 33 to 38 per cent higher than in nonunion mines (1965). Internal dissent in the union and labor–management conflict in succeeding years brought a major deterioration, with the result that in 1975 union mines were 17 to 20 per cent *less* productive than nonunion mines.

Even within the same company unionization per se need not be a plus or minus to productivity. An analysis of productivity at 18 General Motors plants found higher productivity where plant managers rated the industrial relations climate as good or where the rate of grievances filed by workers was low (suggesting that workers viewed the state of labor–management relations as good). A detailed study of paper mills yielded similar results: a plant with a low rate of grievances filed in a given period had notably better productivity than the same plant when it had a high rate of grievances filed. Consistent with this, a third study which examined productivity in nine plants over five years found that a cooperative union management program raised productivity in six of the eight plants for which productivity could be measured (Katz, Kochan and Gobeille, 1982; Ichniowski, 1983; Schuster, 1983).

Of equal or possibly greater importance than the union effect on productivity is the union effect on productivity growth. Here, it is difficult to reach a generalization. There is some evidence that unionism is associated with slower productivity growth but the extant results are in many cases statistically weak and show variation over time. As unionized industries tend to be older smokestack industries, slower productivity growth may reflect industry 'life-cycle' patterns over which unions have little influence. In some industries productivity is advanced by explicit labor–management cooperative ventures. In the men's tailored clothing industry, for example, labor and management established a committee to develop and introduce automatic sewing machines to enable US workers and firms to compete with low-wage foreign competitors, hiring Draper Laboratories, formerly a part of the Massachusetts Institute of Technology, to do the technical work. According to Dunlop:

> The program has several distinct features. The Department of Commerce is contributing financially, although no more than the private-sector contributions from labor and management. The managements and the union in the clothing industry have been joined by two leading textile manufacturers and a leading synthetic yarn company to constitute a broad sectoral group to improve coordination and productivity. These joint responses of labor and management are beyond those that could be achieved at the workplace (Dunlop, 1982).

While joint efforts are relatively uncommon, increased pressures from foreign competitors may induce other industries and unions to engage in similar cooperative activities in the future. Indeed, in the 1980s, as well as earlier, some unions have pressed management to modernize their plants with new investments, as they realize that failure to do so means ultimate loss of jobs.

In sum, a plausible reading of the productivity findings is that what matters is not unionism per se but how management and labor interact at the workplace. Higher productivity in union settings runs hand in hand with 'good industrial relations' and tends to be spurred by competition in the product market while poor labor reactions and protected environments can produce the opposite.

PROFITABILITY

Companies which face organizing drives do not ask if unionism will benefit their workers or the overall economy. They ask what unions do to the corporate 'bottom line.' There is little doubt that unionism reduces company profitability. Indeed, it appears to be one of the major determinants of profitability, with the union effect on wages dominating any positive effect in productivity. Quantitatively, profitability appears to be roughly 20 per cent lower under unionism.

Is this socially good or bad? Persons favoring income redistribution may find it desirable that company profits are lower and worker wages higher. Persons who are concerned with investment and economic growth are likely to worry about what reductions in profits does to the operation of the overall economy.

In part, the answer to this debate depends on the locus of the union impact on profitability. If unions reduce profitability of industries in which firms have sufficient market power to obtain monopoly-level profits, one may place greater weight on the redistributive aspect of the union profit effect. If, on the other hand, unions reduce profits in competitive markets, driving firms out of business, one is likely to place greater weight on the negative effect of profit reductions.

Most studies of the union profit effect find that unions reduce profits largely in sectors where company market power is extensive and thus are more likely to constitute a redistribution of profits than a major force driving firms out of business. When market power changes greatly, however – as occurred in several US industries in the 1980s – it takes considerable concession bargaining by labor and management to keep the firms afloat.

The union impact on profitability is, moreover, by no means always negative. There are two very different types of situations in which unionism is likely to raise rather than reduce profits: when union-induced cost increases in an industry lead the industry to charge monopoly-level prices and when union-induced cost decreases serve to rescue firms on the brink of collapse. In the former case, the union acts, indirectly, as the cartelizing agent in the sector, forcing all firms to act in such a way as to bring the industry closer to the price and output position of a pure product-market monopolist. Since monopoly price increases are socially harmful, the resultant increase in industry profits is socially undesirable. In the latter case, the union behavior, whether reflected in wage reductions or productivity-augmenting activities on the shop floor, is socially desirable.

As an example of an industry in which union wage increases have served to raise industry prices and profits, consider over-the-road trucking during the period of intense Interstate Commerce Commission regulation. When the policy of the commission was essentially to pass union-induced cost increases on to consumers by raising the regulated charges in the sector, profits seem to have been higher than they otherwise would have been. Indeed, profitability in trucking rose after the Teamsters negotiated the nationwide National Master Freight Agreement, which brought virtually all over-the-road drivers into one agreement. Initially, the industry feared such an agreement because of the potential increase in union monopoly power, which many thought could enable the Teamsters to close down trucking in the whole country. In fact, however, the industry as well as its workers benefited from the union's ability to determine all over-the-road wages in one package. In the decade after the agreement, the industry profit rate rose from below the average manufacturing-wide profit rate to a level exceeding the rate for manufacturing.

As an example of more socially desirable union efforts to improve profits in firms, consider the efforts to lower costs under the so-called Scanlon Plan and its close relatives. Under this plan, devised in the 1950s by a former union leader, unions and management work together sharing productivity gains, and in many instances manage to pull companies back from the edge of collapse.

That unions can raise profits by increasing or decreasing costs, with very different consequences for social well-being, demonstrates an important point about the impact of unions on profits: there is little normative content in the direction of the effect per se; rather, what matter are the market conditions and routes by which unionism alters profits.

AN OVERALL ASSESSMENT

Is trade unionism good or bad for the economy? Because unionism has beneficial effects on some aspects of economic performance and harmful effects on others and shifts the distribution of income, there is no simple 'benefit-cost' that can answer our question. What empirical analysis can do is quantify the magnitude of both the pluses and negatives of the institution. In capsule form, extant research suggests the following:

1. Unions raise wages and the cost of labor to firms, with a modest misallocation of resources due to the consequent shrinkage of employment in the union sector.
2. Unions increase fringe benefits desired by workers.
3. Unions reduce inequality of wages in workplaces and across establishments and reduce white-collar/blue-collar pay differentials.
4. Unions reduce quits and increase job tenure, with a resultant modest increase in productivity to firms. The reduction in turnover reflects the extra welfare to workers from unionism.
5. Unions are associated with high productivity in many but not all cases.
6. Unions reduce company profits.

Would the economy function better if it were union-free? The evidence does not support such a conclusion. Would the economy function better if it were dominated by unions? The US experience rejects that view also, as unions – like other institutions – need competition to keep them doing their best.

Perhaps the most sensible conclusion to draw from the evidence is that the economy functions best when there are both union and nonunion sectors. Competition reduces the 'monopoly wage' costs of unionism and encourages the positive aspects of unionism. Competition keeps nonunion firms from taking advantage of their workers and forces them to adopt union-initiated work practices and modes of pay favored by employees to maintain their nonunion status. In the world of perfect full employment and competitive markets, unions would be unnecessary. In the real world in which we live unions can and generally do perform valuable economic functions. An economy is likely to operate efficiently when there is a sufficient number of union and of nonunion firms to offer alternative work environments to workers, innovation in workplace rules and conditions, and competition in the market.

NOTES

1. For examples of economists with generally negative views of labor unions, see Henry C. Simons, *Economic Policy for a Free Society* (Chicago: University of Chicago Press, 1948); Gottfried Haberler, 'Wage policy and inflation,' in P. D. Bradley, ed., *The Public Stake in Union Power* (Charlottesville, Va.: University of Virginia Press, 1959), pp. 63–85; Milton Friedman, *Capitalism and Freedom* (Chicago: University of Chicago Press, 1962), pp. 123–5, and *Free to Choose* (New York: Harcourt Brace Jovanovich, 1980), pp. 228–47; W. H. Hutt, *The Theory of Collective Bargaining* (London: P. S. King, 1930); Fritz Machlup. *The Political Economy of Monopoly* (Baltimore: Johns Hopkins University Press, 1952).

   For examples of economists with generally positive outlooks on labor unions, see Lloyd G. Reynolds and Cynthia H. Taft, *The Evolution of Wage Structure* (New Haven: Yale University Press, 1956); Sumner H. Slichter, James J. Healy, and E. Robert Livernash, *The Impact of Collective Bargaining on Management* (Washington, D.C.: The Brookings Institution, 1960); and Derek C. Bok and John T. Dunlop, *Labor and the American Community* (New York: Simon and Schuster, 1970). Alfred Marshall's views are expressed in *Elements of Economics*, 3rd edition, (London: Macmillan, 1899).

2. The research findings are presented in detail in R. B. Freeman and J. L. Medoff, *What Do Unions Do?* (New York: Basic Books, 1984).

3. The general procedure for estimating welfare loss or gain is described in detail in Arnold C. Harberger, 'Three basic postulates for applied welfare economics: an interpretive essay,' *Journal of Economic Literature* 9 (September 1971), pp. 785–97. Under the assumptions of this approach, the economic cost of the resource misallocation associated with the union monopoly wage effect is:

½ × union wage effect/100	×	decline in employment in union sector due to wage effect/100	×	fraction of labor force in unions	×	fraction of total costs associated

This formula estimates the size of the triangle under the demand curve for union labor, which provides an estimate of what social loss would be if all output were produced under collective bargaining, and then multiplies this amount by an estimate of the fraction of all output produced in unionized settings. Our calculations assume a union wage effect of 20 to 25 per cent, a decline in employment of workers of 13 to 17 per cent, a union share of the workforce of 25 per cent, and a labor share of GNP of three-fourths. Using the formula above we obtain for the social cost:

$$\frac{1}{2} (0.20) (0.13) (0.25) (0.75) = 0.0024 \tag{1}$$

$$\frac{1}{2} (0.25) (0.17) (0.25) (0.75) = 0.0040 \tag{2}$$

Albert Rees' calculations in 'The effects of unions on resource allocation,' *The Journal of Law and Economics* 6 (October 1963), pp. 69–78, yield a similar result, as do those of Robert DeFina using a more complex model in 'Unions, relative wages, and economic efficiency,' *Journal of Labor Economics* 1 (October 1983).

4. Pencavel and Hartsog find essentially no effect of unionism on employment. John Pencavel and Christine Hartsog, 'A reconsideration of the effects of unionism on relative wages and employment in the US, 1920–80,' National Bureau of Economic Research Working Paper No. 1316, 1984; and for a good review of the recent theories see Henry S. Farber, 'The analysis of union behavior,' in *Handbook of Labor Economics* (Amsterdam: North Holland Press, forthcoming).

5. An early analysis of the relationship between the union/nonunion wage differential and the rate of unemployment and the rate of inflation is found in H. Gregg Lewis, *Unionism and Relative Wages* (Chicago: University of Chicago Press, 1914), chapter 5. The impact of these two variables on the wage effect through the 1970s has been analyzed by George E. Johnson in 'Changes over time in the union/nonunion wage differential in the United States' (University of Michigan, February 1981, mimeographed). More discussion of union wage policy through the business cycle is provided by Marten S. Estey, *The Unions: Structure, Development and Management*, 3rd edition (New York: Harcourt, Brace, Jovanovich, 1981), p. 137.

6. The quit rate is much lower for unionized workers than for similar nonunionized workers. See, for example, Francine D. Blau and Lawrence M. Kahn, 'Race and sex differences in quits by young workers,' *Industrial and Labor Relations Review* 34 (July 1981). pp. 563–77; Richard N. Block, 'The impact of seniority provisions on the manufacturing quit rate,' *Industrial and Labor Relations Review* 22 (January 1978), pp. 199–216; Richard B. Freeman, 'Individual mobility and union voice in the labor market,' *American Economic Review* 66 (May 1976), pp. 361–8; Richard B. Freeman. 'The effect of unionism on worker attachment to firms,' *Journal of Labor Research* 1 (Spring 1980), pp. 29–61; Richard B, Freeman, 'The exit–voice tradeoff in the labor market, unionism, job tenure, quits, and separations,' *Quarterly Journal of Economics* 94 (June 1980), pp. 643–73; Freeman and Medoff, op. cit.; Lawrence M. Kahn, 'Union impact: a reduced form approach,' *The Review of Economics and Statistics* 59 (November 1977), pp. 503–7; Duane E. Leigh 'Unions and nonwage racial discrimination,' *Industrial and Labor Relations Review* 33 (July 1979), pp. 439–50; J. E. Long and A. E. Link 'The impact of market structure on wages, fringe benefits, and turnover,' *Industrial and Labor Relations Review* 33 (January 1983); and Olivia S. Mitchell, 'Fringe benefits and labor mobility,' *Journal of Human Resources* 17 (Spring 1982) p. 293.

The quit rate is much lower for unionized industries than for nonunionized industries. See, for example, Charles Brown and James Medoff, 'Trade unions in the production process,' *Journal of Political Economy* 86 (June 1978), pp. 355–78; John Burton and John Parker, Interindustry variation in voluntary labor mobility,' *Industrial Labor Relations Review* 22 (January 1969), pp. 199–216, revised by Freeman; John Pencavel, *An Analysis of the Quit Rate in American Manufacturing*, Industrial Relations Section (N.J.: Princeton University, 1970); V. Stoikov and R. Raimon, 'Determinants of the differences in quit rates among industries,' *American Economic Review* 63, pt. 1 (December 1968), pp. 1283–98.

The job tenure for unionized workers is higher than for nonunionized workers. See, for example, Freeman 'The exit-voice tradeoff . . . ,' op. cit.; Freeman and Medoff, op. cit.

BIBLIOGRAPHY

Bok, D. C., and Dunlop, J. T., *Labor and the American Community* (New York: Simon and Schuster, 1970).

Dunlop, J. T., 'Labor-management response to productivity change', a lecture delivered in Utah State University, 1 April 1982, and published in 'George S. Eccles Distinguished Lecture Series, 1981–2' (Logan, Utah: Utah State University, 1982), p. 34.

Flanagan, R., 'Wage interdependence in unionized labour markets', *Brookings Papers on Economic Activity* (1976), 3, pp. 635–73.

Flanagan, R., 'Wage concession and long-term union wage flexibility', *Brookings Papers on Economic Activity* (1984), 1, pp. 183–222.

Freeman, R. B., 'Union wage practices and wage dispersion within establishments', *Industrial and Labour Relations Review* (October 1982).

Freeman, R. B., and Medoff, J. L., *What Do Unions Do?* (New York: Basic Books, 1984).

Friedman, M., *Capitalism and Freedom* (Chicago: University of Chicago Press, 1962).

Haberler, G., Wage policy and inflation', in P. D. Bradley (ed.), *The Public Stake in Union Power* (Charlottesville: University of Virginia Press, 1959).

Ichniowski, B., 'How do labor relations matter? A study of productivity in eleven paper mills', National Bureau of Economic Research (Summer Workshop, August 1983).

Johnson, G., 'The determination of wages in the union and nonunion sectors', *British Journal of Industrial Relations* (July 1977), 15, pp. 211–25.

Katz, H., Kochan, T., and Gobeille, K., 'Industrial relations performance, economic performance and the effects of quality of working life efforts: an inter-plant analysis', Sloan School Working Paper 1,329–82 (Massachusetts Institute of Technology, July 1982).

Lindblom, C. E., *Unions and Capitalism* (New Haven: Yale University Press, 1949), p. 4.

Mitchell, D. J. B., *Unions, Wages and Inflation* (Washington DC: Brookings Institution, 1980).

Reynolds, L. G., and Taft, C. H., *The Evolution of Wage Structure* (New Haven: Yale University Press, 1956).

Schuster, M., 'The impact of union-management compensation on productivity and employment', *Industrial and Labor Relations Review* (April 1983), 36, pp. 415–30.

Simons, H. C., 'Some reflections on syndicalism', *Journal of Political Economy* (March 1944), 52.

PART IV

LABOR MARKET INSTITUTIONS AND COMPARATIVE ANALYSIS

Are there economies outside of the United States from which one can learn how advanced market economies operate? Anyone conversant with American labor economics would think not. The typical study analyses data for the United States and proceeds to draw conclusions about the way markets function in capitalist economies. If someone from the United Kingdom or Australia, much less Italy or France or Denmark, reports different results for their country, the American economist has one of two responses: either the other guys have screwy data, or their markets are screwy. We do it the real free enterprise way.

The parochialism of concentrating on the experience of only one country is remarkable in a science that purports to rest on a general theory of markets. It limits our progress in understanding how economies function in three ways: first by discarding potential tests of theories (sorely needed in the absence of laboratory experiments); second by ignoring natural experiments in other countries (sorely needed in the absence of laboratory experiments), and third by making economic institutions peripheral rather than major topics of concern.

This part of the book represents my initial efforts to escape the ethnocentrism of American economics and to use experience outside the United States to cast light on American developments and to understand the operation of labor markets elsewhere. The analysis of the evaluation of unionism in the United States (Chapter 11) offers an example of how the experiences of countries can be used to assess the determinants of institutional change in a single country. The study of bonuses on demand for labor in Japan (Chapter 12) exploits the natural experiment of an economy where bonuses constitute a sizeable proportion of pay to evaluate how my co-author Martin Weitzman's share economy might work in practice. The analysis of the differences in labor-market performance between the United States and Western Europe in Chapter 13 is an effort to respond to the major intellectual challenge that comparative analysis offers to the abstract theory of markets: the need to explain the interplay between institutions and markets in which some factors/constraints operate on all labor markets while others allow different societies to produce different outcomes. Hopefully, this represents a first step toward the more general institutional analysis that will, I believe, mark the next phase in labor economics and economic analysis more broadly.

Yes, Virginia, there are economics outside the United States and they offer more than choice spots for conferences.

11 · CONTRACTION AND EXPANSION: THE DIVERGENCE OF PRIVATE SECTOR AND PUBLIC SECTOR UNIONISM IN THE UNITED STATES

The institutional structure of the American labor market changed remarkably from the 1950s and 1960s to the 1980s. In the 1950s and 1960s trade unions seemed permanently established in the private sector of the economy: a third of nonagricultural wage and salary workers and over half of blue-collar workers were union members: hundreds of thousands of workers voted annually in National Labor Relations Board (NLRB) representation elections to join unions; most large firms sought stable collective bargaining relations with their unions. By contrast, in the public sector only 10–12 per cent of workers were union members; fewer were covered by collective bargaining contracts; and most experts regarded public employees as intrinsically nonorganizable. According to AFL-CIO president George Meany, it was 'impossible to bargain collectively with the government' (Kramer, 1962, p. 14).

The massive contraction of unionism in the private sector and expansion in the public sector in the 1970s and 1980s (see Figure 11.1) has produced an utterly different situation today. In the private sector, the proportion of wage and salary workers in unions plummeted to 14 per cent in 1986 – a level comparable to that in the Great Depression; only a minuscule number of workers joined unions through NLRB elections; and national companies openly proclaimed their intent to establish a 'union-free environment', By contrast, in the public sector over a third of the workforce was unionized; some 40 per cent were covered by collective contracts[1] and public-sector unions such as the American Federation of State, County and Municipal Employees, National Education Association, Service Employees International (which became largely public sector in the period) and the American Federation of Teachers were among the largest in the country. With one in three union members working in the public sector, women with master's degrees (largely schoolteachers) more highly

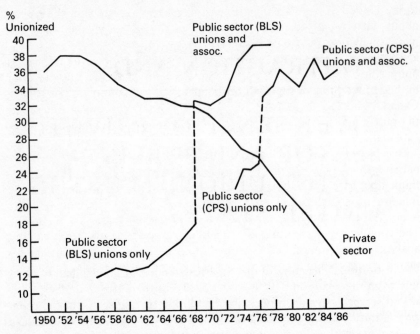

Figure 11.1 Changing percent of nonagricultural workers who are union, by sector.

Sources: Percentage of workers in unions and assoc. in public sector, (BLS) US Dept. of Labor, 1979; Percentage of workers in unions and assoc. in public sector, (CPS) US Bureau of Census, 1973–84 (1982 not available); percentage of workers in union in private sector 1956–82, Troy, Leo and Neil Sheflin, *Union Sourcebook*; Private Sector 1984–6 from CPS, US Dept. of Labor, *Employment and Earnings*, Jan. 1985, 87. Spliced with Sourcebook at 1983.

organized than male high school graduates, and police and firefighters the exemplars of craft unionism, the union movement differed drastically from that headed by Meany in the 1960s.

Because the private sector employs nearly 85 per cent of nonagricultural wage and salary workers in the United States,[2] the contraction of unionization in the private sector dominates the trends for the economy as a whole, with the result that the union proportion of nonagricultural employees fell from 36 per cent in 1956 to 18 per cent in 1986. This decline in union density was larger than that of the 1920s, and thus arguably represents the most significant change in labor-market institutions since the Depression – the effective deunionization of most of the US labor force.

What explains the decline in union representation of private wage and salary workers? Why have unions expanded in the public sector while contracting in the private sector? Is the economy-wide fall in density a phenomenon common to developed capitalist economies, or is it unique to the United States? To what extent should economists alter their views about what unions do to the economy in light of the fact that they increasingly do it in the public sector?

To answer these questions I examine a wide variety of evidence on the union status of public and private workers. I contrast trends in unionization in the United States with trends in other developed countries, particularly Canada, and use these contrasts and the divergence between unions in the public and private sectors of the United States to evaluate proposed explanations.

Because standard economic theory is not normally used to analyze massive changes in the institutional structure of an economy, many may think that an explanation of changing union density requires extensive reliance on social factors that go beyond economics. I argue that this is not the case and base my analysis on economic forces and behavior. The complexity of institutional change does, however, dictate a catholic analytic approach, and I use several lines of argument and evidence rather than a single econometric model or hypothesis test to reach conclusions. In addition, I recognize that a significant residual remains that can and perhaps should be attributed to noneconomic factors such as the abilities of union leaders, public opinion, and the like.

THE DIMENSIONS OF CHANGE

'It is a capital mistake to theorize in advance of the facts.'
Arthur Conan Doyle, recording the words of Sherlock Holmes

Three firm observations can be made about the change in union density in the United States: first, that the decline in density in the private sector has been virtually ubiquitous, encompassing workers in all industries, regions and occupations during the 1980s and earlier; second, that by contrast union expansion in the public sector has been highly uneven, occurring rapidly in some states and occupations but not in others; and third, that the overall drop in union density – the deunionization of the economy – is distinctly American, contrasting sharply with developments in most Western countries.

Table 11.1 documents the claim that union density has fallen among virtually all workers during the 1980s, when the rate of decline was exceptionally severe. The industry figures show the union proportion of workers falling in the areas of traditional union strength such as transportation and public utilities (including trucking, which the Teamsters once dominated); construction (long the preserve of craft unions); manufacturing (where industrial unions have held sway since the organizing drives of the 1930s and 1940s); and services and trade (where proportions organized were so low that even a modicum of union success would raise the union shares).

Table 11.1 Percentage of private wage and salary workers who are members of unions, by industry and occupation, 1980–6

	% Organized	
	1980	1986
Industry		
Mining	32	14
Construction	31	22
Manufacturing	32	24
Transportation, communication, and public utilities	48	35
Trade	10	7
Service	9	6
Occupation		
Professional tech & kindred	23	19
Managers and administrators	8	7
Clerical and kindred	16	14
Sales	4	6
Craft and kindred	39	29
Operatives, except transport	40	33
Transport & equipment	45	31
Non-farm laborers	33	25
Service workers, except protective service[a]	13	10

Note:
a   Protective service excluded because they are largely in the public sector.
    Occupations based on 1980 titles with 1985 estimates for:
    Professional, tech. and kindred = professional Specialty + Tech and related support, weighted by employment;
    Managers and administration = executive, administrator and managers;
    Clerical and kindred = precision production, craft and repair;
    Operatives, except transport = Machine operators, assemblers and inspectors;
    Transport and equipment = transportation and material moving occupations;
    Non-farm laborers = handlers, equipment cleaners, helpers and laborers
Source: US Department of Labor, 1980 and 1987.

The occupation data (which understate declines in private-sector density because they include public-sector labor) reveal a similar trend, with sizeable drops in density among operatives, craft workers, and laborers. As for the longer run, the percentage of production workers in metropolitan areas with collective bargaining contracts fell from 73 per cent in 1960–1 to 51 per cent in 1984, with massive declines in every region of the country ranging from −16 points in the south (48 per cent to 32 per cent) to −32 points in the west (80 per cent to 48 per cent; Goldfield, 1987). These declines show that much more is involved in the contraction of union density in the private sector than changes in the regional mix or production worker share of employment.

Overall, the data indicate that the explanation of the decline in private-sector union density should focus on factors that affect all private employees as opposed to factors that affect employees in some segments of the labor market rather than others.

The rise in public sector union density

Measuring changes in unionism in the US public sector is difficult. One difficulty is that each American state (and the federal government) regulates public-sector labor in its own jurisdiction, producing labor organizations with different legal rights. Whereas in the private sector union membership, collective bargaining representation, and the right to strike are coterminous under the same legal code, in the public sector a worker can be a union member but not be covered by a collective contract in some states (because management can refuse to bargain or to sign an agreement with a union) while being covered in others; be covered by a contract that does not include wages and salaries, as in federal employment; be allowed to strike in some jurisdictions but obligated to resolve disputes through arbitration elsewhere, and so on. Historically, moreover, public-sector worker organizations have ranged from associations opposed to collective bargaining to acting as aggressive unions, with the same organization serving as a union in some localities but not in others (the American Association of University Professors is a case in point). Indicative of the measurement problem the figures on public-sector density in Figure 11.1 show discontinuities when the relevant surveys first included 'associations' with unions in their definition of collective organization. While it might seem misleading to compare union membership in early years with union plus association membership in later years, this comparison does in fact accurately measure the magnitude (though not the timing) of change. This is because in the 1950s and early 1960s most associations – for instance, the NEA or the various police and firefighters' organizations – did not engage in collective bargaining, often rejecting it as 'unprofessional', whereas in the 1980s they embraced bargaining and the other attributes of traditional trade unions.

A final complexity is that the legal environment under which public-sector unions operate has changed over time. From the 1960s through the early 1970s, when public-sector workers joined unions or saw their associations turn into unions, most public-sector labor laws did not require employers to bargain/resolve impasses and outlawed the strike weapon that unions use to force employers to come to agreement. As a result many workers who joined unions did not work under collectively bargained contracts. By contrast, from the mid-1970s to the 1980s more and more union workers (and nonunion workers in organized workplaces) were able to gain contracts from their employers (35 per cent of state and local government workers were covered in 1982, compared to 26 per cent in

1975).[3] At the same time that contract coverage was increasing, however, the proportion of public-sector workers in unions stabilized or fell. In this case, statistics on membership and coverage tell different stories about the trend in union strength. As collective bargaining resulting in a contract has been the essence of American union activity, I stress increased contract convergence rather than membership trends in assessing the 1980s.

Given differences in state regulations of public-sector collective bargaining, it is perhaps not surprising to find that the extent and, by extension, expansion of bargaining has varied across states and among occupations (see Table 11.2). In states with laws favorable to collective bargaining (arbitration or strike permitted laws, and duty to bargain), proportionately more workers are represented by bargaining units than in states that permit but do not require employers to bargain, while representation by unions is low in states that have no collective bargaining provisions and lowest in those that prohibit bargaining. Though these data relate to cross-section differences at a point in time rather than changes over time, we can infer patterns of growth from them. We can do this because contract coverage was sufficiently slight in the earlier period that states/occupations with high density in the 1980s almost always had rapid growth, whereas those in which density was low could not have had such growth. Intepreted in this way, the table shows the uneven expansion of union representation, with proportionately more workers gaining representation in states (and occupations) having laws favorable to collective bargaining than in other states.

The evidence on geographic divergence implies that an explanation of union growth in the public sector must have a geographic dimension related to state laws as opposed to the 'across-the-boards' explanation that seems appropriate for the private sector.

Table 11.2 Geographic variation in percentage of employees represented by bargaining units, by occupation and state law, 1982

State laws from most favorable to least favorable to collective bargaining	No. of states with given labor law (% employees represented by bargaining unit), by occupation:			
	Police	Fire	Sanitation	Street and highway
Arbitration or strike permitted	15 (94%)	18 (94%)	13 (39%)	13 (49%)
Duty to bargain	12 (58%)	11 (62%)	11 (14%)	11 (71%)
Bargaining permitted	11 (45%)	13 (54%)	12 (23%)	12 (19%)
No provisions	8 (29%)	5 (30%)	9 (27%)	9 (44%)
Bargaining prohibited	4 (16%)	3 (18%)	5 (8%)	5 (1%)

Souces: US Bureau of the Census, Survey of Governments, 1982 NBER State Public Sector Collective Bargaining Law Data Set.

Cross-country contrasts

Because the meaning and measurement of union membership differs across countries, the figures in Table 11.3 should be regarded as crude indicators of degrees of unionization. Even read cautiously, however, they clearly contradict the notion that the decline in union density in the United States is part of a general collapse of unions in the developed world; in most countries, union density increased in the 1970s and stabilized or declined modestly in the 1980s at levels above those in earlier years. In Japan, where union density fell in both decades, the rate of decline was half as large as in the United States, and less significant in terms of the entire workforce because the proportion of Japanese working as nonagricultural wage and salary workers increased, maintaining the union share of total employment. In Canada, where many of the same companies and unions operate as in the United States and where living standards and culture (exclusive of Quebec) are similar, union density went from roughly the same to twice the US level from 1970 to 1985. A persuasive explanation

Table 11.3 Levels and changes in union density as a percent of nonagricultural wage and salary across countries, 1970–85

	1970	1979	1984/5	1970–9	1979–85
Countries with sharp rises in density					
Denmark	66	86	98	+20	+12
Finland	56	84	85	+28	+ 1
Sweden	79	89	95	+10	+12
Belgium	66	77		+11	
Countries with moderate rises in density					
Italy (?)	39	51	45	+12	−6
Germany	37	42	42	+ 5	0
France (?)	22	28	28	+ 6	0
Switzerland	31	36	35	+ 5	−1
Canada	32	36	37	+ 4	+1
Australia	52	58	57	+ 6	−1
New Zealand	43	46	?	+ 3	
Ireland	44	49	51	+ 5	+2
Countries with stable/declining density					
Norway	59	60	61	+ 1	+1
United Kingdom	51	58	52	+ 7	−6
Austria[a]	64	59	61	− 5	+2
Japan[a]	35	32	29	− 3	−3
Netherlands	39	43	37	+ 4	−6
United States	31	25	18	− 6	−7

Note:
a No change in union share of total employment due to fall in agriculture employment.
Source: US Department of Labor, Bureau of Labor Statistics, Office of Productivity and Technology, Division of Foreign Labor Statistics and Trade, July 1986, Center for Labor Economics OECD Data Set, updated with respective country statistical abstracts.

of the decline in union density in the United States should also explain why density did not decline in Canada in the same time period. A third country to which I would like to draw attention is the United Kingdom, where density fell in the 1980s, probably at rates above those shown in Table 11.3 (the union figures come from the unions, who exaggerate membership in a period of decline); where organization in the strongest union structure, the closed shop (which requires workers to be union), fell sharply; where an increasing proportion of private manufacturing firms operated non-union; where employment grew more rapidly in low-union density than in high-union density plants; and where proportions covered by collective contracts also fell noticeably.[4] Because union density increased in the 1970s in the United Kingdom, however, these changes have not produced anything like an American-style drop through 1985.

Overall, the patterns of change shown in Table 11.3 highlight the fact that deunionization is largely, if not exclusively, a US development.[5] This fact has important implications. First, it disallows any broad explanation of the decline, say, that 'unions have become obsolete in the modern "post-industrial" market economy' (whatever those grandiose terms mean). Second, it constitutes powerful evidence against the structuralist argument that changes in the composition of the workforce and jobs from (traditionally union) male blue-collar labor to (traditionally nonunion) female, white-collar and service labor underlie the drop. If 'post-industrial' or structural changes inexorably reduce unionization, density would have fallen in Canada and other developed capitalist countries, all of which have experienced essentially the same structural changes as the United States, as well as in the United States. Finally, the divergent country trends also cast doubt on any general macroeconomic explanation of US deunionization: it is hard to argue that the economic problems that followed the oil shock, the inflation of the 1970s, or ensuing deflation caused unions to decline in the United States when the same forces did not reduce union density elsewhere. Put differently, the international data direct attention away from worldwide economic developments to the particulars of American labor relations.

HOW AMERICAN WORKERS ORGANIZE

'No, no! The adventures first,' said the Gryphon in an impatient tone: 'Explanations take such a dreadful time.'

As reported by Lewis Carroll

Before evaluating proposed explanations for the change in union density in the United States, it is important to understand the way in which workers are organized. In contrast to some countries, such as the United Kingdom, where unionization is left largely to private parties, governments in the

United States regulate extensively the process of union representation in both private and public sectors.

The National Labor–Management Relations Act (NLRA) of 1935, amended in 1947 (Taft–Hartley Act) and afterwards, establishes secret ballot representation elections for private-sector workers to choose whether or not to become union and regulates the labor relations conduct of employers and unions in several ways. The Act forbids employers to discriminate against workers for union activity and forbids unions to engage in certain tactics deemed unfair as well, such as secondary boycotts.[6] Under the National Labor Relations Board process, unionization currently takes the following form: a union petitions for an election by producing the signatures of 30 per cent or more (in practice a union will petition for an election only if two-thirds of the employees are willing to request an election). The NLRB decides the set of workers eligible to vote, and, subject to legal objections and appeals that can delay the actual election for several months, supervises the voting. If a majority votes for the union, the NLRB will certify it as the collective bargaining representative of the workforce, which obligates the employer to bargain, though not to come to agreement. To resolve impasses, workers can strike while employers can lock out employees or hire strikebreakers. The NLRB also supervises secret-ballot 'decertification' elections for unionized workers who wish to reconsider their status.

The key to understanding the process is to recognize that although only workers vote in a representation election, management plays an active role in most campaigns, generally trying to convince workers to reject unions. One study of some 200 organizing campaigns in 1982–3, for example, estimated that the direct supervisors of workers played a 'sizeable' or 'extreme' role in two-thirds of the elections, while abstaining in just 6 per cent (AFL-CIO, 1984, Appendix, p. 37). Many managements employ labor–management consulting experts ('union-busters') to convince workers to vote against the union. Determining union status through an adversarial election framework which accords management a major role is a distinctly American process which has contributed, I will argue, to the observed decline of private-sector union density.

The fact that each state has its own public-sector labor law means that there is no uniform method by which workers unionize in the public sector. Indeed, while some states enacted NLRA-type laws that create secret ballot election procedures for workers to decide union status and that require employers to negotiate with the unions, often mandating compulsory arbitration to resolve disputes, other states outlaw unions or collective bargaining.[7] Because state laws often mimic the NLRA, however, the situation is not as chaotic as might first appear. A reasonable generalization is that in states with comprehensive public-sector labor laws, the de jure process of unionization in the public sector is much like that in the private sector, with workers deciding union status through government-sponsored voting procedures. As the method for unionization is comparable between the public and private sectors, an explanation of divergent sectoral trends must explain why comparable processes produce different outcomes in the two sectors.

Finally, US labor law establishes representation elections for workers to choose union status but does not outlaw private agreements between workers and management regarding unionization. Unions and employers can agree that a given workplace will be organized (as GM, Toyota, and UAW have done for the Fremont, California, plant) with an understanding that, if the workers or another union seek an election, management will remain neutral or encourage workers to choose the preferred union. Unions can also sign up workers and demand recognition, threatening a strike should management refuse. In some sectors, moreover, employers are union because they hire from union hiring halls. While non-NLRB modes of organization are likely to become more important in the future, representation elections have been the predominant mode of organization in the past 30 years, making the outcome of the election process critical to union growth in the period under study.

Relating new organization to density

The discussion thus far has dealt with the process by which workers choose to unionize and, hence, with the flow of new union members. As our ultimate concern is with changes in union density it is essential to relate the flows to the 'stock' of union members. The following identity, which makes total union membership a function of the changes in existing membership and of 'investment' through organizing activity, relates the flows to the stocks:

$$\text{UNION}(t) = \text{UNION}(t - 1) - r\text{UNION}(t - 1) + \text{NEW}(t)$$

UNION is the number of union members (persons covered by collective bargaining contracts) in a given year t; r is the rate of change in membership due to changes in employment in organized establishments. It may be negative or positive, though the 'natural' process by which some union plants close yearly (while new plants are born nonunion) suggests that r will be negative, implying a natural depreciation in union membership, even in a growing economy. NEW is the number of new members obtained through organization of new workplaces or lost through decertification of unions at existing workplaces in the period from $t - 1$ to t. For reasons of data availability NEW is best thought of as net members gained through NLRB elections, though in principle one would like to include the result of all new organizing activity.

Dividing both sides of the identity by the number of employees in year t to measure union density (UDENS), and manipulating, one obtains:

$$UDENS(t) = [1/(1 + g)] [(1 - r)UDENS(t - 1) + PCTNEW(t)]$$
$$\approx (1 - r - g)UDENS(t - 1) + (1 - g)PCTNEW(t)$$

PCTNEW is the ratio of workers organized to the workforce in $t - 1$; g is the rate of growth of total employment; and $-(r + g)$ is the net depreciation or appreciation of union density.

The steady state level of union density implied by this difference equation is UDENS = PCTNEW/$(r + g)$, which shows that the permanent level of union density changes whenever $r + g$ or PCTNEW change; that is, whenever economic conditions cause union plants to contract/expand relative to the growth of total employment or when the rate of union organization changes over time. For example, if unions organize 1 per cent of the workforce per annum, as they did in the 1950s, and suffer a net depreciation of density of 4 per cent, the union share of employment would stabilize at 25 per cent. If, alternatively, new organization fell to 0.7 per cent of the workforce, as it did in the 1960s, and $r + g$ remained the same, the union share would drop to 17.5 per cent in the long run.

How important are changes in new organization versus changes in the rate of depreciation of existing union membership in the recent collapse of private-sector union density? Crude calculations applying our difference equation to private-sector union membership and number of workers won through NLRB elections show a rising trend in the depreciation rate in recent years: estimated compound annual rates of $r + g$ for the 1950s of 4 per cent; for the 1960s, 3.4 per cent; for the 1970s, 4.7 per cent; and for 1980–5, 6.1 per cent.[8] Two factors are likely to underlie the increase in $r + g$ in the 1970s and 1980s: the concentration of unionism in slow-growth areas and potential increased death of union plants due to the rising union wage premiums of the 1970s. The crudeness of the data underlying the estimates of $r + g$ makes one leery, however, of taking estimated changes too seriously. What should be taken seriously is the negative value of $-(r + g)$, which implies that unions, lik the Red Queen in *Through the Looking Glass* for whom 'it takes all the running you can do, to keep in the same place', must organize large numbers of workers each year to maintain private-sector density.

That unions have failed to do this through the NLRB electoral process is evident from the statistics summarized in Table 11.4. Columns 1 and 2 measure the success of unions in organizing workers through NLRB representation elections in selected years from 1950 to 1983: column 1 gives the absolute number of workers won by unions in representation elections, while column 2 gives the number of workers won relative to the workforce. These data show that union success in representation elections has declined to the point where virtually no workers are organized through

Table 11.4 Organizing success of unions through NLRB elections

	Workers won (in thousands)	Workers won / nonagr. emp.	% of elig. in union wins	Elig. workers / nonagr. emp.
1950	754	2.0	84	2.4
1955	343	1.0	73	1.4
1960	286	0.7	59	1.2
1965	316	0.7	61	1.1
1970	301	0.6	52	1.2
1975	204	0.4	38	1.1
1980	173	0.2	37	0.5
1983	74	0.1	43	0.3

Source: NLRB Annual Reports.

NLRB procedures. Whereas in the early 1950s unions organized 1 per cent to 2 per cent of the workforce via government-sponsored elections, in the 1960s they organized about 0.7 per cent; in the 1970s, about 0.5 per cent; and in 1983, just 0.1 per cent: 91,000 workers in a workforce of some 90 million! Even these figures, moreover, understate union inability to gain members through NLRB elections for a union electoral victory does not guarantee that workers will obtain a collective bargaining contract. In recent years, in fact, workers voting to unionize failed to gain a contract approximately a third of the time (Weiler, 1985), and thus worked under management-determined rather than collectively bargained conditions. The implication is that in 1983 perhaps only 60,000 workers gained union representation through the electoral process. When account is taken of the 25,000 or so workers who chose to decertify unions in elections, it is apparent that the legally established mode of organizing labor in the private sector of the United States has run dry for trade unions.

Columns 3 and 4 of Table 11.4 decompose the number of workers won by unions in representation elections relative to the workforce into the following: a measure of the union success rate – the number of workers in elections won by unions relative to the number of workers eligible to vote (column 3); and a measure of the extent of electoral activity – the number of workers eligible to vote in elections relative to the workforce. The figures in column 3 show that one factor in the decline in workers organized through representation elections has been a fall in the proportion of workers in elections won by unions (which reflects declines in union win rates and in the average size of union victories).[9] The figures in column 4 show, however, an even greater proportionate drop in the extent of electoral activity: in 1960 some 6,000 NLRB elections covered 1.2 per cent of the workforce; in 1983 4,400 elections covered a bare 0.3 per cent of the workforce. Had unions won all of these elections they would not have gained enough members to increase density.

Turning to the public sector, there are good reasons to believe that both terms in our equation for union density – the net depreciation of existing density – $(r + g)$ and success in organizing new workers – played a role in the speed with which unionization and/or collective bargaining representation grew in the 1970s and 1980s. First, because few government departments, union or nonunion, go out of business, the loss of density due to closure of union workplaces (reflected in r) will be small. Second, the relatively moderate growth of public-sector employment into new areas implies that existing unions do not have to appeal to workers outside their traditional jurisdictions to maintain their share of employment, which also should make $r + g$ smaller in the public than in the private sector. Third, organizing workers into unions has undoubtedly been much easier in the public sector. In part this is because many workers have been historically organized into employee associations, which were readily transformed into unions without massive organizing campaign. More importantly, however, organization is easier in the public sector because politicians and public-sector managers do not contest unionization to the extent that private employers do, for reasons to be laid out shortly. Finally, state laws that require employers to negotiate and mandate impasse procedures guarantee that workers who vote union ultimately receive union representation. Hence, in the public sector, once workers choose union representation, they get what they choose.

With this and the information in the preceding section as background, let us now turn to proposed explanations for the changed union density.

POTENTIAL CAUSES OF CHANGE

'It's rather hard to understand . . . Somehow it seems to fill my head with ideas – only I don't know exactly what they are! However, somebody killed something: that's clear, at any rate.'

Alice, as reported by Lewis Carroll

Researchers have proposed a wide variety of factors to explain the changes in unionization in the United States. Among the hypothesized causes for the decline in private-sector density are the following: structural shifts in the composition of the workforce and mix of jobs; changes in public attitudes toward unions reflected in opinion polls; increased governmental regulation of the labor market substituting for union protection; 'positive labor relations' by nonunion firms; the performance of unions in representing workers and in allocating resources to organizing drives; antiunion policies of the Reagan administration evinced in the air traffic controllers' strike and selection of members to the NLRB; antiunion campaigns by managements. Among the factors said to cause the spurt in public-sector unionism are the following: extension of NLRA-type laws to public-sector workers in many states; extension of some union rights to federal workers by executive order; pent-up demand for unions by workers whose organization level was exceptionally low by US and world standards.

By examining the impact of factors on the changes in the private and public sectors at once, and requiring that the factors have a consistent effect, I eliminate some hypotheses and highlight the role of others.

Structural changes

Because the proportion of the workforce in traditionally nonunion occupations (white collar), demographic groups (females, college graduates), industries (service and trade) and regions (the south) has increased rapidly, various analysts have explored the possibility that the changing structure of the workforce underlies the drop in union density. The tool for this exploration is a fixed coefficient model which decomposes the workforce into a number of groups with varying degrees of unionization at some base time, and explores the impact of changes in the relative size of the groups on aggregate union density under the assumption that the density of each group is fixed at its base level.

Fixed coefficient analyses covering from the 1960s through 1980 attribute 50 per cent to 70 per cent of the decline in private-sector union density to compositional factors with the increase in white-collar employment having a particularly sizeable depressant effect on density. While these calculations would appear to go far toward explaining the decline in unionization, I believe the structuralist analysis is misleading and should be rejected. There are three reasons for rejecting it.

First, the structuralist hypothesis is inconsistent with the rise in union density in other countries (notably Canada) which had structural changes in the workforce similar to those in the United States. Second, surveys of worker desire for unionism show that structural changes cannot explain the decline in union success in NLRB elections, since the groups whose proportion of the workforce increased (such as women and young workers) have as great or greater desire to unionize as do white prime-age male workers (Freeman and Medoff, 1984, p. 228). Third, I reject the structuralist hypothesis because it assumes that the union share of workers in a sector should remain fixed over time. That assumption is inconsistent with the history of union growth, which is one of expansion into nonunion areas, as occurred in the public sector in the period under study. The claim that public-sector workers organized because of pent-up demand for unionization, indeed, implies that unionism 'naturally' grows in new sectors over time. Fixed coefficient calculations sidestep the key issue in the decline in US unionization, which is why unions failed to organize historically nonunion workers in the private sector while doing so in the public sector and in other countries.

Public opinion of unions

The decrease in favorable attitudes toward unions shown in public opinion polls offers another possible explanation for the decline of unionism in the private sector (Lipset, 1986). While public opinion data should not be dismissed out of hand, I do not find this hypothesis persuasive. The timing of the change in opinions and union density are at best weakly related, with public support of unions as measured by the Gallup Poll climbing from 62 per cent in 1949 to 75 per cent in 1953, falling to 64 per cent in 1962, rising to 70 per cent in 1965, falling to 55 per cent in 1981, and rebounding slightly to 58 per cent in 1985. Public favorableness toward unions was 59 per cent in 1973 and 58 per cent in 1985, but union density fell sharply during that time. More damaging to this thesis, perhaps, are responses to the behaviorally more meaningful question of whether workers would vote for a union at their workplace, which show no decline in worker desire for unions: in both 1977 and 1984 about a third of nonunion workers said they wanted unions at their workplace.[10] Finally, a public opinion explanation of union decline is inconsistent with unionization of the public sector, where public opinion could be expected to be especially important.

Substitutes for union protection

Workers join unions for protection against unfair treatment by management, including low wages. This motivation suggests that the development of substitute modes of protection in the form of welfare state interventions in markets (Neumann and Rissman, 1984) or of better personnel practices by management might reduce worker desire for union representation. If government activities substitute for union protection, one would expect unionism to decline most in countries with the greatest welfare state and restrictions on management, in American states with extensive protective labor legislation, and in periods of declining governmental interventions. Further, unions should appeal least to workers who enjoy special legal protections, such as blacks, women, and public-sector employees protected by civil service rules. Changes in union density by country, by states, and over time, and the desire for unions by blacks, women, and public-sector employees protected by civil service rules. Changes in union density by country, by states, and over time, and the desire for unions by blacks, women, and public-sector workers are uniformly inconsistent with these implications (Freeman, 1986b). Hence, I reject the view the governmental regulations and growth of the welfare state underlie the decline in density.

The possibility that 'positive labor relations' practices adopted by many major companies (but too expensive for smaller ones) – paying union-level wages and instituting union-style personnel practices such as seniority, job bidding and posting, grievance systems (Foulkes, 1980) – have reduced worker desires for unions at these workplaces finds better support in the data. Studies of organizing drives show that companies with good personnel practices are more successful than others in defeating unions (AFL-CIO, 1984; Kochan, McKersie and Chalykoff, 1986), although the largest effect of such practices must be in deterring drives in the first place. The increased wage premium associated with size of establishment in the 1970s (Brown and Medoff, 1986), which could be expected to make unionization less attractive to those workers, is, moreover consistent with the declining success of unions in NLRB elections involving large establishments.[11] Still, I doubt that positive labor relations can explain much of the overall decline in union density. Large employers account for a decreasing share of jobs in the United States and unions could increase density greatly without organizing the IBMs of the world.

Government industrial relations policies

Government industrial relations policies have been cited as causing unions to decline in the private sector and to expand in the public sector. For the private sector, some blame (credit) the Reagan administration's operation of the NLRB and destruction of the Professional Air Traffic Controllers Organization (PATCO) as inducing an antiunion climate in the business community. The fact that union density began falling in the private sector before the Reagan administration and that collective bargaining coverage has increased in the public sector during the 1980s would seem to rule out this hypothesis, though it is possible that administration actions may have contributed to the acceleration of the decline in the 1980s.

The argument that state policies toward unionism have played a major role in the expansion of collective bargaining in the public sector has, on the other hand, considerable research support. Numerous studies have found that public sector unionization and collective bargaining contracts are more likely in states with favorable labor laws than in other states (Freeman, 1986b). Other studies – perhaps more persuasive – have shown that unionism has spurted in states following passage of favorable laws (Ichniowski, 1988; Saltzman, 1985, 1988). Even within a city, departments for which state laws are more favorable toward collective bargaining end up with contracts more frequently than 'brother' departments operating under less favorable state law (Freeman and Valletta, 1988). At the minimum, we have an empirical regularity: public-sector collective bargaining coverage and union density increase markedly in the presence of laws favorable to collective bargaining. This finding raises, however, two further questions: why comparable laws induce different outcomes between the public and private sectors, with which I will deal in detail shortly; and why many states enacted laws favorable to unions while 'labor law reform' failed at the national level, which I believe is due in part to the simple fact that a minority of senators, representing states unfavorably disposed to unionism, can stop national legislation but cannot, of course, undo legislation in states that are favorably disposed to unionism.

Union performance

Union performance may have contributed to the decline in union density in three ways. First, unions may have represented members poorly, discouraging nonunion workers from organizing. This hypothesis has little empirical support; it is inconsistent with union success in obtaining wage and benefit increases exceeding those of other workers in the 1970s and with opinion poll data showing union members to be reasonably satisfied with their unions (Kochan, 1979). Second, unions may have failed to allocate sufficient resources to organizing activity in the 1960s and 1970s. This claim has some a priori validity, as organizing expenditures deflated by wages (organizing is labor-intensive) have failed to keep pace with the growth of the increasing nonunion labor force and have been concentrated in sectors in which unions were already strong rather than in new and growing industries (Paula Voos, 1983, 1984). Because decisions to allocate resources to organizing depend in part on the organizing environment and the perceived benefits and costs of organizing campaigns, however, I am leery of attributing a large independent role to union organizing efforts. Union failure to embark on major organizing campaigns may simply reflect rational responses to the low expected rates of success. Third, and paradoxically from the perspective of analyses that treat unionization as a worker decision, the success of unions in raising union wage premiums in the 1970s may have contributed to the decline in density by raising the cost of unionization to firms and thereby intensifying the antiunion activity of management – to which I turn next.

Aggressive antiunion management

Given that the NLRB electoral process allows management to influence results, and that management is likely to prefer to operate nonunion, it is logical to seek an explanation for declining union success in the behavior of management. Did antiunion activity by management increase in the private sector in the period studied? How have public-sector managers behaved?

Figure 11.2 shows graphically that one indicator of management antiunion activity – 'unfair' labor practices under the law – has skyrocketed. While the NLRB data in the graph measure charges of unfair activity rather than actions found illegal in court (raising the possibility that unions

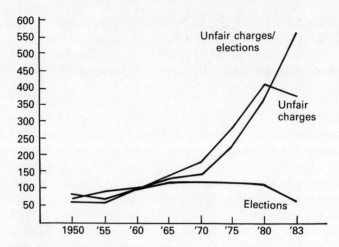

Figure 11.2 Indices of charges of unfair labor practices against management and NLRB elections (1960 = 100).

Source: NLRB Annual Reports.

may simply be filing more unfair charges), the proportion of charges upheld has been roughly constant at 30 to 40 per cent over time (Weiler, 1983), and NLRB statistics on numbers of workers discharged for union activity and ordered reinstated by the NLRB and courts show increases comparable to those in the figure. As for legal management opposition, a Conference Board survey reveals that 45 per cent of firms in their Personnel Practices Forum had 'operating union free' as a labor policy goal in 1983, compared to 31 per cent in 1977, indicating that even over a short period management opposition to unionization has grown substantially (Kochan, McKersie and Chalykoff, 1986).

In the public sector, by contrast, there has been no outburst of anti-union activity by management. Charges of unfair labor practices concern interpretation of state bargaining laws – whether a particular topic is subject to collective bargaining or is a management prerogative – not opposition to the existence of unionism per se. Public-sector managers rarely hire union-preventing firms to discourage organization by their workers. Because of changes in state laws, moreover, the trend in the public sector is toward less rather than more management opposition to collective bargaining.

On the basis of these facts, I argue that the antiunion management offensive in the private sector is the key to deunionization of the United States, and that its absence from the public sector explains the successful organization of public employees. Moreover, I claim that the differential behavior of management in the public and private sectors is explicable by the incentives facing them.

MANAGEMENT OFFENSIVE, UNION WAGE PREMIUMS, AND COST OF OPPOSITION

My proposed explanation can be most easily represented with a simple schematic model (see Figure 11.3), which diverges from many models of union organization by stressing the role of management in unionization and the endogeneity of both management opposition and union organizing. I postulate three basic relations.

The first relation is a production function for organizing success. It

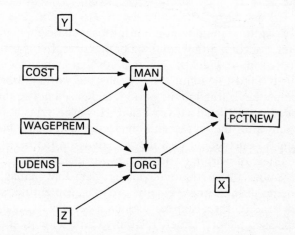

Figure 11.3 Determinants of union organizing activity and management opposition and their effect on unionization on new workers.

The first relation
Determination of organizing success: PCTNEW = f(MAN, ORG, X)
 where PCTNEW = number of workers organized/labor force;
 MAN = resources devoted by management to opposing unions;
 ORG = resources devoted by unions to organizing;
 X = other factors that influence outcomes

The second relation
Management opposition: MAN = g(WAGEPREM, COST, ORG, Y)
 where WAGEPREM = union wage premium;
 COST = cost of opposing union in NLRB elections;
 Y = other relevant factors, largely relating to product market
 factors such as deregulation of industries, etc., which determine effect of unionism on profitability.

The third relation
Union and worker organizing effort: ORG = h(WAGEPREM, MAN, UDENS, Z)
 where UDENS = union density at the beginning of the period;
 Z = other relevant factors, largely relating to labor market.

relates the number of workers newly organized relative to the labor force to the resources devoted by management to opposing unions, the resources devoted by unions to organizing, and a vector of all other factors that might influence the outcome.

The second relation links the resources management devotes to opposing unionization to economic factors likely to affect the profitability of such activity. One such factor is the union wage premium, which is assumed to reduce profits and increase management opposition. Another is the cost of opposing unionism in an NLRB election, which will depend on the 'technology' of battling unions at workplaces (which has changed greatly in the past 15 years due to the advent of labor–management consultants who specialize in training supervisors to pressure workers to oppose unions and in running antiunion propaganda campaigns) and on the legal penalty for committing unfair labor practices. In the private sector the legal penalty is minuscule: the law requires that management reinstate workers unjustly fired for union activity, pay the workers back pay less whatever income they earned in the period, and post a notice that the firm will not engage in such illegal activity again. However, reinstating workers often occurs only after the representation election and many choose not to return. Posting a notice about past illegal activity on the part of the firm often has the effect of warning workers how far management is willing to go to defeat unions rather than convincing them that management will forgo such tactics in the future. Finally, the management decision is also assumed to depend on the resources the union devotes to organizing, and on other unspecified factors, largely relating to product market conditions, that can be expected to make anticipated union wage premiums more or less expensive in terms of lost profits.

The third relationship in my analysis links union (and worker) organizing activity to the following: the wage premium, presumed to raise the attractiveness of unions to workers and thus increase organizing activity; the existing density of union workers, with a lower density assumed to reduce organizing activity because the cost of organizing each nonunion worker is higher to existing union members when there are proportionately fewer unionists among whom to spread the cost; the amount of resources management devotes to opposing unionism; and a catch-all vector of other relevant factors, largely relating to labor-market conditions.

One important feature of this model is that the union wage premium affects the decisions of both the management and union (workers). In the management equation, a higher premium induces more antiunion activity and thus reduces union organizing success. In the union equation, a higher premium induces additional organizing activity and thus raises union organizing success. Given opposing tendencies, is the wage premium likely to be positively or negatively correlated with actual outcomes? To the extent that unions extract rents from firms through monopoly wage increases, the money loss to firms will exceed the transfer to workers (due to the 'triangle inefficiency), giving management a potential incentive to spend more resources to prevent unionization than unions/workers spend to organize (Freeman, 1986a). If expenditures by the two sides have equal effects on outcomes, higher union wage premium will reduce organizing success.

A second important feature of the model is the inclusion of management and union activity in the equations determining the behavior of the other side. This highlights the interactive nature of the organizing struggle – which can be viewed as a two-person (three-person, if one distinguishes workers at an organizing site from the union) game – and thus directs attention to the potential payoff from game-theoretic analyses of union and management strategic behavior that goes beyond the scope of this chapter.

A third aspect of the analysis that deserves attention is the inclusion of union density in the equation for union organizing activity, for it raises the possibility that a fall in union density will produce a cumulative decline, as the increased cost of organizing induces unions to lower organizing activity, while, conversely, rises in union density will have the opposite cumulative effect.

How might one use the model embedded in these relationships to explain the decline in private-sector union density? The most reasonable hypothesis, given the evidence in the previous section, is that management opposition to unionism induced by changes in the cost of unionization and the union wage premium reduced union organizing success, with cumulative effects on union density and organizing effort. For this explanation to be valid, it is necessary that management activity has an important impact on organizing success; and that this activity responds to economic incentives.

With respect to the effectiveness of management opposition, studies by a diverse set of researchers ranging from management groups to the General Accounting Office to the AFL-CIO to academics find that management activity reduces union success in NLRB representation elections and organizing drives (see Table 11.5). The sole exception (Getman, Goldberg and Herman, 1976) has been the subject of considerable controversy, with Dickens convincingly reversing their conclusion in a reanalysis of the underlying data. Even absent this, however, the preponderance of the evidence is that *the extent of management opposition substantially determines the outcomes of organizing campaigns*, as posited. As management devotes considerable resources to opposing unionization, and presumably acts rationally, this makes intuitive sense.

Because the studies in Table 11.5 focus on representation elections/ organizing drives, rather than on the workers gained relative to the workforce (PCTNEW) that enters the union density equation, and do not provide estimates of the extent to which the downward trend in union success can be attributed to management opposition, I have estimated the

Table 11.5 Summary of studies of effects of management activity on NLRB representation election results

Study and sample	Measurement of management activity	Does activity have effect?
1 National Industrial conference Board, 140 union organizing drives of white collar workers, 1966–7	Amount of communication by management	Yes
2 AFL–CIO, 495 NLRB election, 1966–7	Amount of opposition by management	Yes
3 Prosten (1978), analysis of probability of union win in 130,701 elections in 1962–77	Amount of time delay between election and petition	Yes
4 Lawler (1984), 155 NLRB elections, 1974–8	Company hires consultant	Yes
5 Drotning (1967), 41 elections ordered void and rerun by NLRB	Amount of communication by management	Yes
6 Roomkin-Block (1981), 45,155 union representation cases, 1971–7	Delay between petition and election	Yes
7 Seeber and Cooke (1983), proportion of workers voting for union representation by state, 1970–8	Employers object to election district	Yes
8 US General Accounting Office (1982), analysis of 8(a)(3) illegal firings or other discrimination for union involvement in 368 representation elections	Employer committed unfair labor practice	Yes
9 Aspin (1966) study the 71 NLRB elections in which reinstatements were ordered.	Employer fired worker for union activity	Yes, unless reinstated before elect
10 Getman, Goldberg, and Herman (1976) analysis of 1,293 workers in 31 elections in 1972–3	Campaign tactics employer.	Not stat-significant
11 Dickens (1983) study of 966 workers in 31 elections in 1972–3 (using data set in no. 10)	Legal and illegal campaign tactics by employer	Yes
12 Catler (1978) study of 817 NLRB elections	Unfair labor practices and delay	Yes
13 Kochan, McKersie and Chalykoff (1986), 225 firms	Employer emphasizes union avoidance strategy	Yes

impact of the one indicator of management opposition for which time series data exists – unfair labor practices – on workers won by unions as a share of nonagricultural employment. My analysis uses pooled state (industry) time series data, with time dummies included to control for omitted trend and cyclical factors and state/industry dummies to control for omitted state/industry effects, and diverse control variables. The results, summarized in Table 11.6, show that unfair labor practices reduce the number of those unionized relative to the workforce and that the trend

Table 11.6 Estimates of the effect of management unfair labor practices on percentage of the nonagricultural workforce newly organized in the NLRB elections

	Impact of 10% increase in unfair practices / election on proportion of workers newly organized in NLRB elect.	Estimated % decline in organized workforce in NLRB election due to increased management unfair labor practices
Comparison of union success		
Across states, 1950–78	−2.5	28
Within states over time, 1950–78	−3.4	38
Across industries, 1965–80	−3.5	36
Within industries over time, 1965–80	−6.2	62
In US over time, 1950–80	−4.6	51

Source: Lines 1 and 2 from Freeman and Medoff, 1984, p. 238. Lines 3 to 5 from Freeman, 1986a.

in unfair labor practices can account for roughly half of the observed drop in that outcome measure. To the extent that unfair practices substitute for lawful management antiunion activity, this estimate, while sizeable, understates the full impact of management's fight against unions. Alternatively, however, if the growth of unfair practices is positively correlated with the growth of legal management opposition, my estimates overstate the impact of illegal management activity on the decline in union success, though they may accurately measure the impact of management opposition, in total.

The role of changes in the relative cost of union deterrence in simulating the management offensive has not been the subject of extensive research, making conclusions here more speculative. Time series calculations show that some of the rise in unfair practices is explicable by the rise in union wage premiums in the 1970s, but the series is short and the measures are crude (Freeman, 1986a). Estimates of the relation between decline of union density and union premiums at a one-digit industry level indicate that where the premium has risen most, union declines have been greatest (Linneman and Wachter, 1986), which may reflect reduced organizing success or a greater death rate for union plants in those sectors. As for other factors likely to raise the cost of unionism to firms, it is highly plausible that such product market developments as the growth of foreign competition and deregulation have made existing union wages more expensive in terms of lost profits. As increased nonunion competition and management policies against unionized firms in construction indicates, however, new product market competition from any source, not simply trade or deregulation, can significantly reduce union density. Finally, with respect to the determination of union organizing efforts, the major work here – by Paula Voos – suggests that one can treat organizing behavior as rational decision-making.

Is this analysis consistent with the increase in public sector density? There are three basic facts to explain regarding the spread of collective bargaining to the public sector: the geographic variation in unionization associated with different labor laws; the spurt in unionization that followed passage of the laws; and the different behavior of public- and private-sector managers under comparable laws. If the benefits to management of operating with a union relative to the cost of opposing unions are lower in the public than in the private sector, and those costs have decreased over time, we could account for these facts in the same framework used to explain certain developments in the private sector: in terms of the incentives and options for management to oppose unions.

In fact, the incentives for management to oppose unions do appear to be lower in the public sector. First, public-sector workers constitute an especially active political group able to punish or reward the politicians who are their employers at the ballot box, even though they are only a small proportion of voters in most areas. Second, the cost of illegal opposition is likely to be greater for public than for private officials, as public officials who break laws are likely to face possible removal from office. Third, unions can help public-sector employers increase budgets through lobbying for additional public expenditures, creating a greater jointness of interest than in the private sector. Fourth, wage premiums tend to be smaller in the public sector (see Lewis, 1988; Freeman, 1986a). But crudely, management opposition to unions can gain profits in the private sector; in the public sector, it can cost votes. Given this, and the fact that states passed laws favorable to unionization in the 1960s and 1970s that increased the cost of management opposition in the public sector, the spurt of unions there is consistent with the model.

Finally, is this analysis consistent with the differential experience of Canada? While private sector managers are likely to have similar profit incentives to oppose unions in Canada as in the United States (Anderson and Gunderson (1982) show there is no evidence that union wage effects are smaller in Canada than in the United States), the Canadian system for organizing workers differs from the American system by giving management less option to express opposition. Canadian labor boards rely largely on 'card checks' in which unions sign up workers to determine representation at a workplace rather than on adversarial elections and impose harsher penalties on managements that break the laws (Weiler, 1983; Meltz, 1985), with the result that Canada has not experienced anything like the massive outburst of management unfair labor practices that characterizes US labor relations. The difference in institutional procedures highlights the fact that the decline in private-sector unionism in the United States required two factors: increased incentive for management to oppose unions, and the opportunity to turn that incentive into action.

CONCLUSION

As the reader will undoubtedly have observed, not all the pieces for a complete explanation of the decline in private-sector union density and rise in public-sector density in the United States are in place. But the available evidence seems consistent with an explanation of private-sector decline that stresses increased management opposition to union organization, motivated in part by profit-seeking behavior, and augmented by trade union responses; and an explanation of growth in the public sector that stresses reduced management opposition due to passage of comprehensive collective bargaining laws and vote-seeking behavior.

As for the likely impact of the change in unionization on the performance of the economy, two points are worth attention. The first is that the increasingly public-sector locus of American unionism is likely to produce different union effects and modes of operation than have been found for the traditionally private-sector union movement. Public-sector unions have, for example, smaller wage effects and strike rates than private-sector unions and appear to increase rather than reduce employment in union activities (see Freeman and Ichniowski, 1988). Second, without making any judgment of whether a less unionized private sector will perform better or not, one thing should be perfectly clear: analysts who have attributed national economic problems ranging from unemployment to wage inflation to low productivity to unions will have to find a new culprit to blame: unless there is a remarkable renaissance in unionism, critics will not have unions to kick around any more.

NOTES

1. Estimates of organization in the public sector differ somewhat among sources, though all data show greater organization than in the private sector. See Freeman, Ichniowski, and Zax (1988) for a detailed analysis of the various statistics.
2. US employment data come from two basic sources: Current Population Survey data on individuals and establishment data from the Bureau of Labor Statistics. The 85 per cent figure comes from the establishment survey.
3. These data are from the Survey of Governments, which differ from those in the Current Population Survey, as described in Freeman, Ichniowski and Zax (forthcoming).
4. Millward and Stevens (1986) report a rise in the percentage of manufacturing establishments operating nonunion from 18 per cent to 29 per cent (pp.

58–9) and a drop in the percentage with a closed shop from 30 per cent to 18 per cent (p. 103).

5. This is not to say that unions throughout the West do not face serious problems in adjusting to the changing economic climate. They do. The difference between the United States and most other countries is that only in the United States have these problems taken the form of massive deunionization of the private sector.

6. That is, situations where a union tries to pressure an employer by placing economic pressure on a third party, often a customer or supplier.

7. The changes in law are reviewed in Freeman (1986b) and in Freeman and Valletta (forthcoming) in greater detail. The NBER has a computer file on regulations across states, departments, and time, which is available to researchers on request.

8. These estimates are based on the private-sector union membership numbers of Troy and Sheflin for 1950, 1960, 1970, 1980, and a projected 1985 figure based on his 1983 (updated using CPS figures on the percentage change in membership from 1983 to 1985); estimates of private nonagricultural wage and salary workers exclusive of private household workers from the BLS; and the number of members won by unions in NLRB elections in 1951–60, 1961–70, 1971–80, 1981–5 (with 1985 and 1985 assumed to be the same as 1983). I calculated the compound annual rate of depreciation in union membership by comparing actual membership in, say, 1980 with membership in 1970 plus the number of workers won from 1971–80, and then subtracted the compound annual rate of growth of the relevant employment.

9. One can use various identities to decompose the decline in members won/employment (Freeman, 1985).

10. The figures for 1977 are from the Quality of Employment Survey. Those for 1985 are from the Harris Poll.

11. In the 1950s unions had a better record in large units than in smaller ones, but this pattern of success was reversed in the 1970s. The small number of elections in large units in recent years makes the 1980s figures spotty. For data on union win rates by size of unit, see Goldfield (1987).

BIBLIOGRAPHY

American Federation of Labor – Congress of Industrial Organizations, Department of Field Services, *AFL-CIO Organizing Survey* (Washington, DC: April, 1984).

Anderson, J., and Gunderson, M., *Union Management Relations in Canada* (Addison-Wesley, 1982).

Aspin, L., *A Study of Reinstatement Under the National Labor Relations Act*, PhD dissertation (Cambridge, MA: MIT Press, 1966).

Brown, C., and Medoff, J., 'The employer size wage effect', mimeo (Cambridge, MA: Harvard University Press, 1986).

Catler, S., 'Labor union representation elections: what determines who wins?', BA thesis (Cambridge, MA: Harvard University Press, 1978).

Dickens, W., 'The effect of company compaigns on certification elections', *Industrial and Labor Relations Review* (1983), 36, pp. 560–75.

Dickens, W., and Leonard, J., 'Accounting for the decline in union membership, 1950–1980)', *Industrial and Labor Relations Review* (April 1985), 38(3), pp. 323–34.

Drotning, J., 'NLRB remedies for election misconduct: an analysis of election outcomes and their determinants', *Journal of Business* (April 1967), 40(2), pp. 137–48.

Foulkes, F., *Personnel Policies in Large Nonunion Companies*, (Englewood Cliffs, NJ: Prentice-Hall, 1980).

Freeman, R., 'Why are unions fairing poorly in NLRB representation elections?', in Kichan, T. A., ed., *Challenges and Choices Facing American Labor* (Cambridge, MA: MIT Press, 1985), pp. 45–64.

Freeman, R., 'The effect of the union wage differential on management opposition and union organizing success', *American Economic Review* (May 1986a), pp. 92–6.

Freeman, R., 'Unionism comes to the public sector', *Journal of Economic Literature* (March 1986b), vol. XXIV, pp. 41–86.

Freeman, R., and Ichniowski, B., 'When public sector workers unionise: summary of findings', in Freeman, R. and Ichniowski, C., eds, *When Public Sector Workers Unionise* (NBER, University of Chicago Press, 1988).

Freeman, R., Ichniowski, B., and Zax, J., 'Measuring collective organization in the public sector', in Freeman, R., and Ichniowski, C., eds, *When Public Sector Workers Unionise* (NBER, University of Chicago Press, 1988).

Freeman, R., and Medoff, J., *What Do Unions Do?* (New York: Basic Books, 1984).

Freeman, R., and Valletta, R., 'The effects of public sector labor laws on unionisation, wages, and employment', in Freeman, R., and Ichniowski, C., eds, *When Public Sector Workers Unionise* (NBER, University of Chicago Press, 1988).

Getman, J., Goldberg, J., and Herman, J., *Union Representation Elections: Law and Reality* (New York: Russell Sage Foundation, 1976).

Goldfield, M., *The Decline of Organized Labor* (University of Chicago Press, 1987).

Ichniowski, C., 'Public sector union growth and bargaining laws', in Freeman, R. and Ichniowski, C., eds, *When Public Sector Workers Unionise* (NBER, University of Chicago Press, 1988).

Kochan, T., 'How American workers view labor unions', *Monthly Labor Review* (1979), 102(4), pp. 23–31.

Kochan, T., McKersie, R., and Chalykoff, J., 'The effects of corporate strategy and workplace innovations on union representation', *Industrial and Labor Relations Review* (July 1986), 39(4), pp. 487–501.

Kramer, L., *Labor's Paradox – the American Federation of State, Council, and Municipal Employees* (New York: Wiley, 1962).

Lawler, J., 'The influence of management consultants on the outcome of union certification elections', *Industrial and Labor Relations Review* (1984), 38, pp. 38–51.

Linneman, P. and Wachter, M., 'Rising union premiums and the declining boundaries among noncompeting groups', *American Economic Review* (May 1986), 76, 103–8.

Lipset, S. M., 'North American labor movements: a comparative perspective', in Lipset, S. M., ed., *Unions in Transition* (San Francisco: Institute for Contemporary Studies, 1986).

Lewis, H. G., 'Union/nonunion wage gaps in the public sector', in Freeman, R. and Ichniowski, C., eds, *When Public Sector Workers Unionise* (NBER, University of Chicago Press, 1988).

Meltz, N., 'Labor movements in Canada and the United States: are they really that different?', in Kochan, T. A., ed., *Challenges and Choices Facing American Labor* (Cambridge, MA: MIT, 1985).

Millward, N., and Stevens, M., *British Workplace Industrial Relations 1980–84* (London: Gower Publishing, 1986).

National Labor Relations Board, Annual Report (Washington, DC: USGPO).

Neumann, G., and Rissman, E., 'Where have all the union members gone?', *Journal of Labor Economics* (April 1984), 2(2), pp. 175–92.

Prosten, R., 'The longest season union organizing in the last decade', *Proceedings of the 31st Annual Meeting of the Industrial Relations Research Association* (Madison, Wisconsin: 1978), pp. 240–9.

Roomkin, M., and Block, R., 'Case processing time and outcome of elections: some empirical evidence', *University of Illinois Law Review* (1981), VI, pp. 75–97.

Saltzman, G. M., 'Bargaining laws and cause and consequences of the growth of teachers' unions', *Industrial and Labor Relations Review* (1985) 38, pp. 335–57.

Saltzman, G. M., 'The effects of recent bargaining laws in Ohio and Illinois', in Freeman, R., and Ichniowski, C., eds, *When Public Sector Workers Unionise* (NBER, University of Chicago Press, 1988).

Seeber, R., and Cooke, W., 'The decline in union success in NLRB representation elections', *Industrial Relations* (Winter 1983), 22(1).

Troy, L., and Sheflin, N., *Union Sourcebook* (New Jersey: Industrial Relations Data and Information Services, 1985).

US Department of Labor, Bureau of Labor Statistics, *Directory of National Unions and Employee Associations*, various editions.

US General Accounting Office, *Concerns Regarding Impact of Employee Charges Against Employers for Unfair Labor Practices* (Washington, DC: GAO-HRD 82–80, June 21, 1982).

Voos, P., 'Union organizing: costs and benefits', *Industrial and Labor Relations Review* (July 1983), pp. 576–91.

Voos, P., 'Trends in union organizing expenditures, 1953–1977', *Industrial and Labor Relations Review* (October 1984), 38, pp. 52–63.

Weiler, P., 'Promises to keep: securing workers' rights to self-organisation under the NLRA', *Harvard Law Review* (June 1983), 96(8), pp. 1769–1827.

Weiler, P., 'Striking a new balance: freedom of contract and prospects for union representation', *Harvard Law Review* (1985), 98, pp. 351–420.

12 · BONUSES AND EMPLOYMENT IN JAPAN

The bonus payment system, by which Japanese workers receive upwards of one-quarter of their yearly pay in the form of semiannual bonuses, is one of the exotic features of the Japanese labor markets that have long fascinated outsiders. Recently interest has been heightened by the realization that the bonus system may have important macroeconomic implications along the lines of a 'share economy' (Weitzman, 1984, 1985). It is at least conceivable that some part of Japan's remarkable ability to stabilize unemployment at low, steady rates is due to the automatic pay flexibility that comes with profit or revenue sharing. For a subject of such potential importance, the Japanese bonus system has been studied relatively little.

This chapter reports the results of a detailed empirical analysis of Japanese labor-market data designed to address certain fundamental questions about the bonus system. In it we analyze data on bonuses and other labor-market variables at the one- and two-digit industry levels from 1958 to 1983, as well as data from a case study of an individual firm. Our interpretations have been guided by the results of interviews with Japanese employer federation representatives and labor union officials.

BACKGROUND

The purpose of this section is to place the subject of the Japanese bonus system in a broader context. This is important because the bonus system is only one part of the complicated, interrelated web of institutions and attitudes that constitutes Japanese labor relations. Although we have tried hard to guard against a monocausal interpretation of the Japanese labor market, it is quite possible that in analyzing the bonus system we inadvertently overlook other important aspects of the industrial relations system that have also influenced the behavior under study.

The following stylized facts might be taken as roughly descriptive of how the 'Japanese model' of the labor market differs somewhat from others.[1]

First, firms hire workers directly out of school for 'lifetime employment' (the *shushin koyo* system). In fact this is done primarily by the large firms, and only for their so-called 'permanent' or 'regular' employees. In the economy as a whole, 66 per cent of all workers (including self-employed and family workers) and 'regular' employees, of whom 54 per cent are in firms with 50 regular employees or more and 24 per cent in firms with 500 regular employees or more, making the permanent employees a minority of the workforce. Nevertheless, the 'lifetime commitment mentality' seems to be a fair characterization of the Japanese system as a whole.[2]

Second, there is a steep age–earnings profile for permanent workers up to retirement age of 55 or, more recently, 60. Pay is influenced greatly by seniority, but this *nenko* system has begun to erode in many places as it increasingly comes to be viewed as anachronistic and as Japan faces a decline in the number of younger workers relative to older workers.[3]

Third, the Japanese workplace is a relatively cooperative and egalitarian environment. There are few work rules, job reassignments are common, and a high degree of company loyalty motivates productivity-enhancing behavior.[4] Unions are organized along enterprise or company lines and include white-collar as well as blue-collar workers. In addition, blue- and white-collar workers in the same firm are comparatively less differentiated than elsewhere in terms of perquisites, treatment, method of payment (monthly salaries rather than hourly wages – with meaningful bonus payments), and how much they are paid.

Fourth, Japanese society as a whole displays a relatively intense commitment at a grassroots level to maintaining full employment. Moreover, layoffs are not generally by seniority. There appears to be a high degree of social responsibility in wage setting in Japan, as was dramatically shown by labor's heeding the 1975 call for wage restraint in the face of strong inflation caused by the first oil shock. Work sharing is common, as Japanese firms tend to adjust hours more than employment and also to hoard more labor in downturns compared to firms in most other developed countries.[5]

Fifth, bonuses are important quantitatively in the average worker's pay (upwards of one-quarter of pay is in the form of a semiannual bonus). They are also large relative to reported company profits, ranging from 42 to 76 per cent of operating profits before taxes from 1965 to 1983, and have come to constitute roughly 10 per cent of net domestic product.[6]

The typical Japanese worker's pay is divided into two categories. The first component is officially called *kimatte shikyusuru kyuyo*, 'the wage that is surely paid,' which we will refer to simply as base wages, although they are not hourly wages at all, but rather a monthly salary. (Actually, because wages are paid on a monthly basis the concept of 'overtime' payments and work is not sharply differentiated in Japan, suggesting that employment rather than person-hours is the fundamental unit of labor usage for regular workers.) The second component is called 'special cash payments' in the official statistics and the defining characteristic is held to be that it is a payment made 'temporarily, unexpectedly, or erratically at the discretion of the employer.' This category consists overwhelmingly of bonus payments, even though their terms and amount are often established by collective agreements and they are sometimes far from temporary, unexpected, or erratic.

Bonuses are usually paid twice a year – in summer (mostly June and July), and at year's end (December). Insignificant amounts are sometimes paid in August, March, and January. Although before the Second World War blue-collar and low-status white-collar workers often received a lump sum of money twice a year in addition to their regular pay, the small amount of money involved was in no way comparable to the significant semiannual bonuses received by high-status white-collar employees with advanced educational backgrounds. It was only after the war that the payment system emerged in its present form, as part of a broader trend. The main feature of this trend was a deemphasis, to the point of near-elimination, of the invidious status categories of prewar Japan with their implicit legacies of a feudal past. As one by-product of the immediate postwar process of democratizing the workplace, which the unions fully supported, all regular employees – blue collar and white – were henceforth to be paid a monthly salary instead of an hourly wage, supplemented by meaningful semiannual bonuses for every regular employee irrespective of category.[7] The bonus payments constituted less than 2 months' worth of supplement after the war, rose gradually to over 4 months by 1973, and fell back to slightly more than 3½ months currently.[8]

The bonus system is widely viewed as serving three purposes. One purpose, of particular relevance to this study, is that the bonus system provides some pay flexibility to help firms maintain the lifetime employment commitment over bad times and good. Another purpose is to compensate individual effort. Since the bonus is more discretionary than the base wage of the nenko system (which is primarily related to length of service), management typically makes some part of a particular employee's bonus depend on the merit appraisal of the individual worker's job performance (Okuno, 1984). Finally, the bonus emphasizes, symbolically and practically, the common bond linking the company's well-being with the well-being of its regular workers.

The timing of wage decisions and the timing of bonus decisions generally differ. Across many unionized companies base-wage determination is the primary concern of the economy-wide pattern-bargaining spring wage offensive (shunto), which usually starts in February and peaks in April (Grossman and Haraf, 1983). Negotiations over bonuses are typically done after wages are settled; and, according to management and labor representatives, bonuses are more sensitive to a company's or an industry's specific circumstances than base wages, which are primarily dependent on the economy's national performance.

Firms that consistently do well generally succeed in paying a fairly steady number of months' wages as a bonus, so that in prospering sectors and times, their bonuses are unlikely to vary much with cyclical conditions. An oft-cited example of a firm that maintains such a policy is Toyota, which has paid about the same months' worth of bonus in each year since 1968. But for every Toyota Motor Company there are companies in, say, machine tools or shipbuilding where bonuses may vary from 2 to 10 months' pay in extreme economic conditions. At one such firm, Okuma Machine Works, the standard deviation of the percentage change of wages from 1957 to 1985 was 7, compared to a standard deviation of the percentage change of bonuses of 29. Bonuses varied from 9 months to 2 months of pay in postwar years. The majority of firms hold a position in between the positions of Toyota and Okuma. For manufacturing firms in the aggregate, the standard deviation of the log change in bonuses from 1959 to 1983 was 0.072 compared to a standard deviation of the log change of wages of 0.055.[9]

Because our analysis is based on averages of firms within an industry, it is likely that we will understate the variation of bonuses at the level of firms and thus may find less variation with respect to shifts in profits or revenues than would be found in a firm-level study.

To what extent are bonuses directly related to profits through some sort of formula?

Surveys conducted by *Nikkeiren*, the employers' federation, show that most firms think of bonuses as being influenced by profitability. Among corporations that make an explicit agreement with employees about bonus payments, some 15 per cent of such contracts contain profit-sharing clauses.[10]

The key issues

There are three critical issues in evaluating the macroeconomic implications of the Japanese bonus system.

The first is the extent to which bonuses are more 'flexible' with respect to profits or revenues than are wages, and thus operate as a form of profit or revenue sharing.

The second is the effect of bonuses on employment. If bonuses are a cost to employers similar to wages, with no share component, bonuses plus wages are the relevant variable defining labor demand, with increases in bonuses reducing employment just as increases in wages do; contrarily, if bonuses have a nonnegligible profit-sharing component, they might have a very different relation to employment.

The third, and perhaps the most difficult issue to assess, is the contribution of a bonus system that operates along share-economy lines to the overall performance of the Japanese labor market either by itself or relative to other institutional factors, such as the flexibility of the base wage in the annual Shunto negotiations. Our work focuses solely on the potential impact of the bonus system itself on the labor market.

The remainder of the paper examines these three issues. The next two sections analyze the determinants of bonuses and the link between bonuses and employment using data for the entire Japanese economy, for manufacturing, and for more disaggregated two-digit industries, largely within manufacturing. The final section turns to the macroeconomic implications of our findings.

ECONOMIC FLUCTUATIONS AND BONUSES

Are bonuses more responsive to economic conditions than are wages, or are bonuses simply a markup of wages?

One direct way to examine the *relative* flexibility of bonuses and wages to economic conditions is to regress the ratio of monthly bonuses to monthly wages (the number of months of salary paid in bonuses, which is how most Japanese think of them) on measures of aggregate or industry economic conditions, conditional on past values of wages and bonuses.

Table 12.1 contains the results of such an analysis for all industry and for manufacturing in Japan. The dependent variable is the log of the ratio of bonuses to wages from the series of the Japanese Ministry of Labor; it relates to all firms with five or more regular employees. To measure economic conditions we have used the log of profits (π) as reported in the Statistical Survey of Corporate Enterprise series of corporate operating profits for firms of all sizes, and two related measures of revenues: net domestic product (NDP) taken from the Japanese Economic Planning Agency data on net output by industrial origin at market prices, and corporate value added (VA) as reported in the Statistical Survey of Corporate Enterprises. All of the nominal variables are deflated by the wholesale price index (WPI) series of the Bank of Japan, with the total WPI used for the entire economy, the manufacturing price series used for manufacturing, and separate indices for more disaggregate industries. All three indicators of economic conditions are measured over the Japanese fiscal year (April 1 to March 31), which correlates them more closely with the largely springtime determination of upcoming wage and bonus levels than with calendar year data. In addition to the measures of economic conditions, the equations include lagged values of bonuses (B_{-1}) and wages (W_{-1}) introduced separately to allow for differential autoregressiveness of the series. The even-numbered equations include a linear time trend variable while the odd-numbered ones include time and a time-

Table 12.1 Estimates of the effect of economic conditions on log(bonuses/wages), 1959–83[a]

#	Constant	Time	$(Time)^2$	$\ln(\pi)$	$\ln(VA)$	$\ln(NDP)$	$\ln(B_{-1})$	$\ln(W_{-1})$	R^2	SEE
				All industry						
1	−0.08	−0.09	0.001	0.18			0.67	−0.63	0.98	0.018
		(0.03)	(0.0002)	(0.02)			(0.08)	(0.11)		
2	−2.49	−0.01		0.15			0.53	−0.55	0.98	0.020
		(0.004)		(0.02)			(0.07)	(0.12)		
3	−0.29	−0.14	0.001		0.38		0.49	−0.58	0.98	0.019
		(0.04)	(0.0003)		(0.05)		(0.09)	(0.12)		
4	−3.65	−0.01			0.29		0.35	−0.46	0.97	0.024
		(0.004)			(0.06)		(0.10)	(0.14)		
5	1.53	−0.17	0.001			0.42	0.47	−0.45	0.94	0.032
		(0.09)	(0.001)			(0.17)	(0.15)	(0.20)		
6	−2.64	−0.02				0.20	0.41	−0.33	0.93	0.034
		(0.01)				(0.11)	(0.16)	(0.20)		
				Manufacturing						
7	0.62	−0.12	0.001	0.20			0.71	−0.64	0.98	0.021
		(0.04)	(0.0002)	(0.02)			(0.07)	(0.28)		
8	−2.41	−0.002		0.18			0.60	−0.68	0.97	0.026
		(0.006)		(0.03)			0.53	(0.10)		
9	0.94	−0.21	0.001		0.49		0.53	−0.68	0.99	0.018
		(0.03)	(0.0002)		(0.04)		(0.06)	(0.10)		
10	−3.79	−0.004			0.37		0.40	−0.67	0.96	0.030
		(0.007)			(0.07)		(0.10)	(0.18)		
11	2.55	−0.22	0.001			0.38	0.41	−0.25	0.94	0.042
		(0.10)	(0.001)			(0.14)	(0.16)	(0.23)		
12	−2.57	−0.02				0.19	0.40	−0.31	0.92	0.046
		(0.01)				(0.12)	(0.17)	(0.24)		

Note:
a   Equations including π and VA are restricted to 1960–83.
Source: See Data Appendix contained in the journal version of this article. Note that all variables are in 'real' units, deflated as described in the text.

square variable to allow for a more complex 'exogenous' pattern of change in the bonus-to-wage ratio (in particular for the rise, then fall in the ratio shown in the underlying data).

The calculations provide a clear answer to the question of the relative responsiveness of wages and bonuses to economic conditions: in every case, the coefficient on the measure of economic conditions is positive and significant, indicating that bonuses are more responsive than wages to economic conditions. Moreover, the coefficient on lagged bonuses is positive and that on lagged wages is negative, of roughly comparable magnitudes, indicating that a 'partial adjustment' type of model of the bonus-to-wage ratio with persistence of bonuses and wages over time is consistent with the data.

To see whether the results hold up at a more disaggregated level of

Table 12.2 Summary of the coefficients of the effect of profits and revenues on log(bonuses/wages)[a]

		A Bonuses more responsive to profits[b]		B Bonuses more responsive to value added[b]		C Bonuses more responsive to NDP[b]	
		Yes	No	Yes	No	Yes	No
	$\mid t \mid < 1$	2	1	0	1	5	2
$1 < $	$\mid t \mid < 2$	1	0	1	0	4	0
$2 < $	$\mid t \mid < 3$	0	0	4	0	6	0
	$\mid t \mid > 3$	10	0	8	0	0	0
Total		13	1	13	1	15	2

Notes:
a   Based on regressions of log(Bonuses/Wages) on time, log(Bonuses(-1)), log(Wages (-1)), and the log of the relevant measure of economic activity.
b   The figures refer to the number of industries.

analysis, we have estimated equations for the ratios of bonuses to wages for two-digit industries over the same time period. The results of this analysis are given in Table 12.2 in terms of the number of industries in which bonuses are more (less) responsive to the relevant explanatory variable than are wages, categorized by the size of the *t* statistic. As can be seen, the analysis supports the finding that bonuses are more responsive than wages to revenues and profits at the two-digit level of aggregation, with the vast majority of industries obtaining positive and often significant ($t > 2$) impact coefficients. We conclude that although bonuses are not a simple proportion of profits or revenues they depend substantially on those variables, to a much greater extent than wages, and thus vary more with economic conditions than do wages.

How do bonuses and wages, taken as separate variables, respond to economic conditions? Do both wages and bonuses respond positively to conditions with the Table 12.1 results due to the greater responsiveness of bonuses, or are bonuses responsive and wages inflexible? To answer these questions we have estimated the following equations:

$$\log B = A + \lambda a \, \log \pi \text{ (or } R) + (1 - \lambda)\log B_{-1} + cT \qquad (12.1)$$

$$\log W = A' + b\lambda' \, \log \pi \text{ (or } R) + (1 - \lambda')\log W_{-1} + c'T \qquad (12.2)$$

While the results of our analysis, given in Table 12.3, show that bonuses are invariably more responsive than wages to economic conditions, the estimated coefficients tell somewhat different stories for the effect of revenues and the effect of profits on the two measures of pay. While both bonuses and wages are positively related to revenues, only bonuses

Table 12.3 Coefficients and standard errors for effects of net domestic product, value added, and profits on bonuses and wages, 1959–83[a]

Dependent variable	Constant	Time	ln(NDP)	ln(π)	ln(VA)	ln(B_{-1})	ln(W_{-1})	SEE
			A All industry					
1 ln(bonuses)	−0.33	−0.013 (0.005)	0.44 (0.14)			0.64 (0.14)		0.041
2 ln(wages)	1.41	0.002 (0.009)	0.34 (0.13)				0.53 (0.22)	0.051
3 ln(bonuses)	−0.13	−0.009 (0.006)		0.09 (0.05)		0.94 (0.09)		0.048
4 ln(wages)	0.21	−0.01 (0.01)		−0.05 (0.07)			1.12 (0.18)	0.058
5 ln(bonuses)	−1.36	−0.012 (0.005)			0.28 (0.10)	0.74 (0.12)		0.043
6 ln(wages)	0.25	−0.002 (0.01)			0.12 (0.12)		0.81 (0.24)	0.057
			B Manufacturing					
7 ln(bonuses)	0.17	−0.004 (0.006)	0.38 (0.11)			0.63 (0.13)		0.045
8 ln(wages)	1.24	0.002 (0.009)	0.21 (0.09)				0.70 (0.18)	0.045
9 ln(bonuses)	−0.59	−0.004 (0.006)		0.14 (0.04)		0.87 (0.07)		0.045
10 ln(wages)	0.22	−0.012 (0.01)		−0.05 (0.05)			1.14 (0.14)	0.049
11 ln(bonuses)	−2.30	−0.004 (0.005)			0.37 (0.08)	0.63 (0.09)		0.038
12 ln(wages)	0.15	−0.004 (0.01)			0.05 (0.11)		0.94 (0.22)	0.050

Calculated by least squares. The adjusted R^2 for every equation was 0.99.
Note:
a   Equations including π and VA cover 1960–83.

are significantly affected by profits. Since our measure of profits is an 'after-bonus' measure the finding of a positive profit–bonus relation is particularly striking.[11] Finally, note that when the coefficient on the lagged dependent variable is interpreted as a partial adjustment parameter, the implied adjustment parameter λ is invariably larger in the bonus than in the wage equation, strengthening the conclusion that bonuses are more responsive than wages.

Alternative specifications

Thus far, we have estimated models in which bonuses and wages are endogenous variables. Given the timing of negotiations already noted it is also reasonable to examine a model in which wages are exogenous (given, say, by the Shunto Offensive) and bonuses are dependent on wages and economic conditions. If bonuses are simply a markup of wages, as has sometimes been alleged, then the profit or revenue variables would not have a significant effect in this regression. Contrarily, if bonuses were determined solely by 'sharing,' the wage term would not enter significantly.[12]

To examine this possibility we estimate the following equation for all industry and manufacturing:

$$\log B = A + \lambda a \log \pi \text{ (or } R) + (1 - \lambda)\log B_{-1} + \lambda c \log W + dT$$
(12.3)

The results given in lines 1 and 2 and 5 and 6 of Table 12.4 show that while contemporaneous wages are closely related to bonuses, profits or revenues also have highly significant effects, indicating that bonuses depend on both factors. They are neither a pure markup of wages nor a pure markup of profits, although closer to the former than the latter. Finally, in the simple share-economy model workers are presumed to be paid a fixed proportion of profits per worker. To see whether our data are consistent with this view we estimate an equation in which we replace profits and revenues by profits per worker and revenues per worker. We record these results in lines 3 and 4 and 7 and 8 of Table 12.4. In this calculation we have simply divided fiscal year profits (revenues) by fiscal year employment; we have also experimented with calculations using last period's employment (see Table 12.6). As employment is relatively stable and profits are highly variable it does not matter substantially how we model the profit/employment or revenue/employment variable. As can be seen in Table 12.4, the resultant estimates are consistent with our interpretation of bonus determination as paying a share of profits per worker.

Comparing our results to those of other scholars, we are in accord with Weitzman (1986) (who uses somewhat different data) in finding bonuses to depend significantly on profits; in addition, however, we find that bonuses are related to another measure of economic performance, revenues. With respect to the responsiveness of wages to profitability, we cannot find any formal statistical evidence that base wages alone respond to profits, though we do find that wages respond to revenues. Some of the Phillips-curve-like pay-formation regressions in the literature have picked up, we note, a dependence of pay upon profits (Grubb et al., 1983; Koshiro, 1983b; Hamada and Kurosaka, 1985). But in these exercises the authors typically attempt to explain the formation of total pay – defined as wages plus bonuses – and profits may be primarily affecting the bonus component. On the basis of our findings the entire subject of empirical Phillips curve measurements for Japan is worthy of reexamination, with more careful attention focused on separating base wages from bonuses in the pay-formation process.

Table 12.4 Coefficients and standard errors for alternative specifications of the effect of economic conditions on log(bonuses), 1960–83[a]

	Constant	Time	$\ln(\pi)$	$\ln(VA)$	$\ln(W)$	$\ln(\pi/E)$	$\ln(VA/E)$	$\ln(B_{-1})$	SEE
				A All industry					
1	−3.34	−0.02	0.11		0.75			0.43	0.026
		(0.004)	(0.03)		(0.11)			(0.09)	
2	−3.89	−0.02		0.26	0.66			0.33	0.024
		(0.003)		(0.06)	(0.10)			(0.09)	
3	0.89	−0.01				0.07		0.99	0.049
		(0.01)				(0.06)		(0.08)	
4	2.03	−0.01					0.25	0.87	0.046
		(0.006)					(0.13)	(0.11)	
				B Manufacturing					
5	−3.07	−0.01	0.14		0.61			0.52	0.030
		(0.005)	(0.03)		(0.13)			(0.09)	
6	−3.87	−0.01		0.32	0.48			0.40	0.029
		(0.005)		(0.06)	(0.12)			(0.09)	
7	1.41	−0.01				0.14		0.93	0.046
		(0.01)				(0.04)		(0.06)	
8	2.96	−0.01					0.37	0.77	0.041
		(0.006)					(0.09)	(0.08)	

Note:
a   Equations including E are restricted to 1960–1982; the R^2 for every equation was 0.99.

Leaving aside the controversial issue of whether or not Japanese base wages themselves are more responsive to economic conditions than base wages in other countries, we conclude that in Japan bonuses respond more than base wages to economic conditions.

HOW DO BONUSES AFFECT EMPLOYMENT?

The finding that bonuses contain at least some 'share' component raises the possibility that their impact on employment is different from the impact of wages. In this section we estimate several models of demand-for-labor type designed to examine the possibility. We start with a simple null hypothesis: that bonuses are simply part of normal labor costs comparable to wages, so that the appropriate measure of cost is $(W + B)$, with the division of compensation between wages and bonuses having no effect on outcomes. In particular we estimate two comparable partial adjustment forms of a demand relation between employment (E), bonuses (B), wages (W), and measures of the level of demand (X):

$$\ln E = A + b \ln(W + B) + \lambda c \ln B + \lambda dX + (1 - \lambda)\ln E_{-1} + e\text{Time} \tag{12.4}$$

$$\ln E = A' + \lambda'b' \ln W + \lambda'c' \ln(W + B) + \lambda'd'X +$$
$$(1 - \lambda')\ln E_{-1} + e'\text{Time} \tag{12.5}$$

In Equation (12.4), the hypothesis that bonuses are just part of normal labor cost is tested by the coefficient on $\ln(B)$: if the form of compensation is irrelevant to employment and the data are determined by demand forces, the coefficient on $\ln(B)$ will be (approximately) 0 while that on $\ln(W + B)$ will be negative. In equation (12.5), the test of the hypothesis that the composition of compensation is irrelevant to employment is that the coefficient on $\ln(W + B)$ be negative and that on $\ln W$ be zero. Because we include both bonus and wage variables as separate factors in the equation, our model differs from those of other analysts of demand for labor in Japan (Grubb et al., 1983; Koshiro, 1983b; Hamada and Kurosaka, 1985).

As the reader will note, it is the log form of the demand equations that dictates estimation of the two comparable forms. If we modeled demand as a linear equation, one of the two equations would be redundant.

A significant problem with demand relations of this form relates to the measurement of 'level of demand' factors. Some analysts enter output measures or output measures instrumented on other variables to measure the level of demand. Other analysts prefer to exclude such variables due to the production function relation between output and employment. Such exclusions yield reasonable demand relations for some European countries but not for the United States (see Symons and Layard, 1983). To make sure that our results do not depend on how we treat demand-shift variables, we include output measures in some regressions and exclude them from others, with, as will be seen, little effect on our findings.

Another problem with models of this form relates to specifying the causality as going from wages (bonuses) to employment in an aggregate economy with extremely low unemployment. Most analyses of labor demand, in fact, focus on manufacturing where one can plausibly argue that wages are set economywide, making employment a function of wages at the sector level. A priori, one anticipates that a demand model will fit a single sector better than it will fit an entire, essentially full-employment, labor market.

Table 12.5 presents our estimates of the impact of wages, wages plus bonuses, and of bonuses, on employment. Panel A treats the manufacturing industries where our results are particularly striking; Panel B treats the entire economy. The even-numbered equations exclude output; the odd-numbered equations include output as a measure of the level of demand. In addition to the calculations in the table, we experimented with various other demand-shift variables (including profits) and with instrumental variable estimates of demand shifts, instrumenting output on such factors as exports, money supply, etc. Because inclusion of the output variables has only a modest impact on our estimated bonus and wage

Table 12.5 Coefficients and standard errors for estimates of the effects of bonuses and wages on log(employment), 1959–82

	Constant	Time	$\ln(W+B)$	$\ln(W)$	$\ln(B)$	$\ln(NDP)$	$\ln(E_{-1})$	R^2	SEE
				A Manufacturing					
1	7.21	0.0002 (0.002)	−0.37 (0.06)		0.21 (0.05)	0.15 (0.03)	0.59 (0.05)	0.99	0.009
2	10.37	0.0001 (0.003)	−0.33 (0.10)		0.28 (0.07)		0.72 (0.08)	0.98	0.014
3	6.60	0.0001 (0.002)	0.49 (0.15)	−0.65 (0.14)		0.16 (0.03)	0.59 (0.05)	0.99	0.009
4	4.39	0.0008 (0.003)	0.83 (0.23)	−0.87 (0.25)			0.74 (0.08)	0.98	0.015
				B All industry					
5	6.59	0.005 (0.003)	−0.39 (0.16)		0.14 (0.13)	0.32 (0.09)	0.56 (0.14)	0.99	0.019
6	2.80	0.003 (0.004)	−0.20 (0.20)		0.18 (0.16)		0.86 (0.14)	0.99	0.025
7	6.20	0.005 (0.003)	0.14 (0.38)	−0.40 (0.39)		0.33 (0.09)	0.56 (0.14)	0.99	0.019
8	1.99	0.002 (0.004)	0.39 (0.50)	−0.41 (0.51)			0.88 (0.14)	0.99	0.025

coefficients, the way in which we treat demand-shift variables is not a critical issue in the analysis (in contrast to the importance of output terms in US labor demand equations).

The key finding, which runs through all the calculations, is that bonuses and wages have markedly different effects on employment: bonuses obtain *positive* and wages *negative* coefficients in the estimates. When our two variables are bonuses and bonuses plus wages, the coefficient on bonuses is significantly positive while the coefficient on wages plus bonuses is significantly negative. When bonuses plus wages are included with wages, the wage term obtains a negative coefficient while the bonus plus wage yields a positive coefficient.

The strength of our finding differs, we note, between highly cyclical manufacturing and the rest of industry. In manufacturing, the two elements of compensation have such different effects that we can fairly readily reject our null hypothesis. In all industry, the weaker estimated negative effect of wages (wages plus bonuses) on employment gives a more equivocal result, although even here it is apparent that bonuses have a positive impact on employment different from the effect of wages.[13]

What might explain the divergent pattern between all industry and manufacturing? One possibility is that bonuses play one role in a highly cyclical sector and another in the rest of the economy. Another possibility is that the labor supply facing manufacturing is more elastic than is the relatively fixed supply facing the entire economy, permitting bonuses to raise employment more in manufacturing than elsewhere. The first explanation stresses possible differential demand behavior based on cyclical fluctuations while the second stresses differences based on labor supply conditions.

Probing the results

The finding that bonuses are positively rather than negatively associated with employment (in contrast to wages) is sufficiently striking as to merit additional probing. Could the result be due to some type of aggregation bias?

To see if the result holds up at a more disaggregated level we estimated equations like those in Table 12.5 for separate two-digit industries and found results consistent with those in the table. In these calculations bonuses obtain positive coefficients in 6 of 10 manufacturing industries in equation (12.4) and bonuses plus wages obtain positive coefficients in the same 6 in equation (12.5) (3b), with 5 of the positive coefficients having $t >$ 1. In 6 nonmanufacturing industries, by contrast, the results were weaker, which is consistent with the weak economywide results obtained in panel B of the table. Our strongest finding is clearly for manufacturing.

Could the result be due to some form of reverse causality or related problem in which bonuses and employment are positively correlated because increases in employment (reflecting good times) cause higher bonuses?

To examine this possibility we have estimated two lagged models which enable us to 'test' whether employment determines bonuses or bonuses determine employment by examining the lagged impact of bonuses on employment and of employment on bonuses in the spirit of Sims–Granger causality tests. For simplicity, we report results where all variables are defined on a *calendar* year basis; the results with bonuses related to fiscal year variables as in our earlier tables give results comparable to those in the table. The results, given in Table 12.6, suggest that the causal link is from bonuses to employment rather than from employment to bonuses. In manufacturing, lagged bonuses have a positive effect on employment (in contrast to the negative effect of lagged wages on employment), while lagged employment has a negative effect on bonuses. In all industry, bonuses have an insignificant positive impact on employment (contrasted to a negative effect for wages) whereas employment negatively affects bonuses. These results are inconsistent with an employment-causes-bonuses model but are, we note, consistent with a share-model interpretation of the data, as increases in employment reduce workers' earnings from profit sharing in the share model.

Taking our finding of a positive bonus–employment relation at face value, how might we go about interpreting it?

Table 12.6 Alternative models of lagged relations, 1959–83[a]

Dependent variable	Constant	Time	ln(NDP)	ln(E_{-1})	ln(B_{-1})	ln(W_{-1})	ln(B)	ln(W)	SEE
			A Manufacturing						
		Model I: Wages, bonuses, and employment taken as endogenous							
ln(W)	−0.42	0.007	0.19	0.14	0.07	0.56			0.042
		(0.009)	(0.12)	(0.35)	(0.20)	(0.28)			
ln(B)	11.10	−0.017	0.57	−0.77	0.90	−0.22			0.026
		(0.006)	(0.08)	(0.22)	(0.12)	(0.18)			
ln(E)	9.13	−0.003	0.19	0.42	0.12	−0.24			0.013
		(0.003)	(0.04)	(0.11)	(0.06)	(0.08)			
		Model II: Bonuses and employment endogenous; wages exogenous							
ln(B)	7.10	−0.02	0.47	−0.57	0.72		0.14		0.027
		(0.006)	(0.08)	(0.19)	(0.09)		(0.14)		
ln(E)	7.67	−0.002	0.21	0.53	0.08			−0.26	0.010
		(0.002)	(0.03)	(0.07)	(0.03)			(0.05)	
			B All industry						
		Model I: Wages, bonuses, and employment taken as endogenous							
ln(W)	8.09	0.009	0.51	−0.46	0.29	0.14			0.040
		(0.008)	(0.14)	(0.32)	(0.19)	(0.26)			
ln(B)	5.72	−0.01	0.60	−0.48	0.81	−0.18			0.028
		(0.005)	(0.10)	(0.23)	(0.14)	(0.18)			
ln(E)	6.43	0.006	0.23	0.55	0.08	−0.25			0.021
		(0.004)	(0.08)	(0.17)	(0.10)	(0.13)			
		Model II: Bonuses and employment endogenous; wages exogenous							
ln(B)	1.07	−0.016	0.41	−0.22	0.59		0.29		0.027
		(0.004)	(0.13)	(0.21)	(0.10)		(0.16)		
ln(E)	6.87	0.004	0.35	0.52	0.05			−0.32	0.019
		(0.003)	(0.09)	(0.15)	(0.07)			(0.11)	

Note:
a   Equations including E are restricted to 1959–82; the R^2 for every equation was 0.99.

There seem to be two basic modes of interpretation: one in which bonuses are viewed as operating along theoretic share-economy lines; and one in which bonuses are taken as an indicator of the level of demand in a given period.

First, from a share-economy perspective, one may want to read the result as indicating that bonuses, while part of the attractiveness of jobs to workers, are not fully part of the marginal cost of employment to firms. From this perspective the data suggest that we are estimating a mixed supply-and-demand reduced-form equation, with $W + B$ primarily reflecting supply influences on employment and W primarily reflecting demand influences, with the gap between them indicating the 'excess demand' for labor in a share system.[14]

What might one do to test such an interpretation? One approach would be to develop a detailed econometric model of supply-and-demand disequilibrium to estimate the 'structural equations' and to evaluate the predicted excess demand for labor. To implement such a program in practice would require more data on the Japanese labor market than the wage, employment, and bonus series that we have analyzed here. For example, one would want some direct measure of the share parameter that in principle determines the contract, rather than measures of bonuses. (Bonuses differ significantly from share parameters in that they change for two reasons: changes in labor's share of profits (revenues) or changes in the level of profits (revenues).) One would also want direct measures of vacancies by sector and over time to indicate potential changes and differences in 'excess demand for labor' as bonuses vary. It would also be useful to have evidence on patterns of recruitment of new workers. In the absence of such data, and the need to make specific and somewhat arbitrary assumptions about disequilibrium forms, we are loath to pursue this line with our data. Virtually any reasonable disequilibrium formulation will end up with reduced-form mixed supply-and-demand equations like those we have estimated, with predicted coefficients having signs like those we have found.

A second possible interpretation of our finding is that bonuses are a 'proxy' for shifts in labor demand. We do not think that this offers as good an interpretation of the data. First, we have attempted to control for such demand shifts by the explicit inclusion of output terms; yet the signs on bonuses and wages were unchanged. Additionally, the causal lag relation between employment and bonuses we have found is inconsistent with this view. Furthermore, it is not enough for a particular firm or sector to 'demand' more labor in a full-employment economy; a plausible story must be told about how the labor is obtained – e.g., through increased pay ($W + B$) on the supply side. Of course it is still logically possible to argue that bonuses are a superior measure of the level of the labor-demand schedule. (After all, we did find them to vary substantially with the cycle.) Even this interpretation, however, clearly supports the notion that bonuses are *not* part of normal labor cost.

In any case, whatever the ultimate explanation, bonuses are different from wages in Japan, in their effects on employment as well as in their sensitivity to economic conditions. Without pushing the 'share economy' interpretation of the data too far, our results do seem to have the 'flavor' of such a system.

MACROECONOMIC IMPLICATIONS OF THE BONUS SYSTEM

We come now to the difficult question of whether the Japanese bonus system influences macroeconomic performance, and more particularly, whether it helps account for the low unemployment rates found in Japan over the last quarter century.[12] Other things being equal, it stands to reason that the existence of a bonus component of pay with a more automatic procyclical link than base wages should help an economy to maintain a higher level of employment than would be maintained if wages alone were paid. But how important a factor, quantitatively, is this likely to be in the Japanese case? Given the current state of macroeconomics, with widely divergent schools of thought, it is not clear how to pose the appropriate hypothesis formally so that the existing data might, at least in principle, allow us to extricate an answer that is reasonably controversy-free. Rather than trying to confront the issue head on with a formal model, we limit ourselves here to some rough calculations designed to give likely orders of magnitudes of effects.

The bonus itself is about one-fourth of an average worker's total pay. By running regressions in logarithms we have estimated the elasticity of aggregate bonus response to changed aggregate profits at about 0.09 (see line 3, Table 12.3). Converting this parameter to a linear equivalent, we obtain the same elasticity of 0.09 if 9 per cent of the bonus payment is strictly proportional to profits, while the other 91 per cent is like a fixed constant. The following crude imputation can then be made. About 2.25 per cent (9 per cent × 25 per cent) of a Japanese worker's total pay can be treated as genuine profit-sharing income, compared with the other 97.75 per cent, which for economic purposes is better described as being like an imputed base wage.

A rough check on this calculation is possible using our equations linking bonuses to revenues. The elasticity of aggregate bonus payments with respect to aggregate value added, or revenue, was estimated to be about 0.44 (see line 1, Table 12.3). Converting to an equivalent-elasticity linear revenue-sharing formula makes 44 per cent of the bonus payment strictly proportional to revenues, while the other 56 per cent is like a fixed constant. If aggregate imputed base wages are roughly three-fourths of aggregate revenues, that leaves one-fourth for gross profits. By this calculation, 11 per cent (¼ × 44 per cent) of the bonus payment is strictly proportional to profits, while the rest is like a fixed constant. Following this line of reasoning, about 2.75 per cent (11 per cent × 25 per cent) of a typical Japanese worker's total pay can be treated as genuinely proportional to profits, while the remainder is like an imputed base wage.

Splitting the difference between the high (2.75 per cent) and low (2.25 per cent) calculations, we can make the following very rough statement: in any year about 97.5 per cent of an average Japanese worker's total pay is like a fixed imputed base wage, while 2.5 per cent automatically responds directly to profits. If pay contracts are annually renegotiated, the marginal cost to the employer of hiring an extra unit of labor in any given year is just the (imputed) base wage, as opposed to total pay. If the relevant contract adjustment period is more than a year, due to pay parameter stickiness, the profit-sharing component grows in importance relative to the base wage component because of the distributed-lag difference equation. In that case the effect of profit sharing is somewhat more pronounced. Taking the 2.5 per cent as a conservative measure of the pure-profit-sharing part of pay, the relevant theory predicts that the Japanese economy should behave like an otherwise absolutely identical (but hypothetical) wage economy whose wages are 2.5 per cent lower than actual Japanese pay (base wages plus bonus) but whose maintained levels of aggregate demand (autonomous spending, the money supply, and world demand for Japanese exports) are the same.[16] In other words, if someone who thought that Japan was a wage economy and has just now been informed that it is in fact (partially) a revenue- or profit-sharing economy wants to know what difference that makes, the answer is: the same difference as if money wages were perpetually 2.5 per cent lower than what they appeared to be.

While the exact ramifications of a 2.5 per cent wage cut depend on the macro-model in which it is embedded, our reaction is neither to dismiss this effect as negligible nor to argue that it is likely to represent an overwhelming factor in the economy. At one extreme, assume a model in which a 2.5 per cent reduction in wages reduces prices by 2.5 per cent. Supposing, further, that this is equivalent to a 2.5 per cent expansion in output, then employment will increase 2.5 per cent (given constant returns to scale). At another extreme, assume that a 2.5 per cent reduction in wages does not affect prices at all (they are set on world markets) so that the reduction in wages raises employment along a fixed demand curve. If the elasticity of demand is taken conservatively to be about one-half, we would have 1.25 per cent higher employment, giving us a range of employment effects from 1.25 to 2.5 per cent.

Such counterfactual exercises should be understood in proper perspective. First, the calculations are extremely crude. Second, they are based on a particular interpretation of a particular theory. Third, the 'thought experiment' is necessarily artificial. (If there were lower bonuses but higher base wages, it could be argued, wages might become more flexible, timing in the economy might be altered, or fiscal or monetary policy might be changed, perhaps thereby neutralizing some of the effects calculated here.) Limitations notwithstanding, we think the exercise is useful for gaining some rough insight into the likely size of what might be called the 'pure bonus effect.' We interpret the orders of magnitude involved as suggesting that the Japanese bonus system may have exerted a nonnegligible macroeconomic influence by helping automatically to boost employment without inflationary pressure. But the significance of an 'as if' 2.5 per cent money wage cut is not nearly so great as to account for the entire unemployment story, nor to eliminate demand-caused output fluctuations,[17] nor to do away with the need for discretionary policy to maintain full employment, especially in the face of severe economic shocks.

That the bonus system alone cannot possibly be explaining the entire macroeconomic adjustment story is made abundantly clear by the extreme example of Japan's response to the energy crisis. After the first oil shock, in 1974, consumer prices increased by about 25 per cent and wholesale prices by over 30 per cent; output in manufacturing and mining fell by 10 per cent. At first the unions had no better premonition than other groups that a permanent terms-of-trade deterioration was under way, and they were concerned to recoup lost purchasing power as well as to obtain their customary pay increase. In the spring offensive of that year, base wages jumped by 33 per cent while strike days lost were 2.7 per 10,000, a rate double that in previous years and above the rate in the United States in many years. An observer looking simply at these figures would have predicted that the Japanese economy would have been more likely to have gone into a major stagflation decline than the US or European economies. But such was not the case. At this point, when the mechanics of a potentially vicious wage–price spiral started to become evident, the Japanese consensus took over. Government officials, labor experts, businessmen, and labor union leaders began preaching wage and price restraint. The 1975 *shunto* saw base wages increase by only 13 per cent, and they have been held to the single-digit range since then; the consumer price index rate of increase fell to 10.4 per cent, and while output in manufacturing and mining declined by 4.4 per cent in 1975 it rose by 10.8 per cent in 1976. Strike days lost fell sharply to 0.9 per 10,000 in 1976 and to virtually zero in succeeding years.[18]

Because base wages constitute three-fourths of Japanese pay, and only a part of bonuses is responsive to profits (revenue), the deceleration of wage increases was quantitatively more important than the adjustment of bonuses in stabilizing employment. However much the Japanese bonus system may be helping as an automatic employment stabilizer (months-of-bonus pay declined sharply after 1974 while the ratio of bonuses to wages fell from a peak value of 0.35 in 1974 to 0.29 in 1983), in stepping back from high inflation in the mid-1970s Japan relied to a greater extent upon flexible wage setting than upon flexible bonuses, as it had to, given the share of wages in total compensation and the magnitude of the macroeconomic shock.

CONCLUSION

In this chapter we have examined a relatively unique aspect of the Japanese labor market – payment of bonuses which constitute a quarter of workers' pay. Our analysis has rejected the notion that bonuses are just another form of wage payment on two grounds: first, bonuses behave differently than wages over the cycle, responding to profits and responding more to revenues than do wages, and, second, bonuses affect employment differently than wages, having a positive rather than a negative link to employment. While bonuses are not set by pure share-economy principles, they are sufficiently responsive to profits or revenues and affect employment in ways that have the flavor of a share economy. Our estimate is that they contribute somewhat to the success of the Japanese economy by automatically helping to stabilize unemployment at relatively low levels. The importance of reductions in the rate of change of base wages during the first oil crisis, however, makes it clear that, as presently constituted, the bonus system in Japan is by no means the main factor behind Japanese ability to weather severe shocks of that kind better than most other developed countries. This example highlights our basic conclusion. The bonus system helps Japan to maintain relatively tight labor markets, but so too do other, probably complementary aspects of the Japanese system beyond the focus of this study.

NOTES

1. Shimada (1983) gives an excellent survey of the English language literature.
2. Koike (1983a, 1983b, and references therein) sometimes argues the contrary view that Japanese industrial relations, and particularly the lifetime employment system, are not nearly so unique as is sometimes made out. He has a point when he does not push this view too hard. Another view is given by Hashimoto and Raisian (1985). Tachibanaki notes that much of the difference in job tenure in Japan and the United States results from the fact that workers obtain permanent jobs directly out of school in Japan whereas in the United States workers job shop before taking a permanent job. For figures on regular employment see Japanese Ministry of Labor, 'Yearbook of Labor Statistics', 1983, Table 4.
3. For discussion of the *nenko* system, see, e.g., Shimada, 1983, or Shirai, 1983b, Also see Tachibanaki, 1982.
4. For descriptions of the Japanese workplace, see Koshiro, 1983a. See also Koike, 'Skill formation system in the US and Japan: A comparative study', in Aoki, 1984.
5. On many of these points see Shirai, 1983b. Hours adjustments are discussed in Hamada and Kurosaka, 1984.
6. In this calculation we divide bonuses by operating profits. Using a narrower measure of profits, 'current profits,' we get from 56 to 160 per cent between 1965 and 1983.
7. This interpretation is emphasized by, among others, Shirai (1983b, p. 131).
8. See Japan, Ministry of Labor, Monthly Labor Statistics.
9. The Okuma data calculated here are from the union's report to its workers. The standard deviations for manufacturing are calculated from the Ministry of Labor data in the article version of this chapter.
10. Koshiro (1983b), pp. 241–2) gives a good discussion of bonus responsiveness to profits. For figures on firms with explicit profit-sharing see Japanese Ministry of Labor, 'General survey on wage and working hours system'.
11. If there is any resultant error in bonuses, it would induce negative correlation with profits less bonuses.

12. We recognize that bonuses and wages are set separately but since we omitted a relevant variable in both equations, we get wages entering the bonus equation as a proxy for the omitted variable.

13. One interpretation of the 'better' results for manufacturing than for all industry is that we are not identifying a demand equation in a full-employment economy.

14. In terms of the usual supply – demand graph bonuses are a measure of the gap between supply and demand along the cost axis at the point where employment is set in a share economy. Note that such a disequilibrium interpretation does not allow the inference that the employment fluctuations are necessarily amplified due to the existence of a positive statistical relation between bonuses and employment because we are estimating a reduced-form mixed supply-and-demand equation on a disaggregated level.

15. It should be noted that Japan's number one status in having the lowest unemployment rate among major industrialized economies did not emerge until the 1970s. In the 1960s, some other countries like Germany had equally good employment records. There has been some discussion in the literature about the extent to which Japanese statistics may underestimate the unemployment rate by international standards. Taira (1983) and a few others have tried to argue this case. But it is not very convincing (see, e.g., Sorrentino, 1984; Hamada and Kurosaka, 1985). The basic point is that when reasonable adjustment measures are applied uniformly to all countries in an attempt to make international standards more uniform, then all countries' unemployment rates increase slightly, but without much altering their relative standing. Japan's unemployment record remains outstanding even after readjustment.

16. See Weitzman, 1985. The basic idea is that the effect on the firm of converting 2.5 per cent of pay from base wages to profit shares is to lower wages by 2.5 per cent and simultaneously subject the firm to a compensating tax on profits.

17. Depending on how output is detrended from its high growth rates, Japanese output stability might be judged outstanding or mediocre. Actually, Japan has the steadiest growth rate among all OECD countries over the past quarter century if it is measured by relative deviations from a standardized mean. In terms of *absolute* deviations from a nonstandardized mean, Japanese growth shows much more cyclical variability. Note that, with a sprinkling of temporary price stickiness, the relevant model of a profit-sharing economy would predict relatively full employment but some building up of inventories, make-work, or labor hoarding during slack periods. Thus, the large Okun coefficient for Japan (see Hamada and Kurosaka, 1984) is not in itself a theoretical contradiction with share-economy-like interpretations.

18. Data in this paragraph are taken from Japan Productivity Center, 'Practical handbook of productivity and labor statistics' (1985).

BIBLIOGRAPHY

Aoki, M., ed., *The Economic Analysis of the Japanese Firm* (Amsterdam: North-Holland, 1984).

Grubb, D., Jackman, R., and Layard, R., 'Wage rigidity and unemployment in OECD countries', *European Economic Review* (1983), vol. 21, pp. 11–39.

Grossman, H., and Haraf, W. F., 'Shunto, rational expectations, and output growth in Japan', Working Paper no. 1144 (NBER, June 1983).

Hamada, K., and Kurosaka, Y., 'The relationship between production and unemployment in Japan: Okun's law in comparative perspective', *European Economic Review* (June 1984), vol. 25, no. 1, pp. 71–94.

Hamada, K., and Kurosaka, Y., 'Trends in unemployment, wages, and productivity: The case of Japan', paper prepared for the Conference on the Rise in Unemployment (May 1985).

Hashimoto, M., and Raisian, J., 'Employment tenure and earnings profile in Japan and the US', *American Economic Review* (September 1985), pp. 721–35.

Ishikawa, T., and Ueda, K., 'The bonus payment system and the Japanese personal savings', in M. Aoki, (ed.), *The Economic Analysis of the Japanese Firm* (Amsterdam/New York: Elsevier, 1984).

Koike, K., 'Internal labor markets: workers in large firms', in T. Shirai, (ed.), *Contemporary Industrial Relations in Japan* (Madison: Univ. of Wisconsin Press, 1983a).

Koike, K., 'Workers in small firms and women in industry', in T. Shirai, (ed.), *Contemporary Industrial Relations in Japan* (Madison: Univ. of Wisconsin Press, 1983b).

Koshiro, K., 'The quality of working life in Japanese factories', in T. Shirai, (ed.), *Contemporary Industrial Relations in Japan* (Madison: Univ. of Wisconsin Press, 1983a).

Koshiro, K., 'Development of collective bargaining in postwar Japan', in T. Shirai, (ed.), *Contemporary Industrial Relations in Japan* (Madison: Univ. of Wisconsin Press, 1983b).

Okuno, M., 'Corporate loyalty and bonus payments', in M. Aoki, (ed.), *The Economic Analysis of the Japanese Firm* (New York: Elsevier, 1984).

Shimada, H., 'Japanese industrial relations – A new general model? A survey of the English-language literature', in T. Shirai (ed.), *Contemporary Industrial Relations in Japan* (Madison: Univ. of Wisconsin Press, 1983).

Shirai, T. (ed.), *Contemporary Industrial Relations in Japan* (Madison: Univ. of Wisconsin Press, 1983a).

Shirai, T., 'A theory of enterprise unionism,' in T. Shirai (ed.), *Contemporary Industrial Relations in Japan* (Madison: Univ. of Wisconsin Press, 1983b).

Sorrentino, C., 'Japan's low unemployment: An in-depth analysis', *Monthly Labor Review* (March 1984), vol. 107, no. 3, pp. 18–27.

Symons, J., and Layard, R., 'Neoclassical demand for labor functions', London School of Economics Discussion Paper 166, (1983).

Tachibanaki, T., 'Further results on Japanese wage differentials: Nenko wages, hierarchical position, bonuses, and working hours', *International Economic Review* (June 1982), vol. 23, no. 2.

Taira, K., 'Japan's low unemployment: Economic miracle or statistical artifact?', *Monthly Labor Review* (July 1983), vol. 106, no. 7, pp. 3–10.

Wadwani, S., 'The macroeconomic implications of profit sharing: Some empirical evidence', London School of Economics working paper (1985).

Weitzman, M. L., *The Share Economy* (Cambridge, MA: Harvard Univ. Press, 1984).

Weitzman, M. L., 'The simple macroeconomics of profit sharing', *American Economic Review* (December 1985).

Weitzman, M. L., 'Macroeconomic implications of profit sharing', in S. Fischer (ed.), *NBER Macroeconomics Annual* (Cambridge, MA: MIT Press, 1986).

13 · EVALUATING THE EUROPEAN VIEW THAT THE UNITED STATES HAS NO UNEMPLOYMENT PROBLEM

> A session on unemployment in America? Ridicule! The United States has produced 20 million jobs since 1975. If only Europe had America's flexible labor market and 'unemployment'.
>
> Archetypal European economist, circa 1987

Significant differences between the unemployment and employment experiences of the United States and OECD-Europe have made views like the above popular overseas and led many European observers to look longingly at the American labor market as a paragon of decentralized wage and employment flexibility.

Do the labor market performances of the United States and OECD-Europe support this view? How much of the difference between American and European employment and unemployment can be attributed to differences in labor market 'flexibility'?

In this chapter I examine these questions. I review the labor market outcomes that have led many Europeans to see the American economy as having no 'real' unemployment problem; evaluate the claim that greater labor-market flexibility underlies US–OECD-Europe differences in outcomes; and consider the costs that accompanied American employment expansion. My main claim is that the United States paid for its employment expansion with reduced growth of real wages and productivity rather than with relatively costless flexibility. I find that some aspects of flexibility in relative wage setting helped limit US unemployment while others did not, and argue that the disparate experiences of the United Kingdom and Sweden show that a decentralized labor market is neither necessary nor sufficient for employment-enhancing wage settlements.

CONTRASTS IN UNEMPLOYMENT/EMPLOYMENT EXPERIENCES

Three fundamental facts underlie the European view of American unemployment: first, the 1980s reversal of the longstanding pattern of higher rates of unemployment in the United States than in OECD-Europe (see Figure 13.1(a)); second, the growth of employment in the United States, evinced in a rising employment/working age population ratio compared to a declining ratio in OECD-Europe and even more dramatically in employment rates adjusted for the sizeable drop in annual hours per employee in Europe (see Figure 13.1(b)); and, third, the relatively short duration of unemployment spells in the United States, where incomplete spells have averaged from 12 to 20 weeks compared to several years in many OECD-European countries (see Figure 13.1(c)). While spell lengths differ partly because many US spells end in labor force withdrawal (Clark and Summers, 1979), adult male durations are so much longer in Europe than in the United States that this cannot explain the differences (OECD, 1987, Table R).

Youth unemployment is also widely judged to be a greater problem in Europe than in the United States, though differences in schooling and student work behavior creates problems in comparisons. In some European countries, such as Italy, Spain, France, and the United Kingdom (but not Germany), the ratio of youth to adult unemployment rates exceeds that for the United States. The duration of unemployment among European youths also tends to be quite long, exceeding durations for the young blacks who bear a disproportionate brunt of US unemployment. And OECD-Europe had nothing like the United States' 1970–80 6-point *increase* in the employment/population ratio of 16- to 24-year-olds when the influx of baby boomers into the job market could have created massive youth joblessness.

Less widely recognized, US and European patterns of unemployment also differ along gender lines, with the rate of female unemployment relatively lower in the United States than in Europe (save for the United Kingdom and Ireland). Because of the differences in youth and female unemployment rates, adult male unemployment rates in the United States are closer to those in Europe than the average rates shown in Figure 13.1(a), offsetting somewhat the presumptively greater cost of unemployment in Europe due to the long durations (OECD, 1987, Table 2).

Turning to growth of employment, there is a widespread belief that US growth has been concentrated in low-wage Macdonald's-type service jobs. Some hail this as the desirable outcome of flexible wage setting that permits wide variation in pay among industries. Others view it as a sign of American economic decline. In fact, there is nothing special about the growth of service-sector employment in the United States. From 1973 to 1984, OECD data (1986a) show that the service *share* of employment rose by 9 percentage points in OECD-Europe (45 to 54 per cent) compared to an increase of 5 points in the United States (63 to 68 per cent). Moreover, the shift to services has had only a modest impact on average wages, in part because the service sector includes high-paying professional and business services as well as burger joints. Perhaps most telling, employment and

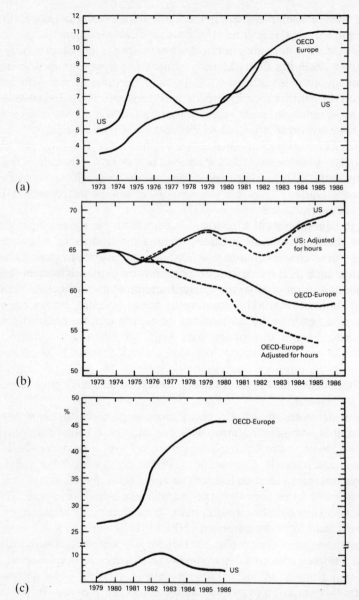

Figure 13.1 US–OECD: European employment and unemployment record, 1973–86: (a) rates of unemployment; (b) employment 15–64 population; (c) percentage of unemployed, 12 months and over.

Source: OECD (1986a; 1987). OECD-Europe figures in panel (b) obtained as a weighted average for countries reporting data with 1985 employment used as weights for all years. OECD–Europe figures in panel (c) obtained as weighted average for all countries reporting data using 1985 unemployment as weights for all years.

wages have grown more in high-level than in low-skill occupations, not what one would expect if the skill structure was deteriorating.

This said, it is the patterns of unemployment and employment shown in Figure 13.1 that has altered European thinking about the American labor market: 'What at the start of the period was being dubbed as a poor labour productivity performance in the United States was being hailed at the end as an impressive job creating performance' (OECD, 1986b, p. 8). Whereas in the 1950s and 1960s analysts rejected textbook claims that decentralized labor market arrangements work best on the basis of actual outcomes ('You say unfettered labor markets, but our ... arbitration tribunals (Australia); bargaining with legal extension (France); shop-floor unionism (United Kingdom) ... produce unemployment far below that in America'), in the 1980s the word is flexibility, US-style.

So, the question is: to what extent is the US unemployment/employment record the result of the flexibility of decentralized labor markets? The answer turns on the ways in which wage setting and employment determination is in fact more flexible in the United States than in OECD-Europe and on the quantitative contribution of those aspects of flexibility to employment. It requires consideration of aggregate wage change and of wage adjustments and labor mobility along disaggregate industry, occupation, region, and so on, lines.

THE CONTRIBUTION OF MACRO FLEXIBILITY

In terms of aggregate wages, recent studies in the Phillips curve tradition suggest that wages in the United States react less to price changes and more to unemployment than wages in many European countries, producing greater 'real wage flexibility' (Bruno and Sachs, 1985; Coe, 1985). As I am uneasy about the robustness of inferences from these time-series regressions, I focus instead on the basic fact that the United States (and Sweden and some other countries) had smaller changes in real wages in the 1970s to early 1980s than most of OECD-Europe and ask: were these modest wage changes (call them the 'flexible' response to the post-oil-shock economic world) associated with differences in employment growth across countries? As Table 13.1 shows, conditional on the growth of real GDP (which increased more rapidly in the United States than in OECD-Europe in total but not in per capita terms), the answer is yes: in each period countries with large increases in real wages (measured by mfg hourly earnings, employee compensation/employees or mfg hourly compensation) had smaller growth in employment or total hours than countries with small wage increases, with elasticities ranging from -0.5 to -0.9. As changes in output per worker and wages are highly correlated across countries, moreover, there is a parallel inverse relation between employ-

Table 13.1 Regression coefficients and standard errors for the impact of real wages and output on employment, OECD countries, 1960–85

Dependent variable	Change in	Change in	R^2
(a) Change in ln employment	In real wage	In GDP	
1960–73	−0.57(0.11)	0.62(0.14)	0.65
1973–9	−0.45(0.11)	0.71(0.17)	0.59
1979–84	−0.54(0.15)	0.62(0.19)	0.56
(b) Change in ln employment	In real labor costs	In GDP	
1960–73	−0.76(0.05)	0.90(0.07)	0.94
1973–9	−0.62(0.10)	0.75(0.13)	0.74
1979–84	−0.53(0.16)	0.88(0.22)	0.53
(c) Comp. annual change, total mfg hrs	Real mfg compensation	Mfg output	
1960–73	−0.53(0.08)	0.62(0.08)	0.86
1973–9	−0.89(0.22)	0.36(0.22)	0.67
1979–85	−0.75(0.24)	0.80(0.13)	0.81

Sources: Panals (a) and (b), 19 OECD countries from London School of Economics Center for Labour Economics–OECD data set. Panel (c), 12 Countries (US, Canada, Japan, France, Germany, Italy, UK, Belgium, Denmark, Netherlands, Norway, and Sweden) as given by A. Neef (1986), with wages deflated by GNP deflator, using OECD data.

ment and productivity growth, with, for example, wages and productivity growing slowly and employment growing rapidly in the United States and Sweden and the converse occurring in Belgium, Spain, and in the United Kingdom in the 1980s, among others.

If one takes country differences in changes in wages as exogenously determined by labor-market institutions (about which I have some doubts) *and* assumes similar rates of exogenous productivity advance in the United States and OECD-Europe, the estimated wage-employment tradeoff schedule suggests that much of the US–OECD-Europe differences in employment growth was 'paid for' by lower real wage growth in the United States. Between 1973 and 1979, for instance, the OECD (1986a) estimates that compound annual rates of GDP growth differed only modestly between the United States and OECD-Europe (2.6 versus 2.4 per cent) while the difference in annual growth in manufacturing wages relative to the GDP deflator was huge (1.0 per cent in the United States versus 4.7 per cent in OECD-Europe), implying a dominant role for the wage-employment tradeoff in the difference in employment growth. While from

1979 to 1984 differences in real wage growth lessened (−0.3 per cent in the United States versus 0.3 per cent in OECD-Europe) and differences in GDP growth widened (2.0 per cent in the United States versus 1.1 per cent in OECD-Europe) the tradeoff still remains important in the employment story.

Now for problems with this interpretation. First, differences in real wage growth cannot be firmly tied to specific labor-market structures. On the one hand, as noted, Sweden and some other countries with quite different labor-market institutions than the United States had similar slow real wage growth and sizeable employment expansion, indicating at the minimum that decentralized US-style labor markets were not necessary for real wage moderation. (Indeed, the performance of Scandinavia and Austria has fueled claims that corporatist economies perform best in this respect.) On the other hand, the United Kingdom – which has the most decentralized and unregulated labor market in OECD-Europe – had sizeable growth of real wages in the 1980s and experienced the employment consequences thereof. Reinforcing this point, OECD countries with disparate labor-market institutions, such as Belgium, Australia, and Italy, reduced their growth of real wages in the early 1980s, some with noticeable employment consequences, but others with no upswing in employment. Second, workers bargain for money wages while real wages depend on prices as well as wages, raising the possibility that country differences in price setting also contributed to observed differences in real wage patterns across countries. As Robert Solow (1986) has stressed in this context, the tradeoff curve can be interpreted as reflecting the joint determination of wages and employment by exogenous aggregate demand factors, suggesting the need to examine differences in those factors across countries and their relation to the observed changes. Regardless of how one interprets the evidence in Table 13.1, however, the wage-employment tradeoff represents the key fact that any explanation of US and OECD-Europe differences must address.

THE CONTRIBUTION OF RELATIVE FLEXIBILITY

Turning to relative wages and employment (where labor economists feel more comfortable as they can get 'in close' to behavior), the evidence suggests that along some dimensions the US labor market has evinced flexibility of the kind likely to be unemployment reducing, while along other dimensions, it has not.

The strongest case for employment-enhancing flexible market responses is found in the changing wage and employment of young workers. Between 1970 and 1983 when baby boomers flooded the US job market, the earnings of the young men fell sharply: real median weekly earnings of workers aged 16 to 24 dropped by 25 per cent between 1970 and 1985, with the result that the premium of men 25 and older to the 16- to 24-year-olds jumped from 43 to 90 per cent (US Department of Labor). On the demand side, the reduced cost of young workers induced employers to increase the youth share of employment in virtually all industries, from manufacturing to services. In several European countries, by contrast, the relative wages of youths rose or remained steady through the 1970s to early 1980s. Regressions of youth unemployment rates on adult unemployment rates and the ratio of youth to adult pay in a pooled time-series cross section of OECD countries shows that countries where relative pay for youths declined, such as the United States, had less youth unemployment than countries without such responses (Bloom, Freeman and Korenman, 1987; OECD, 1986b). While the drop in youth wages presumably affected overall unemployment more modestly (due to substitution among workers of different ages), it more likely than not dampened total unemployment as well.

Relative wages by region tell a different story. Consider, for example, the summary data on the relation between pay, changes in pay and unemployment across geographic units in countries X and Y in Table 13.2: in country Y, wages are higher in high unemployment areas and increases in unemployment only modestly impact wages; in country X, wages are uncorrelated with unemployment at a point in time and declined in areas

Table 13.2 Regression coefficients and standard errors for the relation of wages to unemployment, by area

	Dep. variables:			
	1985–79 Change in wages		1985 Unemployment rate	
	Country		Country	
Independent variables	X	Y	X	Y
1985–79 Change in unemployment rate	−0.92 (0.27)	−0.43 (0.30)		
In wage/earnings, 1985			0.03 (0.06)	0.11 (0.02)
Percent employed mfg, 1985	x	x	x	x
Education of workforce, 1985	x	x	x	x
R^2	0.39	0.51	0.25	0.51

Notes:
For country X there are 61 areas; the wage change variable is the 1979–85 change in ln weekly wage of male manual workers. For country Y there are 50 areas; the wage change variable is the 1979–85 change in ln hourly mfg earnings.
Source: Freeman (1987, 1988).

with relatively rising unemployment – seemingly indicative of a more responsive labor market. Who are the mysterious economies? Country Y is the United States, with states as areas. Country X is the United Kingdom, with countries as areas. While the different pattern of wages might be due to differences in labor-market conditions not reflected in unemployment rates, the data seem prima facie to reject the notion that geographic wage adjustments are more responsive in unemployment-reducing ways in the United States than in the United Kingdom.

It is not only along geographic dimensions, moreover, that the United States does not seem to have more flexibility in the labor market than other OECD countries. While there are sizeable differences in wage differentials between the United States and some countries (for example, dispersion of industry wages is much smaller in Sweden and Denmark than in the United States), analyses of changes in wages by industry in West Germany (Bell, 1986) and in the United Kingdom (Freeman, 1987) show the same factors altering relative wages in those countries with similar magnitudes as in the United States. In addition, in the 1980s pay differentials by skill and by age changed at least as much in the United Kingdom as in the United States (with no sizeable impact on unemployment).

With respect to mobility, the US labor market evinces enormous short-run changes in employment among establishments, with gross employment flows far exceeding the net flows that determine whether aggregate employment expands or contracts (Leonard, 1986). A recent OECD analysis (1987, Chapter 4) estimates that the annual rate of 'job turnover' (the sum of gross job gains and gross job losses among establishment relative to employment) among Pennsylvania establishments averaged 25.8 per cent from 1976 to 1985. If European labor markets were less flexible (say, because of hiring and firing laws), one would expect smaller job turnover rates there. But the OECD reports job turnover rates of 23.3 per cent in France and 23.5 per cent in Sweden. While Germany had a low job turnover rate (16.5 per cent), Japan had the lowest (7.7 per cent) as well as the lowest unemployment – fair warning to anyone who believes that high mobility is necessary for low unemployment.

COSTS OF EMPLOYMENT EXPANSION

If the 1970s' and 1980s' employment growth in the United States resulted from relatively costless flexible labor-market adjustments, the European assessment of the experience 'as an impressive job creating performance' would be difficult to assail. But the evidence suggests, on the contrary, that there were substantial costs associated with the US expansion. First, the cross-country analysis of the wage-employment tradeoff suggests that the United States paid for job creation with slow growth in real wages and productivity. The magnitude of the tradeoff was such, moreover, that despite the fact that employment/population rates and annual hours per employee increased in the United States relative to OECD-Europe, *per capita GDP grew at the same 1.3 per cent rate*. From this perspective, Americans worked harder for the same gain in living standards as Europeans. Second, if, as seems reasonable, some persons entered the labor market in response to low earnings of heads of households (for example, married women with children under one year of age, whose 1987 participation exceeded 50 per cent), their employment reflects a worsening not an improvement in economic well-being. Third, to the extent that the GDP-expansion generated part of employment growth entailed the 'double deficits' that turned the nation into the world's greatest debtor, future living standards will be lower, implying an even higher cost to job creation. Finally, even with employment expansion, the US unemployment rate was markedly greater in the 1980s than in the 1970s, which itself exceeded that in the 1960s, while, as noted, unemployment (and wages) were more unequally distributed along some dimensions than in the past.

In sum, the United States paid more for its improved employment and unemployment position relative to OECD-Europe than is recognized by those who peddle flexible decentralized labor markets, US-style, as the 1980s economic cure-all. There were pluses to the US experience, but there were also costs that make the change in overall economic well-being not so different than in OECD-Europe.

BIBLIOGRAPHY

Bell, L., 'Wage rigidity in West Germany: a comparison with the US', *Federal Reserve Bank of New York Quarterly Review* (Autumn 1986), pp. 11–21.

Bloom, D., Freeman, R., and Korenman, S., 'The labour-market consequences of generational crowding', *European Journal of Population* (1987), 3, pp. 131–76.

Bruno, M., and Sachs, J., *Economics of Worldwide Stagflation* (Cambridge, MA: Harvard University Press, 1985).

Clark, K., and Summers, L., 'Labor market dynamics and unemployment: a reconsideration', *Brookings Papers on Economic Activity* (1979), 1, pp. 13–60.

Coe, D. T., 'Nominal wages, the NAIRU and wage flexibility', *OECD Economic Studies* (Autumn 1985), pp. 87–127.

Freeman, R., 'Are British wages unresponsive to market forces?', unpublished (London School of Economics, 1987).

Freeman, R., 'Labor market institutions, constraints, and performance', *Economic Policy* (April 1988), pp. 63–80.

Leonard, J., 'On the size distribution of employment and establishments', NBER working paper no. 1951 (1986).

Neef, A., 'International trends in productivity, labor costs in manufacturing', *Monthly Labor Review* (December 1986), 109, pp. 12–17.

Organisation for Economic Cooperation and Development, *Statisticques Retrospectives* (Paris: 1986a).

Organisation for Economic Cooperation and Development, *Employment Outlook* (Paris: September 1986b).
Organisation for Economic Cooperation and Development, *Employment Outlook* (Paris: September 1987).
Solow, R., 'Unemployment: getting the questions right', *Economica*, supplement (1986), 53, S23–35.
US Department of Labor, 'Median weekly earnings of full-time wage and salary workers by selected characteristics', various editions.

PART V

METHODS OF EMPIRICAL ANALYSIS

'Give your evidence and don't be nervous or I'll have you executed on the spot.'

The Red King to the Mad Hatter, Lewis Carroll

Issues of methods and techniques of econometric manipulation are to an empiricist what how-to-love manuals are to a playboy: delays in the action. Still, there are times when even the most devoted 'table theorist' feels obligated to draw back from tables of data and assess alternative statistical procedures and methods. Do certain techniques work? How can one improve their value in analysis? What statistical procedures can help actual data analysis? My approach to these questions has, with one exception (Chapter 15), not been in the standard econometrics genre. Instead, I have approached the issues of statistical technique as an empiricist, using *empirical evidence* to assess multi-equation econometric techniques, fixed coefficient models, and so on rather than judging them on their statistical purity.

My general assessment (and that of most empirical economists who are willing to be counted on this issue) is that most high-falutin' multi-equation econometric models have not greatly advanced our stock of knowledge. Although econometricians' criticisms of simple tabulations and least squares regressions have some validity, the empirical evidence demonstrates that the high-powered techniques designed to reveal the 'true structure' of the world all too often fail abysmally in practice to yield reliable and plausible results. Why? Essentially because they force cross-section data into boxes designed to reveal the results of experiments that the world never performed for us. My conclusion is that new data (in the case of unionism, longitudinal information that contrasts the same person in two or more states (Chapter 15)) or new variables – measures of job satisfaction that economists often shun as subjective (Chapter 14) – rather than additional econometric techniques is needed to address the issues that legitimately motivate the multi-equation work.

The chapter on measurement error in longitudinal analysis (Chapter 15) is the one that most closely resembles standard econometrics, though I believe the empiricists' orientation still comes through. This is a paper that I did not initally want to write. When data problems forced the issue to my attention, I asked Gary Chamberlain to analyze the topic, only to be turned down. He had other research on his agenda and thought I should work the problem myself. Damn! What would have taken him two or three weeks to get right took me several months of grinding, particularly during one fruitless stretch when I tried to prove a stronger result than in fact was true. But of course it was worthwhile. Not only did I understand the measurement error problem better than from reading someone else's paper, but I won the approval of my colleagues who are into technique: 'So you are really one of us after all.' Looking over the algebra, I can only reply, thanks, but I hope not.

The final chapter is foray into the history of thought. It is, however, not a standard history of thought piece designed to tell us where sets of ideas came from and how they developed, but rather an effort to evaluate the findings of the 1940s–50s generation of industrial relations-oriented labor economists (a generation that included Clark Kerr, John Dunlop, George Schultz, among others). It contains some thoughts on why economics has not progressed as rapidly as other sciences, which brings us back to the criticisms of empirical economics by my friend the physicist.

14 · JOB SATISFACTION AS AN ECONOMIC VARIABLE

Job satisfaction, while the subject of popular attention, of an extensive sociology and industrial psychology literature, and of theories of 'alienation,' has been studied by relatively few economists (see George Borjas; Daniel Hamermesh; Robert Flanagan, George Strauss, and Lloyd Ulman). Partly, the neglect of job satisfaction reflects professional suspicion of what may be called *subjective variables:* variables that measure 'what people say' rather than 'what people do.' Partly also, economists are leary of what purport to be measures of individual utility.

The purpose of this chapter is to examine these concerns and evaluate the use of job satisfaction (and other subjective variables) in labor market analysis. The main theme is that, while there are good reasons to treat subjective variables gingerly, the answers to questions about how people feel toward their job are not meaningless but rather convey useful information about economic life that should not be ignored. The chapter begins with a brief description of the satisfaction questions on major worker surveys and then considers the use of satisfaction as an independent and as a dependent variable. Satisfaction is shown to be a major determinant of labor market mobility, in part, it is argued, because it reflects aspects of the workplace not captured by standard objective variables. Satisfaction is also found to depend anomolously on some economic variables (such as unionism) in ways that provide insight into how those factors affect people.

THE JOB SATISFACTION VARIABLE

To begin with, Table 14.1 reproduces the job satisfaction questions and distributions of responses from major surveys of workers. The satisfaction questions are quite similar across surveys, asking for an overall evaluation of job satisfaction, and invoked similar distributions of responses. Most persons report themselves as highly or quite satisfied with their jobs, with

Table 14.1 Questions about job satisfaction and responses to questions from major surveys (shown in percent)

Survey and year	Question and response			
National Longitudinal Survey (*NLS*)	'How do you feel about the job you have now?'			
	Dislike it very much	Dislike it somewhat	Like it fairly well	Like it very much
Older men, 1966	2	5	37	56
1971	2	6	45	48
Young men, 1966	3	8	42	47
1971	2	9	50	38
Michigan Work Quality (1968–9) and Quality of Employment (1972–3)	'All in all how satisfied would you say you are with your job?'			
	Not at all	Not too satisfied	Somewhat satisfied	Very satisfied
1968–9	3	11	39	46
1972–3	2	8	38	52
Michigan Panel Survey of Income Dynamics (*PSID*)	'In general would you say your job is:'			

	Not enjoyable at all	Not very enjoyable	Somewhat enjoyable	Mostly enjoyable	Very enjoyable
1972	2	2	21	42	28

Source: Calculated from distribution of answers for the population given by each of the surveys.

only a distinct minority of about 10 per cent reporting dissatisfaction. While there is some indication in the National Longitudinal Survey (*NLS*) longitudinal tapes of declines in satisfaction over time, the Michigan Work Quality and Quality of Employment Surveys shows no such pattern.

The responses to satisfaction questions (and other subjective variables that lack a definite metric) can be scaled in two possible ways in analysis. First, they can be written as *n*-chotomous variables, taking the value 1 if the individual's response fell into the given category and 0 otherwise. When satisfaction is an independent variable, the set of dummies has an a priori ordering of effects with, for example, the third category having a larger effect than the second (relative to, say, the first) and the fourth a larger effect than the third. When satisfaction is the dependent variable, the multinomial probability model can be used to predict the effect of various factors on the probability of giving a certain response. Alternatively, the variable can be rescaled according to a specified symmetric probability distribution, such as the standard normal. With the unit normal transformation, satisfaction becomes a *Z*-score measuring the number of standard deviations between a given response and the mean. This procedure yields a continuous variable that can be entered as a dependent or independent factor in linear regressions, with obvious computational advantages over a maximum likelihood multinomial analysis, and will be followed in ensuing empirical work.

BEHAVIORAL CONSEQUENCES OF JOB SATISFACTION

Do subjective responses to job satisfaction questions contribute to explaining objective economic behavior? If they do, a case can be made for including subjective variables in analyses of economic activity. If they don't, subjective variables can be safely ignored.

To determine the relation between job satisfaction and overt behavior, the effect of job satisfaction on the behavior most likely to be affected by it, quits, has been estimated using the *NLS* and Michigan Panel Survey of Income Dynamics (*PSID*) longitudinal data tapes. These tapes have the advantage of linking satisfaction in one year to *future* mobility, providing a fix on lines of causality and on the *predictive* power of the variable that is not possible with cross-section data. The impact of satisfaction and other determinants of mobility is studied in terms of a logistic probability function, linking the probability P of quitting a job between years t and s to the characteristics of the person and their initial job in $t(X_{it})$, including job satisfaction:

$$P(Q) = 1/(1 + \exp - \Sigma B_i X_{it})$$ (14.1)

The X variables include standard measures of the objective position of the worker (age, race, sex, education, wage, occupation in the initial job) and ignore for simplicity (and to avoid simultaneity issues) the additional information from the new jobs to which job changers move.

Maximum likelihood estimates of the effect of job satisfaction, measured as a standard normal variable, and of several objective economic factors on quits are given in Table 14.2, using the logistic form. All of the calculations are limited to wage and salary workers who remained in the labor force in the period considered and who reported all the relevant information about their base-year job. Column 1 records the frequency of quits in the three samples. Column 2 records the estimated logistic coefficient for the Z-score of satisfaction, scaled so that positive values reflect greater satisfaction; columns 3–5 give the coefficients for *ln* wages, age, and years of tenure with an enterprise. Column 6 lists the other control variables in the calculations, as specified in the table note, while column 7 records the fit of the equation in terms of minus the *ln* of the likelihood function.

The calculations show that, diverse other factors held fixed, the subjective level of job satisfaction is a significant determinant of the probability of quitting, particularly in the *NLS* samples, where it obtains large coefficients

Table 14.2 Maximum likelihood estimates of the coefficients and standard errors of job satisfaction and other variables on the probability of quits, using the logistic form

| Sample Periods and Numbers of observations | Mean Quits | Logistic coefficients and standard errors | | | | | Other variables[a] | Minus ln likelihood |
		Satisfaction	ln wage	Age	Tenure			
NLS Older Men 1966–71 (3284)	0.145	−0.31 (0.06)	−0.37 (0.14)	0.021 (0.013)	−0.05 (0.006)		2–7, 10	2,438
Michigan *PSID* 1972–3 (3730)	0.093	−0.14 (0.06)	−0.89 (0.12)	−0.027 (0.006)	−0.06 (0.01)		1–9, 11	2,585
NLS Younger Men 1969–71 (1742)	0.123[b]	−0.37 (0.09)	−0.62 (0.24)	−0.605 (0.033)	−0.25 (0.06)		2–11	596

Notes:
a Other variables defined as 1 = sex; 2 = race; 3 = years of schooling; 4 = occupation (7 dummy variables in *NLS* samples; 9 in *PSID*); 5 = industry (9 dummies in *NLS* samples. 5 in *PSID*); 6 = number of dependants; 7 = geographic locale (3 region dummies); 8 = years of work experience; 9 = local market conditions (unemployment in area in *NLS* young men sample; 3 variables reflecting unemployment, shortage of workers, and area wage in *PSID*); 10 = Standard Metropolitan Statistical Areas dummy; 11 = union. Sex, race, and union are dummies.
b Quits calculated by a complicated algorithm based on changes from intervening jobs, and is subject to considerable potential error.
Source: Calculated from surveys with questions on satisfaction as described in Table 14.1.

four to five times the standard error. The magnitude of the effect of satisfaction on the probability of quitting can be estimated by differentiating the logistic form (equation (14.1)) with respect to the variable, yielding $dP/dX_i = \beta_i P(1 - P)$ which makes the effect of change depend on the level of P. At the mean level of quits, a one standard deviation change in satisfaction changes the probability by 0.038 in line 1, by 0.012 in line 2, and 0.040 in line 3, all of which are sizeable relative to the means. For comparison, the effect of a standard deviation in the variable most extensively studied by economists, wages, can also be estimated. Multiplying the logistic coefficients in Table 14.2 by $P(1 - P)$ and the standard deviation of the variable yields the following impact parameters: 0.024 (line 1), 0.047 (line 2), and 0.067 (line 3). By this metric satisfaction has a greater effect than wages on quits in the older male *NLS* data set, a noticeably weaker effect in the *PSID* and a moderately weaker effect in the younger male *NLS* set.

Estimates of the effect of satisfaction on two other measures of mobility; employer initiated separations and total separations, consisting of quits and employer actions, were also made using the same equations as in Table 14.2. The results showed only slight effects of satisfaction on employer initiated separations (the largest logistic coefficient was -0.09 with a standard error of 0.06 in the older male *NLS*), but effects on total separations similar to those in the table. By affecting quits, satisfaction alters the overall level of mobility.

While predictive power, statistical significance, and magnitude of effects are not the sole measures of the value of a variable, the evidence on quits in Table 14.2 does provide a clear answer to the question with which we began: it shows that subjective expressions of job satisfaction are significantly related to future overt behavior, which makes satisfaction at least potentially analytically useful.

OBJECTIONS AND EVALUATION

Granting that satisfaction contributes to predicting behavior and is not meaningless, objections can still be raised about its value in social analysis. First, it may be argued that satisfaction is largely a measure of intentions to stay or quit (which could be better captured by a direct 'do you intend to quit' question) and thus that the observed impact of the variable simply relates actions to intentions to act, which does not greatly illuminate the causal forces at work. If mobility were the only variable affected by satisfaction or if the effect of satisfaction were eliminated by inclusion of quit intention questions, this objection would have merit. However, the contrary appears true. The industrial psychology literature relates job satisfaction to such forms of behavior as mental health, absences, and physical ailments (Locke, 1976), suggesting that the variable affects a broader range of phenomena. Inclusion of a direct mobility variable (responses to 'what would the wage or salary have to be for you to be willing to take [another job]?' coded 1 if the person responded at no 'conceivable pay') barely reduced the coefficient of satisfaction in the *NLS* samples (a drop from 0.31 to 0.29 in the older male *NLS*, for example) and contributed less to the explanation of quits than did satisfaction, suggesting that the more general attitudinal variable has greater information content. Inclusion of the variable 'have you been thinking about getting a new job?' in the *PSID*, however, did reduce the satisfaction coefficient in line 2 of Table 14.2 (which was more weakly related to quits than the satisfaction variable in the *NLS*) to insignificance. This would support the objection if the intention variable was unrelated to other forms of behavior.

A related deeper problem is that, as a measure of personal feelings, satisfaction may lack systematic independent variation or links to social variables of concern to economists. Assume, for example, that satisfaction depends only on standard measured variables and random noise but does not exhibit any socially identifiable exogenous variation. Then it would partition the effect of observed variables on mobility into direct and indirect (via satisfaction) routes but provide no information about how mobility could be altered by changing satisfaction. In terms of path analysis, satisfaction would be an endogenous intervening variable of little substantive impact. Only the reduced form equation relating mobility to objective variables would yield meaningful impact parameters.

The response to this objection is that satisfaction does depend on socially identifiable but missing or unobserved factors, which give it systematic exogenous variation. On the one hand, detailed case studies link job satisfaction to a host of very specific aspects of the workplace, such as mode of supervision, physical work conditions, and so forth (Locke 1976; Vroom, 1974) which are not generally measured on large data files, making satisfaction a potential proxy for those *unobserved objective factors*. On the other hand, lack of adequate information on the alternatives facing individuals makes the variable a reasonable indicator of alternative job opportunities, if those with good opportunities are less satisfied than those with poor opportunities. Some insight into the relative importance of omitted characteristics due to changes in the features of the current workplace and of alternatives might be garnered from longitudinal information on changes in the job satisfaction and wages of mobile workers.

The omitted variable argument can be developed further by assuming that mobility depends solely on objective factors, including the omitted variables, and by treating satisfaction as an indicator of the omitted factors. If, as seems reasonable, the omitted aspects of the workplace are correlated with the measured factors, least squares estimates of their effect will be biased. Consistent estimates could be obtained by using satisfaction and other (subjective) variables that depend on the unobserved work characteristics as proxies, using general unobservable models. In this case, the satisfaction variable is needed to correct for econometric problems in estimating the effect of the observed variables. Whatever model structure is preferred, the link between satisfaction and objective but unmeasured variables rescues the satisfaction variable.

Finally, even if the interpretative problems with job satisfaction measures cannot be entirely resolved, the evidence that satisfaction is related to future mobility and other overt behavior (wages and standard variables held fixed) does provide useful clues to individual actions and to needed areas of research. It suggests that nonpecuniary factors are important in mobility and that additional effort be devoted to measuring and analyzing those factors.

JOB SATISFACTION AS A DEPENDENT VARIABLE

The definition of job satisfaction in industrial psychology as a 'positive *emotional state* resulting from the appraisal of one's job' (Locke, 1976, p. 1300), highlights the principal problem in interpreting responses to satisfaction questions: that they depend not only on the objective circumstances in which an individual finds himself but also on his psychological state and thus on aspirations, willingness to voice discontent, the hypothetical alternatives to which the current job is compared, and so forth. Because job satisfaction reflects both objective and subjective factors, it is more complex than standard economic variables and requires more sophisticated and careful analysis. By altering the way in which persons respond to questions, variables like education (which raises aspirations) or collective bargaining (which provides a mechanism for 'voicing' discontent) could have every different effects on job satisfaction than on objective economic conditions. The impact of satisfaction on overt behavior could also differ among groups, depending on the importance of objective and subjective factors in responses.

The distinct features of measured job satisfaction that result from its dependence on psychological as well as objective circumstances might be analyzed by comparing the effect of variables on satisfaction with their effect on overt mobility behavior (satisfaction excluded as an explanatory factor). Assuming that overt mobility depends *solely* on objective circumstances while satisfaction is influenced by subjective as well as objective factors, marked inconsistencies between the effect of variables on the two outcomes could be interpreted as reflecting the dependence of satisfaction on the subjective factor.

Estimates of the effect of various economic variables on job satisfaction (measured, as before, by a Z-score scaled so that positive values reflect increased satisfaction) and on the probability of quits (satisfaction held fixed) were made for the *PSID* and older male *NLS* samples. Because unionism was not available in the older male *NLS* until 1969, the calculations focus on quits from 1969–71. Table 14.3 summarizes the results in terms of the coefficients on variables having markedly different effects on satisfaction and quits.

The principal paradoxical finding is that trade unionism, which reduces quits significantly in the data sets, and thus would be expected to raise job satisfaction, either reduces it significantly (in the *PSID* and in the 1971 satisfaction equation in the older male *NLS*) or has little effect (1969 satisfaction in the older *NLS*). A negative or negligible coefficient of unionism on job satisfaction has also been found in other data sets (Hughes, 1977), including the younger male *NLS*, and has been documented, with a different model, for the older male *NLS* by Borjas (1979). At the 1975 meetings, I suggested that the inverse relation might reflect the role of unions as a 'voice' institution, encouraging workers to express discontent during contract negotiations and to make formal grievances rather than to quit, which would keep the dissatisfied from leaving the employer. If this view is correct, the satisfaction relation lends some support to the exit-voice model of the union (see the author). Since wages are included in the calculation and since a negative relation is found for young as well as older workers, it is difficult to account for the anomalous relation in terms of the flatter age–earnings profile of union workers, or related objective factors.

The other variable with consistently different effects is tenure, which is associated with much lower quit rates (possibly because of selectivity) but which has virtually no effect on job satisfaction. This could reflect the greater aspirations of those in a company due to increased benefits with

Table 14.3 Estimates of the differential effect of unionism and job tenure on satisfaction and quits

	Michigan *PSID*		*NLS* Older Male		
	Satisfaction 1972	P(quit) 1972–3	Satisfaction 1969	1971	P(quit) 1969–71
Union	−0.15 (0.04)	−0.35 (0.16)	0.04 (0.05)	−0.13 (0.05)	−1.93 (0.42)
Tenure	−0.001 (0.002)	−0.06 (0.01)	+0.000 (0.002)	−0.002 (0.002)	−0.16 (0.03)
R^2/ (−*ln* likelihood)	0.067	(2,385)	0.073	0.075	(231)

Notes: All equations include controls used in Table 14.2. The P(quit) estimated on logistic function using maximum likelihood. Sample sizes, as in Table 14.2 except for older male *NLS*, which had 1,735 observations.

seniority, their greater willingness to voice discontent due to job protection, or other subjective factors. While there were other differences in the effect of variables on satisfaction and quits in some of the data sets, there were no other clear patterns for all of the samples. Most variables like age, wages, and a race dummy had the expected opposite coefficients on satisfaction compared to quits.

Overall, the results of comparing satisfaction as a dependent variable with quits indicates that, consistent with economists' suspicion, satisfaction cannot be treated in the same way as standard economic variables. The divergent effects of unions (and to a lesser extent tenure) on satisfaction and quits suggests that at least some economic institutions and variables have very distinct effects on the subjective way in which individuals view their job satisfaction.

CONCLUSION

This chapter has attempted to show that subjective variables like job satisfaction, which economists traditionally view with suspicion, contain useful information for predicting and understanding behavior, but that they also lead to complexities due to their dependency on psychological states. The empirical analysis has found job satisfaction to be a major determinant of labor market mobility and has turned up puzzling relations between certain economic variables, notably unionism, and satisfaction that appear attributable to the subjective nature of the variable.

BIBLIOGRAPHY

Borjas, G., 'Job satisfaction, wages, and unions', *Journal of Human Resources* (Winter 1979), vol. 14, no. 1, pp. 21–39.

Flanagan, R., Strauss, G., and Ulman, L., 'Worker discontent and work place behavior', *Industrial Relations* vol. 13, (May 1974), pp. 101–23.

Freeman, R. B., 'Individual mobility and union voice in the labor market' this volume, Chapter 8.

Hamermesh, D., 'Economics for job satisfaction and worker alienation' in Orley Ashenfelter and Wallace Oates, (ed), *Essays in Labor Market and Population Analysis* (Princeton, 1977).

Hughes, J., *Satisfaction and union voice*, undergraduate honors thesis (Harvard University, 1977).

Locke, E. A., 'The nature and causes of job satisfaction', in Marvin Dunnette (ed), *Handbook of Industrial and Organizational Psychology* (Chicago, 1976), pp. 1297–350.

Survey Research Center, *A Panel Study of Income Dynamics: Study Design, Procedures, Available Data* (Ann Arbor, 1972).

Vroom, V., *Work and Motivation*, 'National Longitudinal Survey 1966–69', Ohio State University (New York: Wiley, 1974).

15 · LONGITUDINAL ANALYSES OF THE EFFECTS OF TRADE UNIONS

> But union members are different from nonmembers in unobserved ways, biasing your estimates. You should ... make a selectivity bias correction ... simultaneously determine union status and economic outcomes ... develop an unobservables model ... *use longitudinal data.* (Archetypical comment on virtually any study of the economic effects of unionism, or suitably modified, on any other empirical subject.)

Longitudinal data, which follow the same worker over time, offer researchers a potentially valuable way to examine often-raised objections to the findings of cross-section studies. Unlike complex 'structural model' approaches to cross-section data problems, which often yield unstable and uninformative results (Freeman and Medoff, 1981), longitudinal data offer a distinctively different 'experiment' for uncovering the effects of changes in economic variables. In the case of unions, what is a more natural way to study what unions do than to compare economic outcomes for workers (firms) before and after they change union status?

This chapter presents a critical analysis of the 'natural experiment.' In contrast to the archetypical comment cited above, it argues that longitudinal analyses do not provide a research panacea for determining the effects of unionism (or other economic forces). The main reason for this is the substantial impact of measurement or misclassification error of the union (other economic) variable on longitudinal work.

The chapter is divided into four sections. The first section develops briefly the statistical models used in this (and other) longitudinal investigations of what unions do. The second section examines the effect of measurement error in union status on estimated effects of unionism in cross-section and longitudinal studies. The next section presents the results of estimating the effect of unionism on outcomes in four longitudinal and cross-section data sets. In contrast to other empirical analyses using longitudinal data, it treats two market outcomes which are at the center of the 'voice-response' face of unionism, dispersion of wages and provision of fringe benefits, as well as wages. The final section considers the argument that cross-section and longitudinal estimates of union effects 'bound' the true impact of unionism.

There are three basic findings:

1. The difference between the cross-section and longitudinal estimates is attributable in large part to random error in the measurement of who changes union status. Given modest errors of measurement, of the magnitudes observed, and a moderate proportion of workers changing union status, also of the magnitudes observed, measurement error biases downward estimated effects of unions by substantial amounts.
2. Longitudinal analysis of the effects of unionism on nonwage and wage outcomes tends to confirm the significant impact of unionism found in cross-section studies, with the longitudinal estimates of both nonwage and wage outcomes lower in the longitudinal analysis than in the cross-section analysis of the same data set.
3. The likely upward bias of cross-section estimates of the effect of unions and the likely downward bias of longitudinal estimates suggests that, under reasonable conditions, the two sets of estimates bound the 'true' union impact posited in standard models of what unions do.

All told, the chapter concludes that because of measurement error and likely selectivity of who changes union status, longitudinal analysis is a useful tool for 'checking on' the result of cross-section studies but may very well yield worse estimates of the parameters of interest.

LONGITUDINAL MODELS OF WHAT UNIONS DO

The standard cross-section analysis of the impact of collective bargaining on the economic outcome or behavior of individual workers (or firms) involves a multivariate statistical analysis of an equation of the form

$$O_i = a + bU_i + cX_i + \varkappa_i \qquad (15.1)$$

where O_i = outcome for person i, U_i = dichotomous unionization variable (1 = covered, 0 = not covered), X_i = control variables (education, sex) assumed constant over time, and $\varkappa_i$ = error term. The recurrent objection to estimates based on equation (15.1) is that because of selectivity of union workers $\varkappa_i$, is likely to be positively correlated with U_i, leading to an overstatement of the union effect. Since, as Abowd and Farber (1982) have stressed, who gets a union job results from the decisions of both employers and workers, the selectivity argument depends on whose decision dominates the hiring process. In the case of wages it is generally assumed that, given high union wages, firms select more able workers from the queue facing them, producing $E(\varkappa_i U_i) > 0$. In the case of nonwage outcomes, it is often claimed that workers sort themselves in such a way that those who have strong desires for union-type work conditions and modes of compensation (and would thus obtain more of those outcomes in nonunion settings than the randomly chosen worker) choose union jobs. In this case firms either are indifferent or prefer those workers as well (since they will be more satisfied).

Longitudinal data provide a way to deal with the correlation between unionism and the error term. Assuming that the part of x_i that is correlated with U_i is an individual effect constant over time, so that $x_{it} = a_i + \epsilon_{it}$ with $E(\epsilon_{it}U_{it}) = 0$, addition of individual constants (which can be viewed as a form of differencing) will eliminate the correlation between x_{it} and U_{it}. In a two-period linear model one obtains

$$\Delta O_{it} = b\Delta U_{it} + \Delta\epsilon_{it} \tag{15.2}$$

where ΔU_{it} takes the values $- 1, 0, 1$. A multivariate analysis of equation (15.2) will yield the desired b as long as the change in union status is properly measured and is uncorrelated with the change in the random part of the error term.

Equation (15.2) can be readily generalized to exploit more fully the longitudinal data by allowing different changes in union status to have different effects on wages. In particular, we can allow changes in outcomes to differ among workers who join unions, leave unions, stay union, and stay nonunion:

$$\Delta O_{it} = a_1 UU + a_2 UN + a_3 NU + a_4 NN + \Delta\epsilon_{it} \tag{15.3}$$

where UU, UN, NU, and NN are dummy variables that take the values 1 or 0 depending on the union status in the two periods: $UU = 1$, if union in both periods; $UN = 1$, if union in period 1, nonunion in period 2; $NU = 1$, if nonunion in period 1, union in period 2; $NN = 1$, if nonunion in each period; and where the constant term has been suppressed.

Equation (15.3) shows that the before/after nature of the experiment permits calculation of three different union effects, each answering a somewhat different question:

1. What happens to nonunion workers who join unions compared to nonunion workers who remain nonunion (obtained as the difference between the coefficients on NU and NN, $NU - NN$, for short)?
2. What happens to union workers who leave the union compared to those who remain union $(UN - UU)$?
3. Among workers who change, what happens to those who join a union as compared to those who leave a union $((UN - NU)/2$ or some other such average)?

It can be readily seen that when union differential is constant over time $(UU = NN)$ and when the effects of joining and leaving unions are the same in absolute value $(|NU - NN| = |UN - UU|)$, equation (15.3) collapses into equation (15.2). Less restrictively, if the only reasons for (15.3) to differ from (15.2) are changes in union differentials over time, the estimated parameters will fulfill the equality in absolute values given above; that is, the only difference between the gains of workers who join unions versus those who leave is the changed union differential over time.

Equations (15.2) and (15.3) can be readily generalized to analyze data covering more than two periods. The natural extension of equation (15.2) is to a fixed-effects model with individual constants (differences from mean values) for each person. The natural extension of equation (15.3) is to a model with dummy variables for all possible classifications of changes in status. For ease of exposition in this paper I treat only the two-period case.

Interpreting longitudinal results

Assuming that $E(\alpha_1 U_i) > 0$, the longitudinal estimates of union impact should be lower than cross-section estimates. In fact, empirical analyses of wages do indeed show a lower impact of unionism in longitudinal than in cross-section data, providing support for the 'omitted ability bias' model given above (among the panel studies are Duncan, 1977, 1979; Brown, 1980; Mellow, 1981; Mincer, 1981; Chamberlain, 1982). In Chamberlain's analysis, for example, addition of individual constants reduces the union coefficient by 32 per cent–44 per cent, indicating 'a substantial heterogeneity (ability) bias.' The union wage effect still stands, but its magnitude is smaller than in traditional cross-section analysis. As the archetypical comment at the beginning of the chapter indicates, many have interpreted the smaller longitudinal estimates as providing better estimates of the true union effects than the larger cross-section estimates. Indeed, under the fixed-effect assumptions that changes in union status are properly measured and that selectivity of changers does not produce a correlation of the error in the change-in-outcome equation with changes in status, the longitudinal estimate is unbiased.

Are these assumptions likely to be valid in empirical work? What does their violation do to longitudinal estimates of union effects? This chapter argues that neither assumption is likely to be valid and that, under reasonable conditions, measurement error and selectivity of changers will bias *downward* longitudinal estimates of union effects. Because in practice measurement error appears to be the principal econometric problem in analysis of longitudinal data, I focus largely on the measurement error issue.

THE PROBLEM OF MEASUREMENT ERROR

In cross-section studies of unionism, one generally ignores measurement error in the union status variable on the assumption that only a small number of workers are likely to be misclassified and thus that any bias in the estimated union coefficient due to measurement error is modest. Misclassification of a small number of workers will, however, produce a much larger error in longitudinal than in cross-section analysis and thus cannot be readily ignored. The reason for the greater error is twofold. On the one hand, random misclassification of workers in two periods will produce a larger number of misclassified workers than random misclassification in one period. On the other hand, by obtaining information on union effects from generally small numbers of changers, the longitudinal analysis will contain a smaller number of correct observations. As a result the proportion of observations in error will be much larger in the longitudinal analysis than in the cross-section analysis, producing a larger bias.

A numeric example illustrates the dramatically different effect of modest misclassification on cross-section and longitudinal estimates. Assume we have a sample of 100 workers, of whom 25 are union members and 75 are not. Assume measurement error is such that 2 union workers are misclassified and 2 nonunion workers are misclassified.[1] Then we have the situation shown in Table 15.1. If the true value of the outcome variable is 1.00 for nonunion workers and 1.30 for union workers, our estimated means would be 1.28 and 1.01, giving an estimated differential of 27 per cent, a value that is 10 per cent below the true impact of unionism.

Table 15.1 Example of measurement error effect: cross-section data set

Observed	True	Number
U	U	23
U	N	2
N	U	2
N	N	73

Assume that 20 workers switch union status in the period, 10 joining and 10 leaving unions. With 4 workers misclassified in each period, so that 8 per cent of union workers and 2.7 per cent of nonunion workers are incorrectly classified, it can be demonstrated (see equation (15.14)) that the longitudinal data set will be approximately as shown in Table 15.2. There are three points to note about this data set. First, the longitudinal estimates of the union effect from NU and UN comparisons are the same: 1.25/1.03 or 21 per cent, which is 30 per cent below the true impact of unionism – an attenuation that is three times as large as that in the cross-section analysis. Second, measurement error produces a pattern of differences in levels of wages between the four sets: for example, workers measured as leaving unions have a lower wage in period 1 than workers who remain union, workers measured as joining unions have a higher wage in period 1 than workers who remain nonunion, and so on. Third, the best estimate of the difference in wages in the data is the comparison of the mean level of wages for the UU set with the mean level for the NN set, which yields essentially the correct 30 per cent differential. For this to be the best estimate of the union effect, however, workers in the two sets would have to be otherwise identical, contrary to the assumed $E(a_iU_i) > 0$.

More formally, I compare what measurement error in the dichotomous union status variable does to the estimated union coefficient in cross-section equation (15.1) to what measurement error in the change in union status variable does to the estimated union coefficient in longitudinal equation (15.2). Because of the restricted values of union status or change in status, the measurement error is correlated with the workers' true status,

Table 15.2 Example of measurement error effect: longitudinal data set

	Observed	Consisting of true	With observed means of 1	2
UU	13	13 UU	1.30	1.30
UN	12	9 UN, 1 UU, 2 NN	1.25	1.03
NU	12	9 NU, 1 UU, 2 NN	1.03	1.25
NN	63	61 NN, 1 UN, 1 NU	1.004	1.004

so that the standard measurement error in regression analysis must be modified, along lines set out by Aigner (1973) and by Marquis et al. (1981).[2]

Consider first measurement error in a dichotomous variable. Let M = measured union status, U = actual status, and e = error. Then

$$M = U + e \qquad (15.4)$$

where possible errors are: -1, if a person's true status is union ($U = 1$), producing a nonunion classification ($M = 0$), and 1, if a person's true status is nonunion ($U = 0$), producing a union classification ($M = 1$).

Now let r_U be the probability that a union worker is misclassified and r_N is the probability that a nonunion worker is misclassified and $1 - r_U$ and $1 - r_N$ be the corresponding probabilities that the workers are correctly classified. Then the relation between the expected error and the true status is

$$E(e) = r_N + (-r_U - r_N)U \qquad (15.5)$$

so that from (15.4)

$$E(M) = r_N + (1 - r_U - r_N)U \qquad (15.6)$$

Hence we can write M as

$$M = r_N + (1 - r_U - r_N)U + v \tag{15.7}$$

where v is a random variable with mean zero and variance σ_v^2.

The effect of regressing an outcome O on M rather than on U can be evaluated by substituting equation (15.7) into the true equation (15.1) and treating the random component of measurement error as an omitted variable. Substitution yields

$$O_i = (b/1 - r_U - r_N)M_i + cX_i - bv_i/(1 - r_U - r_N) + \varkappa_i \tag{15.8}$$

where I have suppressed the constant term.

The bias on the coefficient on M_i from omitting v_i is the coefficient of v_i in equation (15.8) times the regression coefficient of v_i on M_i, holding the X's fixed. Assuming, for ease of presentation, that M is uncorrelated with the X's in equation (15.8), we obtain the coefficient of v_i on M from equation (15.7) as σ_v^2/σ_M^2, the random measurement error component of the measured variance. Then the regression for equation (15.8) yields for the coefficient on M_i ($\hat{b}$)

$$
\begin{aligned}
E(\hat{b}) &= [b/(1 - r_U - r_N)](1 - \sigma_v^2/\sigma_M^2) \\
&= [b/(1 - r_U - r_N)](1 - r_U - r_N)^2\sigma_U^2/\sigma_M^2 \tag{15.9} \\
&= b(1 - r_U - r_N)\sigma_U^2/\sigma_M^2.
\end{aligned}
$$

Since union status is binomial, $\sigma_U^2 = \bar{U}(1 - \bar{U})$, where $\bar{U} = $ mean proportion union. If, as in our numeric example, we assume that $M = U$, which holds whenever $r_U U = r_N(1 - U)$, equation (15.9) simplifies to

$$E(\hat{b}) = b(1 - r_U - r_N) \tag{15.10}$$

When M is correlated with X (r_{mx}) and when the random component of the measured error is independent of $X[E(vX) = 0]$, the comparable equation is

$$E(\hat{b}) = b \frac{[1 - r_U - (r_N)] - b_{UX}b_{XM}}{1 - r_{MX}^2} \tag{15.11}$$

where b_{UX} and b_{XM} are the simple regression coefficients. Here the bias depends on the relation between the X's and both observed and true union status. If we assume that the random component of the measurement error is independent of $X[b_{UX} = 0]$ then, noting that $b_{UX}b_{XM} = r_{MX}^2$, equation (15.11) becomes

$$E(\hat{b}) = b \frac{(1 - r_U - r_N) - r_{MX}^2}{1 - r_{MX}^2} \tag{15.12}$$

Since the bias in equation (15.12) is greater than the bias in equation (15.10), we conclude that as long as the random component of measurement error is uncorrelated with the X's the cross-section estimate of the union effect is biased downward by at least $1 - r_U - r_N$ per cent.[3]

Turning to the effect of measurement error on longitudinal estimates, we proceed in a similar manner to the preceding analysis. In this case, the equation relating measured and true changes in union status is

$$\Delta M = \Delta U + e \tag{15.13}$$

where ΔM = measured change in union status ($= 1, 0, -1$), ΔU = true change ($= 1, 0, -1$), and e = error ($2, 1, 0, -1, -2$).

When r_U and r_N are independent over time, the relationship between the true changes and the measured changes can be written as functions of r_U and r_N and of the true changes from one state to the other T_{ij} ($i, j = U$ or N) as follows:

$$
\begin{aligned}
M_{NN} &= (1 - r_N)(1 - r_N)T_{NN} + (1 - r_N)r_U T_{NU} \\
&\quad + (1 - r_U)r_N T_{UN} + r_U r_U T_{UU} + v_{NN} \\
M_{NU} &= (1 - r_N)r_U T_{NN} + (1 - r_U)(1 - r_N)T_{NU} \\
&\quad + r_N r_U T_{UN} + (1 - r_U)r_U T_{NN} + v_{NU} \\
M_{UN} &= (1 - r_N)r_N T_{NN} + r_N r_U T_{NU} + (1 - r_U)(1 - r_N)T_{UN} \\
&\quad + (1 - r_U)r_U T_{UU} + v_{UN} \\
M_{UU} &= r_N r_N T_{NN} + (1 - r_U)r_N T_{NU} + (1 - r_U)r_N T_{UN} \\
&\quad + (1 - r_U)(1 - r_U)T_{UU} + v_{UU}
\end{aligned}
\tag{15.14}
$$

where v_{ij} is a random error.

Equation (15.14) is the critical equation in our analysis. The three terms in each equation in which an r_i or r_j is multiplied by a $(1 - r_j)$ represent misclassification errors. The terms in which $(1 - r_i)$ is multiplied by $(1 - r_i)$ represent true changes in the measured observations. As before, the error term can take on only a limited set of values, dependent on the value of the true change. The relation between the true values of ΔU and the possible error is defined as in Table 15.3 below. But from this array it can be seen that

$$E(e) = -(r_U + r_N)\Delta U \tag{15.15}$$

so that

$$e = -(r_U + r_N)\Delta U + v \tag{15.16}$$

and

$$\Delta M = - (r_U + r_N)\Delta U + v \tag{15.17}$$

where v is a random measurement error. Substituting equation (15.17) into (15.2) and applying the omitted variable bias formula for omission of v yields for the expected value of the estimated longitudinal impact of unionism ($\hat{b}_L$),

$$E(\hat{b}_L) = b/(1 - r_U - r_N)(1 - \lambda) \tag{15.18}$$

where λ is the ratio of random variance (σ_v^2) to measured variance $(\sigma_{\Delta M}^2)$. From equation (15.17) $\sigma_{\Delta M}^2 = (1 - r_U - r_N)^2 \sigma_{\Delta U}^2 + v^2$, yielding

$$E(\hat{b}_L) = b(1 - r_U - r_N)\sigma_{\Delta U}^2 / \sigma_{\Delta M}^2 \qquad (15.19)$$

According to equation (15.19) the downward bias in the longitudinal analysis will exceed the downward bias in the cross-section analysis as long as $\sigma_{\Delta U}^2 < \sigma_{\Delta M}^2$. Calculating variances we find that

$$\sigma_{\Delta U}^2 = (T_{UN} + T_{NU}) - (T_{UN} - T_{NU})^2 \qquad (15.20)$$

and

$$\sigma_{\Delta M}^2 = (M_{NU} + M_{UN}) + (M_{UN} - M_{NU})^2 \qquad (15.21)$$

Table 15.3 Relation between true value of ΔU and possible error

	Frequency of error assuming true value of ΔU		
Error	1	0	-1
2	0	0	$r_U r_N$
1	0	$(1 - r_N)r_N + (1 - r_U)r_U$	$r_N(1 - r_U) + r_U(1 - r_N)$
0	$1 - (r_N + r_U - r_U r_N)$	$1 - 2((1 - r_N)r_N - (1 - r_U)r_U)$	$1 - (r_N + r_U - r_U r_N)$
-1	$r_N(1 - r_U) + r_U(1 - r_N)$	$(1 - r_N)r_N + (1 - r_U)r_U$	0
-2	$r_U r_N$	0	0

For ease of analysis, assume that the true mean of unionism, $\bar{U}$, is constant over time and that there is no constant response bias, $E(\bar{M}) = \bar{U}$. But it can be shown (Marquis et al., 1981, p. 101) that M_{UN} depends on T_{UN},

$$E(M_{UN}) = (1 - r_U - r_N)^2 T_{UN} + \delta_M^2$$
$$E(M_{NU}) = (1 - r_U - r_N)^2 T_{NU} + \delta_M^2 \qquad (15.22)$$

where $\delta_M^2 = (1 - r_U)r_U \bar{U} + (1 - r_N)r_N(1 - \bar{U})$, the average variance of the measurement error.

With constant $\bar{U}$, $T_{UN} = T_{NU}$. Now let T_c be the proportion of workers changing union status in the sample $(T_c = T_{UN} + T_{NU})$. Then equation (15.21) simplifies to

$$\sigma_{\Delta M}^2 = T_C \qquad (15.23)$$

while substitution of equation (15.22) into (15.21) yields

$$\sigma_{\Delta M}^2 = (1 - r_U - r_N)^2 T_c + 2\delta_M^2 \qquad (15.24)$$

Equation (15.24) is an approximation due to the absence of terms reflecting the equation-specific error terms (v_{UN}, v_{NU} of equation (15.14)).

The key question is, Will $\sigma_{\Delta U}^2$ always be less than $\sigma_{\Delta M}^2$? Examination of equations (15.23) – (15.24) shows the answer to be negative. When measurement error is large so that $(1 - r_U - r_N)^2$ is close to zero and when T_c is large $\sigma^2_{\Delta U} > \sigma^2_{\Delta M}$. For example, let $r_U = r_N = 0.40$ and $\bar{U}\,(= r_U/r_U + r_N) = 0.50$. Then $\sigma^2_{\Delta M} = 0.04\,T_C + 0.48$, so that for $T_C > 0.5\,\sigma^2_{\Delta U} > \sigma^2_{\Delta M}$. In this case, measurement error biases the cross-section estimate more than the longitudinal estimate.

On the other hand, when measurement error is modest – as in our earlier numeric example – $\sigma^2_{\Delta U}$ will be less than $\sigma^2_{\Delta M}$ for moderate values of T_C, producing a greater downward bias in the longitudinal calculation. Since the effect of measurement error on longitudinal as opposed to cross-section analysis thus depends on the magnitudes of the various parameters in the measurement error formula, I turn next to estimates of the critical magnitudes.

Evidence on measurement error

The first parameters needed to evaluate the importance of measurement error are the actual errors themselves $-r_U$ and r_N. I have identified two surveys which provide the type of information needed to estimate r_U and r_N: separate measures of the union status of the same workers at essentially the same time. The first survey is a special supplement to the January 1977 Current Population Survey, which asked workers whether or not they were covered by collective bargaining and then asked their employers the same question. The second is the May 1979 Current Population Survey, which asked workers about their collective bargaining status on the 'dual job' supplement and on the 'pension' supplement. While there are differences in the timing of the questions in both surveys, the time differences are sufficiently slight so that differences in answers provide us with a reasonable first-order approximation to random measurement error in union status.

Table 15.4 Misclassification of union status on two surveys: current population survey, May 1979

Covered by collective bargaining on main survey	Covered by collective bargaining on pension supplement		
	Yes	No	Total
Yes	3,976	272	4,248
Row (%)	93.6	6.4	
Column (%)	91.9	1.9	23.2
No	321	13,688	14,009
Row (%)	2.3	97.7	
Column (%)	8.1	98.1	76.8
Total	4,297	13,950	18,257
Row (%)	23.5	76.5	100

Source: Tabulated from matched sample, *CPS*.

Table 15.5 Misclassification of union status on two surveys: employer–employee matched survey, January 1977

Covered by collective bargaining, by employers	Covered by collective bargaining by employees of household respondent		
	Yes	No	Total
Yes	707	57	764
Row (%)	92.5	7.5	
Column (%)	92.5	2.3	23.2
No	57	2,476	2,533
Row (%)	2.3	47.8	76.8
Column (%)	7.5	97.8	
Total	76.4	2,533	3,297
Row (%)	23.2	76.8	100

Source: Tabulated from January 1977 Employer–Employee Matched Sample.

Tables 15.4 and 15.5 tabulate the responses to these two surveys. They show that while r_U and r_N are, as stated, modest in value, they are sufficiently nonnegligible to produce potentially large response error bias in longitudinal data. In the 1979 CPS sample 6.4 per cent–8.1 per cent of workers in the union category and 1.9 per cent–2.3 per cent of those in the nonunion category are misclassified, giving a value of 8.7 per cent–10.0 per cent for the critical $r_U + r_N$ figure. In the 1977 matched employer–employee sample, 7.5 per cent of workers in the union category and 2.3 per cent of those in the nonunion category are misclassified giving a 9.8 per cent value to $r_U + r_N$.

To check whether the differences in classification on the samples can, in fact, be interpreted as resulting from random measurement error, I have estimated union wage equations for the sample of workers for whom there are conflicting estimates of union status and for the sample for whom there are no such conflicts. If the conflict in responses is due to random misclassification, one would expect no significant union wage effect for persons in the sample in which estimates conflict, compared to a sizeable union effect in the sample for which there are no conflicts in whether a person is union or not. As can be seen in Table 15.6, estimates of standard log wage equations (with the usual demographic and human capital controls) for the samples yield the expected results where the ± before the coefficient reflects the change in sign depending on which estimate of unionism is used as the independent variable.[4]

Finally, taking the magnitudes of the estimated misclassification errors in Tables 15.4 and 15.5 as valid, we can apply the formulas given earlier to evaluate the impact of measurement error on regression estimates of union impacts, given different proportions of workers truly changing union status. As can be seen in Table 15.7, when only 5 per cent of workers change status the longitudinal estimate is less than half the cross-section estimate and just 40 per cent of the true b, whereas if 15 per cent–20 per cent change status the estimates are closer together. Consistent with the preceding analysis, when the proportion changing union status rises to relatively high levels, the longitudinal estimates exceed the cross-section estimates.

Table 15.8 turns to the next obvious issue: the proportion of workers who actually change union status in a longitudinal data set. It examines the proportions *measured* as changing status in four major longitudinal surveys: the May 1974–5 Current Population Survey (CPS), the National

Table 15.6 Estimated effects of unionism on log earnings, by response on union status

	Union status	
	Agreement	Disagreement
January 1977 sample estimated union coefficient (standard error)	0.26 (0.02)	±0.05 (0.07)
May-June 1979 sample estimated union coefficient (standard error)	0.21 (0.01)	±0.06 (0.07)

Table 15.7 Potential impact of measurement error on estimates of union effects

Proportion of workers truly changing union status (%)	Estimated bias in cross-section estimate (a)	Estimated bias in longitudinal estimate (b)	Relative bias (a/b)
5	0.90	0.40	0.45
10	0.90	0.59	0.66
15	0.90	0.70	0.78
20	0.90	0.77	0.86
25	0.90	0.82	0.91
30	0.90	0.86	0.95
80	0.90	1.00	1.12

Source: Calculated using equations (15.10) and (15.24) assuming $r_U = 7.5\%$, $r_N = 2.5\%$, and $\bar{U} = 0.25$, so $\delta_M^2 = 0.036$.

Longitudinal Survey of Men Aged 14–24 in 1966 (NLS) for the period 1970–8, the Michigan Panel Survey of Income Dynamics (PSID) for 1970–9, and the Quality of Employment Panel Survey (QES), 1973–7, and also records estimates of the true proportion changing. The estimates of the true proportions changing are obtained by summing the expected values of M_{UN} and M_{NU} from equation (15.22), which yields

$$E(M_C) = (1 - r_U - r_N)^2 T_C + 2\delta_M^2 \qquad (15.25)$$

Table 15.8 Proportion of workers measured as changing union status in diverse surveys

	Survey (sample size)			
Status	May 1974–5 CPS (7,887)	Michigan Panel Survey of Income Dynamics 1970–9 (635)	National Longitudinal Survey 1970–8 (1,905)	Quality of Employment Survey 1973–7 (543)
NN	0.714	0.400	0.609	0.595
NU	0.028	0.098	0.160	0.057
UN	0.034	0.094	0.087	0.101
UU	0.225	0.408	0.149	0.247
M_C (UN or NU)	0.062	0.192	0.242	0.158
U_1 (UU or UN)	0.259	0.502	0.231	0.348
U_2 (UU or NU)	0.253	0.506	0.309	0.304
Estimated T_C (true UN or NU)	—	0.117	0.210	0.091

Source: Tabulated from relevant survey with estimates of true *UN* or *NU* as described in the text with $r_U + r_N = 0.10$ and that $r_N/(r_U + r_N)$ equal the average rate of unionization in the period; thus, for the NLS, I set $r_N/(r_U + r_N) = \frac{1}{2} (0.231 + 0.309) = 0.27$ and obtain $r_N = 0.027$, $r_U = 0.073$. The same procedure is used for the other data sets. Note the Michigan PSID includes all of the 'poverty' sample, producing a large proportion of union workers.

where T_C is the proportion of true changers, and solving for T_C. In the cases where $\bar{U}$ changes over time, equation (15.25) is still applicable because the impact of changes in U has offsetting effects on $E(M_{UN})$ and $E(M_{NU})$.[5]

In three of the samples, the calculations yielded reasonable estimates of the true proportion changing, and those figures are reported in the table. In the May CPS sample, however, the formulas yielded no estimate, because under the assumptions, measurement error by itself should have produced virtually the proportion of changers observed.

The key finding in Table 15.8 is that whether one looks at the measured proportion of changers or at the estimated true proportion the values are on the low side of the figures in Table 15.7. The measured changes (M_C) range from 6.2 per cent (CPS) to 24.2 per cent (NLS) while the 'true' proportion changing vary from 9.1 per cent (QES) to 21 per cent (NLS). With these changes, measurement error biases downward the longitudinal estimates by 14 per cent (NLS) to 29 per cent (PSID) to 34 per cent (QES) and by even larger amounts in the CPS, according to the estimates in Table 15.3.

In sum, given measurement errors in union status that produce values of $r_U + r_N$ of about 0.10, and true proportions of workers changing status below 0.20, the analysis in this section suggests that longitudinal estimates of the effect of unionism on economic outcomes will be below cross-section estimates and, more important, below the true effect of unionism as well.

COMPARISONS OF LONGITUDINAL AND
CROSS-SECTION ESTIMATES OF UNION EFFECTS

As noted in the first section, there have been several studies of union wage effects using longitudinal data. These studies have found lower union effects than are found in comparable cross-section studies. By contrast, while there is a large and growing cross-section literature on the effects of unions on outcomes other than level of wages, such as dispersion of wages, labor turnover (notably quit behavior), fringe benefits, and the like (see Freeman and Medoff (1981) for a summary), there has been little longitudinal evidence regarding the effect of union membership on these outcomes. This section provides evidence that for two important 'nonwage' outcomes, the dispersion of wages and fringe benefits, and for wages, longitudinal analysis yields smaller estimated union effects than does cross-section analysis, but that the estimated effects are still fairly sizeable and economically significant. This finding leads us to reject criticisms that the results of cross-section studies of the nonwage outcomes are more subject to 'heterogeneity' or fixed-effects bias than are the results of wage studies. As measurement error should reduce the estimated impact of unionism on all outcomes, this is consistent with the models given in the second section.

The analysis treats the four data sets set out in Table 15.8. In each case I sought the largest possible sample for which the outcome variables and the union variable were reported. In the Michigan PSID sample, in which one has a number of possible years to examine, I report the results from a relatively long time span, 1970–9, though I examined shorter spans as well. In contrast to some studies, I include all of the special 'poverty' sample as well as the random sample in the survey. In the NLS sample I also chose a relatively long time span to examine. As the May CPS sample covers one year and the QES covers three years, the result is significant variation in the time span covered and, as seen in Table 15.8, significant variation in the proportion of persons changing union status as well.

Wages

Table 15.9 presents the results of my longitudinal analysis of union wage effects in the four data sets.[6] It records the log wages for the four union-change groups before and after the change, the change in low wages, and the implied union effects and, for comparison, the cross-section estimates of the union wage effect in the same data. While there is some variation among the three types of longitudinal estimates, the general pattern of results is clear: the longitudinal calculations yield lower estimates of the union effects than do cross-section calculations. As many longitudinal

Table 15.9 Log wages, changes in log wages associated with changing union status and estimated union effects

Group and survey	Log wage				Estimated union effects
	Before	After	Δ	Group	
(a) May CPS, 1974–5					
NN	1.24	1.34	0.10	NU – NN	0.09
NU	1.28	1.47	0.19	UU – UN	0.08
UU	1.58	1.67	0.09	(NU – UN)/2	0.09
UN	1.46	1.47	0.01	Cross-section	0.19
(b) National Longitudinal Survey of Young Men, 1970–8					
NN	0.97	1.84	0.87	NU – NN	0.12
NU	0.94	1.93	0.99	UU – UN	0.09
UU	1.34	2.05	0.71	(NU – UN)/2	0.19
UN	1.22	1.84	0.62	Cross-section	0.28
(c) Michigan PSID, 1970–9					
NN	0.95	1.61	0.67	NU – NN	0.08
NU	1.06	1.81	0.75	UU – UN	0.26
UU	1.29	2.02	0.73	(NU – UN)/2	0.14
UN	1.16	1.63	0.47	Cross-section	0.23
(d) QES, 1973–7					
NN	1.38	1.85	0.48	NU – NN	0.19
NU	1.24	1.91	0.67	UU – UN	0.11
UU	1.55	2.00	0.45	(NU – UN)/2	0.16
UN	1.35	1.70	0.34	Cross-section	0.14

Source: Calculated from the surveys. Cross-section estimates based on multivariate regression model with standard set of controls for demographic and human capital variables.

analyses focus on the difference in changes in wages between those joining and those leaving unions, the most significant comparison is between the $(NU - UN)/2$ estimates and the cross-section estimates.[7] Consistent with the results of Mellow (1981), they show a great reduction in the estimated union effect in the May 1974–5 CPS. As this is the group with the smallest measured proportion of changers, this is to be expected from measurement error. There is, however, one aberrant case in the table: in the QES, the $(NU - UN)/2$ comparison yields a larger rather than smaller estimated union effect than does the cross-section analysis. In this case, the cross-section difference in wages was only moderately above the longitudinal difference (UU and NN differ by 0.17 and 0.15) so that inclusion of regression controls reduced the cross-section estimate to the lower level. Note also that the pattern of differences in the log wages themselves, before and after the change, are also generally, although not always, in line with the impact of measurement error. The before-change log wages show that union leavers have lower wages than union stayers, which agrees with the numerical example examined in the second section. The after-change log wages also show that union joiners have lower wages than union stayers in all cases. By contrast, the before and after comparisons of changers with nonunion stayers show a less consistent pattern.

Finally, *if* we assume that the estimates of measurement error used in Table 15.8 apply to these data, we can calculate the proportion of the difference between cross-section/longitudinal coefficients due to measurement error. To do this we estimate the relative bias of longitudinal to cross-section estimates from Table 15.7, using the estimated true proportion of changers from Table 15.8, and multiply the resulting statistic by the cross-section estimate in Table 15.9. This yields 0.24 for the NLS and 0.16 for the PSID as the expected estimates from the longitudinal analyses, if measurement error were the only factor operating. Comparing these figures to the actual longitudinal estimates in Table 15.9, we see that measurement error explains 44 per cent (NLS) to 77 per cent (PSID) of the cross-section/longitudinal differences. While further analysis is required to pin down the specifics of the misclassification effects in each data set, our analysis suggests that measurement error can explain much of the difference between cross-section and longitudinal estimates of union wage effects.

This conclusion, while at odds with the widely used fixed-effects interpretation of the difference between longitudinal and cross-section analysis, is consistent with recent evaluations by other researchers. Chowdhury and Nickell (1982), who correct for measurement error bias in standard covariance estimates by instrumenting unionization on lagged unionization (on the grounds that serial correlation in the U variable is strong but is absent from measurement error), found that a longitudinal estimate of the union effect of 0.10 increased to 0.30 in the instrumental analysis. Their conclusion was that 'omitted quality variables bias the union effect upwards by about as much as measurement error problems bias it downwards and the "old-style" cross-section estimates are of the right order of magnitude after all.' H. Gregg Lewis (1986), in an evaluation of the effect of measurement error on union wages estimates, has also reached a conclusion similar to mine.

Dispersion of wages

The proposition that trade union wage policies are designed to reduce inequality of wages within firms and across firms for workers doing similar work has a long history in labor economics, stretching back to the Webbs. Numerous cross-section comparisons of wage inequality have found that inequality is less in union than in nonunion settings (see, e.g., Hyclak, 1977, 1979; Freeman, 1980, 1982; Hirsch, 1982; Plotnick, 1982). Standard wage regressions provide corroborating evidence, showing that for the most part the impact of most wage-determining variables is smaller on the wages of union than on the wages of nonunion workers. The magnitude of the estimated union impact is sufficiently sizeable to suggest that, despite the increase in dispersion due to union monopoly wage effects, unionism reduces overall inequality of wages.

Do comparisons of dispersions of wages in a longitudinal framework confirm the cross-section results? How much smaller, if at all, is the estimated union effect on dispersion? To answer these questions I have tabulated the standard deviation of the log of earnings for workers by their change in union status in the four data sets referred to earlier. The resulting calculations are given in Table 15.10, which follows the same format as Table 15.9. As can be seen, the longitudinal calculations confirm the cross-section finding of lower wage dispersion under unionism. Dispersion tends to fall when workers join unions and increase when they leave, confirming the reduction in dispersion under unionism. There are, however, notable differences in the magnitude and consistency of the effects by group, with $NU - NN$ and $(NU - UN)/2$ comparisons showing larger union effects than $UU - UN$ comparisons and with the PSID and QES showing more variable results than the other samples. To compare the longitudinal estimates to cross-section estimates, I have made some crude calculations of what a full cross-section analysis (which involves correcting observed differences in variances by observed differences in characteristics) might yield by reducing the difference in standard deviations between UU and NN workers in the before and after data by 30 per cent, a figure consistent with a full analysis of May 1973–5 CPS data (Freeman, 1980, Table 4). Without the adjustment the impact of unionism on dispersion estimated with the longitudinal data is much smaller than the impact estimated with the cross-section data. With the adjustment, the longitudinal estimate is still noticeably smaller, by magnitudes comparable to those obtained in Table 15.9 for wages.

Finally, note that comparisons of the levels of the standard deviations among groups tell a stronger story than did the comparison of the levels of wages.[8] In the before data, workers who leave unions have larger dispersions than those who stay, and workers who join unions have larger dispersions than nonunion workers who remain nonunion. In the after data, workers joining unions have greater dispersion than workers who were always union members while workers leaving unions have less dispersion than workers who remain nonunion. While these patterns could be due to factors other than error in measuring union membership, they are consistent with a pure measurement error interpretation.

Taking all these factors into consideration, I conclude that, as with wages, the impact of unions on dispersion found in cross-section studies is confirmed in a longitudinal analysis and that the magnitude of the effect is commensurably lower, at least partly as a result of error in measuring union status.

Table 15.10 Standard deviation of log wages, changes in standard deviations associated with changing union status, and estimated union effects

Group and survey	Standard deviation in log wages Before	After	Δ	Group	Estimated union effects
(a) May CPS, 1974–5					
NN	0.59	0.58	−0.01	NU − NN	−0.08
NU	0.52	0.43	−0.09	UU − UN	−0.05
UU	0.38	0.35	−0.03	(NU − UN)/2	−0.06
UN	0.46	0.48	0.02	Cross-section	−0.15
(b) National Longitudinal Survey of Young Men, 1970–8					
NN	0.47	0.53	0.06	NU − NN	−0.10
NU	0.39	0.35	−0.04	UU − UN	−0.13
UU	0.29	0.30	0.01	(NU − UN)/2	−0.09
UN	0.32	0.46	0.14	Cross-section	−0.14
(c) Quality of Employment Survey, 1973–7					
NN	0.55	0.55	0.00	NU − NN	−0.23
NU	0.52	0.32	−0.20	UU − UN	0.03
UU	0.38	0.36	−0.02	(NU − UN)/2	−0.07
UN	0.54	0.49	−0.05	Cross-section	−0.13
(d) Michigan PSID 1970–9					
NN	0.46	0.53	0.07	NU − NN	−0.15
NU	0.45	0.37	−0.08	UU − UN	0.01
UU	0.31	0.30	−0.01	(NU − UN)/2	−0.03
UN	0.40	0.38	−0.02	Cross-section	−0.13

Source: Tabulated from the various surveys. The cross-section effect is estimated by taking 70% of the difference in standard deviations between *UU* and *NN* (averaged for before and after). This is an approximate correction for differing characteristics of union and nonunion workers.

Fringe benefits

The third cross-section finding which I examine with longitudinal data in this paper is the finding that unionism increases the fringe component of compensation, particularly those fringe benefits that are most desired by older workers, such as pensions (for studies of fringe benefits, see Duncan, 1976; Goldstein and Pauly, 1976; Donsimoni, 1978; Solnick, 1979; Leigh, 1980; Viscusi, 1980; Freeman, 1981, 1983). As the QES is the only data set which provides fringe benefit figures over time, my longitudinal analysis is limited to that data set. I consider two measures of fringes, the number of fringes reported by workers and the proportion with pensions.

Table 15.11 presents the results of a longitudinal analysis for these two variables, again following the Table 15.9 format. While changes in the list of fringes in the surveys causes the number of fringes reported for the majority of workers to fall, the evidence shows that workers who went from nonunion to union gained fringes, while those going from union to nonunion lost relative to those who remained union. The implied union

Table 15.11 Numbers of fringes, and presence of pensions, changes in numbers of fringes, and presence of pensions associated with changing union status and estimated union effects, QES, 1973–7

Group	Before	After	Δ	Group	Estimated union effects
Number of fringes					
NN	3.01	2.56	−15%	*NU − NN*	32%
NU	2.59	3.02	17%	*UU − UN*	0%
UU	3.64	3.28	−10%	*(NU − UN)/2*	13%
UN	3.16	2.55	−10%	Cross-section	13%
Proportion of workers with pensions					
NN	0.65	0.70	0.05	*NU − NN*	0.34
NU	0.55	0.90	0.35	*UU − UN*	0.02
UU	0.95	0.96	0.01	*(NU − UN)/2*	0.18
UN	0.78	0.77	−0.01	Cross-section	0.25

Source: Tabulated from Quality of Employment Panel, 1973–7. Pension figures based on 429 *NN*s, 185 *UU*s, 66 *UN*s, and 48 *NU*s.

effects are all positive, with, however, considerable difference in magnitude. The *UN − NN* estimate, in particular, greatly exceeds *UN − UU*. The pension coverage figures show a similar pattern, with a sizeable increase in the proportion with pensions for workers joining unions but no real change for those leaving unions. Comparisons of the longitudinal with the cross-section estimates show no difference for number of fringes but the usual diminution of the union effect for provisions of pensions.[9] Finally, note that the pattern of differences in levels of fringes is similar to that found in dispersion for comparisons of *UN*s or *NU*s with *UU*s but is mixed in comparisons of changes with *NN*s.

Taking the results of Tables 15.9–15.11 as a whole, a reasonable generalization is that longitudinal analyses confirm the qualitative findings of cross-sectional analyses, with, however, smaller estimated union effects, possibly due in large part to the greater impact of errors of measurement on longitudinal than on cross-section statistics.

BOUNDING THE TRUE IMPACT?

If, as researchers usually assume, there is a substantial selectivity problem in cross-section analysis, which dominates any problems of measurement error, then cross-section estimates of union effects overstate true union effects. The preceding sections show that if there is a substantial measurement error problem in longitudinal analysis, and if there is no countervailing problem of selectivity of changers, then longitudinal estimates of union effects understate true union effects. When both of these statements are true, we have an important 'bounding' result:

Theorem: Under reasonable assumptions about the impact of measurement error and of selectivity of persons into unions, cross-section estimates of union effects provide an upper bound and longitudinal estimates provide a lower bound on the 'true' union impact in the model under study.

To prove the theorem, it is necessary to show that (a) measurement error biases longitudinal estimates downward to a greater extent than it does cross-section estimates, which is done in the second section; (b) selectivity of unionists in a cross-section biases cross-section estimates upward more than measurement error biases those estimates downward, which I shall assume on the basis of the modest estimated effect of measurement error in the cross-section; and (c) selectivity of who changes union status in longitudinal data either biases longitudinal estimates downward or biases them upward by less than measurement error biases them downward.

In this section I consider proposition (c). I examine the likely impact of selectivity in who changes union status on longitudinal estimates of union effects. I shall argue that under plausible models of the economics of unionism, selectivity of changers biases longitudinal estimates of union effects *downward*, reinforcing rather than weakening or offsetting the effects of measurement error. Hence, as long as (b) holds, the bounding theorem will be valid.

Modeling selectivity[10]

There are two types of selectivity involved in who becomes union or nonunion: workers' choice of working union (nonunion) jobs and employers' choice of workers. I model selectivity on the part of workers, then examine how the analysis changes when employers select workers from the queue desiring union jobs.

Consider the workers' decision to switch from union to nonunion status when the outcomes are determined by

$$O_{Uij} = \bar{d} + d_i + \alpha_i + \epsilon_{Uij}$$
$$O_{Nij} = \alpha_i + \epsilon_{Nij} \tag{15.26}$$

where O_{Uij} = outcome for jth worker in ith period ($i = 1, 0$) when $\bar{d}$ = average union differential, d_i = differential for jth worker relative to average differential with $E(d_i) = 0$, α_i = individual 'ability' effect, and ϵ_{Uij} (ϵ_{Nij}) = error when j works union (nonunion) with expected values 0 and variances σ_U^2 and σ_N^2. A worker will choose to accept a union job when

$$O_{U1j} - O_{N1j} > K \tag{15.27}$$

where K measures cost of mobility. Assume a bivariate normal distribution of the outcome variables. Then the truncated mean gain from working union is

$$E(O_{U1j} - O_{N0j} | O_{U1j} - O_{N1j} > K) = \bar{d} + \frac{\sigma_d^2 + \sigma_U^2}{\sigma^*} \frac{f[(K - \bar{d})/\sigma_*]}{1 - F[(K - \bar{d})/\sigma_*]}$$
(15.28)

where $\sigma_*^2 = \sigma_d^2 + \sigma_U^2 + \sigma_N^2$ and where $f/(1 - F)$ is the 'inverse Mills' ratio correction for truncation. Equation (15.28) overstates the union differential because it averages only over workers with especially high gains.

Similarly, for workers leaving unions, we obtain

$$E(O_{U1j} - O_{U0j} | O_{N1j} - O_{U0j} > K)$$

$$= -\bar{d} + \frac{\sigma_d^2 + \sigma_N^2}{\sigma^*} \frac{f[(K + \bar{d})/\sigma_*]}{1 - F[(K + \bar{d})/\sigma_*]}$$
(15.29)

as the expected mean change.

As our estimate of the union effect we take $(\frac{1}{2})$ $(NU - UN)$, which in the present context is $\frac{1}{2}$ of equation (15.25) minus $\frac{1}{2}$ of equation (15.29). This yields

$$\bar{d} + \left[\frac{\sigma_U^2 f[(K - \bar{d})/\sigma^*]}{\sigma^* 1 - F[(K - \bar{d})/\sigma^*]} - \frac{\sigma_N^2 f[(K + \bar{d})/\sigma^*]}{\sigma^* 1 - F[(K + \bar{d})/\sigma^*]} \right] \Big/ 2$$
(15.30)

where $\bar{d}$ is the union effect and the remaining components reflect selectivity of changers. Assume, for simplicity, that $\sigma_U^2 = \sigma_N^2$ and that there is a true union effect $\bar{d} > 0$. Then the selectivity bias is negative since $f[(K - \bar{d})/\sigma^*]/[1 - F(\cdot)] < f[(K + \bar{d})/\sigma^*]/[1 - F(\cdot)]$ because $K + \bar{d} > K - \bar{d}$. If, as is plausible given our findings on dispersion, $\sigma_U^2 < \sigma_N^2$, the negative bias is enhanced. If, by contrast, $\bar{d} = 0$ and $\sigma_U^2 = \sigma_N^2$, selectivity has – logically enough – no such bias effect.[11]

In this model if there is a union effect, the selectivity of changers biases longitudinal estimates of that effect downward. Even if there is not, we have established that selectivity on the part of workers does *not* bias upward the longitudinal estimate and thus cannot offset the predicted downward bias from measurement error.

What about selectivity by employers? Rather than providing a detailed analysis of this question (which involves complex double integrals), let us simply evaluate the qualitative impact of such selectivity on our previous results. Since only union firms have a queue of workers outside their plants, I assume that the only firm selectivity is selection of workers into union jobs. Firms will choose to hire workers with low d_j's – that is, those for whom the true union effect is smallest (with a fixed union wage effect, this involves picking workers with the highest productivity)[12] – and try to displace those with high d_j's.

With respect to workers who join unions, employer selectivity will augment the downward bias in the longitudinal estimate. This is because firms will be selecting lower values of d_{NUj} from the sample of workers for whom $d_{NUj} > K + \epsilon_{Nij} - \epsilon_{Nij}$. This will reduce the inverse Mills ratio component of equation (15.28).

With respect to workers who leave union jobs, the easiest assumption is that because of seniority rules, firms have no selectivity, leaving equation (15.29) as is. If firms are able to select who leaves, however, there is an additional negative bias component to equation (15.29), so that we can no longer sign the net effect of selectivity in equation (15.30). For the bias in equation (15.30) to remain negative, it is necessary that the effect of firm selectivity on who joins a union dominate the effect of firm selectivity on who leaves. This is plausible given that firms are free to hire whom they want but not to fire or lay off.

All told, our analysis of selectivity in who changes union status suggests that, under reasonable selection criteria but simplified statistical assumptions, the longitudinal estimates of union effects will be biased downward, establishing the bounding theorem.

CONCLUSION

In this chapter I have tried to show that measurement error is a significant problem in analysis of longitudinal data. I have developed some models of measurement error, examined numerical examples, and estimated the impact of measurement error in four data sets. My analysis has not been complete. I gave only cursory treatment to issues of the correlation between the random component of measurement error and control variables and ignored completely the potential impact of standard exclusion rules (such as requiring positive wages and sensible values of explanatory variables) on longitudinal as opposed to cross-section analyses. These errors of omission aside, the analysis suggests that longitudinal analysis is not the research panacea it is sometimes seen to be. While omitted fixed effects bias cross-section estimates of union effects upward, measurement error and possibly selectivity of changers bias longitudinal estimates downward. Under reasonable conditions, the two sets of estimates bound the true impact of unionism and thus should be viewed as complementary research tools. While neither is likely to yield the true parameter, together they enable us to estimate the magnitude of the effects of unionism, which appear to be quite substantial in empirical work.

NOTES

1. The assumption that equal numbers of workers are misclassified implies that the observed proportion union is an unbiased estimate of the true proportion. It is a useful simplifying assumption that appears consistent with actual

measurement error (see Table 15.4) but is not critical to the numeric example or to the ensuing statistical analysis.

2. Much of what follows is based on Marquis et al. (1981). I have also benefited from Aigner (1973).

3. We ask if the following inequality holds:

$$1 - r_U - r_N > \frac{1 - r_U - r_N - r^2_{MX}}{1 - r^2_{MX}}$$

Multiply by $(1 - r^2_{MX})$ to obtain $(1 - r_U - r_N)(1 - r^2_{MX}) > 1 - r_U - r_N - r^2_{MX}$. But simplifying we obtain $(r_U + r_N)\, r^2_{MX} > 0$, which proves the inequality.

4. In the January survey there are two reported wages: one from individuals, the other from employers. I have used the wage reported by the individuals in this analysis.

5. Specifically, the formulas with changes in the value of U between the periods are (Marquis et al. 1981, p. 101) $E(M_{NU}) = r_U(-\Delta U) + (1 - r_U - r_N)^2 T_{NU} + \delta^2_U$ and $E(M_{UN}) = r_U(\Delta U) + (1 - r_U - r_N)^2 T_{UN} + \delta^2_U$, so that the sum becomes $E(M_C) = E(M_{NU}) + E(M_{UN}) = (1 - r_U - r_N)^2 T_C + 2\delta^2_U$.

6. The measurement of wages varies across the data sets. In the CPS I measure wages by the ratio of usual weekly earnings to usual weekly hours; in the PSID, I use average hourly wages; in the NLS, I use the reported hourly rate; while in the QES wages are annual earnings from work divided by hours worked times 52.

7. In regression analyses which impose $NU = UN$, the coefficient is a weighted average dependent on relative numbers changing status. The reader can readily calculate weighted averages for contrast, if desired.

8. A full analysis of the effect of measurement error on dispersion differ somewhat from that of analysis of measurement error in the regression format, but the qualitative effects of error are the same.

9. The cross-section regression for number of fringes is based on regressions using 635 persons with 10 occupation, 6 industry, tenure, tenure squared, education, race, sex, years of schooling, and marital status controls. The regression for proportion with pensions is based on the same sample and model.

10. I have benefited immensely from the comments of John Abowd in this section. The statistical analysis which follows relies extensively on John Abowd (1983).

11. We can also compare the bias in the $NU - NN$ and $UU - UN$ estimates. Following the analysis in the text, we find that the mean for NN is σ^2_N/σ^*. $\{f[(K - \bar{d})/\sigma^*]/\{1 - F[(K - \bar{d})/\sigma^*]\}$, so that the mean for $NU - NN = \bar{d} + \{[(\sigma^2_d + \sigma^2_U - \sigma^2_N)/\sigma^*]f\}/(1 - F)$, which is less than $\bar{d}$ when $\sigma^2_d + \sigma^2_U < \sigma^2_N$, which is likely since the dispersion of wages is less than the dispersion of nonunion wages. Hence, here too we have an underestimate.

12. That is, a reasonable specification is $d_i = -\lambda a_i$, where a_i is our ability indicator with $E(a_i) = 0$.

BIBLIOGRAPHY

Abowd, J. M., 'Comments on the effects of selectivity biases on estimates of union/nonunion effects in a panel setting', review of 'Longitudinal analyses of the effects of trade unions' by Richard Freeman, mimeographed (Chicago: University of Chicago, 1983).

Abowd, J. M. and Farber, H. S., 'Job queues and the union status of workers', *Industrial and Labor Relations Review* (April 1982), vol. 35, pp. 354–67.

Aigner, D. J., 'Regression with a binary independent variable subject to errors of observation', *Journal of Econometrics* (1983), vol. 1, pp. 49–60.

Brown, C., 'Equalizing differences in the labor market', *Quarterly Journal of Economics* (February 1980), vol. 94, pp. 113–34.

Chamberlain, G., 'Multivariate regression models for panel data', *Journal of Econometrics* (1982), vol. 18, pp. 5–46.

Chowdhury, G., and Nickell, S., 'Individual earnings in the US: another look at unionization, schooling, sickness and unemployment using panel data', Discussion paper no. 141, Centre for Labour Economics, London School of Economics (November 1982).

Donsimoni, M.-P. J., *An analysis of trade union power: structure and conduct of the American labor movement*, PhD thesis (Harvard University, 1978).

Duncan, G. J., 'Earnings functions and nonpecuniary benefits', *Journal of Human Resources* (Fall 1976), vol. 10, pp. 462–83.

Duncan, G. J., 'Paths to economic well-being', in *Five Thousand American Families – Patterns of Economic Progress*, ed. by G. J. Duncan and J. N. Morgan, vol. 5 (Ann Arbor: Institute for Social Research, 1977).

Duncan, G. J., 'An empirical model of wage growth', *Five Thousand American Families – Patterns of Economic Progress'*, ed. by G. J. Duncan and J. N. Morgan, vol. 7 (Ann Arbor: Institute for Social Research, 1979).

Freeman, R. B., 'Unionism and the dispersion of wages', *Industrial and Labor Relations Review* (October 1980), vol. 34, pp. 3–23.

Freeman, R. B., 'The effect of trade unionism on fringe benefits', *Industrial and Labor Relations Review* (July 1981), vol. 34, no. 4, pp. 489–509.

Freeman, R. B., 'Union wage practices and wage dispersion within establishments', *Industrial and Labor Relations Review* (October 1982), vol. 36, pp. 3–21.

Freeman, R. B., 'Unions, pensions, and union pension funds', in D. Wise (ed.), *Public Sector Payrolls* (Chicago: University of Chicago Press 1985), pp. 89–122.

Freeman, R. B., and Medoff, James L., 'The impact of collective bargaining: illusion or reality?', in J. Steiber, R. McKersie, and Q. Mills (eds), *US Industrial Relations 1950–1980: a critical assessment* (Madison, Wis.: Industrial Relations Research Association, 1981).

Goldstein, G., and Pauly, M., 'Group health insurance as a local public good', in R. N. Rosett (ed.), *The Role of Health Insurance in the Health Services Sector* (New York: National Bureau of Economic Research, 1976).

Hirsch, B., 'The interindustry structure of unionism, earnings and earnings dispersion', *Industrial and Labor Relations Review* (October 1982), vol. 36, pp. 22–39.

Hyclak, T., 'Unionization and urban differentials in income inequality', *Journal of Economics* (1977), vol. 3, pp. 205–7.

Hyclak, T., 'The effect of union on earnings inequality in local labor markets', *Industrial and Labor Relations Review* (October 1979), vol. 33, pp. 77–84.

Leigh, D. E., 'The effect of unionism on workers' valuation of future pension benefits', *Industrial and Labor Relations Review* (July 1981), vol. 34, pp. 510–21.

Lewis, H. G., *Union Relative Wage Effects: A Survey* (Chicago: University of Chicago Press, 1986).

Marquis, K. H., Duan, N., Marquis, M. S., Polich, J. M., with Meslkoff, J. E., Shwartzbach, D. S., and Stasz, C. M., 'Response errors in sensitive topic surveys: estimates, effects, and correction options', Rand/R-2710/2-HHS (Santa Monica, Calif: Rand Corporation, April 1981).

Mellow, W., 'Unionism and wages: a longitudinal analysis', *Review of Economics and Statistics* (February 1981), vol. 63, pp. 43–52.

Mincer, J., 'Union effects: wages, turnover and job training', *Research in Labor Economics* (2 September 1983), vol. 5.

Plotnick, R. D., 'Trends in male earnings inequality', *Sourthern Economic Journal* (January 1982), vol. 48, pp. 724–32.

Solnick, L. M., 'Unionism and employer fringe benefit expenditures', *Industrial Relations* (February 1978), vol. 17, pp. 102–7.

Viscusi, W. K., 'Unions, labor market structure and the welfare implications of the quality of work', *Journal of Labor Research* (Spring 1980), 1, pp. 175–92.

16 · DOES THE NEW GENERATION OF LABOR ECONOMISTS KNOW MORE THAN THE OLDER GENERATION?

Of course we do. Human capital lifetime optimization models with Hamiltonians. Log-earnings equations at the overtaking age. Longitudinal data. State dependence and heterogeneity in unemployment durations. Efficient labor contracts. NAIRU and natural rates of unemployment. Search theory and reservation wages. Cobweb and rational expectations market adjustments. Implicit contracts. Unobservables. Just open any major labor economics journal (the *Journal of Labor Economics*, for example) and the answer is transparent. Why, the 1950s crowd would have trouble following the invigorating modern discussion of how labor markets operate, much less doing the fundamental research.

Of course we do. Science always progresses, doesn't it? And surely economics is a science. In natural sciences, citations are invariably to articles in the last five years[1] and so too are citations in labor economics. Indeed, my count of citations from the most recent editions of three major labor journals yields a proportion of citations to articles within five years of 67 per cent, 54 per cent, and 52 per cent.[2] Measuring advances in knowledge by the recentness of citations, we must be making as much progress as any of the natural sciences.

Of course we do. The athletes of today are faster, stronger, better fed, and better trained than those of the 1950s; why not labor economists? Put one of those old-timers – Joe Louis, Sugar Ray Robinson, Rocky Marciano – in the ring with a modern champion, and he wouldn't have a chance. Put one of those old scholars – John Dunlop, Clark Kerr, Richard Lester, or Lloyd Reynolds – in with a modern computer whiz, and it would be no contest.

Joe Louis? Sugar Ray Robinson? Rocky Marciano?

John Dunlop? Clark Kerr? Richard Lester? Lloyd Reynolds?

What did the other generation know about the operation of labor markets back then? How does it compare to what we know today? How did they discover what they discovered? How does it compare to our modern methodologies? How much progress have we made on the topics that interested them?

To answer these questions, I have reviewed a significant proportion of the works of Dunlop, Kerr, Lester, and Reynolds (DKLR) and have contrasted their analyses and findings to those in the modern (1970s–80s) literature.

The first thing one notices in such a contrast is the difference in methodology. DKLR and their contemporaries built their picture of the labor market from: detailed knowledge of specific cases, often as a result of personal activity on a war labor board or related public agency; survey analyses of local labor markets, with *both* employers and workers covered by the surveys; carefully reasoned study of simple tabulations, cross-tabulations, and occasional correlation coefficients. Aside from the lack of sophisticated econometric manipulations and mathematical theorizing, the most striking difference between their work and modern analyses is the reliance on informed priors, based on personal observation and common economic sense rather than on econometric tests of competing explanations of behavior (including in some cases, explanations that defy both personal observation and common sense).

A second important difference between DKLR and modern labor economists relates to the use of competitive theory in interpreting empirical results. A large proportion (though not all) of modern labor economists regard their basic task as explaining whatever one observes in terms of competitive theory. Indeed, we ooh and ah at our peers who devise the most clever (far-fetched?) explanation for any regularity that, on the face of it, is inconsistent with the competitive model. When no one can devise a 'good' explanation, some go so far as to question the fact (unemployment is voluntary rather than real) or put it into some sort of intellectual coventry. By contrast, the older generation of labor economists agreed uniformly that the labor market could not be understood as operating according to competitive principles:

> The labor market is by nature an imperfect instrument . . . all kinds of wage distortions exist even under nonunion conditions (Reynolds and Taft, 1956, p. 168).

> The automatic pricing mechanism as model or institution in the labor market is dead (Dunlop, 1944, p. 228).

> Actual wage facts seem contrary to what one might expect according to competitive theory (Lester, 1948, p. 152).

> It (a competitive market-determined wage structure) is a useful norm for theoretical speculations but an unusable departure point for empirical studies (Kerr, 1977, 46).

The third thing one notices is a difference in the weight placed on different topics. DKLR were concerned largely with firm behavior, demand

and wage setting, and broad industrial-relations issues, whereas today's labor economists, schooled in human capital theory and adept at analyzing large computerized data sets, are more concerned with labor supply issues and a wide variety of forms of individual behavior that seemingly go beyond the labor market (demography, crime, and so on). Any comparison of what they 'knew' and we 'know' must as a result differentiate carefully between the topics of concern to them and the topics of concern to us. As the older generation did not work on 'our' topics, I will limit my inquiry to whether or not we know more now on the four broad areas on which they focused their research: *wage determination*, including wage adjustments to economic shocks and the structure of wages; the impact of *collective bargaining* on wages and employment; *labor mobility* and *firm hiring practices*; and the *interrelation among wages, employment, and unemployment*. Since the broad picture of the labor market depicted by DKLR and their generation has been ably synthesized by Segal (1986), I forgo developing my own synthesis and focus on the specific empirical findings which underlie the older generation's picture of how the labor market works. My strategy is to summarize the empirical findings of DKLR, focusing on the results of the analyst(s) whose work concentrated on the particular area, and then to compare those findings with modern work. While I make no pretense to having obtained a complete listing of relevant studies, I believe the comparisons provide a reasonably accurate picture of what they knew and what we know on the relevant topics.

To provide a brief overview, the main conclusion I reach is that while, labor economists are more knowledgeable of labor supply issues than the older generation, we do not know more about firm behavior, labor demand, and the overall functioning of markets. Most ensuing research has supported the empirical generalizations of DKLR, and while we put more mathematical theory and econometrics into our analyses, more math and econometrics does not signify greater understanding of the economic fundamentals.

I conclude the chapter with some speculations as to why we have not made the kind of progress in surpassing our scientific elders, save in technique, as is the case in other scientific endeavors.

SPECIFIC FINDINGS OF DKLR ON MARKET WAGE DETERMINATION

The issue of wage determination was central to the analyses of DKLR. Dunlop's famous maiden paper was on the relation between money wages and real wages, and he later contributed important analyses on wage structure and the relation of wage changes to productivity and price changes. Reynolds dealt with wage structure issues at length in the book with

Cynthia Taft; Kerr examined labor's share of income, while Lester focused on wage differentials among plants.

Table 16.1 gives what I believe to be the central findings of the four analysts on the structure of wages at a moment in time and on changes in the wage structure over time at both aggregate and less aggregate levels.

Table 16.1 Comparison of older generation and modern findings on wage determination and wage structures

Results of older generation	Modern results and partial list of references
1 Wages differ significantly across industries for reasons beyond competitive forces. Therefore the product market as well as the labor market affects wages. (Dunlop, 1957; Reynolds and Taft, 1956)	Industrial wage differentials remain significant when controlling for differences in human capital, including occupation, geographical locale, work conditions and remain in longitudinal as well as cross-section analyses. (Krueger and Summers, 1987a, b; Dickens and Katz, 1987a, b)
2 Wages differ significantly across plants, even within the same industry. (Reynolds, 1951; Lester, 1946a, 1946b)	A sizeable proportion of wage variation within industry is due to employer-based differences. Characteristics of establishments studied in the 1940s and 1950s (size, union affiliation, principal product, technology, and principal pay method), but not growth, can account for at least one-half of measured establishment effects. (Groshen 1986; Osterman, 1982; MacKay et al., 1971; Nolan and Brown, 1983; Brown et al., 1984)
3 Wages differ by firm size for reasons beyond competitive forces (Lester, 1948)	Plant or establishment size and firm size are a major determinant of wages, holding fixed diverse human capital characteristics and other factors. (Brown and Medoff, 1985; Dunn, 1980, 1984; Groshen, 1986; Mellow, 1982; Personick and Barsky, 1982; Miller, 1981; Masters, 1969)
4 Wage rates show some tendency to increase most (least) in industries in which output, employment, and productivity increase most (least); but wages and productivity diverge significantly in the short run. (Dunlop, 1948; Kerr, 1977)	Holding fixed diverse human capital and related variables, industries with rising product prices and physical productivity have relatively rising wages, counter to the standard competitive model of the industry wage structure. (Bell and Freeman, 1985; Kaufman and Stephan, 1987; OECD, 1985)
5 Real wages rise when money wages rise, while a reduction in money wages is sometimes associated with a reduction in real wages. (Dunlop, 1938)	No clear conclusion about real wages over the cycle. (Geary and Kennan, 1982; Grubb, Layard, and Symons, 1984; Bruno and Sachs, 1985)
The structure of wages narrows in full employment and widens in recessions. (Dunlop, 1939)	Wage differentials by industry, education, and age are countercyclical. (Wachter, 1970; Freeman, 1971)
6 Labor's share of national income is countercyclical. (Dunlop, 1944; Kerr, 1977)	Profits are the variable portion of GNP, with labor's share rising in recession and falling in booms.

To begin with, one of the major conclusions which led the DKLR generation of labor economists to reject the competitive model of the labor market was the finding of significant wage differences among workers doing seemingly similar work across industries and among plants within an industry in particular local labor markets (lines 1–3). For a long time, modern labor economists ignored these results. Concerned with estimating the return to investment in human capital in the context of the by-now standard log earnings equation model, many modern labor economists have excluded industry dummy variables from wage analyses on the argument that part of the return to investing in skills is mobility into high-wage industries. The absence of readily available data sets with plant or firm information has discouraged investigation of differences among workers among plants. It is not that human capital analyses have challenged the older findings. They have not. They have rather excluded them from the area of active research concern.

More recently, younger economists interested in wage determination from a broader perspective have reexamined the role of the industry, establishment, and firm in wage determination, with empirical findings totally supportive of the results of the older generation. First, in separate but similar analyses of industry wage structures, Krueger and Summers and Dickens and Katz have analyzed the existence of industry wage differentials and found that no matter what other variables are entered in equations, those differentials were significant and sizeable. Work by Groshen, among others, has confirmed one of the chief findings of Lester's and Reynolds's work – that there are significant wage differentials among plants – and found that these differentials tend to be stable over time. Finally, Brown and Medoff have found that there are significant wage differentials by size of firm that cannot be readily explained by standard competitive theory.

While all the modern analysts, like the older generation, have tried to build competitive stories to explain industry and plant differentials, the broad conclusion they have reached also mimics that of the older generation – namely, that competitive theory cannot explain the observed phenomenon and that labor market analysis must change, accordingly, if it is to deal with the real world.

Turning to changes in wages over time, in an important paper in the 1948 volume in honor of Hansen, Dunlop argued that the wage structure was significantly affected by changes in productivity advances. In later work, he stressed the importance of product prices in wage determination, as well. While Salter (1966) found no such pattern of productivity advances leading to relative wage increases, more recent work has confirmed Dunlop's original insight, though in a modified multivariable context: productivity changes and wage changes by industry are uncorrelated by themselves but are correlated once price changes are held fixed. Alternatively, changes in value productivity rather than physical productivity alter the relative wage of industries.

With respect to cyclical movements in wages, Dunlop's original claim that real wages rise when money wages rise and thus tend to be procyclical rather than countercyclical, as predicted by marginal productivity analysis of a fixed labor demand curve, remains a point of debate in the economics literature. As indicated in line 5, some have presented evidence suggesting that real wages and employment are independent over the cycle, while others have argued the contrary. In part, as Bruno and Sachs note, the issue relates to country, with the United States seemingly more consistent with Dunlop's finding and Western Europe more consistent with the neoclassical pattern. In part, it may also hinge on whether one is concerned with product wages or wages in terms of consumer goods and thus the particular wage deflators used for analyses (consumer prices with/without adjustments for exchange-rate fluctuations; value-added deflators; or producer prices) – issues which, interestingly enough, took up much of Dunlop's article. Finally, the differences in results and continued debate may also reflect actual differences in the behavior of real wages among cycles, depending on the nature of business fluctuations (Malinvaud, 1977; Bruno and Sachs, 1985).

There is, by contrast, general agreement that Dunlop's second claim about wages over the cycle – that wage differentials widen in recessions and narrow in booms – is correct. Such a countercyclical pattern has been found in industry, education, and age differentials.

Finally, the finding that labor's share is also countercyclical, stressed by Kerr (1957) and reported by Dunlop (1944) has also been confirmed in modern work, though issues of labor's share have not been of much concern to American labor economists.

COLLECTIVE BARGAINING

When DKLR were doing their basic empirical research, trade unionism was growing in the United States (from 5 per cent of the private-sector workforce in 1933 to approximately 40 per cent in 1956) and the effect of unions on wage determination, the web of rules that govern labor relations, and the overall functioning of the labor market were major issues in economic analysis. There were those who believed unions would prove disastrous to the competitive system (Lindblom, 1949, Chamberlin, 1958, Simons, 1944, Haberler, 1959) as well as those with favorable attitudes. The DKLR generation provided careful empirical analyses of the actual effects of unions, contrasting the economic outcomes 'between the bargained wage structure and that which actually exists in imperfect non-union labor markets ... [not] with a hypothetical structure which might exist under perfect competition' (Reynolds and Taft, 1956: 168). Together with their contemporary at Chicago, H. Gregg Lewis, they portrayed a union movement that had significant but limited effects on wages under ordinary circumstances. In addition, they stressed that unions had diverse other effects on the labor market, some positive, some negative, and made an effort to model the union as an institution, with Dunlop pushing the importance of economic factors on union policies in his famous debate with Ross and the California school. Kerr noted the different organizations encompassed under unionism, pointing out that 'the type of union and the character of the environment together determine the impact of the union' (Kerr, 1977: 145). Reynolds made the point that the new industrial unions had their principal impact on wages 'through direct negotiations with the employer under threat of strike action' (Reynolds and Taft, 1956: 168) rather than through control of labor supply.

Table 16.2 turns to the findings of DKLR with respect to the impact of collective bargaining on the labor market. As can be seen, most of the nine propositions which I have garnered from their work has been supported in ensuing research.

First, a growing body of evidence based on computer analysis of CPS and establishment-based surveys shows that unions substantially reduce differentials by standard rate policies and indicate that wage differentials across plants are also lowered, though not by as much as the DKLR generation seems to have thought (lines 1 and 2).

Second, modern analyses also show that unions have a greater impact on fringes than on direct pay and have gone on to offer various 'collective goods' and 'median voter' explanations of this impact (line 3).

Third, while the issue of union impacts on labor's share of output has, as noted, not been seriously investigated of late, Bruno and Sachs have attributed some of the 1970s rise in labor's share of GNP in Europe to European union activity, consistent with Kerr's claim that while United States unions have not raised labor's share, European unions have. No one has addressed the issue, on which Kerr speculates, of why some union movements augment labor's share (possibly at the expense of employment) while others do not.

The final wage issues dealt with in Table 16.2 relate to the overall inflationary impact of union settlements and to the effect of unions on industry and occupation wage structures. At a time when some observers believed unions were a threat to the competitive system, DKLR argued that unionism, while important, had much more limited effects than the alarmists believed. This argument has been confirmed by the plethora of studies reviewed by H. G. Lewis (1986). Estimates of the monopoly loss of output due to union wage gains have, moreover, suggested that efficiency losses associated with unionism are slight, with some modern later economists going so far as to suggest that the losses are nil, as unions and

Table 16.2 Comparison of older generation and modern findings on effects of collective bargaining

Results of older generation	Modern results and partial list of references
Wage findings	
1 Unionism reduces personal differentials via standard rates which attach pay to jobs, not to the man. (Reynolds and Taft, 1956: 171)	Freeman (1980d) Freeman and Medoff (1984)
2 Unionism reduces wage differentials across plants (Reynolds and Taft, 1956: 365; Lester, 1948)	Groshen (1986) Freeman (1980d)
3 Fringes are higher the higher the wages, and are greater in union than in nonunion settings. (Reynolds, 1957: 65)	All else the same, the union/monopoly hourly fringe differential is between 20% and 30%. The fringe share of compensation is higher at a given level of compensation. (Duncan, 1976; Freeman, 1981b; Goldstein and Pauly, 1976; Leigh, 1979; Solnick, 1978; Viscusi, 1980)
4 Trade unionism in the United States has no important effect on labor's share, whereas in other countries it has. (Kerr, 1977: 115, 125)	Labor's share in European countries has risen partly as a result of real wage policies of unions. (Bruno and Sachs, 1985)
5 Effect of unions on wage changes does not threaten the competitive system. (Kerr, 1977; Dunlop, 1944)	Union wage effects differ over time but range from 10–25% (Lewis, 1986). The allocative costs are slight (Rees, 1963). Unions may establish efficient contracts (Abowd, 1989; Ashenfelter and Brown, 1986).
6 Unionism has little impact on occupational or industrial differentials. (Reynolds and Taft, 1956: 191, 365; Kerr, 1977: 155)	Nonunion wage structures by industry are hightly correlated with union wage structures (Dickens and Katz, 1987a,b; Krueger and Summers, 1987a,b. Unions reduce white-collar/blue-collar premium (Freeman, 1980d).
Nonwage Rules	
7 Unionized plants have greater reliance on seniority and rely extensively on temporary layoffs, recalling workers by seniority. (Reynolds, 1951: 54–5)	Seniority independent of productivity is rewarded substantially more in promotion decisions among union members than among otherwise comparable nonunion employees (Halasz, 1980; Medoff and Abraham, 1981; Yanker, 1980).
	There is much more cyclical labor adjustment through temporary layoffs in unionized manufacturing firms than in otherwise comparable firms that are nonunion (Blau and Kahn, 1981; Medoff, 1979).
	Terminations are more likely to be on a last-in/first-out basis among employees, ceteris paribus (Blau and Kahn, 1981, 1983; Medoff and Abraham, 1981).
8 Unionism creates 'walls around enterprises,' with lower quits and greater tenure (Reynolds, 1951: 55, 148). Unions reduce interplant mobility in part through	The quit rate is much lower for unionized workers than for similar workers who are nonunion. (Blau and Kahn, 1981, 1983; Block, 1978; Farber OLS results, 1980;

Table 16.2 (contd.)

Results of older generation	Modern results and partial list of references
grievance procedures (Reynolds, 1951: 254).	Freeman, 1978, 1980a, 1980b; Kahn, 1977; Leigh, 1979)
9 Unions are concerned with employment of members to a sufficiently important extent as to trade off wages for employment. (Dunlop, 1944)	Unions have no noticeably negative impact on employment (Pencavel and Hartsog, 1984). Unions weigh employment heavily in wage determination (Farber, 1978; Carruth and Oswald, 1986; Dertouzos and Pencavel, 1981; Pencavel, 1984).

management reach efficient contracts. On the wage structure side, recent work which has used Census of Population and Current Population Survey data to examine industry wage structures has found the structures for union and nonunion workers to be remarkably alike, supporting the DKLR claim that unionism has no great impact on the industry wage structure. On the other hand, the DKLR focus on the wages of manual workers led them to understate the effect of unions on the occupational wage structure. While modern studies support the conclusion that unions have no clear impact on occupational wage differences among blue-collar workers, they show that unions raise blue-collar wages relative to white-collar wages, reducing occupational premium along this dimension.

DKLR stressed throughout their work that unions did much more than raise wages in the labor market, just as they stressed that any labor market contract involved a web of rules and social relations. While this theme was for some time neglected in modern work, it has once again moved to the fore. Lines 7–9 of Table 16.2 summarize the claims of the older generation with respect to some important non-wage effects of unions: seniority and layoff policies under unionism, quit behavior, and employment. Again, we have a general confirmation of results. Indeed, on the key issue of the extent to which unions weigh employment in their negotiations, several studies have found that workers are risk-averse and take account of employment as well as wage gains.

Finally, as I noted in my 1984 review of Reynolds's *The Structure of Labor Markets*, there is one interesting aspect to the agreement between the work of the 1950s and that of the 1970s–80s. Taking the sixth edition of Reynolds's textbook on labor economics, we find him backtracking on two of the points in Table 16.2, writing: 'It is questionable whether collective bargaining has produced a major change in the pattern of labor turnover' (1974: 568), and that 'the specific influence of unionism (on fringes) is hard to determine' (1974: 216–17). These apparent reversals of his views regarding the impact of unions on turnover (point 8 in Table 16.2, and on fringes (point 3) resulted from cross-section industry regressions which found either statistically insignificant or widely divergent coefficients on unionism (in the case of quits, the results were those of Burton and Parker (1969), Stoikov and Raimon (1968), and Pencavel (1970); in the case of fringes, the results were those of Rice (1966). Modern work with data tapes on thousands of individuals and establishments has disproven the industry regressions. The implication is that the surveys, interviews, and informed judgments of the earlier period yielded more reliable results than did efforts to infer union effects from cross-industry regressions, as was common in the 1960s. We should be less willing to surrender conclusions based on case analyses and interviews to aggregative regression analyses than was Reynolds.

Given their knowledge of institutions, one might have expected the DKLR generation to have foreseen the problem of declining private sector unionism that has characterized the 1970s and 1980s, but, like other economists, they were not particularly good seers. In his book, *As Unions Mature*, Lester did not remotely anticipate a reversal in union fortunes, while in *Labor and the American Economy* (with D. Bok), Dunlop did not foresee anything like the current problems facing the union movement.

MOBILITY AND FIRM HIRING PRACTICES

The older generations' work on labor supply and mobility made extensive use of survey and interview data, with Reynolds's *The Structure of Labor Markets* perhaps the most significant piece based on worker interviews and Lester's various surveys of firm practices perhaps the most significant work based on data from firms. In Table 16.3, I have paired the findings from the worker and firm studies, under four broad groupings: internal labor market', correlates of individual mobility, the role of information in the job markets, and the process of job search.

With respect to internal labor markets, the conceptual piece by Kerr, 'The Balkanization of Labor Markets,' offers the broadest statement of the results from the entire spectrum of studies in the period, and I have quoted from it in line 1. Lester's surveys found that the internal market was strong in nonunion as well as in union companies, with large nonunion firms employing the same set of rules as union firms – results confirmed by Foulkes (1980) and Abraham and Medoff (1983). An important aspect of the finding that most workers work in internal markets is that this implies that the bulk of the labor force is effectively 'inframarginal,' and thus unlikely to respond to outside economic incentives in the simple manner represented in the neoclassical labor supply schedule.

In the area of correlates of individual mobility, there has been considerable modern work, in large part because of the availability of large-scale longitudinal data sets. While clothed in quite different statistical

Table 16.3 Comparison of older generation and modern findings on mobility and firm hiring practices

Results of older generation	Modern results and partial list of references
Internal markets	
1 'There is an internal submarket to which persons outside the plant have little or no access.' (Kerr, 1977: 28)	Internal labor markets exist, and are important in determining wages and mobility. (Doeringer and Piore, 1971; Abraham and Medoff, 1984)
2 'Non-union firms seem to follow, more or less closely, the hiring, seniority, and promotional patterns prevailing in similar unionized plants.' (Lester, 1954: 35)	Large nonunion firms have essentially the same personnel practices as union firms. (Foulkes, 1980; Abraham and Medoff, 1984)
3 'Even in good years...something like 80 per cent of manual workers...were not available to other firms.'' (Reynolds, 1951: 83) Management believed that perhaps four-fifths of the employees (were) rather firmly attached to the company...employees with one to three years of seniority rarely leave.' (Lester, 1954: 59–60)	US workers, like those in Japan, tend to stay with the same company for the bulk of their working life (except for job-shopping when they enter the market). (Hall, 1982; Hashimoto and Raisian, 1985)
Correlates of mobility	
4 'Propensity to change employers diminishes rapidly with increasing length of service.' (Reynolds, 1951: 35) 'Attractiveness of alternative employment may be greatly reduced by the need to start ...on the least desirable job and work shift.' (Lester, 1954: 36) 'Unskilled workers change jobs more frequently than the semi-skilled, and those in turn move more frequently than skilled workers. (Reynolds, 1951: 35)	Empirical studies show a strong negative relation between quit rates and job tenure. (Freeman 1980a; Leigh, 1979; Jovanovic and Mincer, 1978; Parsons, 1979; Blau and Kahn, 1981, 1983) Craft workers accrue more tenure than operatives, who accrue more tenure than laborers; workers with more 'specific' human capital quit less and are laid off less. (Parsons, 1972; Pencavel, 1972; Freeman, 1980b)
5 'Satisfactorily employed workers are almost entirely uninterested in...other companies.' (Reynolds, 1951: 85)	Job satisfaction is a key determinant of quit rates. (Mandelbaum, 1980; Freeman, 1978)
6 'The minority of very mobile people accounted for a disproportionate share of the total movement.' (Reynolds, 1951: 27–8)	Substantial core of US labor force is employed in long-term jobs. Unemployment largely due to small minority. (Hall, 1980; Clark and Summers, 1979; Akerlof and Main, 1980)
7 'Inter-plant movement typically involves a reduction in the workers' earnings.' (Reynolds, 1951: 242)	Young workers gain from mobility; older workers roughly hold their own; gains/losses depend on the reason for the change. (Borjas and Rosen, 1980; Bartel and Borjas, 1981)
Information in the job market	
8 'Workers had only a vague and frequently inaccurate idea of wages in other plants.' 'Workers are poorly informed about the job opportunities.' (Reynolds, 1951: 45, 84)	College students have good information on wages for occupations (Freeman, 1971); young people are fairly realistic about wage expectations and well informed about the going hourly pay for the kinds of jobs open to them. (Perrella, 1971)

Table 16.3 (cont.)

Results of older generation	Modern results and partial list of references
9 'A majority (56%) of workers replied they got their information (about jobs) from friends or relatives.' (Reynolds, 1951: 84) 'Gate hiring and internal recruitment are the two methods (used) for the bulk of new hires.' (Lester, 1954: 38)	Personal contact is the predominant method of finding out about jobs (56%); better jobs found through contacts. (Rees and Gray, 1982; Granovetter, 1974) Persons with contacts more likely to be hired by companies. (Freeman, 1981a)
10 'The only way to judge (a job) accurately is to work on it a while. After a few weeks or months of work, one can tell whether a job is worth keeping.' (Reynolds, 1951: 22)	Empirical analysis indicates that there is a strong impact on workers' quitting of. . . aspects of employment for which learning on the job is likely to be of importance. (Viscusi, 1979a, 1979b) Theoretical analysis stresses role of quitting as means to obtain optimal job match. (Mortensen, 1975; Jovanovic, 1979)
Results on process of job search 11 '(The worker) evaluates jobs one at a time, on the basis of his minimum standards, instead of trying to compare each job with the full array of possible alternative "good" jobs; he takes it without worrying over whether a "better" job may be available somewhere else.' (Reynolds, 1951: 85)	Rational search strategy is to search for jobs, taking the job which meets the 'reservation wage.' (Burdett, 1978; Johnson, 1978; Keiffer and Neumann, 1979; Lippman and McCall, 1976, 1980)
12 'The usual pattern is to quit an unsatisfactory job, spend some time in unemployment, then locate a new job.' 'Most workers (80%) change jobs without any unemployment.' (Kerr, 1942: 157)	Majority of all quitters experience no unemployment between jobs. (Mattila, 1974)
13 'Much the best results were obtained by those who had lined up a new job before leaving the old one.' (Reynolds, 1951: 215)	Analyses show employed search more productive than unemployed search. (Mattila, 1974; Black, 1980; Kahn and Low, 1982)
14 Reservation wages depend on: 'workers' earnings on his last job; period of unemployment. . . with a strong inverse relation,' 'The level of (UI) benefit payments seems clearly to influence the minimum supply price.' (Reynolds, 1951: 109, 110)	Asking wage of workers falls modestly with length of unemployment (Kasper, 1967; Barnes, 1975; Sandell, 1980; Stephenson, 1976). Level of UI influences wage changes after unemployment. (Enrenberg and Oaxaca, 1976; Grubel, Maki, and Sax, 1975)

methodology than the older work, these analyses have verified most of the points listed in the table. Seniority, whether for reasons of heterogeneity or state dependence is generally the most powerful determinant of quit and separation rates. As a result of the reduction in turnover with seniority, it is now generally accepted that a large proportion of mobility and unemployment is due to the behavior of a minority, contrary to the earlier assertion

(Feldstein, 1973; Hall, 1976) that high turnover of the workforce is the key to understanding unemployment. Modern analyses of tenure and quit rates also show that mobility is greatest among the less skilled and least among the more skilled manual workers (construction excluded). Not surprisingly, moreover, job satisfaction turns out to be a major determinant of quit behavior, indicating that 'the effective labor supply' does not include the satisfied. The only claim with which modern work disagrees is Reynolds's assertion that workers typically lose, rather than gain, from switching firms – a result reached on the basis of evidence of workers reporting gross weekly earnings on new jobs compared to their previous jobs. This may have been an artifact of the period, city, or group studied; Kerr's analysis of Seattle showed substantial wage gains. Modern work dealing with wage changes and mobility show gains for young workers, roughly no change for older male workers, but with noticeable difference depending on the reason for change. In addition, at least one model (Borjas and Rosen, 1980) suggests that workers who change do better than they would have done by staying on their job.

Turning to the role of information in mobility, the conclusions of DKLR concerning the importance of informal channels of recruitment and of personal contacts in obtaining job market information have been verified in numerous surveys, with analyses of hiring showing that companies prefer workers with relatives or friends in the firm. Moreover, both empirical analyses and diverse models of workers' acquisition of information, most notably Viscusi's Bayesian search models, have put great stress on the importance of actually trying a job in order to obtain accurate information about it.

By contrast, modern work disagrees with a major result of the older generation's view of labor market information: that workers have only vague and inaccurate information about wages. While the specific issue with which Reynolds and others dealt (that is, knowledge by workers of job opportunities in other plants) has not been the subject of major modern study, the general picture of information in the market that emerges from the modern work is quite different. Comparisons of unemployed individuals' expectations of wages available in the market as a whole show striking similarity to actual wages, while my 1971 survey of college students – motivated in large measures by Reynolds's evidence on manual workers – found that students had quite good information about earnings among occupations. Of all the DKLR generalizations, that of the poorly informed worker is the least accepted today.

With respect to job search and selection, Reynolds's *Structure of Labor Markets* – the main piece dealing with the topic – pointed out that workers choose among jobs by comparing each to a 'minimum standard.' While Reynolds seemed to believe that this was not rational, modern models of optimizing search behavior have shown that an appropriate strategy is in fact to compare offers to a reservation wage, accepting the first job with wages above the reservation level.

Modern work diverges from older work in other aspects of mobility behavior as well. For one, modern studies reject Reynolds's conclusion regarding the importance of unemployment in the search procedure – a finding based on his study of New Haven (which some of us who have lived there know cannot be representative) – and support Kerr's contrary finding for Seattle that the sequence of job mobility from employment to unemployment to a new job is less prevalent than job changing from one employer to another. Recent work also finds unemployment to have a much smaller impact on reservation wages than Reynolds obtained with his sample, where 'for people unemployed less than three months, the median expected wage (was) over 90 per cent of the last previous wage. For people unemployed three to six months, the figure dropped to 60 per cent' (1951: 109). On the other hand, several studies have found, consistent with Reynolds, that workers who have a job lined up beforehand are likely to do better than those who do not. Finally, studies of job satisfaction have tended to yield results of a comparable nature to Reynolds's regrading the importance of money income and various nonpecuniary factors in individual's evaluation of the workplace.

Overall, the findings of the DKLR generation with respect to the importance of internal markets, correlates of mobility, and the importance of informal channels of information in the job market have been supported by later work, the primary exceptions relating to worker information, some aspects of job search, and their interpretation of search behavior. Where modern work has gone far beyond the older generation has been in extending analyses to white-collar labor markets, to issues of education and human capital, and to the broader impact of labor market incentives on diverse forms of behavior beyond the interfirm mobility question on which the older generation focused. Here, at least, I think it is safe to say, yes, we do know more than they did.

INTERRELATION OF WAGES AND EMPLOYMENT AND FUNCTIONING OF LABOR MARKETS

The key to the broad picture of the labor market as seen by the DKLR generation – to what Martin Segal has aptly called the 'post-institutional model' – rests with their view that wage rates are only modestly affected by labor market conditions (within boundaries), and thus that the classical market view that wages represent an equilibrium intersection of labor supply and demand is too great an abstraction to be useful for analysis of short- or medium-term problems. As Dunlop (1944) put it, 'The labor market is not a bourse; wage rates are typically quoted prices.'

In my view, there are three components to this 'model.' First, the supply side of the labor market sets 'surprisingly wide' limits to wage differentials, *permitting* firms to pay above market rates. Second, some firms adopt high wage policies for reasons beyond attracting and holding the desired labor force. Third, as a result of permissive supply and wage policies (including those of unions), there is a partial divorce of wage setting from labor market conditions, with such nonneoclassical factors as product market conditions and ability to pay affecting worker compensation.

One striking consequence of this view, which takes on particular importance in light of macroeconomic research, is the denial of the existence of what has come to be called a stable Phillips curve (see line 2 of Table 16.4). I vividly remember John Dunlop pounding the table against the Phillips curve in a graduate labor economics course: he, Reynolds, Kerr, Lester,

Table 16.4 Findings on the interrelation among wages, employment and unemployment

Results of older generation	Modern results and partial list of references
1 'Wage policy is determined by the employed rather than by the unemployed.' (Dunlop, 1944: 69)	The Phillips curve relating wage changes to unemployment is not stable over time. Price changes are a critical determinant of many wage changes (Wachter, 1970; Eckstein, 1969; Medoff and Abraham, 1982; Santomero and Seater, 1978)
Decline in product prices and not unemployment constitute the effective downward pressure on wage structures. (Dunlop, 1944, 1957)	
The level of unemployment has nothing directly to do with the time at which wage increases begin or with the need of advance; this is determined mainly by the commodity pricing mechanism.' (Reynolds, 1951: 23)	It is 'the labor utilization rate that is important for negotiations, rather than the labor utilization rate within the economy.' (Gregory, 1986; Solow, 1980; Okun, 1981)
'The wage market and the job market are substantially disjointed and sometimes do go their separate ways.' (Kerr, 1977: 42–3)	
'A significant gulf exists between company wage policies or practices and economists' wage theories.' (Lester, 1954: 45)	
2 'There was virtually no correlation between the rate of wage increase and the rate of change of employment in individual companies.' (Reynolds, 1951: 223)	Industry wage and employment changes only slightly related. (OECD, 1966; Freeman, 1980c; Ulman, 1965)
'Impediments to intercompany movement tend to make for zones of no reaction between wages and mobility.' (Lester, 1954: 86)	Labor supply curves by industry are relatively elastic; variations of changes in employment exceeds variation in changes in wages. (Implicit in Salter, 1966; Kendrick, 1961; Freeman, 1980c)
'Movement and potential movement of labor seems inadequate to prevent large and persistent differences in aggregate job attractiveness.' (Reynolds, 1951: 246)	There are 'good' and 'bad' jobs; compensating differentials do not equate the values of jobs. (Brown, 1980; Doeringer and Piore, 1971; Bluestone et al., 1973)

and others who based their assessment on firsthand knowledge of wage setting came away with a very different picture of the role of unemployment than that given by 1960s macroeconomists enamored of the Phillips curve. Recent developments and research have supported their assessment about the fragility of the relation between unemployment and wage changes.

Another consequence of the view that wages in many firms are administered prices set above 'competitive rates' is that there need be no relation between changes in wages and changes in employment: GM and IBM, petroleum refining and steel, can attract labor without raising wages – a finding corroborated in various studies of industry wages and employment. While one can interpret the weak correlation between changes in employment and wages as reflecting the operation of competitive labor markets in which firms face infinitely elastic labor supply curves or of simultaneous shifts of supply and demand schedules, such interpretations would be inconsistent with the finding of persistent plant and industrial wage differentials between apparently similar workers and jobs. Such differentials are the key inconsistency between the evidence presented by DKLR and confirmed by modern analysts and the standard competitive market theory, a point which Segal (1986) has emphasized.

CONCLUSIONS AND SPECULATIONS

To summarize matters: on the issues of wage determination, collective bargaining, and the interrelation among employment, wages, and unemployment, which were the principal concerns of the older generation of labor economists, their empirical findings have, with rare exception, been corroborated by modern analysts using sophisticated econometric tools. In one sense, modern human capital earnings models have turned out to be largely 'orthogonal' to the older analyses, adding a supply dimension to our view of labor markets without rejecting the older demand results. Moreover, modern efforts to explain away the key findings of the older generation in terms of competitive market behavior have not succeeded, even in the eyes of some of those offering such explanations (see Krueger and Summers, 1986a, b; Dickens and Katz, 1986a, b). With respect to supply-side issues, which were of less concern to the older generation (save for Reynolds), the basic finding that labor supply has a largely passive effect on wage determination has been accepted in most respects, although observed job search and labor mobility has been interpreted as reflecting a more rational form of behavior. Only in issues which attracted little attention from the older generation – investment in human capital, economics of discrimination, dynamics of unemployment, to name a few topics – have we clearly surpassed our elders.

From one perspective, corroborating the results of the older generation on *their* issues is encouraging, as it indicates that neither the passage of time nor development of new techniques and data sets gives the profession a dramatically different picture of the labor market. That is not, however, the perspective from which I see our confirmation – our rediscovery – of the older results. In advancing science, one does not reconfirm or rediscover the facts of the previous generation; one builds on their analyses to obtain additional fact and new and deeper understanding about the way the world works. We should know a *lot* more about the labor market than the older generation, not only on issues they rarely addressed but on their central issues as well. But, despite our considerably more powerful tools of analysis, we don't know more than they do.

Why? Does our failure to make greater progress surpassing the older generation lie in the nature of our science? In our methods and approaches? In the structure of rewards given economists?

Without a detailed comparison of the sociology (epistemology?) of economics with that of other sciences, which goes far beyond the confines of this chapter, one can offer no more than speculations on these fundamental questions.

My speculation is that part of the problem resides in the nature of empirical economics, which is endemic to our endeavor, but that part of the problem also resides in the way in which we have proceeded in recent years.

The basic problem with accruing knowledge about how labor markets (other aspects of economies) work is that economic events are on-going, with the world continually performing 'experiments' for us under ever-changing conditions. Since the economic environment always changes (at the minimum because agents have additional past history from which to form expectations), there is a sense in which we always have to 'replicate' the findings of older generations to see if they hold up under modern conditions. Unlike physical scientists who can take certain 'facts' as given and build on them, we must make sure that patterns and relations found in the past hold under different environments. Because we cannot perform controlled experiments and, in one sense, are not terribly interested in the results of such experiments (we want to discover robust relations – ones which hold under many possible conditions – more than we want to discover ceteris paribus relations), our stock of knowledge can depreciate in ways unknown to scienists who conduct controlled experiments. The continued way in which macroeconomic developments overturn accepted doctrine is a case in point, with the history of the Phillips curve (here Monday, gone Tuesday, back Wednesday) indicating the problem in interpreting wage and unemployment relations. From this perspective, corroboration of the main findings of the older generation in today's economic world is no mean accomplishment. We do 'know' more than the older generation, for we know that their findings on the labor market hold not only under the conditions of the 1930s, 1940s, and 1950s but also under the conditions of the 1960s, 1970s, and 1980s. We know, for example, that even with computerized personnel departments and economies that have avoided anything like the Great Depression or a World War II boom, interplant differentials are as large and inexplicable in simple competitive terms as they were in the postwar reconstruction years when DKLR did much of their detailed empirical work. Our progress in surpassing the previous generation is slow in part because we are obligated by the nature of economic evidence to verify in 'modern times' what they found in older days.

Our progress is also slow, however, because of a pronounced tendency to neglect the work of those who came before us. How many graduate students read older empirical work? How many *can* read studies that are not presented with formal models and described in 'regressionese'? How many believe results that are not written with the newest mathematical jargon and put through the latest econometric sieve? One sure way to depreciate our stock of knowledge, and thus reduce the likelihood that we 'know' more than our predecessors, is to ignore their work.

Third, I fear that in part our failure to make greater advance with more powerful techniques is itself due to our inamorata with those techniques – a devotion to mastering and demonstrating our mastery of techniques as opposed to studying our subject itself – that a Marxist (we all have heard of them) might call 'techniques fetishism.' In econometrics, there is of course some justification for assessing old facts with new techniques because our 'experiments' are imperfect, but in light of the past two decades, experience with structural equations, corrections for sample selection, and the like, it is clear that fancier techniques are not the way to increase knowledge rapidly. In theory, I find the justification for techniques fetishism even weaker, for all too often what happens is that old principles are restated in new mathematical language. This is not to say that advances in techniques cannot be useful and fun. Some are useful. Some are fun. To some people. With a limited amount of research resources, however, the extent to which ours are devoted to techniques as opposed to discovery has, I believe, slowed progress. Valuing mathematical elegance and consistency, we surpass our predecessors in mathematical elegance and consistency, but not necessarily in understanding.

Does the new generation of labor economists know more than the older generation? On their issues, perhaps not. But that does not, I warn you, mean that when we disagree with them you should believe what they say. According to Edward Leamer's (1975) theory of random access-biased memory, quite the contrary. John Dunlop may have a storehouse of knowledge on a particular issue – dozens of specific cases that he can marshal like soldiers in an argument – while Richard Freeman may know only one fact. But as a result, Dunlop will *always* be able to recall instances consistent with whatever point he is making, and thus (inadvertently, of course) give a biased picture of the world. Freeman's one example is, by contrast, unbiased. Now, if we could model the access-biased memory path . . . and develop a multivariate statistical correction procedure for memory selection bias . . . or teach Freeman something more.

NOTES

1. See Derek de Solla Price, *Science Since Babylon* (New Haven, Conn.: Yale University Press, 1975) and *Little Science, Big Science* (New York: Columbia University Press, 1965).
2. *Industrial Labor Relations Review* (July 1986), 67 per cent; *Journal of Labor Economics* (July 1986), 54 per cent; *Journal of Human Resources* (Winter 1986), 52 per cent.

BIBLIOGRAPHY

Abowd, J., 'The effect of wage bargains on the stock market value of the firm', *American Economic Review* (February 1989).

Abraham, K., and Medoff, J., 'Length of service, terminations and the nature of employment relation', *Industrial and Labor Relations Review* (October 1984), vol. 38, no. 1.

Akerlof, G. A., and Main, B. G. M., 'Unemployment spells and unemployment experience', *American Economic Review* (December 1980), vol. 70, pp. 885–93.

Alexander, K., 'Market practices and collective bargaining in automotive parts', *Journal of Political Economy* (February 1961), vol. 69, pp. 15–29.

Barnes, W. F., 'Job search models, the duration of unemployment, and the asking wage: some empirical evidence', *Journal of Human Resources* (Spring 1975), vol. 10, pp. 230–40.

Barron, J., and McCafferty, S., 'Job search, labor supply and the quit decision', *American Economic Review* (September 1977), vol. 67, pp. 683–91.

Bartel, A., and Borjas, G., 'Wage growth and job turnover: an empirical analysis', in S. Rosen (ed.), *Studies in Labor Markets* (Chicago: University of Chicago Press, 1981).

Behman, S., 'Interstate differentials in wages and unemployment', *Industrial Relations* (May 1978), vol. 17, pp. 168–88.

Bell, L., and Freeman, R., 'Does a flexible industry wage structure increase employment?: the US experience', Cambridge, MA: National Bureau of Economic Research, working paper 1604 (1985).

Black, M., 'Pecuniary implications of on-the-job search and quit activity', *The Review of Economics and Statistics* (May 1980), vol. 62, pp. 222–9.

Blau, F., and Kahn, L., 'Race and sex differences in quits by young workers', *Industrial and Labor Relations Review* (July 1981), vol. 34, pp. 563–77.

Blau, F., and Kahn, L., 'Unionism, seniority, and turnover', *Industrial Relations* (Fall 1983), vol. 22, pp. 362–73.

Block, R., 'The impact of seniority provisions on the manufacturing quit rate', *Industrial and Labor Relations Review* (July 1978), vol. 31, pp. 474–88.

Bluestone, B., Murphy, W. M., and Stevenson, M., 'Low wages and the working poor' (Ann Arbor: The Institute of Labor and Industrial Relations, University of Michigan, policy paper 22, 1973).

Borjas, G., 'Job satisfaction, wages and unions', *Journal of Human Resources* (Winter 1979), vol. 14, pp. 21–40.

Borjas, G., 'Job mobility and earnings over the life cycle', *Industrial and Labor Relations Review* (April 1981), vol. 34, pp. 365–76.

Borjas, G. and Bartel, A., 'Middle age job mobility: its determinants and consequences', in Seymour Wolfbein (ed.), *Men in the Preretirement Years* (Philadelphia: Temple University Press, 1977), pp. 39–97.

Borjas, G., and Rosen, S., 'Income prospects and job mobility of younger men', *Research in Labor Economics* (1980), vol. 3, pp. 159–81.

Brown, C., 'Equalizing differences in the labor market', *Quarterly Journal of Economics* (November 1980), vol. 62, pp. 529–38.

Brown, C., and Medoff, J., 'The employer size wage effect' (Cambridge, MA: Harvard University, unpublished, 1985).

Brown, J., 'Expected ability to pay and the interindustry wage structure in manufacturing', *Industrial and Labor Relations Review* (October 1962), vol. 16, pp. 45–62.

Brown, W., Hayles, J., Hughes, B., and Rowe, T., 'Production and labor markets in wage determination: some Australian evidence', *British Journal of Industrial Relations* (July 1984), vol. 22, pp. 169–78.

Browne, L., 'Regional unemployment rates – why are they so different?', *New England Economic Review* (November/December 1978), pp. 35–53.

Bruno, M., and Sachs, J., *The Economics of Worldwide Stagflation* (Oxford: Basil Blackwell, 1985).

Bunting, R., *Employer Concentration in Local Labor Markets* (Chapel Hill, NC: University of North Carolina Press, 1962).

Burdett, K., 'A theory of employee job search and quit rates', *American Economic Review* (March 1978), vol. 68, pp. 212–20.

Burton, J., and Parker, J., 'Inter-industry variation in voluntary job mobility', *Industrial and Labor Relations Review* (January 1969), vol. 23, pp. 199–216.

Carruth, A., and Oswald, A., 'Miners' wages in post-war Britain: an application of a model of trade union behavior', *Economic Journal* (December 1985), vol. 95, pp. 1003–20.

Carruth, A., and Oswald, A., 'A test of a model of union behavior: the coal and steel industries in Britain', *Oxford Bulletin of Economics and Statistics* (February 1986), vol. 48, pp. 1–18.

Chamberlin, E., 'The economic analysis of labor union policies', in *Labor Unions and Public Policy* (Washington, DC: American Enterprise Institute, 1958).

Clark, K., and Freeman, R., 'How elastic is the demand for labor?', *Review of Economics and Statistics* (November 1980), vol. 47, pp. 509–20.

Clark, K., and Summers, L., 'Labor market dynamics and unemployment: a reconsideration', *Brookings Papers on Economic Activity*, vol. 1 (1979), pp. 13–60.

Cohen, H., 'Monopsony and discriminating monopsony in the nursing market', *Applied Economics*, vol. 4, (1972), pp. 39–48.

Dertouzos, J., and Pencavel, J., 'Wage and employment determination under trade unionism: the international typographical union', *Journal of Political Economy* (December 1981), vol. 89, pp. 1162–81.

Dickens, W., and Katz, L. F., 'Interindustry wage differences and industry characteristics', in K. Long and J. Leonard (eds), *Unemployment and the Structure of Labor Markets*, London: Basil Blackwell, (1987a).

Dickens, W., and Katz, L. F., 'Interindustry wage differences and theories of wage determination', Cambridge, MA: National Bureau of Economic Research, working paper 2271 (1987b).

Doeringer, P., and Piore, M., *International Labor Markets and Manpower Analysis* (Lexington, MA: Lexington Books, 1971).

Duncan, G., 'Earnings functions and nonpecuniary benefits', *Journal of Human Resources* (Fall 1976), II, pp. 462–83.

Dunlop, J., 'The movement of real and money wage rates', *Economic Journal* (September 1938), vol. 48, pp. 413–34.

Dunlop, J., 'Cyclical variations in wage structure', *Review of Economics and Statistics* (February 1939), vol. 21, pp. 30–9.

Dunlop, J., *Wage Determination Under Trade Unions* (New York: Augustus Kelley, 1944).

Dunlop, J., 'Productivity and the wage structure', in *Income, Employment and Public Policy, Essays in Honor of Alvin H. Hansen* (New York: W. W. Norton, 1948), pp. 341–62.

Dunlop, J., 'The task of contemporary wage theory', in George Taylor and Frank Pierson (eds), *New Concepts in Wage Determination* (New York: McGraw-Hill, 1957), pp. 117–39.

Dunn, L. F., 'The effects of firms and plant size on employee well-being', in J. Siegfried (ed.), *The Economics of Firm Size, Market Structure and Social Performance* (Washington, DC. Federal Trade Commission, 1980), pp. 348–58.

Dunn, L. F., 'The effects of firm size on wages, fringe benefits and worker disutility', in H. Goldschmid (ed.), *The Impact of the Modern Corporation* (New York: Columbia University Press, 1984), pp. 5–58.

Eckstein, O., 'Money wage determination revisited', *Review of Economic Studies* (April 1969), vol. 35, pp. 133–43.

Ehrenberg, R., and Oaxaca, R., 'Unemployment insurance, the duration of unemployment, and subsequent wage growth', *American Economic Review* (December 1976), vol. 65, pp. 754–66.

Farber, H., 'Individual preferences and union wage determination: the case of the united mine workers', *Journal of Political Economy* (October 1978), vol. 68, pp. 923–42.

Farber, H., 'Unionism, labor turnover and wages of young men', *Research in Labor Economics* (1980), vol. 3, pp. 33–53.

Farber, H., 'The analysis of union behavior', in O. Ashenfelter and R. Layard, eds, *Handbook of Labor Economics* (Amsterdam: North Holland, 1986).

Feldstein, M., 'The economics of the new unemployment', *The Public Interest* (Fall 1973), vol. 33, pp. 3–42.

Foulkes, F., *Personnel Policies in Large Nonunion Companies* (Englewood Cliffs, NJ: Prentice-Hall, 1980).

Freeman, R., *The Labor Market for College Trained Manpower* (Cambridge, MA: Harvard University Press, 1971).

Freeman, R., 'Job satisfaction as an economic variable', *American Economic Review* (May 1978), vol. 68, pp. 135–41.

Freeman, R., 'The exit-voice trade-off in the labor market: unionism, job tenure, quits and separations', *Quarterly Journal of Economics* (June 1980a), vol. 94, pp. 643–76.

Freeman, R., 'The effect of unionism on worker attachment to firms', *Journal of Labor Research* (Spring 1980b), vol. 1, pp. 29–62.

Freeman, R., 'An empirical analysis of the fixed coefficient manpower requirements model, 1960–1970', *Journal of Human Resources* (Spring 1980c), vol. 15, pp. 176–99.

Freeman, R., 'Unionism and the dispersion of wages', *Industrial and Labor Relations Review* (October 1980d), vol. 34, pp. 3–23.

Freeman, R., 'Changing market for young persons: who gets hired? A case study of the market of youth', Washington DC: Department of Labor, Final Report Grant no. 21-25-78-19 (1981a).

Freeman, R., 'The effect of trade unionism on fringe benefits', *Industrial and Labor Relations Review* (July 1981b), vol. 34, pp. 489–509.

Freeman, R., 'Union wage practices and wage dispersion within establishments', *Industrial and Labor Relations Review* (October 1982), vol. 36, pp. 3–21.

Freeman, R., 'The structure of labor markets: a book review three decades later', in Gustav Ranis, et al. (ed.), *Comparative Economic Perspectives* (Boulder, Colo.: Westview, 1984), pp. 201–26.

Freeman, R., and Medoff, J., 'The impact of collective bargaining: illusion or reality', in J. Steiber, et al. (eds), *US Industrial Relations 1950–1980: A Critical Assessment*, pp. 47–97 (Madison, Wis.: Industrial Relations Research Association, 1981).

Freeman, R., and Medoff, J., *What Do Unions Do?* (New York: Basic Books, 1984).

Geary, P. T., and Kennan, J., 'The employment-real wage relationship: an international study', *Journal of Political Economy* (August 1982), vol. 90, pp. 854–71.

Goldstein, G., and Pauly, M., 'Group health insurance as a local public good', in R. Rosett (ed.), *The Role of Health Insurance in the Health Services Sector* (New York: National Bureau of Economic Research, 1976), pp. 73–110.

Granovetter, M., *Getting a Job: A Study of Contacts and Careers* (Cambridge, MA: Harvard University Press, 1974).

Green, J., and Kahn. C., 'Wage employment contracts', *Quarterly Journal of Economics* (1983), vol. 98, Supplement, pp. 173–87.

Greenberg, D., 'Deviations from wage-fringe standards', *Industrial and Labor Relations Review* (January 1968), vol. 22, pp. 197–209.

Gregory, R., 'Wage policy and unemployment in Australia', *Econometrica* (1986), Supplement: pp. 553–74.

Gronau, R., 'Information and frictional unemployment', *American Economic Review* (June 1971), vol. 61, pp. 290–301.

Groshen, E., *Sources of Within Industry Wage Dispersion: Do Wages Vary By Employers?* (Cambridge, MA: Harvard University, unpublished PhD dissertation, 1986).

Grubb, D., Layard, R., and Symons, J., 'Wages, unemployment, and incomes policy' (London: Centre for Labour Economics, discussion paper 168, 1984).

Grubel, H., Maki, D., and Sax, S., 'Real and insurance induced unemployment in Canada', *Canadian Journal of Economics* (May 1975), vol. 8, pp. 174–91.

Haberler, G., 'Wage policy and inflation', in Philip Bradley, (ed.), *The Public Stake in Union Power* (Charlottesville, Va.: University of Virginia Press, 1959), pp. 63–85.

Halasz, P., 'What lies behind the slope of the age-earnings profile?', (Cambridge, MA: Harvard University, senior honors thesis, 1980).

Hall, R., 'Why is the unemployment rate so high at full employment?', *Brookings Papers on Economic Activity* (1970), vol. 3, pp. 709–64.

Hall, R., 'The importance of lifetime jobs in the US economy', *American Economic Review* (September 1982), vol. 72, pp. 716–24.

Hamermesh, D., 'Econometric studies of labor demand and their application to policy analysis', *Journal of Human Resources* (Fall 1976), vol. 11, pp. 507–28.

Hamermesh, D., 'Economics of satisfaction and worker alienation', in O. Ashenfelter and W. Dates (eds), *Essays in Labor Market and Policy Analysis* (Princeton: Princeton University Press, 1977), pp. 53–72.

Hashimoto, M., and Raisian, J., 'Employment tenure and earnings in Japan and the US', *American Economic Review* (September 1985), vol. 75, pp. 721–35.

Haworth, C., and Rasmussen, D., 'Human capital and inter-industry wages in manufacturing', *Review of Economics and Statistics* (November 1971), vol. 53, pp. 376–9.

Johnson, W., 'A theory of job shopping', *Quarterly Journal of Economics* (May 1978), vol. 92, pp. 261–78.

Jovanovic, B., 'Firm specific capital and turnover', *Journal of Political Economy* (December 1979), vol. 87, pp. 1246–60.

Jovanovic, B., and Mincer, J., 'Labor mobility and wages', in S. Rosen (ed.), *Studies in Labor Markets* (Chicago: University of Chicago Press, 1981).

Kahn, L., 'Union impact: a reduced form approach', *The Review of Economics and Statistics* (November 1977), vol. 59, pp. 503–507.

Kahn, L., and Low, S., 'The relative effects of employed and unemployed job search', *Review of Economics and Statistics* (May 1982), pp. 234–41.

Kasper, H., 'The asking wage of labor and the duration of unemployment', *Review of Economics and Statistics* (May 1967), pp. 165–72.

Kaufman, B. E., and Stephan, P. E., 'Determinants of interindustry wage growth in the seventies', *Industrial Relations* (Spring 1987), vol. 26, pp. 186–94.

Keiffer, N., and Newmann, G., 'An empirical job search model with a test of a constant reservation wage hypotheses', *Journal of Political Economy* (Feburary 1979), vol. 87, pp. 89–107.

Kendrick, J., *Productivity Trends in the US* (New York: National Bureau of Economic Research, 1961).

Kerr, C., *Migration to the Seattle Labor Market Area: 1940–1942* (Seattle: University of Washington Press, 1942).

Kerr, C., *Labor Markets and Wage Determination* (Berkeley: University of California Press, 1977).

Krueger, A., and Summers, L., 'Reflections on the interindustry wage structure', in K. Lang and J. Leonard, (eds), *Unemployment and the Structure of Labor Markets* (London: Basil Blackwell, 1987a), pp. 17–47.

Krueger, A., and Summers, L., 'Efficiency wages and the interindustry wage structure', *Econometrica* (March 1987b), pp. 259–93.

Landon, J., and Baird, R., 'Monopsony in the market for public school teachers', *American Economic Review* (December 1971), vol. 61, pp. 966–71.

Landon, J., and Pierce, W., 'Discrimination, monopsony, and union power in the building trades: a cross-sectional approach', in Industrial Relations Research Association, *Proceedings of the Twenty-Fourth Annual Winter Meeting* (Madison Wis.: Industrial Relations Research Association, 1971), pp. 254–61.

Leamer, E., 'Explaining new results as access biased memory', *Journal of American Statistical Association* (1975), vol. 70, pp. 85–93.

Leigh, D., 'Racial discrimination and labor unions: evidence from the NLS sample of middle-aged men', *Journal of Human Resources* (Fall 1978), vol. 13, pp. 568–77.

Leigh, D., 'Unions and non-wage racial discrimination', *Industrial and Labor Relations Review* (July 1979), vol. 32, pp. 439–50.

Lester, R., 'Trends in southern wage differentials since 1890', *Southern Economic Journal*, (April 1945), vol. II, pp. 317–44.

Lester, R., 'Shortcomings of marginal analysis for wage-employment problems', *American Economic Review* (March 1946a), vol. 36, pp. 63–72.

Lester, R., 'Wage diversity and its theoretical implications', *Review of Economics and Statistics* (August 1946b), vol. 28, pp. 152–9.

Lester, R., *Company Wage Policies: A Survey of Patterns and Experience* (Princeton: Princeton University, Industrial Relations Section, 1948).

Lester, R., 'A range theory of wage differentials', *Industrial and Labor Relations Review* (July 1952), vol. 5, pp. 483–500.

Lester, R., *Hiring Practices and Labor Competition* (Princeton: Princeton University, Industrial Relations Section, 1954).

Lester, R., *As Unions Mature* (Princeton: Princeton University Press, 1958).

Levinson, H., 'Pattern bargaining: a case study of the automobile workers', *Quarterly Journal of Economics* (May 1960), vol. 74, pp. 296–317.

Lewis, H. G., *Union Relative Wage Effects: A Survey* (Chicago: University of Chicago Press, 1986).

Lindblom, C., *Unions and Capitalism* (New Haven: Yale University Press, 1949).

Lippman, S.A., *Studies in the Economics of Search* (Amsterdam: North Holland, 1980).

Lippman, S. A., and McCall, J. J., 'The economics of job search: a survey', *Economic Inquiry* (September 1976), vol. 14, pp. 155–89.

Mackay, D. T., Boddy, B., Brack, J., Diack, J. A. and Jones, N., *Labour Markets Under Different Employment Conditions* (London: Allen and Unwin, 1971).

Malinvaud, E., *The Theory of Unemployment Reconsidered* (Oxford: Basil Blackwell, 1977).

Mandelbaum, D., 'Responses to job satisfaction questions into why workers change employers' (Cambridge: Harvard University, unpublished undergraduate thesis, 1980).

Marston, S., 'Anatomy of persistent local unemployment', draft paper prepared for the National Commission for Employment Policy Conference, 1980.

Marston, S., 'Two views of the geographic distribution of unemployment', (Ithaca: Cornell University, working paper 225, 1981).

Masters, S., 'An interindustry analysis of wages and plant size', *Review of Economics and Statistics* (August 1969), vol. 51, pp. 341–5.

Mattila, J., 'Job quitting and frictional unemployment', *American Economic Review* (March 1974), vol. 64, pp. 235–9.

Medoff, J., 'Layoffs and alternatives under trade unions in United States manufacturing', *American Economic Review* (June 1979), vol. 69, pp. 380–95.

Medoff, J. and Abraham, K., 'Experience, performance, and earnings', *Quarterly Journal of Economics* (December 1980), vol. 69, pp. 703–36.

Medoff, J. and Abraham, K., 'The role of seniority at US work places: a report on some new evidence', Cambridge: Harvard University, unpublished paper, 1981a.

Medoff, J. and Abraham, K., 'Are those paid more really more productive? The case of experience', *Journal of Human Resources* (Spring 1981b), vol. 16, pp. 186–216.

Medoff, J. and Abraham, K., 'Unemployment, unsatisfied demand for labor, and compensation growth in the US, 1956–1980', in M. Baily (ed.), *Workers, Jobs and Inflation* (Washington: Brookings Institution, 1982).

Medoff, J., and Fay, J. A., 'Labor and output over the business cycle', *American Economic Review* (September 1985), vol. 75, pp. 638–55.

Mellow, W., 'Employer size and wages,' *Review of Economics and Statistics* (August 1982), vol. 64, pp. 495–500.

Miller, E., 'Variation of wage rates with size of establishment', *Economics Letters*, vol. 8, (no. 3), (1981), pp. 281–6.

Mincer, J., *Schooling, Experience and Earnings* (New York: National Bureau of Economic Research, 1974).

Mortenson, D., 'The turnover implications of learning about attributes on the job', Evanston, Ill. Northwestern University Discussion Paper, 1975.

Nolan, P., and Brown, W., 'Competition and work place wage determination', *Oxford Bulletin of Economics and Statistics* (August 1983), vol. 45, pp. 269–88.

Organization for Economic Cooperation and Development, *Wages and Labor Mobility*, Paris, 1966.

Organization for Economic Cooperation and Development, *Employment Outlook* (September 1985), Paris.

Oi, W., 'Heterogeneous firms and the organization of production', *Economic Inquiry* (April 1983), vol. 21, pp. 147–75.

Oi, W., and Raisian, J., 'Impact of firm size on wages and salaries', unpublished paper, 1985.

Okun, A., *Prices and Quantities: A Macroeconomic Analysis* (Washington, DC: The Brookings Institution, 1981).

Osterman, P., 'Employment structures within firms', *British Journal of Industrial Relations* (November 1982), vol. 20, pp. 349–61.

Parsons, D., 'Specific human capital: an application to quit rates and layoff rates', *Journal of Political Economy* (November/December 1972), vol. 80, pp. 1120–43.

Parsons, D., 'Quit rates over time: a search and information approach', *American Economic Review* (June 1973), vol. 63, pp. 390–401.

Parsons, D., 'Models of labor turnover', *Research in Labor Economics* (Greenwich, Conn.: JAI Press, 1979).

Pencavel, J., *An Analysis of the Quit Rate in American Manufacturing* (Princeton: Princeton University Press, 1970).

Pencavel, J., 'Wages, specific training and labor turnover in US manufacturing industries', *International Economic Review* (February 1972), vol. 13, pp. 53–64.

Pencavel, J., 'The trade-off between wages and employment in trade union objectives', *Quarterly Journal of Economics* (May 1984), vol. 99 pp. 215–32.

Pencavel, J., and Hartsog, C., 'A reconsideration of the effects of unionism on relative wages and employment in the United States, 1920–1980', *Journal of Labor Economics* (April 1984), vol. 2, pp. 193–232.

Perrella, U. C., 'Young workers and their earnings', *Monthly Labor Review* (July 1971), pp. 3–11.

Personick, M. E., and Barsky, C. B., 'White collar pay levels linked to corporate work force size', *Monthly Labor Review* (May 1982), pp. 23–8.

Peterson, D., 'Economics of information and job search: another view', *Quarterly Journal of Economics* (February 1972), vol. 86, pp. 127–31.

Phelps, E., 'Money-wage dynamics and the labor market equilibrium', *Journal of Political Economy* (July/August 1968), vol. 76, pp. 678–711.

Quinn, R., and Staines, G., *The 1977 Quality of Employment Survey* (Ann Arbor: University of Michigan, 1978).

Rees, A., 'The effects of unions on resource allocation', *Journal of Law and Economics* (October 1963), vol. 6, pp. 69–78.

Rees, A., and Gray, W., 'Family effects in youth employment', in Freeman, R., and Wise, D., *The Youth Labor Market Problem: its natural causes and consequences* (Chicago: University of Chicago Press, 1982).

Reynolds, L., *The Structure of Labor Markets* (New York: Harper, 1951).

Reynolds, L., *Labor Economics and Labor Relations*, 6th edn (Englewood Cliffs, N. J.: Prentice-Hall, 1974).

Reynolds, L., and Taft, C., *The Evolution of Wage Structure* (New Haven: Yale University Press, 1956).

Reza, A. M., 'Geographical differences in earnings and unemployment rates', *Review of Economics and Statistics* (May 1978), vol. 60, pp. 201–8.

Rice, R., 'Skill, earnings and the growth of wage supplements', *American Economic Review* (May 1966), vol. 54, pp. 583–93.

Salter, W. E. G., *Productivity and Technological Change* (Cambridge, England: Cambridge University Press, 1966).

Sandell, S., 'Job search by unemployed women: determinants of the asking wage', *Industrial and Labor Relations Review* (April 1980), vol. 33, pp. 368–78.

Santomero, A. A., and Seater, J. J., 'The inflation-unemployment trade-off: a critique of the literature', *Journal of Economic Literature* (June 1978), vol. 16, pp. 499–544.

Schultz, C., 'Has the Phillips curve shifted? Some additional evidence', *Brookings Papers on Economic Activity*, (1979), vol. 2, pp. 452–67.

Scully, G., 'Pay and performance in professional baseball', *American Economic Review* (December 1974), vol. 64, pp. 915–30.

Segal, M., 'Post institutionalism in labor economics: the forties and fifties revisited', *Industrial and Labor Relations Review* (April 1986), vol. 39, pp. 388–403.

Seltzer, G., 'The United Steelworkers and unionwide bargaining', *Monthly Labor Review* (February 1961), pp. 129–36.

Simons, H., *Economic Policy for a Free Society* (Chicago: University of Chicago Press, 1944).

Solnick, T., 'Unionism and fringe benefit expenditure', *Industrial Relations* (February, 1978), vol. 17, pp. 102–7.

Solow, R., 'On theories of unemployment', *American Economic Review* (March 1980), vol. 70, pp. 1–11.

Stephenson, S., 'The economics of youth job search behavior', *Review of Economics and Statistics* (February 1976), vol. 58, pp. 104–11.

Stigler, G., 'The economics of information', *Journal of Political Economy* (June 1961), vol. 69, pp. 213–25.

Stoikov, V., and Raimson, R., 'Determinants of the differences in quit rates among industries', *American Economic Review* (December 1968), vol. 58, pp. 1283–98.

Ulman, L., 'Labor mobility and the industrial wage structure in the post-war United States', *Quarterly Journal of Economics* (February 1965), vol. 67, pp. 73–97.

Viscusi, W. K., *Employment Hazards: An Investigation of Market Performance* (Cambridge: Harvard University Press, 1979a).

Viscusi, W. K., 'Job hazards and worker quit rates: an analysis of adaptive worker behavior', *International Economic Review* (February 1979b), vol. 20, pp. 29–58.

Viscusi, W. K., 'Labor market structure and the welfare implication of the quality of work', *Journal of Labor Research* (Spring 1980), vol. 1, pp. 175–92.

Wachter, M., 'Cyclical variation in the interindustry wage structure', *American Economic Review* (March 1970), vol. 60, pp. 75–84.

Yanker, R. H., 'Productivity versus seniority: what is the determining factor in regard to wages and promotion?', Cambridge: Harvard University senior honors thesis, 1980.

ACKNOWLEDGEMENTS

PART I: MARKETS FOR EDUCATED LABOR

1. Supply and salary adjustments to the changing market for physicists
   First published in the *American Economic Review* (March 1975).
2. Functioning of the college graduates job market
   First published in the *Over-educated American* (New York: Academic Press, 1976).
3. Expectations and marginal decision-making
   First published in *The Market for College-Trained Manpower* (Cambridge, MA: Harvard University, Press, 1971).
4. The effect of demographic factors on age–earnings profiles
   First published in the *Journal of Human Resources* (1979), vol. XIV, no. 3.

PART II: DISCRIMINATION AND POVERTY

5. Black economic progress since 1964
   First published in *The Public Interest* (Summer 1978).
6. Young blacks and jobs
   Written with H. J. Holzer and first published in *The Public Interest* (Winter 1985).
7. Permanent homelessness in America?
   Written with Brian Hall and first published in *Population Research and Policy Review* (1987), vol. 6, pp. 3–27, © Martinus Nijoff Publishers (Kluwer), Dordrecht, Netherlands.

PART III: MARKETS UNDER TRADE UNIONISM

8. Individual mobility and union voice in the labor market
   First published in the *American Economic Review* (May 1976).

9. The exit–voice tradeoff in the labor market: unionism, job tenure, quits and separations
First published in *The Quarterly Journal of Economics* (June 1980).
10. Effects of unions on the economy
First published in S. M. Lipset (ed.), *Unions in Transition* (San Francisco: Institute for Contemporary Studies, 1986).

PART IV: LABOR MARKET INSTITUTIONS AND COMPARATIVE ANALYSIS

11. Contraction and expansion: the divergence of private sector and public sector unionism in the United States
First published in the *Journal of Economic Perspectives* (Spring 1988).
12. Bonuses and employment in Japan
Written with M. L. Weitzman and first published in the *Journal of Japanese and International Economics* (1987), vol. 1, pp. 168–94, © 1987, Academic Press Inc.
13. Evaluating the European view that the United States has no unemployment problem
First published in the *American Economic Review* (May 1988).

PART V: METHODS OF EMPIRICAL ANALYSIS

14. Job satisfaction as an economic variable
First published in the *American Economic Review* (May 1978).
15. Longitudinal analyses of the effects of trade unions
First published in the *Journal of Labour Economics* (1984), vol. 2, no. 1.
16. Does the new generation of labor economists know more than the older generation?
First published in B. E. Kaufman (ed.), *How Labor Markets Work* (Lexington: Lexington Books, 1988).

INDEX